In Praise of Skeptic

In Praise of Skepticism

Trust but Verify

PIPPA NORRIS

OXFORD
UNIVERSITY PRESS

OXFORD
UNIVERSITY PRESS

Oxford University Press is a department of the University of Oxford. It furthers the University's objective of excellence in research, scholarship, and education by publishing worldwide. Oxford is a registered trade mark of Oxford University Press in the UK and certain other countries.

Published in the United States of America by Oxford University Press
198 Madison Avenue, New York, NY 10016, United States of America.

Library of Congress Cataloging-in-Publication Data
Names: Norris, Pippa, author.
Title: In praise of skepticism : trust but verify / Pippa Norris.
Description: New York, NY : Oxford University Press, [2022] |
Includes bibliographical references and index.
Identifiers: LCCN 2022018801 (print) | LCCN 2022018802 (ebook) |
ISBN 9780197530115 (paperback) | ISBN 9780197530108 (hardback) |
ISBN 9780197530139 (epub)
Subjects: LCSH: Trust—Social aspects. | Skepticism.
Classification: LCC HM1204 .N67 2022 (print) | LCC HM1204 (ebook) |
DDC 302/.12—dc23/eng/20220613
LC record available at https://lccn.loc.gov/2022018801
LC ebook record available at https://lccn.loc.gov/2022018802

DOI: 10.1093/oso/9780197530108.001.0001

1 3 5 7 9 8 6 4 2

Paperback printed by Lakeside Book Company, United States of America
Hardback printed by Bridgeport National Bindery, Inc., United States of America

Contents

List of Figures

List of Tables

Preface and Acknowledgments

Trust is a perennial issue of concern in the social sciences and in society more generally. I have written about trust for many years now, including in an edited volume, *Critical Citizens*, published more than two decades ago by Oxford University Press. It seems timely to revisit the topic, given the latest wave of deepening anxiety about the contemporary state of trust, sparked by reflections on deepening social intolerance, growing party polarization, rising populism, and democratic backsliding. Accordingly, this book seeks to take a fresh look at trust and trustworthiness, challenging both the standard normative perspective in contemporary social theory and bringing new evidence from a wide range of diverse open and closed societies around the world to bear in understanding the drivers of this phenomenon.

Skeptical judgments reflect reasonably accurate and informed predictions of the future actions by agents based on evidence of their past performance and safeguards against deviant behavior. We should cautiously trust but verify. Unfortunately, our assessments of risks are commonly flawed. Both *cynical* beliefs (underestimating performance) and *credulous* faith (overestimating performance) involve erroneous judgments reflecting a combination of legacy cultural values, inadequate cognitive skills, and information echo chambers. These claims are tested using new empirical evidence drawn from interviews with more than 650,000 respondents in the European Values Survey/World Values Survey. Public opinion is compared over four decades in more than 100 societies, including in a diverse range of closed societies and autocracies, as well as in open societies and liberal democracies. The book concludes that the grave dangers arising from the public's credulous faith in incompetent, corrupt, and self-serving authorities are commonly underestimated.

Research for this book would not have been possible without the survey data gathered by the European Values Survey and the World Values Survey over successive waves. Sadly, we have lost Ronald Inglehart, who left an enduring legacy through his vision in founding the World Values Survey, his seminal intellectual insights into understanding the cultural roots of social change, and his warm friendship and engagement with friends, colleagues, and students around the globe. I am particularly grateful to everyone involved in the European Values Survey and the World Values Survey Association for release of seventh wave World Values Survey (1981–2021) time-series data set and the Joint EVS/WVS 2017–2021 data set.[1] These projects are international research programs devoted to the scientific and academic study of social, political, economic, religious, and cultural values of people around the world. I particularly acknowledge the invaluable contribution of the WVS Executive Committee, Christian Haerpfer, Alesandro Moreno, Chris Welzel, Kseniya Kizilova, Jamie Diez-Medrano, Marta Lagos, and Bi Puranen. The massive survey could not be produced without the global network of hundreds of national Principal Investigators, research teams, survey organizations, sponsors, and funding organizations supporting the work in each country, and also all the team of colleagues involved in the European Values Survey.[2] Research funding the inclusion of new batteries of questions on trust in WVS surveys in a dozen selected authoritarian states was generously supported by the United Kingdom's Economic and Social Research Council grant No. ES/S009809/1 for the TrustGov project (www.TrustGov.net), working in conjunction with Will Jennings and Gerry Stoker at the University of Southampton.

In addition, the core ideas for the book have benefited immensely by invitations to present draft chapters at a series of workshops, panels, and talks around the world, in many cases virtually in recent years. The feedback from all these events has been immensely helpful in sharpening the argument and presentation of the evidence, and I am most grateful to all the organizers, discussants, and participants. Finally, as always, the support of Oxford University Press has proved invaluable, particularly the patience and enthusiasm of Angela Chnapko, the book's editor, as Covid-related delays prolonged production, as well as the helpful comments of the reviewers.

PART I
INTRODUCTION

1

Two Faces of Trust

According to a well-known fable, a scorpion wants to cross a river but cannot swim, so it asks a frog to carry it across. The frog hesitates, afraid that the scorpion might sting, but the scorpion argues that if it did that, they would both drown. The frog considers this argument and agrees to trust the scorpion. The frog lets the scorpion climb on its back and then begins to swim. Midway across the river, the scorpion stings the frog anyway, dooming them both. The dying frog asks the scorpion why it stung despite knowing the consequence, to which the scorpion replies: "I couldn't help it. It's in my nature."

Trust is usually expected to be mutually advantageous. The extensive contemporary literature by leading scholars from multiple disciplines has generated a litany of beneficial consequences claimed to arise from trust within advanced industrialized societies, including for sustaining love (Larzelere and Huston), overcoming collective action problems within local communities (Putnam), lubricating the wheels of economic markets (Arrow, Fukuyama), managing organizations (Mayer, Davis, and Schoorman), overcoming gridlock in Washington, DC (Hetherington and Rudolph), legitimating governments (Gamson), underpinning rule of law (Tyler), and facilitating international collaboration, underpinning the democratic peace (Russett).[1] Trust, it is widely claimed, enables open communications and voluntary cooperation while reducing transaction costs in situations that involve risk and uncertainty.

It follows logically that signs of low or eroding trust are of widespread concern if this makes it harder for us to work together in society, to fix urgent problems through democratic governance, and to avoid bloody conflict in international relations. Who, after all, could be against something believed to facilitate passion, prosperity, and peace?

But the time is long overdue to rethink conventional assumptions underpinning all these popular claims. For agents, trust is always beneficial. For principals, however, a broader perspective reflected in the fable recognizes that in fact trustworthiness has two faces, not one. Blind trust in anti-vax posts weaken herd immunity, putting lives at risk. Faith in Q-Anon conspiracy theories triggered a violent insurrection attacking the US Capitol. Equally disastrous consequences can follow from gullible belief in fake Covid-19 cures like ingesting bleach and the Ivermectin anti-parasitic drug for livestock, investing life savings in Madoff pyramid schemes, Putin's claims to denazify Ukraine, or the Big Lie about pervasive electoral fraud in America. Trust also has a dark side.[2] Habitual faith in the rectitude of authorities such as bad cops, disgraced priests, and quack physicians is foolish, at best, and dangerous, at worst. The tale of the scorpion and the frog teaches children to beware of strangers. Flawed judgments of trustworthiness are closely related to more general problems of misinformation, where theories of motivated reasoning by cognitive psychologists suggest that citizens often actively seek to reject contrary facts which challenge their preconceived beliefs, while accepting confirmatory evidence to buttress their views.[3] Like faith in many other types of misinformation, trust in the untrustworthy often has malign consequences; after all, thousands of unvaccinated Americans died from Covid-19 after betting on conspiracy theories over scientific evidence presented by Dr. Anthony Fauci.

What is "trustworthiness"? This book distinguishes between *trust* as a quality of the individual and *trustworthiness* as a feature of dyadic relationships. The study focuses on "trustworthiness," defined as *an informal social contract where principals authorize agents to act on their behalf in the expectation that the agent will fulfill their responsibilities with competency, integrity, and impartiality despite conditions of risk and uncertainty.* This conceptualization emphasizes that trustworthiness is not about you or me—it is about us.[4] Trust delegates actions both to agents (individuals) as well as to agencies (institutions). Are friends and neighbors likely to help in a family crisis? Will parties keep their promises? Will the police keep us safe? Will vaccinations work? Will foreign countries honor multilateral treaties? And in cases where agents and agencies fail to fulfill their responsibilities, will effective accountability mechanisms and institutional warranties protect my interests anyway? Will I get refunds for broken products? Will physicians lose their license for gross misconduct? Will elections or impeachment kick out incompetent leaders? Will states violating international human rights treaties face sanctions imposed by the UN Security Council? If these sorts of judgments are positive, then it makes sense to authorize agents to act on our behalf, whether for individuals to hire the professional services of a defense attorney or heart surgeon, for customers to deposit their life savings in a bank or brokerage account, for voters to re-elect politicians, and for countries to sign bilateral trade agreements with other states.

I. Types of Judgments

Decisions that agents or agencies are trustworthy, in this conceptualization, involve estimating the risks and benefits of delegating authority to others. Skeptical judgments, the antithesis of blind faith, use some evidence to cautiously trust but verify. This process seeks to arrive at reasonably accurate and informed predictions about future actions by agents based on their past performance, as well as safeguards ensuring against deviant behavior. Skeptical processes of decision-making weigh and sift information to assess the reputation of the agent or agencies. Several questions guide critical thinking. Is the agent *competent*, with the skills, resources, and capacity to deliver on their responsibilities? Do they have *integrity*, behaving in ways which are honest, ethically upright, and truthful? Are they *impartial* in their role, with actions serving the interests of the principal rather than their own? Finally, do broader institutional *guardrails* and oversight mechanisms offer effective protection from betrayal of these standards?

The question which arises is whether ordinary people have the capacity for skeptical thinking about these matters, such as when deciding to trust strangers as well as friends, novel products from start-up companies as well as established brands, or new political challengers as well as familiar incumbents. All predictions involve guesswork, to a greater or lesser degree. It is well known from cognitive psychology and behavioral economics that under conditions of uncertainty, humans are prone to errors of judgment when estimating the probability of many common long-term risks.[5] Mistakes can arise from multiple sources: reliance upon inaccurate, incomplete, or contradictory information sources; outdated cultural values; motivated reasoning; confirmatory bias; prejudicial stereotypes; partisan loyalties; affective blinders; ideological worldviews; or misleading heuristic shortcuts.[6] Both consistent errors and random noise can and do let the heart govern the head, generating imprudent everyday decisions. We often mistakenly overestimate the risks of short-term threats, while also underestimating longer-term hazards, for example of lung cancer from smoking, the odds of becoming a victim of terrorist violence, the jeopardies of investing in market bubbles, or the dangers of getting vaccinated against the coronavirus.[7] It is the same when struggling to calculate whether someone (an agent) or something (an agency) will probably prove trustworthy.

This book focuses on understanding the reasons underlying types of perceptual bias in judgments of trustworthy relationships, where decision errors are understood as a mismatch between assessments of the likely future actions of somebody (an individual agent) or something (a collective agency), and the safeguards protecting against betrayal, compared with indicators of whether agents will actually fulfill their responsibilities, and the strength of accountability mechanisms guarding against failure to do so. Whether our judgments of trustworthiness reflect the true and accurate state of the world is the central concern of this book. The problem is that we can and do commonly make wrong predictions, for multiple reasons, and thereby risk being defrauded by smooth-talking con men, swindled by seasoned liars, and duped by silver-tongued demagogues. It's easy to fall victim to propaganda from foreign enemies, misinformation from the internet, or faux promises of quack cures. Limits on our rationality, information, and cognitive capacities lead to erroneous beliefs which either underestimate trustworthiness (generating cynical biases) or else overestimating it (producing credulous biases). The theory developed in this book predicts that accurate estimates of trustworthiness—subsequently confirmed as true—are most likely to be strengthened by several conditions which commonly facilitate informed decision-making in multiple contexts. *Open societies* provide environments with multiple channels of communications and "two-sided" sources of alternative viewpoints, expanding access to diverse opinions, sources of evidence, and independent news media. This is most likely to avoid information echo-chambers most common in closed societies which repress freedom of expression, use state censorship, and limit critical voices. Adherence to legacy *cultural values and attitudes* in any society are also expected to play a negative role through affective feelings and adherence to fixed ideological convictions which fail to be updated in the light of contemporary performance. Finally, *education* is likely to prove important by facilitating the cognitive abilities, reasoning skills, literacy and numeracy proficiencies, and prior knowledge facilitating the individual capacity for critical deliberation and rational decision-making. Propositions flowing from this core argument are tested against empirical evidence in over 100 diverse societies around the globe, using the rich resources from the pooled time-series European Values Survey/World Values Survey (EVS/WVS), conducted in seven waves from 1981 to 2021. This massive data set draws upon interviews with over 650,000 respondents. The theory developed in this study can be applied to multiple types of actors and agencies. This study examines empirical evidence by comparing public trust against government performance. This involves both subjective perceptions and objective performance indicators monitoring the record of governments when delivering economic prosperity and development, and also the quality of democratic governance, as the primary mechanism for political accountability, in a wide range of open and closed information societies around the world.

The book's core fourfold typology of judgments of trustworthy relationships is illustrated schematically in Figure 1.1. This simple heuristic model suggests that in any informal social contract, judgment by principals about whether the future performance of agents or agencies will meet their responsibilities can be either positive (trusting) or negative (mistrusting). And the agent or agencies' actual record of performance may subsequently prove to be either negative (incompetent, dishonest, and/or self-interested, without accountability, and thus untrustworthy) or else positive (displaying competency, integrity, and impartiality, with accountability, and thus trustworthy). Congruent categories, where evaluations accurately reflect performance, reflect either skeptical trust or skeptical mistrust. But this model identifies two key types of mismatched decision-making errors, arising from cynicism and credulity, distorting our forecasts.

		PRINCIPALS' JUDGMENTS OF AGENCY TRUSTWORTHINESS	
		Negative	Positive
PERFORMANCE BY AGENCY	Positive	CYNICAL MISTRUST	SKEPTICAL TRUST
	Negative	SKEPTICAL MISTRUST	CREDULOUS TRUST

Figure 1.1. Conceptual typology of trust relationships.

Cynics persistently *underestimate* trustworthiness. Irrationally gloomy and overly cautious expectations prevail, irrespective of the positive reputation of agents when fulfilling their obligations and the strength of effective institutional mechanisms of accountability deterring betrayal by deviant actors. When mentally calculating the risks and rewards of delegating responsibilities to others, in vulnerable situations, cynics gloomily exaggerate the hazards, for example whether decisions about hiring a babysitter (will they look after my kids?), getting vaccinated (what are the side effects?), consulting a defense attorney (will they be competent?), electing governments (will politicians fulfill their promises?), or traveling abroad (will I be safe?). Like weather forecasts, multiple factors can skew predictions. People may be brought up to be extremely cautious and risk-averse. Psychological feelings of fear, anxiety, and insecurity, direct experience of genuine dangers and threats, or learned cultural values and ideological worldviews which sway basic cognitive processes and shape attitude formation, may drive cynics to adopt a dark Hobbesian view of the world where life is regarded as "poor, nasty, brutish and short." The book theorizes that cynical errors and false beliefs are likely to be exacerbated by inadequate cognitive skills and lack of sufficient knowledge to make sound judgments, as well as by living in closed societies without access to plural sources of information and diverse viewpoints. The consequences of toxic cynicism are harmful for individuals, governance, and society. Extreme misanthropists share a pessimistic Weltanschauung, doubting the benevolence of friends and strangers alike, an outlook minimizing vulnerability to risks but also limiting opportunities for mutually beneficial social relationships. Cynicism corrodes faith in others but also in government authorities, weakening the willingness to obey the law voluntarily, to cooperate collectively in civic affairs, and to feel a sense of political legitimacy. The problems of excessive cynicism are widely recognized and well known in the extensive literature on trust.

What most standard accounts of trust underestimate, however, are the dangers to individuals, democracies, and societies arising from the opposite error of *credulity*, among those who consistently and naïvely *overestimate* trustworthiness. This Panglossian perspective reflects a rose-tinted optimistic bias which incautiously expresses gullible faith in everyone and everything, even deceptive actors likely to do harm, such as believing Nigerian fraudsters promising fake get-rich-quick schemes, the fake Covid-19 remedies offered by quack physicians, QAnon conspiracy theories, the honeyed lies of corrupt demagogues ("Trust me"), or paper treaties signed by ruthless tyrants.[8] Credulous people are too ready to have faith in another agent or agency's honesty, competency, or sincerity, without sufficient critical scrutiny of their record or guardrail warranties, thereby becoming vulnerable to exploitation. This orientation has been conceptualized by psychologists as an "optimistic bias" among individuals, giving rise to unrealistic expectations and lack of precaution against risk.[9] Problems of credulous decisions are theorized in this study to be exacerbated by similar sources of bias as cynicism, namely restrictions on pluralistic information sources in closed societies, cultural values and ideological worldviews which distort cognitive processes and accurate judgments, and lack of the cognitive skills that facilitate critical thinking involved in complex judgments.

The contemporary era is widely thought to have weaponized the risks of misinformation for the gullible, through the spread of online media bubbles.[10] But there is nothing new about the underlying process; well before QAnon, conspiracy theories flourished in Salem during the 1692 witch trials. From Chaucerian and Shakespearian times to the Prohibition era of Damon Runyon, fictional stories have long warned about the world's knaves, quacks, mountebanks, hustlers, tricksters, con artists, crooks, flimflam artists, and swindlers, while denigrating innocent victims as fools, dupes, patsies, stooges, suckers, mugs, and chumps. In *Candide*, Voltaire mocked Panglossian optimism which preached that everything which happens is for the best in the best of all possible worlds.

The economic costs of credulity can be substantial; thousands of people and companies have fallen hook, line, and sinker for misleading scams like identity theft, ransomware, phishing, and Ponzi pyramid schemes. The damage to financial markets are far from minor; for example, the FBI's division handling cybercrime estimates that American victims lost around $4.2 billion in 2020 alone; it has received around 5.7 million victim complaints since 2000.[11] In July 2021 a single massive ransomware cyberattack on Kaseya by REvil, a Russian gang, hit up to 1,500 companies around the world, with demands for $70 million to restore IT data.[12] The dangers to democracy can also be severe, as exemplified by the series of polls reporting that months after the courts and Congress certified President Trump's defeat in the 2020 US presidential election, two-thirds or more of Republicans believed right-wing media commentators and leaders that the outcome was "rigged" or "stolen."[13] False claims do not just undermine the legitimacy of President Biden's victory, exacerbate partisan gridlock, and weaken confidence in future American elections, they reportedly motivated the rioters who stormed the US Capitol in the fatal insurrection of January 6, 2021.[14]

The broader costs of misinformation for public health have proved tragic, a process dramatically illustrated by the aggressive resurgence of Covid-19 infections in the United States and Europe months and months after scientifically tested vaccinations had become widely available in these countries, as discussed further in Chapter 6. After the initial distribution of vaccines in these societies, almost all Covid-19-related hospitalizations and fatalities in these societies have subsequently occurred among those who refused to inoculate themselves from known risks, with many deaths blamed on misinformation that disseminated unsubstantiated claims and false cures.[15] Cross-national surveys suggest that trust in fellow citizens, government authorities, and science predicts people's willingness to comply with official regulations, to change their behavior, and thereby to limit the spread of the virus, such as by social distancing, wearing masks, and getting inoculated.[16] The other side of the coin is excessive faith in anti-vax misinformation spread by right-wing media and leaders.[17] Wild conspiracy theories about Covid-19, especially the risks of vaccination, have proliferated widely, prompting the World Health Organization to warn of an "infodemic."[18] For example, polls report that one in five Americans (and half of those refusing to be vaccinated) believed that the Covid-19 vaccine was a government plot to microchip citizens.[19] Claims that 5G mobile phone towers cause Covid-19 symptoms led people to set these ablaze. Naïve victims believe untrustworthy news and rabble-rousers, becoming susceptible to misinformation, thereby neglecting to protect themselves, their society, and their country from the world of scorpions and parasites seeking to exploit the credulous. The central problem is not just the supply-side dissemination and exploitation of propaganda, conspiracy theories, and lies by leadership elites, or the rapid spread of misinformation and disinformation in legacy and social media. It is also faith in its credibility by the gullible. And lack of compliance by the large minority of anti-vaxxers means that societies fail to achieve the collective protection of herd immunity that would safeguard lives and livelihoods.

The book argues that both excessive cynicism *and* credulity pose hazards, by under- or over-estimating the risks of placing confidence in others. Social theorists often unconsciously echo the normative biases of leadership elites, where excessive cynicism in the public is regarded as potentially problematic since this makes ordinary people more cautious about delegating decisions and more hesitant about obeying authorities, such as listening to advice in the

Covid-19 pandemic from public health experts, elected leaders, and international agencies such as the World Health Organization. But for ordinary *citizens*, rather than elites, blind compliance probably raises the greatest dangers of trusting the authorities if there are potential conflicts of interest, the risks arising from mistaken decisions are high, information about the past reputation of agents is unreliable, and formal accountability mechanisms are fallible. In such conditions, young children are taught that the default option is to be wary about strangers offering sweets, who may or may not prove benevolent. In a perilous world, the potential jeopardies of compliance (overestimating trustworthiness) heighten vulnerabilities more than the cautious hazards of cynicism (underestimating trustworthiness).

II. Skeptical Decisions of Trustworthiness

In contrast to these orientations, the book regards prudent *skepticism* as the most beneficial stance. Skeptics don't take reputations for granted by relying upon affective feelings of habitual trust for authority figures such as the police, clergy, or doctors, learned from parental cues and agencies of cultural transmission during childhood, or from the predominant attitudes, values, and norms absorbed from societal cultures. Instead, skeptics use updated information reviewing the performance of agents or agencies, including their past reputation and their record of competence, integrity, and impartiality, as well as the strength of the institutional guardrails protecting against failures in any informal social contract. Skeptics delegate authority only after weighing information and cautiously calculating whether agents are likely to prove trustworthy in their future actions. In short, reversing the Russian adage, skeptics verify and then trust. They learn from experience of interacting with police officers, teachers, banks, or local bureaucrats. They check alternative product reviews on Amazon. They carefully read the fine print on warrantees. They seek references before hiring plumbers. They weigh opposing views in op-ed columns. They examine the government's past record in power against alternative choices before casting a ballot. In short, skeptics are critical thinkers making strenuous efforts to avoid herd mentalities, conventional thinking, and learned preconceptions. Based on this conceptualization, it follows that skeptics should have the capacity to provide logical reasons for their decisions whether to trust or mistrust others, demonstrating evidence of internal consistency in their deliberative and cognitive processes. Their decisions should also display evidence of external consistency against credible performance benchmarks from independent sources of objective factual evidence, such as the governing party's record of delivering on their promises and the effectiveness of competitive elections to "throw the rascal out" if they fail to do so.

It should be acknowledged that *from the viewpoint of elite agents*, even blind trust generates some positive external consequences, as many scholars have emphasized, such as maximizing social cooperation and collective actions in local communities, civic engagement in the public sphere, and willingness to obey the authorities. But this book argues that *from the viewpoint of ordinary citizens*, not all forms of trust are equally valuable, and both cynical and credulous estimates of trustworthiness pose twin dangers. By contrast to these, skeptical calculations are more likely to generate prudent evaluations of the risks involved in any trust relationship, thereby minimizing the dangers and maximizing the benefits for the principal as well as collectively for the functioning of society and democracy as a whole. Normatively this argument reframes the conventional view; it suggests that what matters is less whether individuals express feelings of trust or mistrust, and whether trust has eroded—the focus of so much of the extensive research literature—but whether judgments about trustworthy relationships are based on sound or erroneous predictions. Contra pervasive assumptions, from the perspective of principals, this implies that evidence of either low or escalating mistrust among the public should not necessarily be regarded as problematic if caution is indeed warranted, such as when walking barefoot through a scorpion pit.

The general conception of "skepticism" used in this book is far from novel; instead, it builds upon a long tradition developed by many of the earliest philosophical thinkers about epistemology, including Rene Descartes and David Hume.[20] The ancient philosophical root of skepticism and its role in the Enlightenment and in modern scientific methods emphasize the value of doubt over certainty, suspended judgment over gullible acceptance of herd mentalities, bold conjectures, and attempted refutations, and the willingness to search for reasoned truth over blind faith.[21] This perspective provides the core foundation for the scientific mindset and the open society. Although a long-standing normative ideal widely celebrated in the modern age, it often remains difficult to achieve. The notion implies approaching future relationships with an agnostic lens, suspending judgment, and expressing uncertainty, especially in situations involving serious threats and vulnerabilities. Skeptics decide about trustworthiness only after the cognitive process of searching cautiously for reliable information about the past reputation of the agent, and awareness of the institutional safeguards ensuring against losses from bad actors. Slow thinking is used to estimate what is trustworthy on reasonably prudent grounds, authorizing agents and agencies after calculating the potential costs and benefits of any social contract. Skeptics are motivated by the desire to make a correct decision, avoiding the pitfalls of confirmatory bias.[22]

Of course, we can never predict anything about other people's future actions with absolute certainty. What degree of effort is "reasonable" in this process is not fixed in stone; instead, it depends upon the severity of the risks of getting judgments wrong. The greater the dangers arising from mistaken bets which eventually prove unduly optimistic or pessimistic, the more effort should be invested in gathering reliable information. Choosing a physician for an annual flu shot may not matter much, for example, but erroneous decisions may be life-threatening when selecting a heart surgeon. Trusting strangers may be a sensible rule of thumb in safe neighborhoods of Stockholm, Zurich, and Oslo, where there are effective sanctions against lawbreakers and a low crime index—but foolish in the violent streets of Kabul, Pretoria, and Tijuana.[23] Skepticism toward authorities is the equivalent of adopting an agnostic stance in religion, as skeptics seek to steer between the Charybdis of paralyzing doubt (like atheists) and the Scylla of misplaced certainty (like blind faith).[24] To avoid information overload, sensible pragmatism is needed to make good-enough prudent judgments, especially concerning routine low-risk decisions. Both cognitive skills and the broader information environment in open societies facilitate skeptical judgments.

Establishing empirical evidence to understand when public assessments of trustworthy relationships are well-informed and prudent—and where and when and why blind faith or cynical mistrust skew judgments—is the central puzzle unpacked at the heart of this book. The research design uses survey data from the EVS/WVS, gathered in seven successive waves over four decades since the early 1980s in around 120 societies worldwide, covering diverse contexts. This is used to gauge how far, and under what conditions, the public's evaluations of agents' reputations and accountability guardrails are indeed skeptical. This quality is not observed directly; instead, it is demonstrated indirectly by how far decisions of trustworthiness meet several criteria. First, skeptical decisions should be *internally consistent*, understood as displaying evidence of deliberative logical thinking about the reasons underlying these judgments. Second, skeptical estimates should be *externally consistent*, meaning that they are derived from some sources of reliable information and therefore observed to be correlated with objective macro-level performance indices for agents and agencies. Skeptical evaluations also should be observed to be responsive to new information, adjusting thermostatically in reaction to medium- and short-term "shocks" in agency performance, like major scandals, economic downturns, or policy blunders, so that they represent a running tally or iterative learning process updated over time. Alternatively, both cynical and credulous judgments fail these criteria; they lack evidence of deliberative internal reasoning, are more weakly correlated with performance indices, and display stable patterns of trust irrespective of changes in agency performance. Cynical and credulous biases in trust judgments can be thought either to arise from long-standing personality predispositions or inherited traits, as classic psychological theories suggest, or to be acquired as stable cultural attitudes and ideological viewpoints from socialization processes during the formative years of early childhood and adolescence within societal cultures, as sociological theories argue.

The motivation for writing this book did not start from the a priori assumption that skeptical judgments of trustworthiness will necessarily be pervasive in most societies; indeed I thought that, in fact, given our proclivity to make common errors in decision-making about many complex matters, and in a world awash with misinformation, they may well prove to be the exception rather than the rule. Social psychological theories emphasize that errors in rational calculations about risks and rewards commonly arise from reliance upon affective dispositions, whether arising from habitual loyalties, motivated reasoning, social identities and prejudicial stereotypes, selective perceptions, media misinformation, or gut instincts. Accurate evaluations of trustworthiness can be expected to be even more difficult for illiterate populations living in closed societies, replete with state propaganda, limits on access to independent media, and the suppression of dissent. Under these conditions, both cynicism and compliance are particularly likely to flourish. No simple "magic bullet" can fix decision biases, rid the world of misinformation, or protect the gullible from exploitation by powerful predators. But similarly, recognizing the realistic limits of skepticism is not a recipe for fatalistic "do-nothingism." The conclusion argues that accurate judgments of trustworthy relationships can be built most effectively by improving analytical, cognitive, and information-processing skills through processes of critical education, as well as by bolstering plural debate and viewpoint diversity in open societies.

III. Road Map of the Book

Subsequent chapters proceed to expand upon this argument. Part I of the book clarifies the general theory of skeptical trust sketched here, develops the conceptual framework, and describes the sources of empirical evidence and measures. Part II builds upon this foundation by examining alternative explanations of trust relationships, testing core theoretical propositions against empirical evidence, and presenting the key findings for different arguments. The conclusion in Part III summarizes the key theoretical argument and findings, and considers how skeptical assessments of trustworthiness can be strengthened, as well as discussing the broader implications and consequences of this phenomenon. Given the acknowledged importance of trustworthy relationships, it is vital and timely to revise our conventional understanding and to think anew about how far, where, why, and how these are gained, sustained, and lost.

Theoretical Framework

Chapter 2 develops the normative and theoretical framework. It summarizes debates about the consequences of trust in the extensive research literature and explains how the account presented in this study differs, both normatively and empirically, from previous perspectives. Three explanations of trust are common in the scholarly literature, including *psychological* accounts at the micro-level, which treat trust as a fixed characteristic or innate personality trait of the individual derived from birth or early childhood; *sociological* theories at the macro-level, emphasizing both the role of socialization processes and agencies of cultural transmission in the acquisition of stable values and predominant beliefs within societies, as well as the importance of social networks; and, by contrast, *performance* theories focused on how far decisions about agents' trustworthiness are based on judgments about their past record.[25]

The logic of performance theories can apply to any type of trustworthy agent, such as decisions to trust neighbors and strangers, civil society organizations like labor unions, banks, and major corporations, security forces such as the police and military, and other nations and peoples. The most extensive research literature has applied the theory to determine the links between levels of political trust (monitored by social surveys) and government performance. The latter has been measured in empirical studies mainly by subjective and objective empirical indicators of *economic policy outcomes* (such as satisfaction with the provision of public services and the management of the economy, and official statistics on rates of growth in per capita GDP and unemployment), as well as *procedural* indicators associated with accountability (such as satisfaction with democracy and perceived levels of state corruption, and institutional indicators about rule of law and good governance).[26] Building upon this literature, the book expands standard performance theories by emphasizing how skeptical judgments of trustworthiness for diverse agents can be understood as based upon public perceptions of both their past record of delivery on their responsibilities and the strength of accountability guardrails providing redress against bad actors. Intermediate conditions which strengthen the capacity of citizens to make reliable judgments of trustworthiness include cognitive skills and open societies.

Chapter 3 sets out the study's research design, how the core concepts are operationalized and tested empirically, and the main sources of evidence. The chapter evaluates the pros and cons of many approaches to studying trust, including randomized and survey experimental designs, game simulations, narrative case studies, as well as national, longitudinal, and cross-national social surveys.[27]

Survey Data

The primary data source used for analyzing micro-level and macro-level public opinion in this book is the pooled EVS/WVS, with fieldwork conducted among over 650,000 respondents in seven waves spanning four decades from 1981 until 2021.[28] This evidence facilitates comparison of almost 120 societies (including 114 independent nation-states and 5 dependent territories like Hong Kong and Puerto Rico). Overall, the pooled EVS/WVS data set for all seven waves includes 435 "country-year" surveys as units of comparison. The global scope facilitates individual-level analysis of public opinion in all inhabited continents and cultures around the globe.

Representative surveys of the adult population have been conducted under varied macro-level contexts, including in liberal democracies and electoral autocracies, as well as in both low-, middle-, and high-income economies, and in open and closed societies, all conditions theorized in this study as important to understand the role of the societal-level information environments. The time-series data also allow comparisons of the cultural evolution in trust over successive waves in countries experiencing processes of political and socioeconomic development, in some societies extending over four decades from 1981 to 2021. All countries were not included across all waves, however, as the contents of the survey questionnaire have been updated and revised over time to monitor new themes. The analysis of trust and trustworthiness of government in Chapters 5 and 6 focuses on the seventh-wave survey data. But several measures of social, institutional, and international trust have been carried consistently from the first wave onward. The pooled data set therefore allows us to monitor the evolution of longitudinal trends, and the impact of specific medium-term and short-term "shocks," from events, on public opinion over successive decades in many diverse developing and postindustrial societies across the world.

Measuring Trust

For the dependent variables, the book analyzes multiple items about trust and confidence contained in the pooled EVS/WVS survey. Previous studies have commonly focused upon one dimension of this phenomenon, such as generalized trust toward social out-groups, trust in exchanges in economic markets, or confidence in government. But analysis of a broader range of data suggests that, in fact, trust relationships are multidimensional, with public opinion distinguishing among different types of agent or agency. The chapter therefore develops trust scales for six distinct aspects, serving as the dependent variable in the book. This includes:

(i) *Social trust toward "in-groups,"* like family, friends, and neighbors most familiar to us;

(ii) *Social trust toward "out-groups,"* like peoples of other faiths, races, ethnicities, and nationalities;

(iii) Confidence in *civic society institutions* (actors mediating between citizens and the state, such as social movements, voluntary associations, religious organizations, banks, major corporations, television, and newspapers);

(iv) Confidence in *state security agencies* concerned with enforcement (the armed forces, police, and courts);

(v) Attitudes toward the *core agencies of governance* within the nation-state (functioning as channels of representation and policymaking, including parliaments, the government, public-sector bureaucracy, and political parties); and also

(vi) Confidence in the agencies of *global governance* at the supranational level, involving multilateral intergovernmental organizations in the international community (such as the United Nations, the World Bank, the World Trade Organization, and major regional bodies like the European Union and equivalent).

Reliability Tests

For reliability tests of measures of trust, the study uses survey item count experiments. This seeks to test whether responses to survey questions measuring public trust can themselves be trusted, especially when fielded in closed societies and repressive states limiting free speech. The problem of potential measurement errors and response biases commonly arise in many contexts, however, especially for survey questions monitoring sensitive issues such as sexuality, corruption, or racial prejudice, if respondents express inauthentic answers or use self-censorship to disguise their genuine views. This potential risk must be treated as especially serious when survey questions about trust in government or the political authorities are asked in authoritarian societies. To examine this issue, list experiments were embedded as part of the TrustGov battery added to the standard WVS questionnaire in the surveys conducted in 2020 in diverse electoral autocracies which suppress open dissent and free speech, including Ethiopia, Kyrgyzstan, the Philippines, Nicaragua, Iran, Kenya, and Zimbabwe. Survey respondents were randomized in split samples in each country. The comparison of responses across groups in each society helps to determine data reliability and potential response bias in self-reported trust of political leaders.[29] For additional external validity and replication checks, the measures of trust in the EVS/WVS are also compared with the results of other surveys using identical or similar questions in the same countries. Where independent studies point in a similar direction, with highly correlated national estimates, this strengthens confidence in the consistency of the survey data and the generalizability of the findings.

What Explains Trust Relationships?

Why did the frog decide to trust the scorpion? Part II of the book goes on to tackle a series of alternative explanations. Building upon the conceptual and theoretical framework outlined in the introductory chapters, Chapter 4 lays out the groundwork by painting the big picture of cross-national and time-series patterns of trust compared across diverse cultures and societies worldwide during the last forty years. The book then tests empirical evidence for the core theory seeking to explain trust relationships in politics, including indicators of government delivery and accountability (Chapter 5), and the quality of democratic governance (Chapter 6).

Cultural Values and Societal Trust

Chapter 4 starts to unpack the survey evidence considering by describing observed cross-national comparisons in patterns of trust in societies around the world, as well as the dynamics of longitudinal trends over successive decades. Cultures are commonly thought to drive patterns of trust observed around the world—reflecting the enduring legacy of predominant values observed in different societies. The cultural explanation of trust draws upon classic socialization theories which emphasize that attitudes, beliefs, norms, and values are learned during the formative years of childhood and adolescence within each society.[30] In this view, the propensity to trust is an affective orientation acquired from role models such as parents and family, neighbors, colleagues, and peers, as well as from exposure to the agencies of cultural transmission, including schools and colleges, interpersonal, group and mass communications, religious organizations, social networks, and the workplace and local community. In adulthood, however, cultural theories suggest that the learning process for individuals slows. Trust is regarded as an enduring individual orientation, like other core attitudes, values, and beliefs. Cultural change in society is thought to arise primarily from long-term demographic processes of generational replacement, population turnover, and migration. Hence, compared with the attitudes of their parents and grandparents, Inglehart argues that the younger college-educated generation growing up in secure postindustrial societies are far less trusting of traditional forms of hierarchical authority, such as the institutions of political parties, elections, parliaments, governments, the army, the church, and the police.[31] Due to demographic trends, he argues, trust in these traditional pillars of political and moral authority has gradually eroded in affluent societies, as one birth cohort succeeds another. Along similar lines, the work of Putnam also attributes the decline of social capital and interpersonal trust in the United States largely to longitudinal demographic and cultural trends.[32] His theory of social capital attributes the erosion of generalized trust primarily to the replacement of the "Silent" generation of Americans, who built networks of trust and communitarian values based on shared the collective experience of living through the immense disruption of two world wars and the Great Depression, by the younger generations growing up in the 1960s and 1970s during the television age, with privatized leisure and more individualized values.

Cultural theories suggest several propositions which can be examined in this chapter with the empirical cross-national longitudinal survey data. First, cultural accounts suggest that trust within each society should display either stable trends over time, where cultures are fixed, or else slow-moving evolutionary linear decline, indicative of secular demographic change or processes of generational population turnover. Moreover, long-standing cultural contrasts should be observable as persistent patterns at the macro-level between, say, trusting attitudes toward people and politics, which are thought to predominate in Nordic societies, compared with more cynical views, believed more common in Southern Europe.[33] Finally, similarities should also be observed within world regions among nations sharing similar levels of human development, historical legacies, and religious traditions, such as contrasts between Protestant and Muslim societies.

This chapter starts by documenting societal trends and confirms that the empirical evidence often fits these predictions, with clear contrasts observed worldwide among global regions. But there are also observable patterns of trendless fluctuations over time, even among relatively similar societies. Trust also varies substantially across different agencies. It is important to explore further to understand the meaning of the data, how far fluctuations in trust reflect performance, and the underlying causes of trustworthiness.

Competency

Chapter 5 focuses upon the evidence for performance theories where citizens are expected to trust individual agents and collective agencies based on their past reputation for competency in meeting their responsibilities, serving as proxy guides to their future actions. Previous studies of performance theories have focused mainly on comparing trust with the economic record of governments, where national rates of unemployment, growth, and inflation serve as objective measures of policy performance. Citizen satisfaction with the government's handling of the macroeconomy has also commonly been used to gauge subjective perceptions of performance. Where governments meet targets and prove adept at steering the nation's economy, and more generally are effective in delivering a broader basket of public goods and services like improved healthcare, better education, and stronger security, this is widely assumed to bolster public confidence. This thesis has influenced government attempts to strengthen satisfaction among citizens, and thus restore political trust, through reforming public-sector management and service delivery. The logic is straightforward, yet the results of empirical studies testing these claims seem sensitive to the particular choice of indices, comparative frameworks, and methods, rather than proving robust.[34]

Building on this foundation, this chapter theorizes that public perceptions of government competency will be mediated by the type of information environments. Open societies, with plural sources of alternative viewpoints and freedom of expression, are most likely to facilitate more informed and accurate public judgments of government competency. In these contexts, political trust is likely to be most strongly correlated with objective performance indicators. By contrast, closed societies are characterized by limits on freedom of expression, state control of the media, and the repression of critical voices. This context generates conditions where public judgments of political trust are less likely to reflect the government's objective record in managing the economy and development. The chapter seeks to re-examine and update the empirical evidence testing this thesis using new data covering around eighty diverse societies worldwide.

Chapter 6 turns to investigate whether public evaluations of government trustworthiness are based on the criteria of integrity and impartiality, and the effectiveness of accountability mechanisms if the authorities systematically fail to meet these standards. One way to consider this question is to compare individual-level trust in political institutions with subjective evaluations of the procedural quality of democratic governance, such as satisfaction with the state of democracy and perceptions of state corruption. The previous literature suggests strong correlations can be observed; however the direction of causality in this association is impossible to untangle from cross-sectional survey data alone, due to issues of reciprocal relationships. More rigorous approaches compare public trust in any society with objective macro-level indicators of the quality of democratic governance, such as measures of levels of corruption, rule of law, liberal democracy, and the quality of public-sector management, provided by the Varieties of Democracy project and the World Bank Institute. Theories predict that citizens will be more trusting of political institutions where regimes score highly, according to standard indicators of good governance. By contrast, public dissatisfaction is predicted to be evident in states where governments routinely perform poorly according to procedural criteria, exemplified by repressive regimes which employ rigid coercion and govern by arbitrary rule, and where there is evidence of corruption. To develop this argument, the theory developed in this book predicts that this relationship will also be mediated by the information environment in each society, as well as by cognitive skills, education, and knowledge.

Much work on trust has been conducted in postindustrial societies and liberal democracies, with freedom of the press and plural media outlets. But a global perspective highlights the importance of the information environment in open and closed societies, including freedom of expression and the availability of alternative viewpoints and sources, as well as freedom of the press and state control of the airwaves, censorship of freedom of expression on social media, the degree of media pluralism providing alternative sources of information, and the type of democratic or autocratic regime. The broader macro-level context of the information environment in open and closed societies is predicted to be important for judgments of trust by serving as necessary but not sufficient intermediary conditions for skeptical decision-making. Thus, more knowledgeable decisions about trustworthy political leaders, political parties, civil service officials, and state authorities are likely to be maximized in open societies with freedom of expression, media pluralism, and accountability mechanisms, all closely associated with the type of democratic or autocratic regime governing each state, combined with levels of human development, expanding literacy, schooling, and media access in each society. By contrast, in closed societies the free exchange of information is constrained by the regime, independent journalism critical of the authorities is repressed, and the state controls the media.

Cognitive skills are also likely to strengthen skeptical judgments of trust. A large body of experimental research in behavioral economics, decision sciences, and cognitive psychology emphasizes that many heuristic short-cuts are common in how people use even minimal information to make social trust judgments, such as learned cultural cues derived from social identities, partisan loyalties, or media frames, which may or may not prove an accurate and reliable guide to decision-making.[35] The capacity to form unbiased and accurate trust judgments is plausibly strengthened by levels of formal schooling and the knowledge and reasoning skills which come from education. Building upon these ideas, two decades ago I predicted that growing literacy, cognitive skills, civic knowledge from formal schooling, and access to plural sources of mediated information, in particular, would encourage the rise of "critical citizens," where the younger generations in many postindustrial societies become increasingly skeptical about the actual performance of the core institutions of representative democracy, notably political parties, parliaments, and governments, while still adhering strongly toward democratic ideals and values.[36]

For all these reasons, Chapter 6 examines evidence for the relationship between the quality of democratic government and judgments of trustworthiness, and the mediating effects of formal education and the information environment. Finally, comparative case studies of government responses to the outbreak of the Covid-19 pandemic illustrate the risks facing both individuals and societies arising from cynicism toward scientific expertise and public health authorities, and credulous reliance upon incompetent leaders, misinformation, and conspiracy theories.

In Praise of Skepticism

The concluding chapter summarizes the main argument and empirical findings, considers their implications, and highlights the next steps in the broader research agenda. A shared consensus about the value of trust, alongside widespread concern about its supposed decline, has become ubiquitous in popular commentary. The scholarly literature in diverse disciplines reflects the predominant narrative. The literature is overwhelmingly skewed toward blaming lack of public trust for multiple sins, whether for individuals, liberal democracies, markets, or societies. Hence, corruption and failure to comply voluntarily with the law are attributed to mistrust of the police and courts. Social intolerance is blamed on distrust of strangers from different lands, languages, and faiths. Eroding membership in voluntary organizations is ascribed to weakening social bonds connecting neighbor with neighbor in local communities. Falling support for liberal democracy and the rise of authoritarian populism are explained by eviscerating confidence in governments, political parties, and indeed the rejection of politicians as a class.[37] In politics, any significant loss of trust is conventionally thought to be important for many reasons, not least by eroding civic engagement and conventional forms of political participation,[38] reducing support for progressive public policies,[39] potentially heightening the risks of democratic backsliding, and facilitating the resurgence of strongman leaders and authoritarian forces.[40] Weakening multilateral cooperation in the European Union is credited to a rising tide of nativism and xenophobia. And so on. If trust maximizes human happiness and well-being, prosperity, cooperation, and sociability, then any loss should surely be lamented. Concern has fueled an extensive body of applied policy research which has sought to understand how public trust could potentially be restored, for example by strengthening citizen engagement on the demand-side, such as through civic education, or else by improving process or policy performance, through implementing structural reforms to governance on the supply-side.[41] At the same time, however, harder scrutiny of the conventional "declinist" wisdom raises important questions—normative, methodological, and empirical—which deserve to be addressed.

By contrast, the argument developed in this book suggests that some of the conventional concern about a crisis of low and/or declining trust may be misplaced. In particular, deep cynicism can be dysfunctional for society and for democracy, but equal dangers arise from the opposite extreme, among credulous citizens believing agents blindly, irrespective of their dishonest, incompetent, and corrupt performance ("Trust me—I alone can fix it"), whether because of affective partisan loyalties, feelings of shared social identities, cultural values, belief in media misinformation, motivated reasoning, selective perceptions, and/or the persuasive power of seductive rhetorical appeals. The reconceptualization proposed in this study counterbalances the conventional view prevalent in the empirical literature by emphasizing the two faces of trust, and the value of skepticism, reflecting trust only after a process of weighing the available evidence with an agnostic mind open to persuasion.

This understanding of the two faces of trust carries certain implications for our interpretations and evaluations of this phenomenon. In particular, concern about the erosion of trust and confidence has become the conventional mantra, repeated so often by liberal scholars and commentators that it has become an orthodox cliché which deserves critical rethinking. The underlying assumption in these accounts is that citizens should have more faith in their delegated agents, whether the advice of scientific experts, the willingness of elected representatives to serve the public interest, or the capacity of international organizations to strengthen peace and prosperity. Alternatively, however, this chapter argues that deep reservoirs of blind trust should not necessarily be celebrated—nor indeed should concern be expressed about either low or eroding public trust per se. If trust is reframed as having confidence that specific institutions or individuals will deliver certain desired outcomes, then the key problems arise where trust by principals fails to match agency performance, within some reasonable margin of error. At the same time, it should be acknowledged that there are multiple barriers to achieving skeptical trust relationships—and the different ways by which this can be strengthened to guard against both blind trust and corrosive cynicism are not clear-cut. The conclusion reviews the main empirical results throughout the book and considers their broader implications for social relationships, for liberal democracy, and for international cooperation.

2

The General Theory of Skeptical Trust

For many decades the conventional view has overwhelmingly celebrated the positive consequences of trust, which is believed to oil the wheels of personal relationships, to provide the foundations for democratic legitimacy, and to facilitate cooperation across national borders. Scholars and popular commentators, both liberals and conservatives, usually express deep concern where there are plausible signs of either excessive cynicism within particular societies, and/or signs of declining trust over time within a country.

To consider these issues, Section I of this chapter discusses debates in the contemporary literature about the causes of trust, summarizing the extensive body of empirical research published by social scientists in diverse disciplines. Three alternative schools of thought have long been debated in the social sciences. *Social psychologists* regard generalized trust as an affective feeling, rooted in individual personality predispositions and innate characteristics, associated with other positive traits such as sociability, optimism, and cooperation. Alternative *cultural sociologists* emphasize the role of early childhood socialization processes for the acquisition of enduring values, cognitive and moral beliefs, social attitudes, and behavioral norms, including trust toward other people, social groups, institutions, and nations. These orientations are thought to persist as stable worldviews within each society. Evolutionary changes in social cultures are attributed to long-term secular trends of societal modernization and generational replacement of successive birth cohorts within the population, more than period or life-cycle effects. By contrast, *performance* theories, common in political economy and behavioral economics, suggest that trusting attitudes are more fluid, reflecting rational calculations in decision-making processes. In particular, judgment of trustworthiness is thought to reflect evaluations of the governing party's past competency in managing public goods and services, as well as the quality of accountability institutions and processes, monitored by objective indicators such as levels of corruption, rule of law, and democracy.

Section II describes the core thesis developed in this book, which builds upon the performance arguments in the literature and considers its applicability in the political sphere. As argued in the previous chapter, judgments of trustworthiness reflect estimates of the future actions by agents and institutions. Skeptical judgments of trustworthiness, whether positive or negative, are theorized to rest on critical evaluations of the past performance of agents and agencies, especially their established record for delivering on their responsibilities, reflecting the criteria of competency, integrity, and impartiality, along with the strength of institutional accountability guardrails, which serve to mitigate the risks of bad actors. By contrast, errors of judgments can arise for many reasons, with cynical judgments systematically underestimating future agency performance, while credulous evaluations overestimate it.

After developing the core typology, Section III theorizes that individual cognitive skills and knowledge, as well as the broader information environment found in open societies, help to strengthen accurate evaluations of trustworthiness, avoiding biased errors of judgment associated with both the Scylla of corrosive cynicism and the Charybdis of naïve credulity. This argument challenges the prevalent normative assumptions about the intrinsic or instrumental value of trust prevalent in the modern literature and reframes our interpretation of the empirical evidence. This lays the foundations for the next chapter, which outlines the study's research design, sources of empirical data, and how judgments of trustworthiness are operationalized and tested against performance indicators.

I. Debates about the Origins of Trust

What theories illuminate the drivers of trust and trustworthiness? Three schools of thought have predominated in social science debates in the literature, including *psychological* explanations based on individual personality predispositions, *sociological* theories emphasizing the role of socialization processes and learning within collective societal cultures, and *performance* theories focused upon public evaluations of agency reputations and the strength of accountability safeguards.[1] How do these accounts differ? And rather than treating these artificially as separate rival perspectives, can they be reconciled and integrated to generate a richer and more holistic theoretical framework?

Trusting Individuals

The early psychological literature regarded interpersonal trust (among people) as critical for nearly all social dealings, the foundation for happy, well-functioning relationships in the home, workplace, and public sphere. The early work was individualistic, where trust was seen as an enduring affective trait hardwired into our brain that forms part of our basic personality and is largely independent of our adult experience of the external world.[2] The concept of "personality" is understood by psychologists as consistent patterns of attitudes and behavior, a largely stable orientation enduring throughout one's lifetime, whether inherited genetically from parents, or else learned during the early formative years.[3]

Psychological accounts therefore emphasize that some people are born trusters and others are born cynics. Both carry their genetic predispositions around with them as adults, affecting how they interact with friends and strangers, and how much they are open or closed toward other groups and nations.[4] Thus, trusters have an open and sunny disposition with a propensity toward believing the best in others and rarely suspecting hidden intent. Because of their psychological history and makeup, and their early life experiences, trusting individuals are thought to have an optimistic view of life and they are willing to help others, to cooperate, and to be sociable. Personality types are regarded as stable across contexts, so that an individual who is trusting toward friends and family is also likely to trust neighbors and strangers, displaying cooperative behaviors, like civic engagement and cooperation to build better societies. Cynics, by contrast, have personality traits suspecting that others are likely to betray them. Their personality tends to be more pessimistic and misanthropic, guarded or alienated, more distrustful and cautious of others, and pessimistic about social affairs and about people and politicians in general. Both trust and cynicism are thought to be traits rooted in personalities and thus fixed and enduring, without much reference to social contexts and life's lessons.

The early psychological literature treated individual-level trust and institutional confidence (or distrust and lack of confidence) as basic stable aspects of personality types.[5] According to Erikson, for example, feelings of inner goodness, trust in others and oneself, and optimism form a "basic trust" personality trait formed in the first stages of psychological development as a result of the mother-baby feeding experience. These childhood personality traits, it is argued, are enduring and general, influencing many aspects of adult behavior, including social relationships.[6] The capacity to develop intimacy in adulthood is thought to be influenced by formative socialization experiences with parents early in life, learning from childhood bonds of intimacy that others will protect us, with experiments suggesting that even three- and four-year-old children have the capacity to differentiate between people who are trustworthy and those who aren't. Seminal work of the social psychologist Morris Rosenberg also argued that alienation, trust in people, and beliefs that people are fundamentally cooperative and inclined to help others combine to form a single "trust in people" scale.[7] Some individuals are thought to have an optimistic view of life and are willing to help others, to cooperate, and to be trusting because of their psychological history and makeup, and their early life experiences. Others are thought to be more pessimistic and misanthropic, guarded or alienated, more distrustful and cautious of others, and generally pessimistic about social affairs and about people and politicians. In this regard, trust is seen as an affective and persistent orientation that forms part of the DNA of our basic personality, whether genetic or learned in the formative years of childhood and adolescence, although subsequent experiences in new roles and adult experience of the external world may also influence feelings of trust.[8] Other classic accounts in the mid-twentieth century can also help to explain trust and deference toward those in authority, such as Soloman Asch and Stanley Milgram's seminal experiments illustrating the power of conformity when compliantly following the crowd in adopting false beliefs.[9]

Contemporary psychologists continue to research the roots of interpersonal trust among children and adolescents, and how this affects, and is affected by, their interaction with parents and siblings, peers and social groups.[10] Hence Ulsaner argues that generalized social trust is an enduring affective orientation learned during the formative years of childhood: "Trust is a moral value that does not depend upon personal experience or on interacting with people in civic groups or informal socializing. Instead, we learn to trust from our parents, and trust is stable over long periods of time. Trust depends on an optimistic world view: the world is a good place and we can make it better."[11] This cheerful predisposition is thought to have beneficial consequences for civil society, irrespective of whether or not the world actually *is* a benign place. Faith in societal cooperation is assumed to make this more likely to happen. In Uslaner's words, "Moralistic trusters believe that the world is a benign place, that other people are generally well motivated, and that they share similar moral premises. In the words of the standard survey research question, they believe that 'most people can be trusted.' Such beliefs ease the way toward getting people to work together to make their communities (and the larger society) a better place."[12] By contrast, this view regards "strategic" trust, based on utilitarian evaluations of performance, as of limited value, because this is unlikely to have beneficial social consequences, like giving to charity or volunteering service.

During the last two decades, psychologists have considered how trust is related to the "Big Five" personality traits, including Extraversion, Agreeableness, Conscientiousness, Emotional Stability, and Openness to Experience, which are regarded as stable aspects of individuals persisting through the life cycle that shape how people respond to the world across diverse situations.[13] Trust is understood within this framework as a trait linked with Agreeableness, reflecting pro-social and communal feelings toward others, rather than antagonism.[14] For Yamagishi and Yamagishi, interpersonal trust is defined as "a belief in the benevolence of human nature in general."[15] These psychological characteristics are thought to predict human relationships as well as patterns of political behavior, such as civic engagement and political activism.[16]

Challenges to Psychological Accounts

The classic psychological approach continues to influence our understanding of trust, yet this approach can be challenged in several important regards.

First, if trust is largely fixed and inherited from birth or acquired in early childhood, hardwired into our basic personality, the account is unable to explain any sharp fluctuations in public opinion observed to occur at individual or societal levels, for example why trust in government suddenly rebounded in America in a "rally-around-the-flag" effect observed after 9/11, or how political trust in national governments and the European Union responded to the events of the 2008 financial recession in Europe or the Covid-19 pandemic.[17] Responses to surveys, the psychological approach assumes, tell us something about the individuals who express feelings of trust rather than something about the world in which they live and the trustworthiness of agents. Psychological research using this approach has also focused mainly upon interpersonal and generalized trust (of unknown others, such as strangers and foreigners), rather than upon its institutionalized forms. Studies have sought to identify the micro-level characteristics of trust—such as differences by age/birth cohort, sex/gender, education, race/ethnicity, and socioeconomic status/income—and related affective traits such as feelings of self-esteem, well-being, and security—but more rarely on macro-level factors that may be expected to drive fluctuations in trust, like long-term changes in demography and cultural values in society, or short-term changes in economic and political events, government performance, media frames, or international developments.[18]

In addition, the focus on innate characteristics can also be seen as largely deterministic, so that it becomes difficult to identify effective practical social interventions or political reforms which could be implemented to strengthen feelings of trust. As Freeitag and Bauer say: "If we agree that personality traits are, to a certain extent, rooted in biology and that certain personality traits affect trust judgments, it also means that trust is also inherited to a certain degree."[19] Biological genetics can be regarded as destiny.

Finally, there are normativity issues. If feelings of trust are relatively fixed and stable from birth, or are inherited from parental role models in early childhood, this may still have certain positive benefits. In particular, from the perspective of the authorities, this orientation can be expected to encourage feelings of solidarity and willingness to cooperate, as well as encouraging citizens to comply obediently with formal laws, rules, and informal social norms. But indiscriminate trust of both the untrustworthy and trustworthy alike can also potentially generate negative consequences for individuals. The credulous, characterized by a sunny and open view of the world, are left unprotected from exploitation by bad actors, like the lies of demagogues, identity-theft thieves online, and conspiracy theories from QAnon. Similarly, cynical individuals inheriting overly negative or wary predispositions are also at risk, if they feel unable to delegate decisions and rely upon the advice of others, like anti-vaxxers rejecting science, even when agents are actually competent, benevolent, and honest.[20]

Tests of causal claims in psychological theories using empirical micro-level evidence have employed different techniques, such as individual-level longitudinal panel surveys, lab experiments, or dyadic parent-child or paired twin studies to trace inherited characteristics, early parent-child relationships within the family, or adolescent learning and development. These techniques cannot be analyzed in this book from the data available through cross-national surveys of the adult population. But the thesis does generate several empirically testable propositions which can be re-examined against the comparative survey evidence. If trust is indeed a basic personality trait or stable predisposition, these attitudes can be expected to be closely related to other types of psychological indicators of affective well-being, also included in surveys, such as feelings of life satisfaction, happiness, personal security, and sociability. Moreover, individuals with trusting personalities should also be expected to display indiscriminately positive attitudes toward a wide range of diverse agents and institutions, irrespective of their specific functions and past record, for example, consistently trusting both friends and strangers, as well as expressing confidence in political parties, parliament and governments, and UN agencies of global governance. Some aspects of this influential approach can therefore be reexamined within this study.

Or Trusting Societal Cultures?

Sociological theories, by contrast, focus upon the macro-level, emphasizing that societies stamp enduring cultural values and social norms upon those growing up within each local community, nation-state, and world region, generating enduring geographic contrasts in trust that are evident across societies. Cultural theories seek to explain enduring cross-national contrasts in attitudes and values observed in social surveys, such as why Danes, Swedes, and Norwegians are generally characterized by high levels of interpersonal trust and social tolerance, a deep reservoir of confidence in democratic government which persists through good times and bad, while those living in the Nordic region also support international cooperation with the UN agencies of global governance. By contrast, citizens in equivalent postindustrial societies in the southern Mediterranean, such as those in Italy, Greece, and Spain, have long expressed minimal generalized trust, far greater suspicion of state institutions than their Nordic cousins, and greater dissatisfaction with how their democracy works.[21] The comparative sociological tradition, rooted in the earliest work by Lerner (1958) and by Almond and Verba (1963), suggests that cultural attitudes, values, and beliefs persist since they are reproduced in each society for decades, or even for centuries, by social conditions and by collective agencies of cultural transmission.[22] Thus individualistic Southern Europeans come to see government and politics as threatening and corrupt, while Northern Europeans, favoring the values of solidarity and cooperation, learn to regard the democratic state more benevolently as a way to work together for common goals.

Sociological accounts overlap with psychological accounts which suggest that trust, like many other related attitudes, values, and beliefs, is learned individually through early socialization processes and thus derived from formative role models like parents and family, neighbors and peers during childhood and adolescence. The values which parents seek to instill through childrearing practices are thought to instill habitual feelings of generalized trust or mistrust among their children which persist throughout their lifetime. But cultural accounts also place greater emphasize on how trusting orientations are acquired from experience of the collective agencies of cultural transmission within each society, including from levels of societal development and security, the role of formal education in schools and colleges, moral teachings from religious organizations and faith communities, information acquitted from the mass and social media, informal networks and social norms learned through participation in voluntary organizations and community associations, and experience in the workplace and local community.[23]

In particular, theories of modernization suggest that the social conditions under which people grow up in each society are critical for the acquisition of enduring cultural values. Early experiences of security, from growing up in affluent postindustrial economies with long-established democratic states and comprehensive cradle-to-grave welfare states with universal benefits, are expected to lead toward more trusting attitudes.[24] By contrast, deep mistrust is expected in these accounts to be evident among those with formative experiences during childhood and adolescence of being raised among poorer and less secure sectors in developing nations, as well as for citizens in authoritarian states governed by repressive and corrupt rulers, and in deeply divided urban communities afflicted by conflict, crime, and violence. This perspective suggests that trusting orientations toward other people and government can be expected to evolve slowly in society over time. For example, Bergh and Öhrva report that trust persisted as a sticky trait, even among expatriate Swedes living abroad in developing countries with unstable societies and corrupt governance.[25] Similarly, Algan and Cahuc suggest that among contemporary Americans, those claiming a Nordic family heritage are likely to display considerable trust today compared with those with migrant roots descended from Southern and Eastern Europe.[26] In adulthood, cultural theories suggest that the learning process slows, with value change in society arising primarily from demographic processes of generational turnover, as the entry of younger birth cohorts into the population gradually replaces older cohorts, rather than from life-cycle effects associated with aging, like experience of marriage, home ownership, and entry into the workforce, or period effects attributed to the impact of "shock" events.

Modernization theories developed by Ronald Inglehart, and accounts of social capital by Robert Putnam, provide the classic paradigms for understanding these processes. Hence Inglehart argues that the social and economic conditions under which people grow up are important for the acquisition of enduring cultural values among different generations. Processes of societal modernization and human development are theorized to transform cultural attitudes and beliefs, especially citizens' relationships with the state. Economic growth profoundly transforms poorer societies, bringing many characteristics of advanced industrialized societies, including expanded affluence and leisure time, growing access to higher education, and the proliferation of media information.[27] Modernization theories posit that economic growth, technological development, rising levels of education, and the expansion of mass communication in postindustrial societies transform citizens' civic skills and value orientations, weakening attachments to political parties and traditional interest groups, and diminishing voting participation, while swelling the propensity to engage in direct forms of activism such as consumer politics and mass demonstrations.[28] Inglehart argues that, compared with the attitudes of their parents and grandparents, the younger college-educated generational cohorts growing up in secure postindustrial societies are far more likely to question traditional forms of hierarchical authority, such as the institutions of elections, parliaments, governments, the army, and the police. Through demographic replacement, as younger generational cohorts succeed older ones, the reservoir of political trust in government is thought to gradually erode.[29]

Similarly, Putnam's explanation of the decline of social capital in America attributes this largely to processes of social development and generational change. In particular, he emphasizes the importance of the gradual replacement of the "Silent" generation of Americans, who shared the collective experience of living through the immense disruption of two world wars and the Great Depression, with the younger generations of Americans growing up with more individualistic values and privatized leisure habits in the 1960s and 1970s, following the rise of the television age.[30] Putnam argues that the older generations were often active through belonging to a wide range of local voluntary organizations, working together with neighbors upon collective problems; by contrast, the younger generations were less likely to join and become active in these groups and associations.

Cultural theories suggest several predictions open to testing against new survey data in subsequent chapters. Most broadly, this perspective suggests that a legacy of similar attitudes of social, political, and international trust should be observed at the macro-level in countries and world regions sharing common values and norms. This includes cross-cultural linkages such as those derived from shared religious legacies in Protestant and Catholic Europe or Muslim societies in the Middle East, linguistic ties shared across national borders in Anglophone and Francophone Africa, processes of economic development and democratization experienced in Asia, historical legacies derived from patterns of colonial settlement in sub-Saharan Africa and Latin American nations, and memories of the Soviet state in central and eastern Europe. These residual attitudes can be expected to be deep-rooted historically, evolving closely, and thus persisting over many decades as sticky shared cultural orientations toward trust in nations and global regions, almost irrespective of the contemporary short- or medium-term performance of regimes and states, such as the disruption triggered by rapid opening of market economies in central Europe, transitions from authoritarianism in the third-wave era, or processes of democratic backsliding in recent years. As a result, cultural attitudes and values are predicted to be path dependent, so that observed patterns of social, political, and international trust reflect past societal experiences—but legacy attitudes and beliefs are unlikely to respond to contemporary changes in social conditions, like sudden upticks or downturns in levels of unemployment and growth, or to shifts in governance, like the downfall of dictators or the sudden rise to power of authoritarian populist leaders.

Or Agency Performance?

The final alternative perspective expounded in this book builds upon the extensive literature in political economy which has examined empirical evidence for performance theories. This account can be applied to multiple agents, but it has most commonly been applied to understand trust in government. In these accounts, political trust is explained either by subjective public perceptions or objective indicators of the competence, integrity, and impartiality of governments.

The first approach predicts that citizens will have greater confidence in state institutions where governing parties have established a track record demonstrating competence in delivering on their campaign promises, especially by managing the effective delivery of essential public goods and services. Short-term upturns and downticks in economic performance, like the effects on employment of the Eurozone banking crisis in 2007–2008 and from the outbreak of the Covid-19 pandemic, are expected to be correlated with subsequent thermostatic shifts in public confidence in government and political institutions like parliaments and parties, as well as general satisfaction with democracy.[31] This view is similar to standard theories of economic voting which assume that citizens are able to recognize and respond to changes in economic conditions attributable to public policies, in order to assign responsibility, and reward or penalize governments accordingly at the ballot box.[32] Empirical studies have usually defined performance fairly narrowly when analyzing standard aggregate indicators from official statistics measuring the government's competency in managing the macroeconomy, such as by expanding the national economy, as well as by minimizing inflation, unemployment, and poverty.[33] Researchers have examined individual-level survey data to see whether trust relates to subjective satisfaction with the state of the national and household economy.[34] Based on these sorts of claims, Kettl suggests that governments could earn back public trust by getting better at doing what he calls the retail-level functions of delivering, operationally, policies that are fair and effective, connected to what people want.[35]

But when evaluating government performance, does the public care most about policy outcomes—or are they also concerned about political procedures, reflecting how power and authority are exercised in any state?[36] A second strand of the research literature has studied the performance of government decision-making processes. Many researchers have focused on whether generalized social and political trust is strengthened by what is commonly termed "good" government or the "quality" of government, including institutions concerned with implementation and enforcement, like the quality of rule of law, transparency, and oversight, which seek to protect the integrity and impartiality of policymaking processes and prevent the abuse of power by any branch of government.[37] Others suggest that public confidence is also influenced by the function of institutions and processes on the "input" side of liberal democracy that channel citizen's demands into the policymaking process, like the integrity of free and fair elections, the inclusiveness of channels of political participation, and competition among political parties.[38]

At the same time, however, standard performance theories also face considerable challenges. In particular, there are several reasons why it is difficult to establish convincing empirical evidence connecting subjective perceptions of government competency, integrity, and impartiality with subsequent levels of social and political trust among citizens.

Policy outcome studies using cross-national comparisons usually assume that the public decides whether governments are trustworthy based on their country's economic record compared against the benchmark of equivalent conditions in similar neighboring states or countries—such as how well the Biden administration handled the economic disruption in the United States caused by the Covid-19 pandemic compared with the experience of equivalent disruptions in the United Kingdom, Spain, or Germany. But it remains unclear what values and information citizens use to evaluate the government's performance. Do voters judge the economic record of their government against the benchmark and targets which governing parties promised to achieve in their campaign, party manifesto, and leadership election speeches? Or is economic management evaluated retrospectively by the public as doing better or worse than the past performance of successive administrations and leaders within a country, thus comparing pandemic cases, fatalities, and mitigation measures under the Trump and Biden administrations? Similar considerations face studies of the impartiality and integrity of government procedures.

Moreover, for studies of competent policy delivery, what issues count? Are economic conditions the most salient criteria used by the public to evaluate the government's record and competence, as is often assumed, or should studies expand their scope by also monitoring the impact of government decisions and actions on a far broader range of salient non-economic issues which the public regards as the most important problems facing the country, such as the provision of public welfare services like healthcare and education, challenges of environmental protection and climate change, or foreign policies such as engagement in international cooperation and conflict?[39] Similarly, does the public care most about procedural issues of corruption, fairness, or inclusion?

In addition, even when strong correlations are observed to link public trust and government performance indices, challenges of causal inference arise in our interpretation of the direction of causality involved in the core relationships. Many studies have used subjective evaluations of policy and procedural performance, such as public opinion surveys monitoring satisfaction with the government's handling of the state of the economy, the state of corruption, the fairness of elections, and so on.[40] It would not be surprising, however, if our feelings of trustworthiness prove to be closely associated with such *subjective* perceptions of the past performance of agents. Indeed, this is commonly observed; thus people expressing confidence in their personal financial position and in the state of their nation's economy are often also more willing to trust political institutions, as well as expressing more satisfaction with the workings of democracy.[41] Yet the direction of causality in this complex relationship remains indeterminate; interpretations based on surveys taken at a single point of time face issues of endogeneity where prior beliefs and preferences may color assessments of good or bad performance. Do perceptions of a strong economic performance lead me to be more trusting about the government? Or because I trust a particular party or leader, am I more likely to be positive when assessing their economic record?

Finally, even if the direction is demonstrated to run from prior subjective assessments of performance to subsequent feelings of trust, this in itself cannot be regarded as providing skeptical and informed assessments, not least because many other factors covary. The links connecting subjective feelings of economic satisfaction with political trust are complex to interpret with cross-sectional survey data alone due to issues of reciprocal causation.[42] Among US Republicans, for example, Pew surveys report that optimism about the state of the American economy shot up one month after President Trump won the November 2016 US election. Three-quarters of Republicans predicted that the economy would get better, up from 29% the previous June, even though there was no change in the underlying economic indicators.[43] Similarly, Pew surveys in September 2018 report that perceptions that presidents are honest and trustworthy are closely conditioned by partisanship, with around three-quarters of Republicans believing that Trump is trustworthy, compared with one in ten Democrats.[44] Challenges can also arise when inferring causal links between trust and objective measures of performance, since again reciprocal relationships may operate, for example if more generalized trust in society serves to make markets more efficient, thereby strengthening prosperity. Attempts to overcome these limitations involve using longitudinal panel surveys repeatedly interviewing the same

respondents over an extended period of months or years, applying instrumental variables, as well as by using laboratory, field, or population-based
survey experiments.[45]

II. The Theory of Skeptical Trust

Each of these standard accounts contributes toward the debate about the
origins of trust, but each also has certain important limitations. Building
upon performance theories, it is timely to conduct a major reassessment of
the concept, drivers, and consequences of this phenomenon.

Several related concepts are often used interchangeably to describe the
underlying phenomenon, and these deserve to be clarified more precisely.
The notions of "confidence" and "trust" can be defined as the belief that certain future outcomes will probably happen. Weather forecasts predict an 80%
chance of rain. The World Bank projects that rising rates of global economic
growth are likely. The Centers for Disease Control and Prevention (CDC)
expects fatal risks from Covid-19 variants to fall. And so on. The related concept of "trust" also means the expectation by principals that agencies (collective institutions) or specific agents (individuals) are expected to achieve
certain outcomes. More precisely, building upon these ideas, the central
notion of "trustworthiness" used at the heart of this study is understood to
involve *an informal social contract where principals delegate authority to agencies (collective institutions) or to agents (specific individuals) to act on their behalf in the expectation that they will fulfill their responsibilities, even in risky
and uncertain situations.* This process is expected to generate certain goals,
whether for themselves, their family, and local community, for their government and society, or for the world. Decisions about trustworthiness may involve expectations about the behavior of family, friends, and neighbors in the
local community (in cases of social trust). Or they may concern the actions
of expert elites, groups, and organizations in civil society, the private sector,
or government (in cases of institutional trust). Or they may be about predictable relations with other countries, world leaders, or the role of multinational
agencies, like the World Health Organization and United Nations (in cases of
international trust).

The key empirical question which arises is whether public assessments
of trustworthiness are relatively accurate and informed, as indicated by

their being systematically correlated with subjective perceptions and/or to independent objective measures of agency performance. The latter can be monitored through internationally standardized indicators gauging a range of policy *outputs* (like levels of public-sector spending on healthcare and schools as a proportion of GDP) and policy *outcomes* (such as rates of maternal and child mortality, literacy, rates of Covid-19 fatalities, and growth in per capita GDP).[46] The direction of causality in any association remains to be determined. But observing any significant and strong correlations would provide proxy evidence that trust judgments by the general public are systematically related to the performance of agencies.[47]

And, equally importantly, an important distinction can be drawn between agency actions and regulatory processes.[48] Given imperfect information to judge future vulnerability to risk, and the existence of a few bad apples in any bag, do reliable and effective procedural guardrails ensure against the risks of potential scorpions by deterring or punishing bad actors? The strength of *accountability guardrails* can be expected to provide structural safeguards against potential risks arising from betrayal by incompetent, self-interested, or dishonest agents. Others have also emphasized the importance in this regard of impartiality and integrity to hinder the abuse of executive power.[49] Are there formal mechanisms of accountability and redress, for example effective legal sanctions through the courts if investment advisors abscond with funds? Do professional medical boards strip licenses of physicians who violate ethical standards? Do elections allow citizens to "kick the rascals out" if politicians are caught red-handed in corruption scandals? Are there bureaucratic penalties if dishonest UN officials take bribes? These types of considerations are not about trusting individuals, such as the skills and experience of specific lawyers or doctors, or being satisfied with the competency of the government's delivery of public goods and services, or having confidence in particular international agencies such as the World Health Organization. Rather, procedural trust is more about confidence in the integrity and impartiality of the institutions and processes ensuring collective accountability, in the event of any individual incompetence and performance failure. In assessing the competency, integrity, and impartiality of governments, this study can take advantage of the recent proliferation of cross-national performance indicators, disseminated by international monitoring agencies and academic research projects, gauging the delivery of specific policy goals and the quality of *processes* of accountable governance, such as those gathering expert perceptions of liberal democracy, corruption, press freedom, levels of electoral integrity, and rule of law in each nation-state.

Determining Errors in Judgments of Trustworthiness

Why, when, and where do people predict trustworthiness accurately? Why do they fail? In many ways, human errors and biases about trustworthiness can be expected to arise for similar reasons as any other flawed risk-reward assessments of the consequences arising from our actions, for instance whether estimating the hazards of driving over the speed limit, the threat of side effects from Covid-19 vaccines, or the risks of burning fossil fuels for climate change. Following in the footsteps of Simon (1956), and Tversky and Kahneman (1974), researchers have long sought to understand the limits of rational information processing and the use of heuristic shortcuts for decision-making under conditions of risk and uncertainty, such as those based on simplified strategies of bounded rationality and satisficing.[50] Skeptical forecasts about trustworthiness are understood in this study as reasonably reliable decisions about the reputation and past performance of agents, and the accountability safeguards in place should agents fail. This forms the basis of preliminary decisions about the agent's likely future behavior, with these appraisals adjusted sequentially in a running tally as further reliable information comes to light. Such estimates reflect open vigilance against misleading claims and incorrect beliefs, a vital process to sort out truth from falsity in a world of misinformation and disinformation.[51]

What explains systematic biases in flawed decisions about trustworthy relationships? The "mediated performance model" depicted in Figure 2.1 summarizes the book's core analytical theory. To build upon previous rational choice performance theories, this study argues that it is important to unpack mediating conditions which can help to understand the intervening steps and the causal chain within the "black box" performance model more fully. As van der Meer argues, it is insufficient to study only the links connecting subjective public perceptions of procedural fairness with political trust, or to examine only the links connecting objective indicators of the actual quality of governance with public perceptions; instead, research ideally needs to establish the complete sequence of steps in the causal chain.[52] As illustrated in Figure 2.1, the theory suggests that in the first step, agency performance

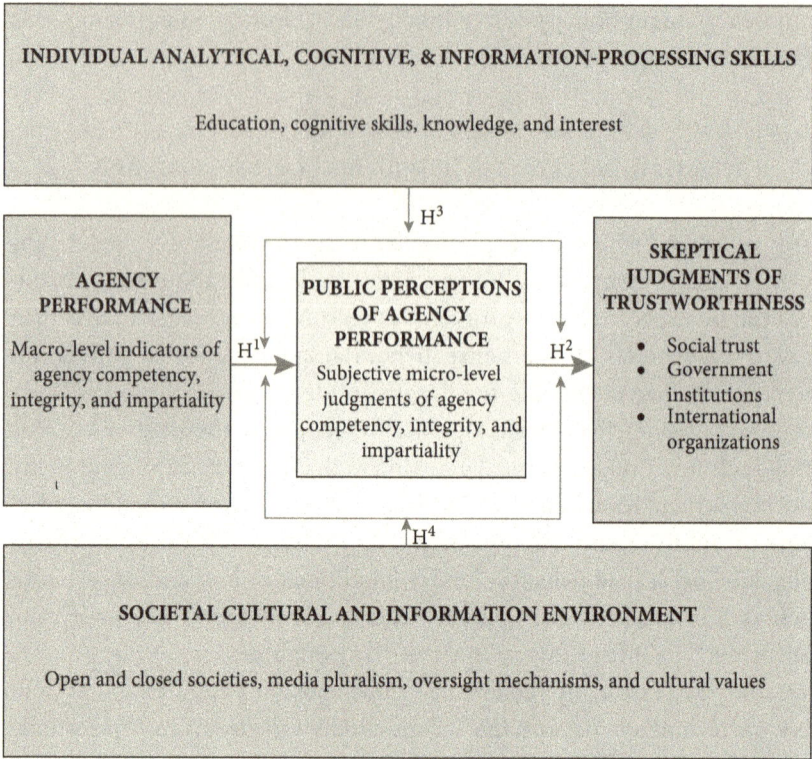

Figure 2.1. Heuristic model of skeptical judgments of trustworthiness.

and accountability safeguards (measured by objective indicators) are likely to affect public perceptions (monitored by subjective judgments) (H^1). In the second step, subjective public perceptions are expected to influence their views of agency trustworthiness (H^2).

The fourfold typology illustrated in Figure 1.1 in Chapter 1, categorizing biases in types of decisions about potentially trustworthy relationships, is operationalized and the empirical evidence tested through two criteria. First, skeptical judgments are defined in practice as those which display a reasonable degree of *external* consistency. This is measured by how strongly public judgments about trustworthiness are correlated with objective macro-level benchmarks of agency performance and with the effectiveness of accountability mechanisms. Second, skeptical judgments are also expected to display process of *internal* deliberation (the reasons given for trust decisions) involving judgments about the competence (capacity), integrity (honesty), and impartiality (neutrality) of the agent.

Internal Consistency

One way to open the black box, and to identify the rationality of our judgments, is to establish whether assessments of trustworthiness reflect processes of internal deliberation. Skeptical citizens should be able to offer reasonably coherent and consistent reasons for their assessments, to explain logically why they believe that agents or agencies are or are not trustworthy. Others have argued that perceptions of impartiality are likely to prove particularly important in this regard, and indeed a series of studies has demonstrated the empirical link between public perceptions of corruption and political trust.[53] But this is only one possible criterion for evaluating the process of government and vulnerability to the abuse of power. For example, many leaders may be regarded as scrupulously honest yet deeply incompetent. Or indeed they may be acknowledged as deeply corrupt and morally flawed, but still effective at delivering public goods rewarding their supporters.

The three standard key criteria of performance identified for this purpose in previous research, as summarized by Mayer et al., include perceptions about the agents' *competence* (their technical knowledge, skills, aptitude, and training strengthening their ability to deliver), *impartiality* (or benevolence and altruism in serving on behalf of the principal, setting aside self-interest), and *integrity* (the agent's ethical reputation for honesty, fairness, and truthfulness).[54] For example, are political leaders seen as able to fulfill their campaign promises, while serving the public interest and being transparent and open in their dealings? If decisions about trustworthiness are strongly associated with these criteria, this suggests a more deliberative and thoughtful process of skeptical evaluation. On the other hand, if political leaders are regarded as trustworthy despite being perceived as lacking these qualities, this suggests that affective projections and cultural values may play a stronger role, for example if feelings toward political leaders are driven mainly by negative partisanship (dislike of the other side), by ideological views about the role of government, or by identity cues derived from shared personal characteristics and social traits. While long regarded theoretically as some of the main components of trust decision in previous research, it is important to establish the weight which citizens give to competence, impartiality, and integrity when assessing the past reputation of agents, as well as their subjective views about the strength of the accountability mechanisms if they fail to prove trustworthy in the future. It is also important to determine whether such judgments play a similar role for different agents—and across diverse cultures and contexts.

External Consistency

The capacity of people to provide logical reasons consistent with their evaluations of agency performance and their decisions about trustworthiness encourages us to infer an internal process of skeptical deliberation. Yet this provides only a relatively weak test that performance matters. The underlying psychological motivations and cognitive processes for arriving at trust judgments cannot be observed directly through this method, and decisions may involve a circular process of rationalization. Thus, positive characteristics like competence, impartiality, or integrity may be attributed to agents based on affective orientations, such as loyalty, partisanship, selective perceptions, or gut instincts. As noted earlier, many previous researchers have linked subjective judgments of the government's economic performance with judgments about political trust and confidence. But some degrees of reciprocity in cognitive processes is likely to occur in this process. For example, surveys suggest that when Democrats and Republicans evaluated the conditions of the US national economy, their opinions responded rapidly to changes in the White House, driven by partisanship, irrespective of stable economic indices like jobs and growth.[55] Comparative studies report that this is fairly typical since people often perceive national rates of unemployment, economic growth, and crime more positively when their preferred party or leader is in power.[56] Motivated reasoning is likely to filter perceptions of agency performance. Partisanship and other related heuristic cues can influence information processing and knowledge of factual matters, especially judgments about matters like foreign affairs, where ordinary people lack cues from direct experience.

Tests of external consistency, where judgments of trust by principals correlate with objective indicators of agency performance, provide more rigorous evidence of rational judgments of trustworthiness. The typology of trustworthy judgments at the heart of the book uses this approach, and correlations are categorized by both the direction and strength of any observed relationships. As illustrated heuristically in Figure 1.1 in Chapter 1, skeptical judgments of trustworthiness are indicated where public assessments of trustworthy agents and agencies are strongly and significantly correlated with objective performance indices of agency competency, integrity, and impartiality, with observations falling on the line. The direction generates either relationships of *skeptical trust* (observed where public trust and performance indices are both strongly positively correlated) or of *skeptical mistrust* (where they are both strongly negative).

Errors in Assessments of Trustworthiness

By contrast, where public assessments of agency trustworthiness diverge sharply from indicators of agency performance, this can potentially generate two types of errors. One concerns overly *cynical* biases, where citizens are too critical in their judgments, failing to express confidence in benevolent actors, even to the detriment of their own individual interests and societal well-being. Dogmatic anti-vaxxers, for example, risk their own lives and the safety of their family and community despite scientific evidence about the threats from Covid-19 and the effective protection offered by approved vaccines. Cynical citizens who falsely believe that elections are rigged may refuse to vote, empowering illiberal strongmen. Or xenophobes may be afraid to travel abroad, missing cultural pleasures and new experiences. This orientation is indicated in the illustration by weakly negative correlations (representing outliers to the line of fit) linking positive objective performance indices with low public assessments of trustworthiness.

The other response, which is more rarely highlighted in the literature, concerns overly *credulous* relationships of blind trust, where the public harms their own interests by being too trusting, deferential, and cult-like toward malevolent agents, like investing faith in the false promises of snake-oil charlatans, surrendering savings to confidence tricksters, and falling for the promises of demagogic political leaders—all scorpions. Through gullibility, a person is easily tricked or manipulated to believe harmful propositions unsupported by valid factual evidence and objective standards of reality, for example believing former president Trump's suggestion that drinking bleach will prevent Covid-19. This orientation is indicated in the typology by weakly positive correlations (or outliers to the line of fit) linking public assessments of high trustworthiness with poor performance indices by agents.

The performance model, depicted in Figure 2.1, is relatively straightforward and parsimonious.[57] At the same time, however, the black box model and the heuristic typology also raise multiple questions about the conditions influencing judgments of trustworthiness.

III. Intermediary Conditions

The mediated model depicted in Figure 2.1, at the heart of this study, predicts that several *intermediary conditions* operating at micro and macro levels are likely to expand the capacity to make skeptical and unbiased judgments of trustworthiness, strengthening the external consistency of objective performance indices and citizens' judgments of trustworthiness.

Cognitive Skills and Education

First, *analytical, cognitive, and information processing skills derived from education* are expected to be useful in helping to sort truth from falsehoods (H³), thereby increasing the rationality of skeptical judgments of trustworthiness, so that there is a closer correlation linking public assessments with performance indices.[58] These capacities can be inferred indirectly by proxy measures, including years of formal education as well as knowledge, interest, and information derived from interpersonal discussions and attention to news and social media as information sources.

Many researchers have observed that more educated people are generally more likely to trust other people.[59] The 2020 Global Attitudes Survey by Pew Research compared fourteen postindustrial societies and reported that in every country but one (Japan) social trust was lower among people with less education than among those with more education, and in most places the education gap was 10 percentage points or more.[60] Nevertheless, the links between education and judgments of political trust are less well established. The theory developed in this book suggests that knowledge reduces uncertainty about the world—and thus the risks of trusting others, assuming that, in the absence of information (like dealing with strangers), the default position is one of cautious mistrust. Over and above this effect, however, in making complex judgments of agency trustworthiness, formal learning is also likely to expand logical capacities and sophistical thinking skills, an important consideration in societies replete with disinformation and misinformation. Education and knowledge are expected to be particularly useful resources for facilitating slow, effortful, and reflective thinking processes associated with open vigilance toward accepting new arguments and beliefs.[61] The more educated are also expected to be more sensitively attuned to reading signals of social untrustworthiness.[62] Therefore, formal education, as a proxy for analytical, cognitive, and information-processing skills, is predicted to serve as one of the important intermediary conditions strengthening the accuracy of both public perceptions of agency performance and also the capacity to make wise judgments of trustworthiness.

Freedom of Expression in Open Societies

Beyond these capacities, however, the broader macro-level context of the information environment in open and closed societies is predicted to be even more important by serving as necessary but not sufficient intermediary conditions for skeptical decision-making (H[4]). Thus, more informed decisions about trustworthy political leaders, political parties, civil service officials, and state authorities are likely to be maximized in open societies with freedom of expression, media pluralism, and accountability mechanisms, all closely associated with the type of democratic or autocratic regime governing each state, combined with levels of human development, expanding literacy, schooling, and media access in each society. By contrast, in closed societies the free exchange of information is constrained by the regime, independent journalism critical of the authorities is repressed, and the state controls the media. In this context, citizens may respond either cynically, typically by dismissing any positive news about the government's performance as the product of propaganda and misinformation, or else may react compliantly, by credulously believing state propaganda suggesting that the authorities are benevolent and trustworthy, even when, in fact, leaders and institutions are deeply corrupt, incompetent, and self-serving.

As well as freedom of expression and media pluralism, transparency and accountability in the public sphere are expected to be strengthened by institutions of "good governance," as exemplified by judicial independence and rule of law, anti-corruption laws, and professional standards regulating public-sector management.[63] In contrast, if elected or appointed officials have repeatedly failed to fulfill their responsibilities and if they have betrayed the public interest in the past, through proving venal, scandal-ridden, or narcissistic, then skeptical citizens should conclude that they will probably prove untrustworthy in the future. This type of assessment goes beyond discontent with particular policy decisions and actions, or the delivery of specific outcomes like economic growth, welfare, and national security, to tap into more deep-rooted perceptions about how governments generally work and safeguards against the abuse of power. Similar considerations concern accountability mechanisms for other types of agents and agencies, such as the role of press councils in maintaining professional standards in newsrooms, medical associations monitoring cases of medical malpractice by physicians, and safety standards agencies protecting workers and consumers from risk of injury in the corporate sector.

The book's theory therefore predicts that the public's judgments of trustworthiness are likely to be more accurate in open democratic societies, characterized by legislative oversight of the executive and courts, investigative journalistic watchdogs, and independent oversight agencies monitoring maladministration and malpractices by state and local authorities. Unfortunately these accountability mechanisms are expected to prove less effective in countries where these types of oversight bodies and the independent news media have come under growing attack. Some of the most troubling indications of democratic backsliding in recent decades concern increasing restrictions on freedom of expression and civil liberties, including through state censorship of the independent media, unofficial government harassment of critical journalists, and expanded libel or defamation laws, illustrated in cases such as Hungary, Turkey, and Poland.[64] Levitsky and Ziblatt suggest that the readiness of illiberal rulers to undermine the unwritten norms and institutional guardrails of democracy is sign of a growing drift toward authoritarian practices in recent decades. This problem is exemplified by the former president Trump's repeated depiction of the mainstream news media as "enemies of the people," dismissing critical coverage of his administration as biased and inaccurate "fake news," and subjecting several individual journalists to a barrage of vitriolic attacks and even inciting violence toward them.[65] Monitoring agencies such as Freedom House have documented growing attacks on press freedom in many countries during the past decade: "The media have fallen prey to . . . nuanced efforts to throttle their independence. Common methods include government-backed ownership changes, regulatory and financial pressure, and public denunciations of journalists. Governments have also offered proactive support to friendly outlets through measures such as lucrative state contracts, favorable regulatory decisions, and preferential access to state information. The goal is to make the press serve those in power rather than the public."[66] Reporters without Borders report that more extreme practices suppressing freedom of expression and the role of the independent media are evident in some of the world's most closed societies and repressive autocracies ruled by dictators bent on staying in power at any cost, with countries such as Eritrea, North Korea, Turkmenistan, and China ranked worst in their 2021 Press Freedom Index. These techniques of propaganda and censorship are exemplified by Putin's draconian clampdown on press freedom in Russia following his military invasion of Ukraine. In these types of cases, human rights monitors like Amnesty International report that states commonly disseminate misinformation, attack investigative journalists, activist bloggers, and pro-democracy campaigners, imprison or exile critics of the regime, restrict public access to foreign media and digital communication channels, and promote one-sided propaganda emphasizing the benevolence and wisdom of the country's leaders.[67] Where voices critical of the regime are restricted, the public lacks access to two-sided information essential to evaluate the performance of the authorities with any degree of accuracy. Even in open societies, however, information echo chambers exist, especially where media systems are both fragmented into multiple platforms and also highly polarized. This generates media systems with external diversity, reflecting different partisan and ideological viewpoints spread across a wide range of newspapers, television channels, social media, and digital platforms. But users can self-select in this environment so that they are not exposed to a diversity of alternative viewpoints and sources.

Cultural Lags

This theory does not seek to deny that the enduring imprint of cultural biases and long-standing beliefs in each society may well persist as sticky phenomena or lagged attitudes shaping contemporary judgments of the performance and thus trustworthiness of the authorities—and of friends, neighbors, and strangers, or of civil society organizations and other countries. Culture matters, of course. Long-standing values, shared beliefs, and similar attitudes observed among countries within global cultural regions are expected to evolve gradually over time, rather than responding immediately to short-term changes in performance. But a major disconnect between cultural attitudes and the actual competency, impartiality, and integrity of agents and agencies can generate overly cynical citizens who fail to comply with trustworthy agents, such as those people refusing to go along with prevention and mitigation measures against Covid-19 despite the advice of medical authorities and the scientific evidence confirming the life-saving properties of preventive treatments. Or a major disconnect can induce the opposite sin of compliant citizens, trusting the untrustworthy, such as those expressing blind faith in medical quackery, uncritically accepting the word of political leaders and media commentators pursuing partisan advantage over the public interest, and believing online conspiratorial theories.

The theoretical framework remains relatively parsimonious—many other factors may be associated with skeptical evaluations of trustworthiness. It remains unclear from the wealth of previous research on social, political, and international forms of trust how far public judgments of trustworthiness are indeed commonly skeptical—meaning displaying signs of processes of internal deliberation and external consistency with objective performance indicators—or how far feelings of cynicism or credulity generally predominate in diverse societies. The theory developed in this book makes no a priori claims about the overall distribution of types of trustworthiness. That is to say, this investigation does not start from the assumption that many or most estimates of agency trustworthiness are or are not the result of skeptical processes of reasoning. The theory does predict, however, that both individual cognitive skills and societal information environments are likely to strengthen the skeptical rationality of trustworthy judgments, as measured empirically by the strength of the correlation linking objective output and process performance indices with subjective assessments of agencies—and ultimately with public predictions of trustworthiness. In short, biased errors generating inaccurate predictions of future trustworthiness based on past performance, and thus both the cultural biases associated with overly negative cynicism and unduly positive credulity, are expected to arise most commonly where (i) individuals lack cognitive skills, awareness, and knowledge from education and literacy, and where (ii) they live in closed societies and media communities lacking multiple sources of alternative information and viewpoint diversity, so that inaccurate cultural biases are reinforced and people believe false promises, one-sided propaganda, and disinformation. Flawed estimates of trustworthiness are predicted to be especially evident in places where both conditions prevail. On these grounds, judgments of trustworthiness reflecting cultural biases are expected to be most commonly

observed in closed societies lacking freedom of expression and media pluralism, as well as in low-income developing societies among social sectors
lacking literacy and education, cognitive skills, and civic awareness.

This argument establishes the foundation for the next chapter. Chapter 3
summarizes the pros and cons of experimental and observational comparative methods and evidence, describes the research design for the empirical
analysis and the measurement of the key concepts in this study, and considers
how far survey indicators of trust can themselves be regarded as reliable and
trustworthy, especially in closed societies and repressive autocracies.

3

Evidence

What evidence would allow the general theory of skeptical trust to be tested empirically? This chapter describes the data used to operationalize the book's typology and analyze how far trust relationships are based on informed calculations, evidence, and logical reasoning, and the conditions most conducive to skeptical judgments.

To start, Section I reviews alternative techniques and methods commonly used in previous research to understand trust. This includes game simulations, field observations, laboratory and field experiments, case studies, formal modeling, expert surveys, longitudinal macro- and micropanel surveys, and cross-sectional comparative surveys. Debate continues about the pros and cons of using experiments facilitating causal inference, widely employed in behavioral economics and social psychology, and using descriptive observational data from social surveys, maximizing generalizability in any observed relationships, an approach common in political science, comparative sociology, and studies of public opinion.

Section II outlines the research design at the heart of the book, which uses survey evidence both to operationalize the typology of trust relationships and to test the theorized impact of agency reputation and accountability guardrails on trust decision, with individual cognitive skills and the broader information environment serving as the main intermediary conditions expected to strengthen skeptical judgments.

Section III explains how the core concepts are operationalized from sources of macro- and micro-level data. This includes describing the dependent variables—six dimensions of trust and their components. For data, the study draws on the pooled European Values Survey/World Values Survey (EVS/WVS), covering 120 societies around the world in the seven waves since the study was established in the early 1980s. The independent variables gauge agency performance through both subjective evaluations, including micro-level satisfaction and perceptions of agency integrity, capacity, and benevolence, and objective macro-level indices, such as levels of economic growth and corruption in each society.

Section IV discusses the reliability of the survey data since response biases may arise from many sources, including question phrasing, item order, and self-censorship on sensitive questions. The EVS/WVS responses to items on confidence in parliament, political parties, the police, and the courts are compared with equivalent items in the European Social Survey, and confirmed to be highly correlated at national level. With self-censorship, when asked to express their views about the authorities, for fear of potential penalties, the public may be particularly reluctant to give authentic answers, especially in societies governed by repressive regimes which restrict freedom of speech. To examine this issue, an item-count experiment was included in WVS-7 surveys in selected authoritarian regimes. Finally, the conclusion in Section V summarizes how the research design used in this study differs from many previous studies.

I. Alternative Methods for Understanding Trust

What empirical methods allow researchers to examine theories of trust and trustworthiness? Varied techniques, analytical approaches, and data sources have been used in diverse disciplines, including game simulations, field observations, laboratory and field experiments, case studies, formal modeling, macro and micro-level longitudinal panel surveys, instrumental variables, and cross-sectional comparative surveys.[1] Each has its own strengths and limits.

Experimental Designs

Perhaps the most common approach, used by social psychologists and behavioral economists to support strong causal inferences, examines micro-level interpersonal trust relationships by utilizing experimental game simulations within artificial laboratory settings. Experiments control the recruitment, random assignment, and measurement of subjects randomized into treatment groups to maximize causal inference. This approach is exemplified by the canonical Prisoner's Dilemma role-playing exercise, designed by Berg et al. to model the willingness of pairs of individuals to engage in hypothetical forms of cooperative behavior, treated as a proxy measure of expectations about the trustworthiness of other people.[2] In a widely cited study conducted among Harvard undergraduates, Glaezer and colleagues manipulated trust games among senders and receivers involving small monetary rewards.[3] They concluded that trusting behavior (the return of a monetary gift) was not predicted by attitudes of social trust, using standard survey questions. Experiments manipulating key variables in treatments, such as selecting groups of subjects based on their gender or race, or varying the risks and rewards in any hypothetical simulation, are thought to allow researchers to pinpoint alternative causes and conditions of trust. To strengthen the external validity, robustness, and generalizability of any findings, trust simulations have been implemented in different countries and contexts—and the results compared with survey data among representative populations.[4] These methods are most useful for precise control of the experimental conditions, holding other aspects constant, and thus for making causal inferences about individual behavior with a reasonable degree of confidence, ruling out confounding conditions.[5] Laboratory experiments monitor hypothetical forms of interpersonal cooperative behavior among individuals, treated as a proxy for social or interpersonal trust, as well as the background characteristics of those who trust, such as their education, race or ethnicity, or age cohort.[6]

Nevertheless, game simulations and lab experiments have several key limitations for our purposes.

First, the artificial lab setting facilitates precise control of interpersonal social trust relationships, but it is less suited to monitor dimensions of trustworthiness which cannot be easily manipulated, due to practical or ethical constraints.[7] Experimental games have been used to study the effect on trusting behavior of introducing various rules, such as sanction systems[8] and binding contracts.[9] Simulations like the Prisoner's Dilemma game are designed to provide reliable insights into human motivations, since "actions speak louder than words." In practice, however, willingness to engage in cooperative behaviors may be the result of multiple factors other than trust. Participants may choose to return monetary gifts due to their preference for risk aversion, perceptions of socially desirable behaviors, or altruism toward others, as much as any judgments of reciprocal trustworthiness.[10]

Moreover, it is hazardous to generalize about human behavior on the basis of hypothetical reactions among atypical local groups, such as students or paid volunteers. The randomization process selects participants into control and treatment groups to determine group similarities and differences in response to the treatment. But this does not necessarily allow broader generalizations beyond the selected populations; the reaction of young college students in Iowa or paid local volunteers in Michigan to any treatment condition may well be expected to differ from that of older Americans in Florida or black rural populations in Mississippi, let alone the response of diverse peoples living in other cultures and countries worldwide.

Comparativists emphasize that the broader cultural, institutional, and societal context is critical for trust and trustworthy relationships, as illustrated by the well-established high social and political trust observed in Scandinavia and Northern Europe, compared with far greater mistrust commonly recorded in post-Communist Europe and Latin America.[11] Some large-scale cross-national field experiments have been conducted among the general public, exemplified by the global "dropped wallet" study.[12] Population-based survey experiments are growing in popularity as these combine the advantages of generalizability from a representative sample of the general adult population, with the rigor from random allocation of survey respondents to control and treatment groups.[13] Section IV in this chapter discusses the results of just such a cross-national survey experiment, using the technique of item list counts to test for response bias in leadership approval. Unfortunately, despite its strengths, survey experiments are costly to implement, especially across societies, so they remain far less common than those conducted among small groups in artificial laboratory settings.[14]

Researchers have also taken advantage of longitudinal panel surveys which monitor changes in the attitudes and opinions of the same individual respondent over successive waves to take advantage of naturally occurring random events, maximizing realism. For example, this approach has been used to examine the dynamics of American trust before and after the events of 9/11,[15] to examine trust among Leave and Remain voters in the United Kingdom pre-post the Brexit referendum,[16] to determine how far trust influences people's willingness to vote for protest parties,[17] and whether the quality of political institutions influences subsequent levels of generalized trust.[18] But in practice the impact of real-world "shock" events may also prove far from randomly distributed. For example, the Covid-19 pandemic caused US states to expand balloting facilities, like no-excuse postal and advance voting, which could be expected to increase convenience and thus state voter turnout. Overall levels of electoral turnout in the 2020 US presidential election were the highest in the United States since 1960. But the adoption of these facilities was far from uniform across the country, generating confounding conditions, since Democratic-controlled states were more likely to implement advance voting than Republican-controlled ones, and the initial spread of the virus during the spring of 2020 was more severe in urban areas and coastal regions of the United States than in isolated rural counties.

The Comparative Framework

The classic logic of comparative politics is to observe judgments of trustworthiness toward different types of agents among diverse groups, including those living in a wide variety of open and closed societies, cultures, and institutional contexts, providing a high degree of generalizability.[19] Most cross-national studies using survey data about trust have focused upon liberal democracies, where survey data sets have long been established, such as the Eurobarometer, European Social Survey, the International Social Survey Program, and national election studies. This book also compares a wide range of affluent postindustrial societies, open societies, and long-established liberal democracies, where reliable time-series survey data have traditionally been most plentiful, such as Germany, the United States, and Sweden, to replicate and update previous research. But seeking to generalize from Western countries alone unintentionally distorts our understanding of this global phenomenon, by focusing upon a truncated and skewed distribution of cases. Experimental studies report that if you lost a wallet full of cash in Geneva, Oslo, or Stockholm, for example, you could safely bet that someone will probably seek to return it to you or to hand it in to the police. But the same calculation could well prove foolhardy in, say, Lima, Rabat, or Nairobi.[20] Generalizing based on affluent and secure open societies alone is problematic, especially to understand trust and trustworthiness under repressive rulers and authoritarian states. We ideally need to expand the comparison to include diverse high-risk contexts, including among poor communities in the world's developing societies, like in rural Bangladesh, Ethiopia, Myanmar, and Zimbabwe, where too often life for millions proves dangerous, there are threats of ethnic conflict, and many people are vulnerable to humanitarian and natural disasters, with endemic poverty, social inequality, and short life expectancy. The risks of trusting the authorities are highest among closed societies governed by repressive rulers, with minimal domestic guardrails against the abuse of executive power, especially in major states resistant to international pressures, and with state control of media.

For the theory developed in this book, the cross-national framework needs to be able to compare contrasts in the information environment characteristic of open and closed societies, since these conditions are predicted theoretically to be important for trust judgments.

Since this study's design seeks to generalize about social, political, and international trust across multiple diverse cultural contexts, including comparing levels of trust and trustworthiness in the world's most open and closed societies, it uses pooled data from the EVS/WVS. The pooled data set across all waves, used for the next chapter, facilitates comparison of cross-national and longitudinal survey data gathered from representative samples of the adult population in 120 societies around the world over successive waves from 1981 to 2021, as illustrated in Figure 3.3 later in the chapter. The book focuses in particular on analyzing on the most recent (7th) wave of the EVS/WVS pooled survey, where new items on trust were included, with data gathered in over 70 societies during 2017–2021.[21] Both these data sets include varied societal contexts, for example to compare absolute levels of trust commonly observed among the public living in open and closed societies under different types of democratic and authoritarian regimes, as well as across Protestant, Catholic, and Muslim religious cultures, in countries with long-established shared collective identities and social stability compared with deeply divided societies with a legacy of conflict, as well as in rich and poor societies with different levels of human development. The EVS/WVS contains numerous items monitoring absolute levels of social trust, confidence in a wide range of national institutions, and trust in international organizations.

The Information Environment

At the macro level, skeptical and affective judgments of trust in agents are predicted to vary according to the role of the media and the broader information environment in each society. In particular, in open societies, freedom of the press, the role of the media and investigative journalism as the fourth estate, and the existence of plural legacy and social media can all be expected to provide richer and more diverse sources of information which can facilitate the basis of rational trust judgments. By contrast, in closed societies, state control over the media through practices of censorship and propaganda can be expected to polarize trust in authorities, both reinforcing blind loyalties among supporters of the regime while also sowing distrust among their critics and opponents. The information environment in open and closed societies can be expected to prove important for what we learn about fellow people, national authorities, and the agencies of global governance. After all, beyond some routine dealings with local services, most of us have little direct experience or information which would allow us to evaluate the overall performance of national agencies, such as parliaments, governments, or the civil service. The primary agencies of cultural transmission include interpersonal communications among family and friends and the role of the news and social media when covering public affairs.

Thus, skeptical trust and mistrust can be expected to be conditioned by the availability of freedom of information in any society, including the absence of government censorship, the existence of pluralistic news media, and the protection of rights to freedom of expression and publication. Ipso facto, more severe limits on information pluralism in closed societies are expected to foster both more cynical *and* more credulous citizens, since one-sided messages from state propaganda and restricted media criticism of the regime are likely to condition public judgments of trustworthiness. The information environment, including the legacy news media and social media platforms, varies markedly under different types of regime. Monitoring organizations highlight major contrasts between open and closed societies in respect to freedom of expression, the use of official censorship and intimidation, constraints on journalism, and the role of intermediary watchdogs over the powerful, strengthening transparency and accountability.[22] Levels of economic and human development are also expected to be important, by expanding the population's access to education, literacy, and information.[23] Testing the contrasts between open and closed societies expands the comparative framework well beyond the common focus on contemporary democracies and affluent postindustrial societies.

At the same time, the role of the mass and social media on trust has long been a matter of contention, including the impact of the positive or negative direction of any media messages. Hence in the 1970s, theories of video-malaise by Michael Robinson claimed that extensive exposure to typical television entertainment and news was the root cause of a "mean world" effect, weakening trust in other people and in government and generating a broader sense of political malaise.[24] The typical negative slant of news coverage, especially "gotcha" journalisms focusing upon personal scandals, policy failures, and public-sector waste, has been blamed for damaging the image of government.[25] A steady diet of negative news is thought to encourage a rising tide of political disenchantment.[26] But this has been challenged by the "virtuous circle" counterargument theorizing that repeated exposure to the news media led to positive reinforcement over time, by increasing political awareness of processes, institutions, and actors, thereby encouraging greater knowledge and trust in the political system.[27] Debate remains, in part because of the difficulty of disentangling long-term processes of learning from media exposure from selection effects in the choice to switch on news media. As a result, some cross-sectional studies across or within societies have observed that the consumption of legacy and online news media is usually associated with higher political trust, but these findings have been challenged by others finding either decreased political trust or no effects.[28]

To measure the availability of plural sources of information, the Varieties of Democracy (V-Dem) annual estimate of Freedom of Expression and Alternative Sources of Information Index for each country is matched to the year of measuring government trust in the pooled EVS/WVS. The Index is designed by V-Dem to measure how far governments respect press and media freedom, the freedom of ordinary people to discuss political matters at home and in the public sphere, as well as the freedom of academic and cultural expression. The composite Index is formed from the V-Dem subindicators gauging media censorship effort, harassment of journalists, media bias, media self censorship, print/broadcast media critical, and print/ broadcast media perspectives, freedom of discussion for men/women, and freedom of academic and cultural expression. For the analysis in this chapter, nations are classified into "open" and "closed" societies based on dichotomizing the V-Dem Index around the mean score.

The mean scores for each society and the categorization into open and closed societies are illustrated in Table 3.1. Thus states such as China, Tajikistan, and Egypt are estimated to have the most restrictive freedom of expression scores. In China, for example, state and privately owned media are under the Communist Party's ever-tighter control, while the administration creates more and more obstacles for foreign reporters. Monitoring reports by Reporters without Borders rank China worst in the world for press freedom in 2020, with over 100 journalists jailed, many in life-threatening conditions.[29] In Tajikistan, pressures from President Rakhmon's government,

Table 3.1 Classifying Open and Closed Societies

CLOSED SOCIETIES	Mean	OPEN SOCIETIES	Mean
Croatia	0.74	Denmark	0.97
Lebanon	0.73	Germany	0.96
Poland	0.73	South Korea	0.96
Bulgaria	0.73	Switzerland	0.96
North Macedonia	0.72	United Kingdom	0.96
Philippines	0.71	Estonia	0.96
Bosnia Herzegovina	0.71	Sweden	0.96
Hong Kong SAR	0.71	France	0.96
Brazil	0.70	New Zealand	0.96
Iraq	0.70	Canada	0.95
Montenegro	0.69	Norway	0.95
Ukraine	0.68	Italy	0.95
Colombia	0.68	Portugal	0.95
Myanmar	0.67	Finland	0.95
Malaysia	0.66	Spain	0.94
Kyrgyzstan	0.66	Netherlands	0.93
Hungary	0.63	Austria	0.93
Albania	0.62	Cyprus	0.93
Ethiopia	0.62	Slovakia	0.92
Jordan	0.61	Greece	0.92
Pakistan	0.60	Iceland	0.92
Guatemala	0.75	Argentina	0.91
Bangladesh	0.53	Peru	0.91
Serbia	0.43	Lithuania	0.90
Thailand	0.42	Tunisia	0.89
Zimbabwe	0.41	Czech Republic	0.89
Kazakhstan	0.34	United States	0.89
Singapore	0.33	Australia	0.88
Iran	0.32	Georgia	0.88
Nicaragua	0.30	Mongolia	0.88
Belarus	0.29	Taiwan ROC	0.86
Russia	0.27	Armenia	0.85
Azerbaijan	0.25	Japan	0.85
Turkey	0.19	Chile	0.84
Vietnam	0.18	Romania	0.83
Egypt	0.18	Kenya	0.83
Tajikistan	0.16	Indonesia	0.81

Table 3.1 *Continued*

CLOSED SOCIETIES	Mean	OPEN SOCIETIES	Mean
China	0.08	Mexico	0.81
		Nigeria	0.81
		Slovenia	0.81
		Ecuador	0.81
		Bolivia	0.77
Total	0.49	Total	0.90

Note: Societies in wave 7 of the EVS/WVS surveys are classified based on the Varieties of Democracy Freedom of Expression and Alternative Sources of Information (0/1) index, matched to the year of the survey and dichotomized into binary categories around the mean. The table displays the categories and mean score on the index.

Sources: World Values Survey 7 (2017–2021), 81 societies (N. 124,641); Varieties of Democracy project (V-Dem 11.0).

compounded by an economic crisis, have resulted in the closure of most independent media outlets, as well as a great deal of self-censorship, and the departure of dozens of journalists into self-imposed exile. Harassment by the intelligence services, intimidation, and blackmail are now part of the daily routine for the journalists who have stayed behind, and some have reportedly been blacklisted as "terrorists."[30]

By contrast, a range of open societies such as Denmark, Germany, and South Korea score highly on V-Dem's Freedom of Expression index. Most open societies are among the most affluent in the world and are long-established democratic states, such as Switzerland and Canada, but others, like Estonia, Argentina, and Slovakia, are middle-income economies and younger democracies. (The relationship between V-Dem's estimates of Freedom of Expression Index and their Liberal Democracy is shown in Figure 3.4 later in the chapter.) There is a strong association between these measures (R = .824 ***), not surprisingly since freedom of the press is an essential component of liberal democracy. Nevertheless, liberal democracy requires many other institutions as well, like the independence of parliament and courts, so that these indices are not perfectly correlated. Several countries, including Ecuador, Nigeria, and Ukraine, have relatively strong freedom of expression and alternative sources of information, according to the estimates, while still lacking several other effective institutions of liberal democracy. The comparison allows us to examine how far the characteristics predicting trust vary in divergent information and media environments.

Types of Regimes

In addition, the societies included in the EVS/WVS allow attitudes and beliefs to be compared in a wide variety of regimes. There is a long debate about the most appropriate way to classify regimes. For more than forty years, Freedom House has used a tripartite distinction of "Free," "Partly free," and "Not free" countries and territories, based on expert annual assessments of levels of civil liberties and political rights worldwide.[31] But the middle category of "hybrid" states is ambiguous and imprecisely conceptualized, mixing apples and oranges.[32] Others favor a minimalist binary categorization, reducing potential errors from more subjective judgments, distinguishing democracies from autocracies based on the criteria of Schumpeterian electoral competition.[33]This approach has been complicated by the rise in the number of states around the world holding multiparty elections for legislative and executive offices, but with major electoral malpractices strongly skewing the outcome in favor of the ruling party, accompanied by weak judicial and parliamentary institutions of checks and balances on executive powers.

To classify states, the book uses the Regimes of the World categories developed by researchers at the V-Dem project (Table 3.2).[34] This uses a fourfold typology. *Closed autocracies* lack multiparty elections for the chief executive or national legislature. *Electoral autocracies* hold competitive elections for these offices, but these are flawed by major electoral malpractices, such as violence at the polls, fraud, or manipulation of the results. *Electoral democracies* hold contests with high levels of electoral integrity, but other liberal democratic institutions still remain weak and underdeveloped, such as oversight of the executive by the legislature, the independence of the judiciary and rule of law, freedom of the press and association, and respect for individual liberties and minority rights. And *liberal democracies* fulfill all the requirements embedded in Dahl's conceptualization. The type of regime was matched to the year of the survey; for example, both Tunisia and Myanmar were electoral autocracies at the time of the survey but they subsequently experienced military coup d'états, changing their status. As the comparison shows, the survey allows comparison of five absolute autocracies, exemplified by the one-party Communist states of Vietnam and China. The survey also covers around two dozen electoral autocracies, from diverse world regions, cultural and religious traditions, and levels of socioeconomic development, such as Russia, Turkey, Egypt, and Iran. The comparative framework includes about the same number of equally varied electoral democracies, including Argentina,

Table 3.2 Classifying Types of Regimes

Absolute Autocracy	Electoral Autocracy	Electoral Democracy	Liberal Democracy
China	Armenia	Albania	Australia
Hong Kong	Azerbaijan	Argentina	Austria
Jordan	Bangladesh	Bolivia	Canada
Thailand	Belarus	Bosnia-Herzegovina	Chile
Vietnam	Egypt	Brazil	Cyprus
	Ethiopia	Bulgaria	Czech Republic
	Hungary	Colombia	Denmark
	Iran	Croatia	Estonia
	Iraq	Ecuador	Finland
	Kazakhstan	Georgia	France
	Kyrgyzstan	Guatemala	Germany
	Lebanon	Indonesia	Greece
	Malaysia	Lithuania	Iceland
	Montenegro	Mexico	Italy
	Myanmar	Mongolia	Japan
	Nicaragua	Nigeria	Netherlands
	Pakistan	Northern Macedonia	New Zealand
	Philippines	Peru	Norway
	Russia	Poland	Slovenia
	Serbia	Portugal	South Korea
	Singapore	Romania	Spain
	Tajikistan	Slovakia	Sweden
	Turkey	Tunisia	Switzerland
	Zimbabwe	Ukraine	Taiwan
			United Kingdom
			United States
5	25	24	27

Note: Societies in wave 7 of the EVS/WVS surveys are classified based on the Regimes of the World categories (V-Dem), matched to the year of the survey.
Sources: World Values Survey 7 (2017–2021), 81 societies (N. 124,641); Varieties of Democracy project (V-Dem 11.0).

Bulgaria, Mongolia, and Ukraine. Finally, the survey conducted surveys in twenty-seven liberal democracies, including long-established regimes such as Germany, Denmark, and Switzerland, as well as third-wave democracies such as Estonia, South Korea, and Chile.

Measuring Trust

Can beliefs about trust and trustworthiness be monitored reliably through survey data? Psychological studies have focused primarily on understanding social trust, reflecting interpersonal relationships in society, such as ties among friends and neighbors, family and work colleagues, as well as trust in the media, online networks, and digital platforms, and confidence in civic institutions, such as churches, banks, and corporations.[35] Political science, by contrast, has focused more attention on citizens' trust toward authorities such as leaders and elected representatives, confidence in institutions such as governments, the civil service, courts, political parties, and parliaments, and also attitudes toward the principles and performance of democratic regimes.[36] A growing literature in international relations is also emerging to study transnational dimensions of trust, including toward other peoples and nation-states, as well as attitudes toward the institutions of global governance, like the European Union and the United Nations.[37] The general theory developed in this study has the capacity to span these disciplinary boundaries, synthesizing our understanding of this phenomenon and integrating the research literature across diverse subfields. But are these distinct dimensions of the concept of trust—or are attitudes closely correlated?

Social Trust

To measure absolute levels of social or interpersonal trust, the survey asked the standard binary question which is used in longitudinal studies like the US General Social Survey (GSS) and all previous waves of the EVS/WVS, namely whether respondents agreed that "Most people can be trusted (1)" or "you can't be too careful in dealing with people (0)." This provides longitudinal data over many decades, as the item has been widely used since it was first developed in 1956.[38] But the measure is also limited, as it is not clear whom respondents are thinking about when referring to "most people." It has commonly been treated as a measure of "generalized" trust, toward people unlike oneself, but this is not strictly implied in the wording, where respondents could be thinking that "most people" refers to those like friends, neighbors, and family. The meaning may also vary cross-nationally; for example, Asians may have different groups in mind than American or European respondents.[39] Based on experimental game studies, some scholars have argued that the standard measure of social trust is an unreliable predictor of cooperative behaviors.[40] Other researchers contend, however, that beliefs and expectations of trustworthiness monitored through game experiments do relate to the standard survey measure of trust, once this is distinguished from other preferences, like risk aversion.[41]

In addition, it is important to test the "radius of trust" thesis, which suggests that social trust is not necessarily all of one piece but instead it is expected to vary by the distance of the agent, with trust usually believed to be greater among more familiar circles of cooperation, like friends and family, rather than strangers or foreigners. Fukuyama suggested that these different forms of trust could have important consequences; the in-group trust based on shared norms of cooperation among narrow circles, like clans, tribes, and kin, may prove positive, but it may also reduce the ability of people to develop social relationships with perceived "outsiders," like immigrants, with the potential for generating negative externalities for society as a whole.[42] In particular, Fukuyama suggests that in-group ties may encourage moral judgments which justify serving the interests of the group, such as engaging in cronyism and corrupt acts, at the expense of outsiders. By contrast, out-group trust may generate broader circles of cooperation and empathy.[43] To gauge this distinction, we also tapped into the WVS battery which asks "How much do you trust . . ." a list of five different objects, including "your family," "people you know personally," "your neighborhood," to "people of another nationality" and "people of another religion," measured on 4-point scales from "do not trust at all" (1) to "trust completely" (4). While particularized trust toward "in-groups" like family and friends is important, it is generalized trust in "out-groups," and thus people unlike us in certain regards, which is expected to strengthen broader bridging relationships, to facilitate social cooperation and democracy, and to deepen social tolerance in local communities and cosmopolitan networks.

Institutional Confidence

As discussed in Chapter 2, the concept of "confidence" relates more precisely to the expectation that something will probably happen, minimizing uncertainty, irrespective of whether future outcomes are desirable.[44] For example, cynics might express confidence in their beliefs that 99% of politicians will probably act in a corrupt and dishonest manner, without endorsing this form of behavior. Nevertheless, this study follows the long-standing standard practice which treats expressions of confidence as closely equivalent, although not strictly identical, to one type of expectation, namely the notion of "trust," understood as a belief that agents will act in a way which serves the interests of the principal. The WVS questionnaire asks the following: "I am going to name a number of organizations. For each one, could you tell me how much confidence you have in them: is it a great deal of confidence, quite a lot of confidence, not very much confidence or none at all?"[45] The survey lists a wide range of governance organizations within the nation-state, including absolute levels of trust in the government, political parties, and parliament, as well as in state agencies responsible for security, like the courts, police, and armed forces, and a range of civil society organizations, such as the new social movements concerned with environmental protection and women's rights, as well as banks and major companies in the private sector, television, and the press, and trust in multilateral agencies of global governance, such as the United Nations and the World Health Organization (WHO).

To check the dimensionality of responses, all the thirty-three selected items on social trust and institutional confidence contained in the seventh wave of the individual-level EVS/WVS (V1.0) were subjected to Principal Component factor analysis with varimax rotation.[46] If trust is a simple affective orientation or personality trait, as psychological accounts suggest, then we might expect to observe a unidimensional pattern indicating that respondents fail to distinguish among different agents and agencies. Instead, the results presented in Table 3.3 suggest that responses fell into six dimensions, reflecting trust or confidence in six different types of actors:

(i) *Agencies of global governance* within the international community, such as the World Trade Organization, the World Bank, the North Atlantic Treaty Organization (NATO), and the United Nations, as well as regional intergovernmental organizations like the Organization of American States (OAS), the European Union (EU), and the African Union (AU);

(ii) *Agencies of national governance*, including parliament, political parties, the government, elections, and the civil service;

(iii) *State security agencies*, including the police, armed forces, and the courts;

Table 3.3 Dimensions of Trust

	Global Governance Agencies	National Governance Agencies	State Security Agencies	Civil Society Agencies	Out-Group Trust	In-Group Trust
The World Trade Organization (WTO)	0.82					
The World Bank (WB)	0.82					
North Atlantic Treaty Organization (NATO)	0.81					
International Criminal Court (ICC)	0.80					
International Monetary Fund (IMF)	0.79					
The World Health Organization (WHO)	0.78					
The United Nations (UN)	0.73					
Parliament		0.82				
Political parties		0.79				
The government		0.71				
Elections		0.69				
The civil services		0.46				
Armed forces			0.83			
The police			0.64			
Justice system/Courts			0.45			
Major companies				0.43		
The women's movement				0.74		

Continued

Table 3.3 Continued

	Global Governance Agencies	National Governance Agencies	State Security Agencies	Civil Society Agencies	Out-Group Trust	In-Group Trust
Charitable or humanitarian organizations				0.72		
The environmental protection movement				0.69		
Television				0.55		
Banks				0.47		
The press				0.47		
Churches				0.40		
People of another nationality					0.84	
People of another religion					0.84	
People you meet for the first time					0.67	
Your neighborhood						0.77
Your family						0.58
People you know personally						0.53

Note: Principal Component Analysis: Varimax with Kaiser Normalization, excluding coefficients below .39.

Source: World Values Survey 7 (2017–2021), 81 societies (N. 124,641).

(iv) *Civil society agencies*, including the women's movement and environmental groups, banks, major corporations, the press and television, and religious organizations;

(v) Social trust toward *in-groups* (like family and neighbors); and finally,

(vi) Social trust toward *out-groups* (such as people of different faiths and nationalities).[47]

The survey items identified listed in Table 3.3 were summed and turned into standardized 100-point scales for each dimension, where higher scores reflected the expression of greater absolute trust, allowing consistent comparison of standardized mean scores across each component. It should be noted that not all items were carried across each of the seven waves of the survey, but sufficient items were asked in each wave to facilitate consistent time-series analysis. Table 3.4 shows the correlation across the six scales, demonstrating that all scales are significantly related. In particular, not surprisingly, both dimensions of social trust toward in- and out-groups are strongly correlated. The institutional scales are also strongly interrelated, including trust in civil society organizations, state security agencies, national government, and global governance. The analysis suggests that trusting attitudes do fall into distinct dimensions, but these are not wholly separate, with the primary division between social and institutional trust.

Table 3.4 Correlation among Trust Scales

	In-Group Trust	Out-Group Trust	Trust in Civil Society Organizations	Trust in State Security Agencies	Trust in Government Institutions
Out-group trust	.475**				
Trust in civil society organizations	.239**	.171**			
Trust in state security agencies	.267**	.177**	.566**		
Trust in government institutions	.224**	.184**	.626**	.622**	
Trust in agencies of global governance	.192**	.208**	.687**	.412**	.555**

Note: ** Correlation is significant at the 0.01 level (2-tailed).

Source: World Values Survey 7 (2017–2021), 81 societies (N. 124,641).

It should be noted that in the United States the standard approach to measuring trust in government has deployed several other items originally developed by the American National Election Studies (ANES), carried in this two-year series since 1958, and subsequently replicated in some other national election studies.[48] These items were designed by Donald Stokes to monitor how the public feels about the performance of public officials in terms of their ethical standards, capacity, and integrity. The ANES asks Americans to assess whether the "government in Washington" can be trusted to do *what is right*, whether "people running the government" *waste taxes*, whether government is run *for the benefit of a few big interests*, or whether public officials are "crooked."[49] The ANES standard "trust in government" items have come to be regarded in the United States as the canonical measures for analyzing trends in public opinion toward the federal government.

Nevertheless, interpreting these measures raises several issues of conceptual validity, both in the United States and in comparative election surveys. The referent of these items is clearly worded to be incumbent-oriented ("the people in the government," "the government in Washington," "the people running the government").[50] But it is unclear exactly what is understood here by respondents living under a federal system of government divided among branches and levels, for example, Democrats are likely to disapprove of the former president Trump and the GOP-controlled Senate, but they may still approve of the Democrat-controlled House of Congress and their local representative, as well as state and local governments. Moreover, as Levi and Stoker point out, although commonly assumed to reflect *trust* in government, in fact the measures tap other related sub-dimensions of trust, such as the ability and efficiency of public officials (to do "what is right"), as well as their ethical qualities (to be honest or crooked), and the responsiveness of government (toward special interests or the general good).[51] The general concepts of trust and trustworthiness, Levi and Stoker note, never featured in the original design of these items.

Another conventional distinction has commonly been drawn in the American literature between trust and confidence in "public" institutions, such as Congress, and in "private" institutions, such as major corporations.[52] Since 1973, the US GSS conducted by NORC has monitored confidence in "the people running" the executive branch of government, the US Supreme Court, Congress, and the military, as well as private-sector agencies, such as major companies, medicine, banks and financial institutions, the press, television, and labor unions.[53] Disaggregating the specific agency makes this question more precise than the ANES series asking about "government." Yet this public/private dividing line is complicated to compare cross-nationally, as it depends upon the degree of state control in each society, for example whether a country has public service or commercial television broadcasters, public-sector or private-sector healthcare, and whether religious institutions are disestablished.[54] There are also many institutions, like NGOs, charitable bodies, and trade unions, located in the "third" nonprofit sector. Accordingly, the EVS/WVS data set provides a broader range of items measuring diverse dimensions of trust which are better designed for comparative purposes.

Operationalizing the Concept of Skeptical Judgments of Trustworthiness

Cross-national studies which rely primarily upon survey evidence have used several approaches to operationalizing the core notion of *skeptical* judgments of trustworthiness.

The first method uses directional scales. When Mishler and Rose studied the attitudes of many citizens living through post-Communist transitions in Central and Eastern Europe, they described the most common approach toward civil and political institutions as one of "skepticism," measured by the authors as people taking middling positions on 7-point trust scales, rather than opting for either of the poles reflecting either very positive scores (a score of 6 or 7 is understood as implying wholehearted trust) or very negative scores (where a score of 1 or 2 is taken to mean deep distrust).[55] Cook and Gronke adopt a similar approach in a 2002 US survey.[56] Using 0–10-point trust scales, Americans who expressed a midpoint response (5) were classified as skeptical, meaning that they neither trusted nor distrusted the agent. At the same time, this method may identify moderates, or those unwilling to offer an opinion, rather than skeptics per se, since the underlying reasons for adopting the middle response were not established, nor did the surveys measure the certainty of any beliefs, nor the correlations with independent performance indices. For example, if a government agency has a poor record and reputation in its delivery of public goods and services, then the most accurate rational assessment in public opinion should be to award it poor marks, which does not reflect a cynical response.

Another approach to this measurement issue relies upon variability in responses, understood to reflect the degree of discrimination in trust judgments. Wu and Wilkes sought to identify "critical trusters" by scrutinizing the consistency of citizens' response patterns to survey questions about trust in different agencies.[57] The authors argue that discriminatory judgments, defined as those displaying variations in trust responses, suggest that people actively distinguish among different actors, such as having confidence in the courts but not the police, expressing little faith in government but more confidence in local representatives, or trusting friends but not strangers.[58] The authors use standard deviations from the mean across composite trust scales as a proxy indicator of discrimination. On the other hand, individuals with a propensity toward usually trusting friends, neighbors, and family may also express confidence in different agencies, such as government officials, political parties, and the news media. The consistency of positive responses may imply that trust reflects sticky predispositions or habitual character traits, like feelings of hopefulness and optimism, irrespective of any considerations about agency performance, as social psychological accounts suggest.[59] Or alternatively this response pattern could mean that in societies such as Sweden and Denmark, most agents and agencies are, in fact, trustworthy.

In an alternative study, Hu and Yin classified Chinese citizens into a four-fold typology of political trusters based on variability in Eastonian levels of diffuse and specific systems support.[60] In this, "compliants" are defined as those with high levels of both diffuse and specific forms of support, for example approving of both particular authorities as well as the political institutions of the regime. By contrast, "critical citizens" have high diffuse support (for regime principles) but low specific support (for officeholders). "Contingents" have low diffuse support but high specific support. And "cynics" are categorized as those who have consistently low specific and diffuse support.

These studies provide useful ways to think about citizen orientations toward their political system, which could be operationalized through cross-national surveys and applied to many countries and types of regimes. It is indeed important to determine the internal consistency of trust judgments, and the subjective reasons behind these evaluations, as indicative of deliberative thinking. But these approaches are also unfortunately ultimately flawed, as they provide invalid measures of the concept of trustworthiness. They rest on the notion that skeptical trust is a quality of the individual (and thus can be measured by survey data alone), rather than reflecting the dyadic relationship between the principal and agent. Hence in dangerous contexts surrounded by many life-threatening risks and dangers, for those living in Yemen or Syria, for example, it may be perfectly rational to be consistently cautious and deeply mistrusting. By contrast, for those fortunate to live in secure and comfortable surroundings, with cradle-to-grave welfare states, like many citizens of Sweden or Germany, it may be perfectly rational to be consistently trusting. It would also be logical for many Chinese citizens to approve of the outcome performance of the regime institutions, since China has a very effective state, as demonstrated by its capacity to generate substantial economic growth, lifting millions out of poverty, while still decrying its procedural performance, shown by the country's record of abusing human rights and repressing political freedoms. But this tells us nothing about the concept of *trustworthiness*, which is used in this study to mean probabilistic expectations that collective institutions (agencies) or specific individuals (agents) are likely to deliver certain desired individual and public goods. Skeptical and well-informed judgments of trustworthiness can only be measured satisfactorily, therefore, by supplementing subjective indicators of the *internal* consistency of deliberative processes with measures of *external* consistency, linking the level of trust by the principal with subjective and objective indices monitoring the performance of the agent when delivering individual or collective goods and the effectiveness of structural guardrails and accountability mechanisms protecting against agency failure. What matters for trustworthiness, from this point of view, is not the endpoint judgment reached by ordinary citizens—but rather the decision pathway traveled.

Based on this reasoning, the research design in this study can be summarized schematically as a three-step process, illustrated in Figure 3.1.

The first step involves analyzing survey data at the micro level to monitor the degree of social, political, and international trust among citizens living in diverse countries, as well as trends over time. The EVS/WVS data facilitate comparison by nation-state and world regions at different levels of development, for example to contrast attitudes in affluent Scandinavia, middle-income Latin American nations, and poorer developing societies. Standard socio-demographic characteristics can also be examined to establish whether these factors predict individual-level patterns of trust, especially the indicators of cognitive skills, knowledge, and information, cultural values, and media use, which may be expected to influence attitudes toward government authorities, or feelings of interpersonal trust toward friends and strangers.

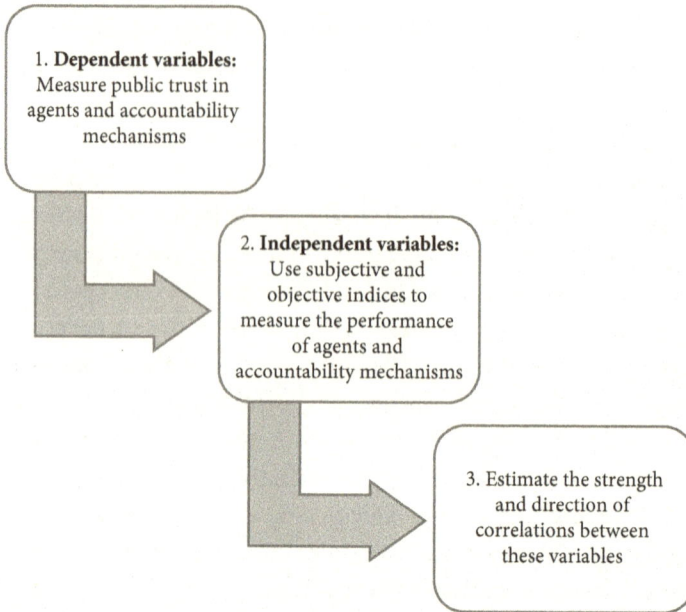

Figure 3.1. Steps for identifying skeptical trust.

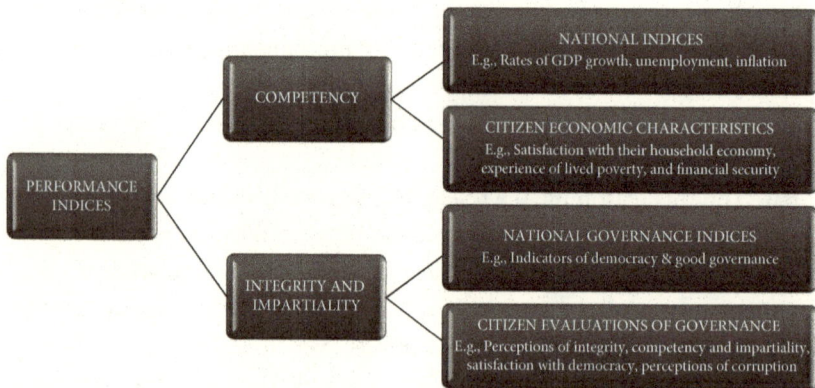

Figure 3.2. Types of performance indices.

The second step involves analyzing evidence to determine whether trust judgments accord with performance indicators. As illustrated in Figure 3.2, these can be divided into evaluations of the agent or agent's reputation for competency, as well as indications of the strength of institutional guardrails underpinning integrity and impartiality, like accountability mechanisms if actors or agencies prove corrupt, incompetent, or self-interested. A further distinction can be drawn between subjective evaluations at the individual level (like satisfaction with household finances or perceptions of corruption monitored through social surveys) and objective indices measured at the macro level (like annual changes in per capita levels of GDP as a measure of national economic growth, derived from official statistics). The data monitoring trusting attitudes are compared in this study with both subjective micro-level perceptions of performance contained in the EVS/WVS survey and with macro-level objective performance indicators from sources such as the World Bank and the V-Dem project, as discussed in detail in subsequent chapters.

Evidence for *internal consistency* involves the subjective reasons underlying trust decisions, suggesting processes of deliberative judgment and logical thinking. For example, do people trust strangers more if they feel secure and believe that they live in safe neighborhoods? Are people less trusting of the news media if they suspect that many journalists are corrupt? Do they have more confidence in elections if they think that there are effective and fair appeal mechanisms like judicial bodies charged with adjudicating any disputes? And so on. In addition, the book can also draw on new data in the WVS-TrustGov surveys conducted in authoritarian states for how far agencies are thought *competent* in delivering on their delegated responsibilities and keeping their commitments, *impartial* by serving the public interest rather than lining their own pockets, and serving with *integrity* so that they are ethical and transparent in their dealings, thereby delivering the outcomes that their clients prioritize. Examining the consistency of these sorts of attitudes provides insights into the reasons closely associated with trust judgments. At the same time, complex recursive processes can be expected to underlie these relationships so the direction of causality linking trust with subjective attitudes cannot be inferred from cross-sectional survey data collected at one point in time. For example, do positive evaluations of the competence and honesty of government leaders and local officials lead people subsequently to judge them as generally trustworthy—or do habitual feelings of trust strengthen subsequent positive evaluations of their performance? Use of lagged independent variables in dynamic models and panel surveys of the same respondents over an extended period of time have sought to unravel complex recursive processes in these complex relationships.[61]

In the final step of the research design, this step seeks to compare the correlations between public judgments of trustworthiness and objective performance indicators about the agency's record of actions taken and the processes used to arrive at these decisions (H^1). Data can be derived from the wealth of macro-level measures which are now available, for example the links connecting political trust in public opinion polls with aggregate indicators of good governance and the delivery of common universally desirable policy outputs and outcomes, like economic growth, longevity, education, and health.[62] Thermostatic dynamic shifts in agency performance can furnish important insights to monitor the stability of trust over successive survey waves, for example to determine whether sudden societal shocks, such as the impact of the Covid-19 pandemic on public health, or the occurrence of major economic downturns, are related to subsequent changes in public confidence in the agencies of national and international governance responsible for managing these problems. Similarly, major scandals and controversies damaging the reputations of agencies provide a shock event which can be related to subsequent downturns in public trust. The degree of fit suggests the *external* consistency of skeptical judgments, reflecting the correlation between public estimates of trustworthiness and objective indices of agency performance (H^2). Cynical judgments reflect minimal trust in agents, despite their relatively positive performance in delivering public goods. Compliant judgments reflect considerable trust, believing agents to be competent, honest, and impartial, despite many performance failures.

Comparative Framework and Case Selection

The pooled EVS/WVS data set covers all inhabited continents around the globe, as illustrated in Figures 3.3 and 3.4. At the same time, to deepen and expand our understanding about the drivers of public judgments of trustworthiness in authoritarian states, the seventh wave of the WVS conducted surveys of selected cases of such regimes sponsored by the European Social Research Council (ESRC)-funded TrustGov project. This initiative also added an innovative list count experiment monitoring trust in political leaders, described later, and new batteries of questions about trust were included in the standard WVS questionnaire to measure whether perceptions of competency, integrity, and impartiality contribute toward trust judgments.[63]

Country cases were selected by the TrustGov project to probe more deeply into trust in different types of closed societies. These are governed by electoral autocracies, defined as regimes with elections for national office, but lacking many fundamental freedoms and human rights characteristic of electoral and liberal democracies, like independent judiciaries, effective opposition parties, and respect for constitutional checks on executive powers. These selected cases included surveys conducted in various world regions including in Southeast Asia (such as in Myanmar, the Philippines, Vietnam), Africa (Zimbabwe, Kenya, Ethiopia, Libya, Morocco), Central Asia (Iran, Tajikistan and Kyrgyzstan), and Latin America (Nicaragua, Venezuela).

Tables 3.5 and 3.6 illustrate the characteristics of the selected cases and provide a snapshot comparison of these societies. The chosen cases include varied authoritarian regimes, including presidential and parliamentary republics, a theocracy, and a one-party Communist state. In terms of the V-Dem index of liberal democracy, as shown in Figure 3.2 illustrating levels of democracy and economic development in all the societies included in the survey, in 2020 the selected TrustGov states are all ranked relatively low on both dimensions, with Iran, Libya, Nicaragua, Venezuela, Vietnam, and Tajikistan the most autocratic, while higher index scores were given to Kyrgyzstan, the Philippines, Kenya, and Myanmar (before the military coup d'état in February 2021). In terms of per capita GDP, Ethiopia, Zimbabwe, and Tajikistan are also among the poorest developing societies under comparison, and therefore with vulnerable populations facing some of the greatest existential risks of insecurity.

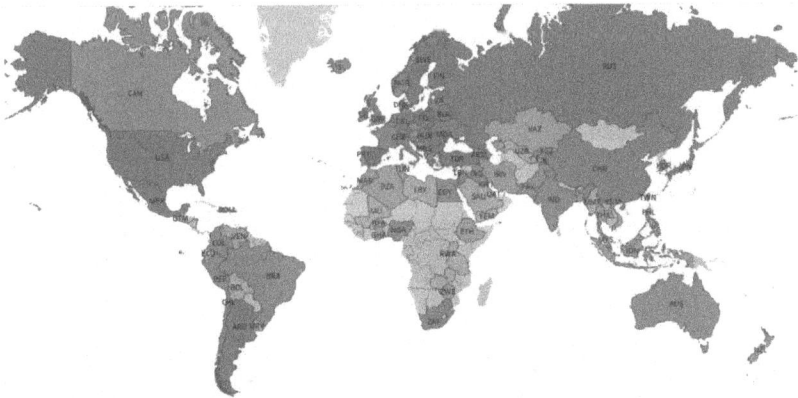

Figure 3.3. Societies in the EVS/WVS pooled surveys.

Notes: The map illustrates the geographic coverage of the pooled European Values Survey/World Values Survey (EVS/WVS), 1981–2001. In total, 120 societies are labeled if they contain at least one survey. Darker and lighter shades of gray indicate the number of survey waves (1–7) conducted to date in each society.

Source: www.worldvaluessurvey.org.

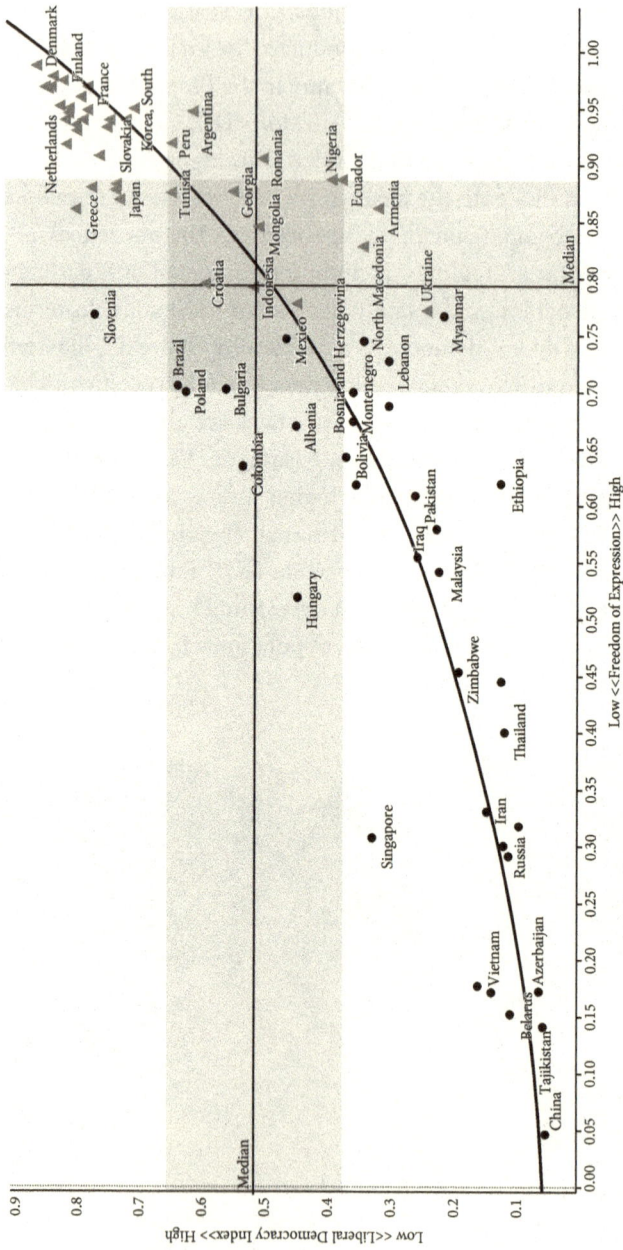

Figure 3.4. Liberal democracy and freedom of expression.

Note: Vertical axis: Liberal Democracy 0–100-point index, 2020. Horizontal axis: Freedom of Expression and Alternative Sources of Information Index.

Sources: Varieties of Democracy 11.1 dataset, https://www-dem.net/en/.

Table 3.5 Types of Regimes and Leaders in the Selected TrustGov Autocracies

Nation	Year	Type of Regime (2020)	Head of State (2020)	Head of Government (2020)
Ethiopia	2020	Federal parliamentary republic	President Sahle-Work	Prime Minister Abiy Ahmed (*)
Iran	2020	Theocratic republic	Supreme Leader Ali Hoseini-Khamenei	President Hasan Fereeidun Rohani (*)
Kenya	2021	Presidential republic	President Uhuru Kenyatta (*)	President Uhuru Kenyatta (*)
Kyrgyzstan	2020	Parliamentary republic	President Sooronbai Jeenbekov (*)	Prime Minister Ulukbek Maripov
Libya	2022	Transitional Presidential republic	Chair Pres Council, Mohammed Al Menfi	Prime Minister Abdul Hamid Dbeiba (*)
Morocco	2021	Parliamentary monarchy	King Mohammed VI	Prime Minister Saad Eddine El Othmani (*)
Myanmar	2020	Parliamentary republic/military junta	President Win Myint	State Counsellor Aung San Suu Kyi (*)
Nicaragua	2020	Presidential republic	President Jose Daniel Ortega (*)	President Jose Daniel Ortega (*)
Philippines	2019	Presidential republic	President Rodrigo Duterte (*)	President Rodrigo Duterte (*)
Tajikistan	2020	Presidential republic	President Emomali Rahmon	Prime Minister Qohir Rasulzoda
Venezuela	2021	Presidential republic	President Nicolas Maduro (*)	President Nicolas Maduro (*)
Vietnam	2020	One-party Communist state	President Nguyen Phu Trong (*)	General Secretary Nguyen Xuan Phuc (*)
Zimbabwe	2020	Presidential republic	President Emmerson Mnangagwa (*)	President Emmerson Mnangagwa (*)

Note: (*) The year of the survey fieldwork, the names of the incumbent leaders specified in the list experiments, and the types of regimes, at the time of the survey.

Source: World Values Survey 7 in the 10 selected TrustGov authoritarian states (N. 12,092).

The selected cases also display diverse trajectories of democratization, as shown in Figure 3.5. Several states remain relatively stable autocracies, according to the V-Dem data. This includes Viet Nam under the control of the Communist Party, Iran with some erratic liberalization under the Supreme Leader Ali Khamenei, and Tajikistan, a small, mountainous, and predominately Muslim Central Asian republic bordering Afghanistan and China,

Table 3.6 Characteristics of the Selected TrustGov Autocracies

	Liberal Democracy Index, 2020 (V-Dem)	Change in the Liberal Democracy Index 2000–2020 (V-Dem)	Freedom of Expression, 2020 (V-Dem)	Rank in Press Freedom Worldwide (Reporters without Borders, 2021, 180 Countries)	GDP per Capita, $ ppp 2019 (WB)	Pop. 2018 (WB)
Ethiopia	0.16	0.05	0.62	101	$2,319	109,224,559
Iran	0.14	−0.03	0.33	174	$12,937	81,800,269
Kenya	0.37	0.12	0.82	102	$4.521	51,393,010
Kyrgyzstan	0.29	0.12	0.68	79	$5,485	6,315,800
Libya	0.15	0.10	0.63	165	$15,845	6,678,567
Morocco	0.24	0.03	0.59	136	$7826	36,029,138
Myanmar	0.27	0.25	0.77	140	$5,369	53,708,395
Nicaragua	0.06	−0.33	0.32	121	$5,646	6,465,513
Philippines	0.28	−0.17	0.62	138	$9,302	106,651,922
Tajikistan	0.05	−0.03	0.14	162	$3,529	9,100,837
Venezuela	0.07	−0.25	0.29	148	$7,704	28,870,195
Vietnam	0.11	0.00	0.17	175	$8,041	95,540,395
Zimbabwe	0.19	0.00	0.45	130	$3,206	14,439,018

Sources: Varieties of Democracy 11.1 data set https://www.v-dem.net/en/; World Bank World Development Indicators, https://datacatalog.worldbank.org/dataset/world-development-indicators.

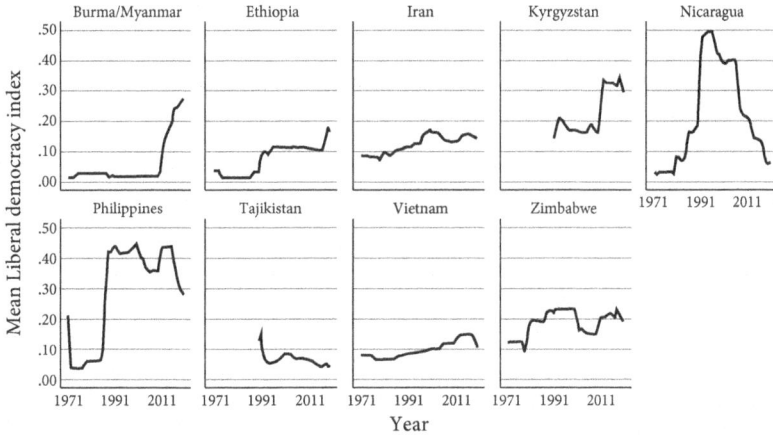

Figure 3.5. Trends in liberal democracy in the selected TrustGov autocracies.
Note: The Liberal Democracy index is the Varieties of Democracy (V-Dem) 0-100-point scale during 1971–2020.
Sources: Varieties of Democracy 11.1 dataset (2021), https://www.v-dem.net/en/.

ruled by strongman President Emomali Rahmon since his election in 1994. Other selected cases, including the Philippines, Nicaragua, Myanmar, and Ethiopia, experienced more volatile political trajectories and periods of liberalization which subsequently failed. In Nicaragua, for example, the revolutionary Sandinista National Liberation Front seized power from the ruling Somoza family in 1979. Following President Daniel Ortego's election in 1984, the country experienced growing freedoms, before he was defeated by the opposition in 1990. After a series of unsuccessful bids, he was re-elected again in 2006, with the strong support of the poor. Democracy backsliding occurred once he aligned himself with leftist populist Venezuelan president Hugo Chavez, then restricted news coverage, amended the constitutional ban on presidents standing for a second term, and increased executive power. Authoritarian rule has strengthened in recent years as Ortega, governing with his wife as vice president and the advice of a small circle of loyalists and family, forced nongovernmental organizations (NGOs) to close, violently repressed protests, disqualified opposition parties from running for election, and arrested rival presidential candidates.

Myanmar saw modest liberalization from military rule, as a political reform program and new constitution permitting multiparty elections were implemented in 2010. The National League for Democracy (NLD) contested the subsequent 2015 general election, winning an absolute majority of seats under its leader, Aung Sun Suu Kyi, although the military remained powerful. Hopes for liberalization were dashed on February 1, 2021, when the leader and elected members of NLD were arrested and deposed by the military, which declared a state of emergency. The selected cases therefore provide varied types of regimes to compare how far the process of democratization and backsliding affected trends in political trust in each society.

II. Reliability Checks

But can we trust the survey data as a reliable reflection of public opinion? One simple crosscheck is to compare the questions asked in the EVS/WVS about confidence in several political institutions with equivalent items asked in twenty-five countries in an independent study, the European Social Survey (ESS). The items are measured using different scales, and the EVS/WVS asks about "confidence" in these institutions whereas the ESS asks about "trust." Despite this, and many other differences in the questionnaire, survey design, and fieldwork procedures and dates, nevertheless, as illustrated in Figure 3.6, there is a remarkably strong and significant correlation across both surveys, lending confidence to the robustness of these measures. The simple Pearson correlations (R) across both surveys on the national estimates are .899 for trust in parliament, .813 for trust in political parties, .929 for trust in the police, and .931 for trust in the legal system/courts.

Questions about the veracity of responses by survey participants arise when monitoring trust, as with any sensitive questions where candid and truthful answers are at odds with perceived social norms, or where other negative consequences may arise, like potential social penalties for the expression of certain extreme political views. The "spiral of silence" theory by Elisabeth Noelle-Neuman (1974, 1984) suggested that perceptions of being in the majority or minority in opinions within any group or society affect processes of interpersonal communications, especially the open expression of attitudes and beliefs about deeply polarizing issues. Social pressures, both implicit (unspoken) cues and explicit viewpoints, are predicted to influence the willingness to speak out with confidence or to be more reticent.[64] Questions about the reliability of surveys monitoring confidence in political institutions and elites are particularly salient in the world's most repressive authoritarian states which routinely restrict freedom of expression and silence criticism.[65] The risks of self-censorship multiply among citizens living in closed societies

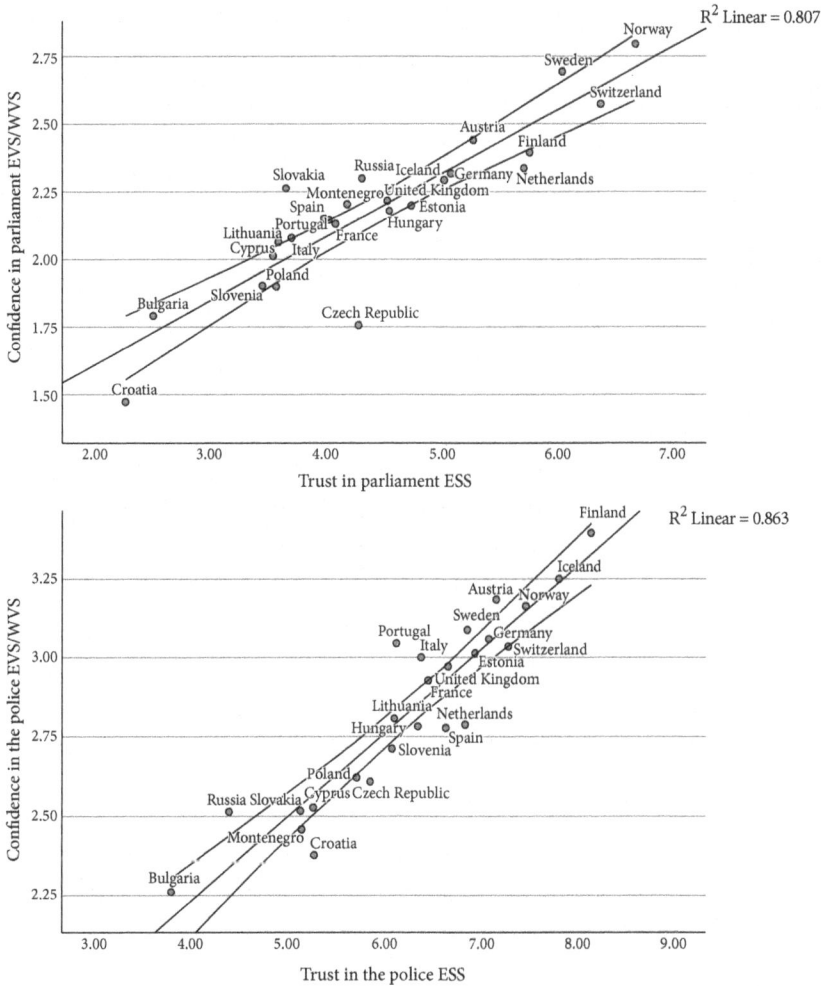

Figure 3.6. Correlations in survey measures of institutional trust and confidence.

Note: EVS/WVS, Wave 7 (2017–2021); European Social Survey mean (2015–2020).

lacking free speech, where outspoken dissidents face serious risks of imprisonment or exile. In this context, respondents who are being asked to express confidence in their government, support for the governing party, or approval of their political leader may fail to express their authentic feelings out of fear that their replies may be reported to the official authorities, despite promises of anonymity, with sanctions or other punishments applied to government critics. There are therefore good reasons to be suspicious about the reliability of survey data monitoring sensitive political attitudes, beliefs, and behavior in authoritarian societies, and measurement equivalence, even when polls are officially sanctioned by government authorities and conducted by reputable companies with a long tradition of maintaining professional standards. In this context, preference falsification may occur, where private and public preferences toward a regime may differ.[66]

To examine these issues, one approach is to use reliability tests comparing estimates of trust, using similar or identical questions across independent surveys in each country. Measures of trust and confidence are available for comparison from many time-series cross-national surveys, including the ESS, the Standard Eurobarometer bi-annual surveys, and the US GSS. Replication tests employed in subsequent chapters suggest that the more that similar results are recorded from similar or functionally equivalent questions monitored by independent surveys conducted in the same country and time period, the greater the confidence in the generalizability of the findings. At the same time, if there is a general tendency for preference falsification, then this may occur repeatedly across all the available surveys.

List Survey Experiments

Social scientists have developed a number of indirect question techniques, including list experiments (item count techniques), endorsement experiments, and randomized response techniques, designed to reduce desirability biases which can arise from direct questions.[67] The risks of self-censorship, which prevent the expression of authentic beliefs and attitudes, arise with many direct survey questions which raise socially sensitive issues, for example concerning types of risky sexual behavior, domestic violence, drug abuse, illegal behavior like tax avoidance or petty theft, racial animus, or engagement in corrupt acts like vote-buying.[68] Respondents are thought likely to provide "politically correct" answers about such questions, lying about their attitudes or behavior to avoid violating perceived common norms and thereby suffering from social sanctions. The dangers of response bias may be expected to be heightened in certain contexts, especially where citizens living in repressive societies fear that they may well face punishment from the official authorities for expressing overt criticism of their own government and political leaders. List experiments using the item count technique provide a way to detect truthful expressions and monitor potential response bias. In

Russia, for example, Frye et al. used this method to test whether Putin's popularity in the opinion polls was inflated because respondents were lying to pollsters, with the results suggesting that the favorability ratings were probably genuine.[69] An evaluation in a survey on reported voting behavior in an anti-abortion referendum in a US state found that, when compared with the actual vote share, the list count technique generated a smaller bias than direct questioning.[70]

Accordingly, to examine trust in leaders in several selected authoritarian states, the TrustGov project added a list experiment to the WVS standard questionnaire. To employ this technique, respondents who were representative of the general population in the selected autocracies were randomly distributed into either a treatment group or a control group.[71] Respondents in the control group were asked to read a short list of four non-key items. Participants in the treatment group were then presented with an identical list, with the addition of one key item about the sensitive issue of interest. Both groups were then asked to tell the interviewer the *number of items* applicable to themselves, but (most importantly) not to specify which items apply. For example, in studies designed to monitor the use of racist language, respondents may be asked to say how many terms they use personally to describe ethnic minorities, with the treatment group including an additional racist epithet in the list. The comparison of the mean scores across the randomized treatment and control groups can be attributed to positive responses by the treatment group on the key item. A list experiment does not tell us about the attitude of any individual respondent, but it tells us about the prevalence of the sensitive attitude in the survey population.

To use this method, list experiments were embedded in the seventh wave of the WVS survey questionnaire in ten closed societies with autocratic states and low- or middle-income economies located in different world regions. As illustrated in Figure 3.3, these states are classified as electoral autocracies, scoring below .40 according to the V-Dem Liberal Democracy index. It was not possible to survey trust in leaders in extreme cases such as North Korea, Syria, Eritrea, and Turkmenistan, which annual reports from monitoring agencies like the Committee to Protect Journalists and Reporters without Borders suggest have the most draconian state censorship, but which also censor the inclusion of politically sensitive survey questions. Nevertheless, all the selected TrustGov list experiments were conducted in states which had limited media pluralism, restrictions on the independent press, and abuses against journalists. For example, as Table 3.6 shows, the 2021 World

Press Freedom Index reports that out of 180 nations worldwide, Iran ranked 174th, Zimbabwe 130th, and Ethiopia 101st.[72]

Many types of trust relationships could be examined by the list experimental method, but survey questions about trust in political leaders is the issue which could potentially be *highly* vulnerable to response bias in closed societies which silence dissent and freedom of expression, potentially leading respondents to self-censor their authentic views. The new list experiment monitoring this issue was designed to replicate Frye et al.'s study of Russian support for President Putin.[73] Accordingly, in the first step the WVS questionnaire asked respondents in the selected cases to say directly how far they trusted the leader of their government, defined by the name of the national head of state in their country, using the list contained in Table 3.5), using a scale from "No trust at all" (0) to "A great deal of trust" (10). The scale was collapsed into binary categories, where a score more than five is classified as trusting.

The results in Table 3.7 show that responses measuring directly expressed trust in their leader varies a lot across cases, from a mean score of 27% trusting the Venezuelan president, Nicolás Maduro, to a high of 76% saying

Table 3.7 Direct Measure of Trust in the Country's Head of State

	No Trust at All %	1 %	2 %	3 %	4 %	5 %	6 %	7 %	8 %	9 %	A Great Deal of Trust	% Trusting (6–10)
Ethiopia (Ahmed)	23	1	2	3	3	15	5	5	6	3	34	53
Iran (Rohani)	22	5	5	5	8	22	3	7	9	4	11	34
Kenya (Kenyatta)	15	5	7	9	9	18	10	8	7	3	11	39
Kyrgyzstan (Jeenbekov)	16	3	3	4	4	22	5	5	6	3	31	50
Libya (Dbeiba)	1	2	7	7	7	18	14	10	10	6	19	59
Morocco (El Othmani)	14	7	10	13	17	16	16	14	7	3	1	41
Nicaragua (Ortega)	34	4	4	4	5	11	5	6	4	6	18	39
Philippines (Duterte)	2	2	2	2	3	13	7	10	15	11	33	76
Venezuela (Maduro)	38	11	4	3	5	12	6	3	6	6	6	27
Zimbabwe (Mnangagwa)	29	4	5	3	4	14	5	4	4	4	24	41

Note: Q: "How much you trust [name of the head of state]?" For the name of the Head of State or Head of Government, see Table 3.5. It should be noted that this measure could not be included in the surveys in Myanmar, Tajikistan, and Vietnam.

Source: World Values Survey 7 (2017–2021) in 10 selected TrustGov autocracies (N. 12,092).

that they trusted the Philippines president, Rodrigo Duterte. The mean across all cases was 46% reporting that they trusted their head of state. The distribution suggests that, despite limits on freedom of speech in these authoritarian states, nevertheless almost one-fifth of survey respondents (19%) felt free to express no trust at all in their leader. This was similar in size to the group expressing "a great deal" of trust (19%).

For the survey list experiments, in the second step, WVS respondents were randomized in the selected national samples and divided into the treatment and control groups. Respondents in each group were then asked the following question:

[Control group] I am going to read out a list of world leaders. Can you tell me **how many** *you generally trust?*
Control sample (50% of respondents, randomly assigned):
    Angela Merkel, chancellor of Germany
    Donald Trump, president of the United States
    Vladimir Putin, president of Russia
    Xi Jinping, president of the People's Republic of China
    Responses:
    [0]   [1]   [2]   [3]   [4]

Treatment group (50% of respondents, randomly assigned):
    Angela Merkel, chancellor of Germany
    Donald Trump, president of the United States
    [Name of national head of state, president, prime minister, or equivalent in each country]
    Vladimir Putin, president of Russia
    Xi Jinping, president of the People's Republic of China
    Responses:
    [0]   [1]   [2]   [3]   [4]   [5]

Thus, in this indirect list experiment, respondents were only asked to specify the *number* of government leaders they generally trusted, without revealing the names of the specific government leaders whom they trusted. Trust in their own head of state is thus obscured in the recorded answers. The design provides a "Chinese wall" on the assumption that respondents consciously know their own attitudes toward their own leader, but they do not want to be associated in public with the answer. There are some potential risks of cultural or political bias in the selection of leaders contained in the list, for example, if citizens of Kyrgyzstan are generally more favorable or knowledgeable toward Putin and Xi than citizens of the Philippines or Kenya. Pew global surveys suggest that there are substantial cross-national differences in how far the public expresses trust and confidence in different world leaders such as French president Emmanuel Macron, Russian president Vladimir Putin, and German chancellor Angela Merkel.[74] To ensure measurement equivalence, the question listed well-known and high-profile world leaders, all of whom represented major world powers, selected from both democratic and autocratic states. It is not the comparisons across countries, but rather the difference *within* each country between the mean responses expressed by the control and the treatment sample groups which provides the critical test of the key item, enabling indirect estimates of the authentic level of trust in government leaders. For example, within a country, if the mean number of trusted leaders is 2.67 in the treatment group, compared with 1.96 in the control group, this implies that 71% of respondents (2.67 − 1.96 = 0.71) trusted their own government leader. Potential response bias is measured as the difference between this indirect estimate and replies to the standard question which asks directly about trust in the government leader in their own country.

The results in Table 3.8 suggest that significant response biases were detected in half of the cases, although the size of this bias varied across societies, ranging from 14% in Morocco to 39% in Ethiopia. The reasons for these observed differences suggest respondents may fear informal social sanctions or formal retribution from the authorities in these cases, if respondents perceive a lack of anonymity and worry that their response will reveal the sensitive item. Awareness of the world leaders contained in the list may also generate contrasts across in societies with different levels of education, knowledge of world affairs, and literacy skills. Moreover, the results were not consistent across all cases, since in five countries the estimated bias was modest in size (below 6%) and statistically insignificant, meaning that this could also arise for multiple unrelated reasons, such as measurement error.

The list experiment therefore serves to confirm the thesis that positive estimates of trust in their own leader are likely to be inflated in many (but not all) closed societies by direct survey questions; respondents may exaggerate their genuine level of trust when recording direct answers about their head of state if they are living in repressive authoritarian states lacking free speech. By implication, similar processes of self-censorship may also influence other

Table 3.8 Estimates of Response Bias

	Control**	Treatment	Indirect Item Count Estimate of Trust in Their Head of State	Direct Measure of Trust in Their Head of State	Response Bias
	Mean	Mean	%	%	%
Ethiopia	1.00	1.14	14	53	39
Iran	0.82	1.18	36	34	−2
Kenya	1.26	1.69	43	39	−4
Kyrgyzstan	1.72	2.19	47	50	3
Libya	0.46	0.89	43	59	16
Morocco	2.19	2.43	27	41	14
Nicaragua	0.74	0.79	5	39	34
Philippines	1.20	1.71	52	76	24
Venezuela	0.87	1.09	22	27	5
Zimbabwe	1.11	1.47	36	41	5
Mean	1.17	1.52	33	46	13

Note: For the direct measure of trust, see Table 3.7

Source: World Values Survey 7 (2017–2020) TrustGov battery in 10 selected authoritarian societies (N. 12,092).

politically sensitive attitudes, such as reporting trust in government, public agencies, or state security authorities, like the military and police. At the same time, equivalent response biases from the expression of negative views are less likely to arise concerning survey questions monitoring non-political dimensions of trust, such as toward friends and neighbors, civil society institutions in the private sector such as banks and corporations, or confidence in international organizations like the United Nations.

In addition, the spiral of silence theory suggests that pressures to conform with the predominant culture, and thus response biases in survey research, may arise for socially sensitive issues irrespective of the type of regime, and so in democracies as well as in authoritarian states. Elisabeth Noelle-Neumann's classic concept of a "spiral of silence" was developed almost four decades ago in social psychological and interpersonal communication studies.[75] This idea describes situations where, for fear of social isolation or loss of status, people are hesitant to express authentic opinions contrary to prevalent social norms, producing self-censorship of unpopular views. The more that individuals feel confident that their opinion reflects majority opinion and prevalent social norms, however, the more willing they become to voice their views in public discourse, without fearing the penalty of social sanctions. Concern about the contemporary concept of "cancel culture" echoes this tendency.[76] Hence citizens living in democratic states may give "politically correct" answers when asked about all sorts of socially sensitive questions, for fear of violating prevailing norms, such as when expressing support for illiberal practices, disapproval of gender or racial equality, negative attitudes toward the rights of LGBTQ or ethnic minorities, or when reporting experience of corruption, rape, or domestic violence.

In short, therefore, response biases are an important factor when monitoring political trust in authoritarian states and interpreting the meaning of the survey questions concerning political institutions—although these considerations are far from unique to this context and to this issue. Expressions of political trust and confidence in governing authorities are more likely to be exaggerated in closed than in open societies. This is one important source of error which features in later chapters when interpreting attitudes toward government performance in a range of repressive authoritarian states. On this basis, Chapter 4 goes on to describe and compare multidimensional levels of trust, and trends over time; subsequent chapters will explore the reasons for these variations.

III. Conclusions

What is distinctive about the approach used in this research design compared with many previous studies?

First, an *interdisciplinary* perspective is adopted. Many scholars have focused upon one or other dimension of this phenomenon, such as sociologists studying trust in friends, families, and neighbors within local communities,[77] scholars of international relations focusing on trust in the United Nations and related international organizations,[78] or political scientists analyzing confidence in political institutions, such as the US Congress or the European Commission.[79] In the extensive research literature, disciplines in the social sciences have differed in their focus and methodological approaches to these questions, focusing on diverse objects of trust.

Thus, psychologists and sociologists have typically emphasized social or interpersonal forms of trust, understanding how far and why people trust each other, including in-groups like friends and family, and out-groups like strangers (generalized trust). Traditionally, early theories in psychology treated trust as an affective characteristic rooted in individual personality traits, inherited from parents, similar to feelings of optimism, extroversion, and agreeableness.[80] By contrast, accounts in sociology have often regarded trusting attitudes as an enduring orientation, acquired from socialization processes during the formative childhood years, although the learning process can continue during the adult years, for example where people move into new workplaces or communities and adapt prevailing social norms.[81] Cultural accounts of trust regard societies as evolving incrementally over many decades, or even centuries, leaving an enduring imprint, although these orientations also evolve through processes of demographic change and generation replacement. As such, the key question is why societies like Sweden and Norway are typically observed to be high in trust when compared with others like Italy. Explanations typically focus on contrasts among peoples, local communities, and nation-states.

Political scientists have commonly examined public confidence in political institutions within the nation-state, including governments, parliaments, and parties, and trust in civil society organizations, including the media, traditional interest groups, and new social movements. Many have focused on public perceptions of procedural fairness, including the role of corruption, as well as policy performance.[82] Most recently, studies have emphasized the role of populist rhetoric and political polarization in weakening feelings of public trust for the core institutions of liberal democracy, like elections and the media.[83] Scholars of international relations, by contrast, have analyzed trust among peoples and nation-states, as well as the perceived legitimacy of agencies of global governance, like the United Nations, WHO, and NATO, and whether a backlash against globalization and rising nationalism has been weakening support for multilateral cooperation.

Alternative perspectives in communication studies have often treated mistrust as the product of media messages, exemplified by theories of the so-called classic mean world effect of television common in the 1970s. Contemporary concern has focused upon the impact of fake news and conspiracy theories, online misinformation and disinformation, and populist rhetoric. Explanations focus on the effects of exposure and attention to processes of communications.

In addition, many accounts across diverse disciplines have traditionally emphasized the *affective* nature of trust and mistrust, akin to faith, gut feelings, or instinctive reactions, whether derived from innate psychological predispositions, learned cultural attitudes in each society, or the unfiltered absorption of negative communications. By contrast, contemporary accounts in cognitive psychology and in behavioral economics emphasize the role of heuristic shortcuts used to simplify decision-making in the face of complex choices, high uncertainty, information overload, and limited attention spans. As such, the key question becomes why people trust, with explanations focusing on core personality traits (in older accounts), on societal cultures (in comparative sociology), and on reasoning processes (in several more recent studies).

But a comprehensive general theory should ideally be able to explain the broader aspects of the trust relationship, irrespective of the specific type of principal or agent. The book aims to offer a comprehensive cross-disciplinary approach useful to understand interpersonal or generalized social trust, as well as confidence in political institutions in the nation-state, and trust in the agencies of global governance. Important contrasts can be expected to be observed in each of these dimensions—but a systematic general theory should seek to take account of these. In this regard, the study seeks to offer a more comprehensive approach, cutting across conventional disciplinary boundaries.

This conceptualization also drives the choice of a *multilevel research design*. Using a loose market metaphor, previous studies of the attitudes and values of individual citizens have often drawn upon evidence from individual-level social surveys. This traditional approach has been supplemented more recently in social psychology, decision sciences, and behavioral economics by the growing use of lab, field, and survey experiments, primarily to monitor the causes and consequences of social or interpersonal trust.[84] Fewer experiments have tested trust in government institutions—or between the publics in different states. The underlying assumption of much of the individual-level analysis is that any shifts in levels of public trust involve changes in the psychology of ordinary citizens, for example due to rising cognitive skills in knowledge societies, information processing, or changing cultural values among younger generations, which are believed to have led to diminished respect for traditional forms of authority.[85]

By contrast, a more satisfactory and comprehensive approach that requires *multilevel analysis* to understand trust relationships should also involve taking account of the performance of agents as trustworthy, including their past record of delivery, competency, integrity, and impartiality, and the formal structural guardrails which ensure these standards.[86] In this regard, explanations for any erosion of trust may rest not upon shifts in the psychology of individual citizens, or the evolution of cultural values in society, but rather in contextual conditions. For example, lack of trust may arise from the gap between public expectations and government performance, if the capacity of governments to steer the economy has been eroded by the forces of globalization. Any research design ideally requires a multi-method comparative approach, using triangulated sources of qualitative and quantitative evidence, where principals and agents are understood to function within a broader context. At the macro level of the nation-state, the overarching institutional and societal context plays a potentially important part in shaping trust relationships, through providing procedural guardrails, including constitutional designs, legal regulations, and entrenched informal social norms protecting accountability and enforcement, the role of communications in media landscapes, as well as the risks arising from living in fragile states with corrupt, repressive rulers and insecure surroundings.

Finally, in the light of these considerations, the *comparative framework* for the cross-national and longitudinal study ideally needs to extend well beyond the prevalent focus on established democracies, such as Anglo-American and European societies. This study also analyzes trust relationships in a diverse range of local communities, nation-states, and types of regimes around the world. This raises several analytical challenges, not least that the richest body of longitudinal survey data to monitor trends is available in Western societies. Cross-national social surveys have greatly expanded their coverage, facilitating a growing literature examining trust elsewhere in the world, including among those living in states governed by electoral democratic and electoral autocratic regimes, such as in post-Communist states in Central and Eastern Europe,[87] in sub-Saharan Africa,[88] and in China and other East Asian societies.[89] The book therefore adopts a global comparative framework and integrates many methods and analytical tools which can provide more reliable and robust insights into this phenomenon, including macro-level indicators of performance and representative surveys of the general public in many diverse states around the world.

PART II
WHAT CAUSES TRUST?

4

Comparing Trends in Trust Worldwide

The general theory of skeptical trust at the heart of this study has important implications, by challenging prevalent normative assumptions and reframing our understanding of the meaning of the observed evidence. This chapter focuses on comparing absolute levels of trust in public opinion across a wide range of societies worldwide to establish the cross-national patterns, especially contrasts in a range of open and closed societies, as well as establishing the dynamics of trends over successive decades. This lays the foundation for subsequent chapters, seeking to understand some of the key drivers influencing judgments of relative trustworthiness.

Section I considers debates about whether any long-term decline in trust has occurred. Ever since the tradition of comparative social and political surveys was first established by Almond and Verba in the mid-twentieth century, a substantial literature has discussed whether the core foundations for the civic culture have eroded over time.[1] To update previous analyses of the evidence, Section II compares global patterns of trends in trust using data from the pooled European Values Survey/World Values Survey (EVS/WVS), 1981–2021.[2] The key advantage of the data is that they provide the broadest evidence of multiple dimensions of trust in all inhabited continents worldwide, with longitudinal trends monitored in this chapter across fifty-three varied societies. This facilitates generalizations about the dynamics of value change across diverse contexts, including regions with varied cultural histories and religious legacies, levels of economic development, and types of regimes. The survey monitors trends in multiple dimensions of trust identified in the previous chapter. This includes confidence toward: (i) several agencies of *global governance* (including the United Nations, the World Health Organization, and the World Bank); (ii) political trust in *core governance agencies of the nation-state* (such as parliaments, governments, civil service, and political parties); (iii) trust in *state security agencies* (including the police, courts, and military); (iv) trust in *civil society agencies* (such as in new social movements, the press and television, religious organizations, banks, and corporations); (v) social trust in *out-groups* (generalized trust) (such as toward strangers and people of other faiths and nationalities); and finally, (vi) social trust toward *in-groups* (such as friends and neighbors). Section III describes the individual-level social and demographic characteristics most closely associated with the dimensions of trust. The conclusion in Section IV summarizes the key findings from this chapter and considers their implications for theories seeking to explain trust and trustworthiness.

I. Debates about Trends in Trust

Understanding the trajectory of trust across different societies and establishing the pace of change are important for insights into the causes of trust. In particular, time-series trends can provide theoretically important insights. As we have discussed earlier in Chapter 2, scholars from different disciplines continue to debate developments. If social trust in friends and neighbors, confidence in political institutions, and trust in agencies of global governance reflect an enduring set of values, beliefs, attitudes, and norms acquired from agencies of cultural transmission in each society, as sociologists suggest, then we would expect to observe slowly evolving trends in trust over successive decades, which occur in response to generational shifts and demographic turnover, as well as seeing persistent contrasts among societies and global regions due to historical cultural legacies, like enduring contrasts between Northern and Southern Europe.[3] If trust reflects judgments which are more responsive to medium- and short-term forces, however, as performance theories contend, then greater volatility in levels of trust should be observed. These could be attributed to the public's response to major events, for example, if changes in American attitudes toward the police occur following news media reports and mass protests by the Black Lives Matter movement over issues of racial justice. Similarly, if polls report significant shifts in trust in the European Commission and European Parliament, depending upon their timing, performance theories suggest that this could be explained as the public's response to their handling of the 2008 financial crisis, the 2015 refugee crisis, and the 2020 Covid-19 pandemic.[4]

It is also important to document observed trends over time because the consequences of any signs detecting declining trust also generate considerable concern for governance and democracy.[5] Thus hostility to Covid-19 regulations regarding masks and vaccines has recently been attributed to doubts about the scientific and public health authorities.[6] Similarly, the rise of support for authoritarian populist parties and leaders has been widely linked with growing loss of public confidence in mainstream parties on the center-left and center-right, signaling widespread discontent with liberal democracy.[7] Apprehension about the potential risks arising from any loss of trust is far from new, however, as concern has ebbed and flowed periodically over the decades, escalating during the late 1960s and early 1970s, the early 1990s, and again today.

A Crisis of Governability in the 1960s and 1970s?

Anxiety about the state of social and political trust was heightened by turbulent politics during the 1960s and the early 1970s. In the United States, this was exemplified by the explosion of race riots igniting conflagrations in Black areas of major US cities, the assassinations of Rev. Martin Luther King, President John F. Kennedy, and Senator Bobby Kennedy, and President Richard Nixon's resignation over Watergate. On divisive issues of racial justice and gender equality, environmentalism, and war, this era saw massive protests, political strikes, and student demonstrations mobilized on the streets of Chicago and Washington, DC, which quickly spread to London, Paris, and Tokyo. Reflecting on these events, in the mid-1970s, Michel Crozier, Samuel Huntington, and Joji Watanuki published their classic *The Crisis of Democracy* report for the Trilateral Commission, which highlighted growing political alienation and democratic malaise across many Western states.[8] The report claimed that many political problems confronting America arose from an "excess of democracy," while European governments were believed to be "overloaded" with demands, and thereby incapable of responding to new voices and new issues. Studies in political participation, which had traditionally focused on conventional acts like voting, contacting, and party activism, expanded to explore the roots of protest politics, mass demonstrations, political strikes, new social movements, and direct forms of activism by new social movements.[9] Crozier et al. argued that these developments served to undermine confidence in the authority of core political institutions, generating massive shocks to the foundations of social order and a so-called crisis of governability.

The Decay of Social Capital and Trust in Government in the 1990s?

The early 1990s witnessed another outbreak of alarm about civic ills in Western societies. This built on theories of social capital theories developed by sociologists Pierre Bourdieu and James Coleman, drawing attention to the effects and consequences of human connectedness.[10] The core concept of social capital was reformulated and amplified by Robert Putnam's seminal work warning about its attrition in the postwar United States.[11] In this account, Putnam defined social capital as "features of social organizations, such as networks, norms and trust that facilitate action and cooperation for mutual benefit."[12] He argued that the health of social connections and cooperation in American society was under growing threat, in particular that the post–World War II generation were far less willing than their parents and grandparents to join local philanthropic groups, voluntary associations, and civic community organizations. These institutions were believed to provide the sort of face-to-face interactions thought to build "bridging" forms of social capital across diverse local groups within local communities, thereby fostering the roots of societal cooperation, tolerance, and trust. As a result, he concluded, American society had seen flagging interpersonal bonds, waning engagement in local community groups, falling membership and activism in traditional voluntary and philanthropic organizations like Parent-Teacher Associations, and the forfeiture of public trust in the federal government.

Concern about the state of social capital struck a chord and proved immensely influential at a time when political trust in the US federal government was also reported by pollsters to have plummeted, especially confidence in Congress.[13] This decline persisted and went far beyond conventional explanations emphasizing the impact of particular contingent events occurring during previous eras, such as falling confidence attributed to deep divisions in the United States over the Vietnam War, race relations and civil rights, or Watergate.[14] The notion of social capital had bipartisan appeal during the 1990s both to moderate conservatives like President George H. W. Bush, aiming to shrink the size of the federal government and address social problems through engaging nonprofit organizations in local communities, as well as to Clintonite "Third Way" Democrats, seeking to revive local activism as a way of "reinventing government."

Commentators were quick to draw parallels concerning signs of democratic disaffection thought to be confronting European societies on the other side of the Atlantic. Hence Russell Dalton conducted a widespread review of the survey evidence and concluded that European citizens had ". . . grown distrustful of politicians, skeptical about democratic institutions, and disillusioned about how the democratic process functions."[15] In 2004, Schmitter and Trechsel echoed these sentiments: "Today, one of the most striking features of European democracies is an apparent widespread feeling of political discontent, disaffection, skepticism, dissatisfaction, and cynicism among citizens."[16] And Torcal and Montero concurred with the diagnosis: "Public skepticism about politicians and government is spreading to virtually all the advanced industrialized societies."[17] Citizens in the West were believed to have grown increasingly disillusioned with the way that representative institutions worked in liberal democracies, including the role of political parties, the news media, parliaments, and governments. There was also widespread concern that disaffection with these agencies could spread upward, like the fish rotting from the tail, generating growing public doubts about the workings of democratic regimes and even the value of democratic principles in general.[18] Dogan's review, drawing upon the EVS in 2001, concluded: "Surveys conducted in almost all of the European countries have shown that a large part of the citizenry, in some cases the majority, have 'none' or 'little' confidence in the principal institutions and organizations of the political regime: parties, government, parliament, high-level administration, courts, army, police, unions, big business, churches, television and printed mass media."[19]

Yet debate about the interpretation of trends was far from settled; in particular, electoral democracies were rapidly spreading around the world during the early 1990s, especially the rapid transformation of many Central and Eastern European states following the fall of the Berlin Wall, as well as process of democratic consolidation observed in Latin America.[20] Reflecting a more optimistic perspective, the large-scale *Beliefs in Government* project, involving an extensive network of scholars who conducted an exhaustive study of beliefs in postwar Europe until the early 1990s, challenged the gloomier interpretations of the challenges confronting representative democracy. Klingemann and Fuchs concluded that European citizens had indeed become more critical of politicians and parties, and more willing to use direct actions to mobilize and organize around their issue agenda. These well-established developments were regarded as a positive political transformation with the capacity to strengthen representative democracy, if citizens thereby became more active and effective in the political process, generating greater responsiveness by major political actors and collective actors, rather than a deterioration in the relationship between citizens and the state.[21] Several scholars have challenged the more pessimistic claim that trends in American cynicism toward government are a universal pattern observed across Western societies. Hence comparative studies of political attitudes taken from the annual Eurobarometer survey, including indicators of social trust, confidence in political institutions, and support for democracy, have concluded that trendless fluctuations can be observed over time in Europe, rather than a consistent downward erosion, while persistent contrasts in trust distinguish several postindustrial societies, such as Norway and Italy.[22] According to Andeweg and Aarts: "The legitimacy crisis has some of the characteristics of the Loch Ness monster: there are regular reports of sightings by villagers and tourists, but repeated scientific expeditions using the latest technology all fail to come up with solid evidence."[23] Similarly, Van Ham et al. conclude that claims of a "legitimacy crisis" constitute a powerful and tenacious "myth" more than reflecting reality, at least according to survey data in European Union member states.[24]

Deepening Mistrust Fueling Authoritarian Populism during the Past Decade?

Recent decades have seen widespread popular alarm about the functioning of political institutions essential to protect liberal freedoms, including rule of law, judicial independence, and media independence, concern about democratic norms being undermined, even in long-established democracies, and the vulnerability of Third Wave electoral democracies to backsliding into authoritarian practices. Popular accounts often assume that interpersonal trust has frayed in many Western societies over time, accompanied by a steadily rising tide of public disenchantment with national and global institutions of governance, and growing lack of confidence in other private and nonprofit-sector civic society institutions, like the news media, banks, and major companies. In a survey monitoring annual trends in trust in government, the media, business, and NGOs in around two dozen countries, for example, the 2021 Edelman Trust Barometer reports that the Covid-19 pandemic has accelerated "an erosion of trust around the world" and produced "an epidemic of misinformation and widespread mistrust of societal institutions and leaders."[25] The conservative columnist David Brooks argues that in a world where institutions failed, financial system collapsed, and families were fragile, America has been experiencing a moral convulsion: "Levels of trust in this country—in our institutions, in our politics, in one another—are in precipitous decline. And when trust collapses, nations fail. Can we get it back before it's too late?"[26] Alternatively, however, many scholars argue more cautiously that closer scrutiny of the polls suggests more complex and nuanced patterns of trendless fluctuations over time and substantial cross-national contrasts. Hence after comparing survey data for four decades since the mid-1970s across relatively similar European postindustrial societies, van Ham and Thomassen concluded that in the region, "despite the wealth of data and research on political support, scholars have not been able to reach agreement . . . we find no consistent evidence for declining political support . . . rather than a clear long-term decline in legitimacy that is apparent across all established democracies, we find large variations between countries, both in levels of political support and trends over time."[27]

American research has traditionally analyzed longitudinal indicators, drawing upon the US General Social Survey (GSS), opinion polls, and the American National Election Study (ANES).[28] Numerous commentators have repeatedly highlighted plummeting American confidence in the federal government; in 2019, for example, Pew reported that less than one-fifth of Americans said that they can trust the government in Washington to do what's right "just about always" (3%) or "most of the time" (14%).[29] Of all the branches, Congress has the worst ratings; the proportion of Americans expressing "a great deal" or "quite a lot" of confidence in the legislative branch in Gallup polls plummeted from around 40% during the early 1970s to the nadir of just 7% in 2014.[30] For many, this decline indicates a dysfunctional Congress, increasingly facing gridlock and hyper-partisan polarization, that has lost much of its legitimacy in the eyes of the people it serves.[31] The US insurrection on Capitol Hill on January 6, 2021, fueled by former president Trump's repeated challenges to electoral legitimacy, deepened alarm about the risks of domestic terrorist threats in the United States. Problems may be even deeper and more widespread; for example, Foa and Mounk compared several Anglo-American societies based on the sixth-wave WVS and argued that faith in democratic principles, and support for democratic values, had slumped most precipitously among the younger generation, interpreted as signals of "democratic deconsolidation," although the evidence for this claim has been strongly challenged by other scholars.[32] Lack of public trust in the police and the courts was highlighted by the death of George Floyd on May 25, 2020, while in police custody in Minnesota, triggering massive coast-to-coast demonstrations demanding racial justice and police accountability.

In many countries, a rising tide of political cynicism in recent years has been widely blamed for both facilitating, and also accelerating, a Pandora's Box of authoritarian-populist forces erupting in many societies.[33] These forces feed from, and stoke, the fires of social intolerance, division, and mistrust.[34] Leaders typically express anger directed "upward" to criticize "the establishment," including the "fake" news media, the "partisan" judiciary, "corrupt" politicians, and out-of-touch center-left and center-right parties.[35] The rhetoric heightens polarizing "Us–Them" fears, emphasizing trust and deferential loyalty toward leaders *within* the tribe, but simultaneously denigrating *outward*, whether "Other" peoples are defined by nationality, race and ethnicity, religion, gender identities, or sexual orientations. White Nationalist movements seek to challenge liberal democratic norms, values of pluralism and diversity, the rules-based world order, and agencies of global cooperation.[36] Populist rhetoric typically claims that mainstream politicians are dishonest and corrupt, elites are out of touch with the concerns of ordinary people, and the core institutions of representative democracy, like the media, courts, and parliament, are illegitimate.[37]

This phenomenon is exemplified in the United States by heightened party polarization and racial tensions, record numbers of violent hate crimes,[38] and a white supremacist backlash rejecting growing ethnic diversity.[39] Anger and disgust with Washington, DC ("Drain the Swamp") is one of the conventional explanations for Trump's rise to power in 2016.[40] His subsequent claims that the 2020 election was stolen by massive voter fraud encouraged the deadly Capitol Hill insurrection on January 6, where an angry pro-Trump mob sought to overturn the Congressional certification of Biden's victory in the 2020 presidential election. These events were followed by months of escalating protests and threats of violence by Trump supporters directed against State capitals, electoral officials, school boards, and elected representatives. But the potential risks to political stability, party polarization, and democratic norms which authoritarian-populism poses is far broader than America; votes and seats for parties and leaders using populist rhetoric and promoting authoritarian practices have surged in long-established democracies as diverse as Sweden and Norway, affluent Scandinavian welfare states, Italy and

Greece in Mediterranean Europe, Germany and France in Western Europe, as well as Hungary and Poland in post-Communist Europe.[41] Populist leaders such as Alberto Fujimori, Hugo Chavez, Evo Morales, Narendra Modi, Victor Orbán, Recep Tayyip Erdoğan, and Nicholas Maduro have shattered basic human rights and liberal freedoms.[42] In the United Kingdom, Brexit generated intense polarization and paralysis among (and within) parties, and a rising tide of public discontent and anger among both Leave and Remain camps.[43] Moreover, this is not a new phenomenon generated by the 2016 Brexit referenda; Jennings et al. claim that there has been a sustained growth in political discontent in the United Kingdom over more than half a century, based upon evidence from multiple polls.[44] In the European Union, as well, authoritarian-populist forces have deepened divisions among member states over how best to cope with the refugee crisis. The rules-based world order has also been threatened by a nationalist revival, challenging long-standing international alliances over free trade, human rights, climate change, security, and defense, exemplified by the Trump administration's withdrawal from the Paris Climate Change accord and the Iranian nuclear deal, as well as Hungarian refusals to conform with European Union policies over open borders, refugees, and population migration.

The dangers are thought to be far graver in electoral democracies, where a series of monitoring reports by international agencies like Freedom House, the Economist, International IDEA, and Human Rights Watch have blamed eroding public faith in mainstream governing parties, heightened party polarization, and electoral instability for heightening the risks of democratic backsliding, most evident through restrictions on civil liberties, the independent judiciary, and press freedom, and even occasional regime reversals.[45] The Varieties of Democracy (V-Dem) expert survey data estimate that several states which had transitioned toward electoral democracies during the early 1990s have subsequently slid back into electoral autocracies, exemplified by developments in Hungary, Turkey, the Philippines, Venezuela, and Russia.[46] In their 2022 annual report, Freedom House warns that democracies around the world are battered and weaker, with more losses than gains in recent years: "The long democratic recession is deepening. The impact of the long-term democratic decline has become increasingly global in nature, broad enough to be felt by those living under the cruelest dictatorships, as well as by citizens of long-standing democracies. Nearly 75 percent of the world's population lived in a country that faced deterioration last year."[47] Deep alarm about the political consequences of the state of the contemporary civic culture has intensified; for many international monitoring agencies, and for many leading scholars of comparative politics, the Doomsday Clock for liberal democracies is now pointing toward two minutes to midnight.[48] Hence International IDEA's report, *The Global State of Democracy 2021*, concluded: "The world is becoming more authoritarian as non-democratic regimes become even more brazen in their repression and many democratic governments suffer from backsliding by adopting their tactics of restricting free speech and weakening the rule of law, exacerbated by what threatens to become a 'new normal' of Covid-19 restrictions. For the fifth consecutive year, the number of countries moving in an authoritarian direction exceeds the number of countries moving in a democratic direction. In fact, the number moving in the direction of authoritarianism is three times the number moving towards democracy."[49] International threats to democratic states from armed interventions are also heightened by Putin's aggressive invasion of Ukraine and President Xi's heightened rhetoric toward Taiwan.

At the same time, however, important qualifications to the more pessimistic prognostications again deserve to be highlighted. Many studies have established that public mistrust in political institutions helps to drive voting support for more populist parties, defined as those parties campaigning on anti-elite and anti-corruption platforms.[50] Yet it remains an open question whether authoritarian populist forces should be regarded in general as the cause, or the consequence, of deepening political disaffection.[51] One reason is that the electoral success of these parties may provide an outlet for those previously feeling excluded from mainstream politics.[52] For example, during the first two years of the Trump administration, despite the president's repeated attacks on "the establishment" like the "fake media" and "corrupt politicians," Gallup polls reported a modest but consistent *recovery* of American trust in Congress, the Supreme Court, and the presidency, not a further decline, as significant gains among Republicans outweighed the loss among Democrats.[53] The lowest point in trust in the presidency recorded in the Gallup series from 1975–2021 occurred in 2014, under the Obama administration.[54] Moreover, the US GSS suggests minimal change in American feelings of social trust in recent decades, not any erosion, despite heated polarizing rhetoric during the Obama and Trump years.[55] The links connecting populist parties with social and political trust may therefore prove contingent and more complex than is often assumed in popular commentary.

Interpreting Trends

The interpretation of trends in trust also continues to be debated among scholars. Genuine differences in interpreting the available empirical survey evidence can arise for many reasons, including the use of different data sets and questions, the baseline starting points and endpoints used in longitudinal studies, the choice of model specifications and controls, and the comparative framework.

During the last four decades, the WVS has monitored longitudinal trends using several common indicators which are widely regarded as valid and reliable measures of trust, including levels of interpersonal (generalized) trust toward other people, confidence in public and private-sector institutions, and trust in the agencies of global governance.[56] It should be noted, however, that trust is a complex concept, so that measures may not be equivalent in meaning across diverse cultures, regimes, and societies.[57] The analysis of the trajectory of public opinion also helps to provide theoretical insights. On the one hand, if societal levels of trust are observed to be largely unchanged over successive decades, and persistent contrasts are observed even among relatively similar neighboring states within a world region such as the Middle East or Latin America, this suggests that trust is a largely stable orientation. This observation would be consistent with social psychological accounts suggesting that children grow up fearing the worst or hoping for the best in other people, so that trust is an individual personality trait, like affective feelings of openness or caution, introversion or extroversion, largely irrespective of adult experiences and the performance of governments in the public sphere.[58] Thus, for decades, or even centuries, those living in Nordic societies may be born optimists, trusting strangers into their homes, while by contrast those in Mediterranean Europe may be born cynics, bolting their doors tight shut against outsiders.[59] By contrast, survey evidence suggesting a consistent long-term erosion of trust over time observed in many countries, clear contrasts in trust among rich and poor societies, and/or distinct generational differences across birth cohorts would lend credence to sociological theories emphasizing long-term cultural shifts.[60]

Alternatively, however, if medium- and short-term fluctuations in levels of trust are observed to occur over successive surveys in the same country, generating both volatile upticks and downturns around the mean, this points more strongly toward performance-based explanations. It becomes more plausible to expect that the public is probably responding to perceptions about the trustworthiness of agents—such as their assessments about the government's record of managing jobs, healthcare, and security, as well as public confidence in the accountability guardrails protecting against bad actors. The performance-based explanation becomes more credible where public trust is observed to tick upward or downward in the immediate aftermath of highly disruptive "shocks."[61] Random, unpredictable events may generate abrupt shifts or period effects which are expected to have major consequences. When the governing party or leader is accused of major money-in-politics scandals, for example, such as in Japan, Spain, or Brazil, do longitudinal series of public opinion surveys in these societies register a subsequent sharp surge in subjective perceptions of the extent of corruption *and* fall in levels of public trust in government? Similarly, does public trust respond to crisis events, such as in debtor countries like Greece when the Eurozone banking and financial crisis occurred, or in Italy and Brazil when hospital intensive care units (ICUs) were overwhelmed by a surge in Covid-19 patients? And was the election of Donald Trump followed by a sharp uptick in political trust among his supporters—but a parallel dive among Democrats? A series of studies have used cross-national time-series survey data to explore how far public opinion responds to major event shocks, including trends in attitudes concerning confidence in institutions, regime support, leadership popularity, and support for democracy following major economic downturns such as the 2007–2008 banking crisis and eurozone recession in Mediterranean Europe.[62] Many other types of events may serve as equivalent jolts, however, such as the timing of the initial outbreak of the Covid-19 pandemic and subsequent mitigation efforts such as lockdowns,[63] the impact of major terrorist attacks, as exemplified by 9/11,[64] the onset of political scandals in the United States, Brazil, and Japan,[65] or the consequences of leadership change and major regime transitions, like those experienced following the downfall of the Soviet Union or during the Arab Spring.[66]

Observed trends over time and the cross-national patterns of trust cannot be regarded as definitively confirming theories of skeptical judgments of trustworthiness, based on this evidence alone. Any sudden fluctuations in trust could always be the product of random noise, for example due to measurement error associated with technical changes in survey fieldwork, question order, and sampling procedures, rather than linked to rational evaluations of variations in performance per se. Complex processes of cognitive reasoning need to be considered when testing the links connecting objective performance indices, subjective public evaluations of agency performance, and levels of trust, as scrutinized in the next chapter. Nevertheless, the observed cross-national societal patterns, and trends in public opinion, on the "demand-side" of the trust equation, deserve a more thorough investigation in subsequent chapters.

II. Comparing Evidence of Trends and Patterns of Trust Worldwide

Social Trust

What evidence would help to update the analysis of longitudinal and global comparisons of trust? Data visualizations of trends over successive waves of the EVS/WVS, broken down by agency and country, provide a rich basis for descriptive comparisons, and the size and significance of the net change are calculated by the difference between the mean level of trust in the earliest and latest survey wave, as summarized in Table 4.1 later in the chapter. Net time-series trends can be compared most straightforwardly by examining the fifty-three EVS/WVS country surveys included in both the second (1989–1993) and seventh waves (2017–2021), with an interpolation line in the graphs for any cases not surveyed in any particular intermediate wave.

Turning first to the global comparison of social or generalized trust over time, the widely used standard item has been carried in successive waves of the EVS/WVS since the early 1980s. This binary question asks: "Generally speaking, would you say that most people can be trusted or that you need to be very careful in dealing with people?" Trends are available for comparison in fifty-three diverse postindustrial and developing societies from all over the world. As discussed in the previous chapter, there are pros and cons of using this measure, but analysis allows comparisons updating many previous studies. Change is estimated by the proportion responding "Most people can be trusted" in each nation from the earliest to the latest wave, spanning four decades. Trends in social trust using this question can be compared in eighteen societies worldwide included in the earliest and latest waves of the EVS/WVS, spanning over four decades, including several affluent postindustrial societies, as well as some middle-income countries, such as Argentina, Mexico, and Hungary. Previous comparative studies have established that Nordic countries are usually exceptionally high in absolute levels of social trust, while by contrast trust has typically been found to be lower in post-Communist Europe and Latin America.[67] But is this a persistent pattern today and, given the concern over eroding social trust, what has changed over time?

Figure 4.1 shows that far from absolute levels of social trust falling consistently over the years, as pessimistic views claim, in fact variable trends are observable across these fifty-three societies. Thus, the smaller welfare states in Northern Europe and Scandinavia are not only relatively high in absolute levels of social trust—contrary to widespread expectations, *they have also experienced net growth in trust during these four decades*, with substantial rises recorded in Denmark (+26%), Iceland (+23%), the Netherlands (+19%), Finland (+15%), Germany (+14%), and Norway (+12%). The net change has sometimes been dramatic; for example, the proportion expressing social trust rose from around half of the Danish respondents in the early 1980s to over three-quarters today. This development in Denmark has been attributed to growing levels of education, improvements in the quality of state institutions, and processes of generational replacement.[68] By contrast, net social trust can be observed to erode steeply in several developing societies over these years, notably in Indonesia, Bulgaria, Albania, and Mexico. A lot of concern about social capital focused on the United States, based on GSS evidence of trends from the 1970s to the early 1990s. But the EVS/WVS data show only a modest net erosion in social trust from the early 1980s to the early 1990s in the United States, followed by a largely flat profile. This confirms trends observed since the early 1990s in the annual US GSS, where about one-third of Americans agree that most people can be trusted, while two-thirds report that it depends or you can't be too careful.[69] In many other nations under comparison, observed absolute levels of social trust usually display either a pattern of trendless fluctuations around the mean (such as in Australia, Spain, the Czech Republic, and the United Kingdom), or else fairly stable but relatively low levels of social trust (for example, in Italy, Japan, the Philippines, and France).

The contrasts in levels and trends observed among several neighboring European Union member states with similar economic and social characteristics during recent decades, such as trust rising in Germany compared with stability in France, or differences apparent in Italy and Spain, appear to challenge some of the standard explanations based on long-term secular trends transforming postindustrial societies, like the role of communications or the impact of generational shifts in cultural values. Most of the high and rising trust cases in Figure 4.1 are typically prosperous and secure postindustrial

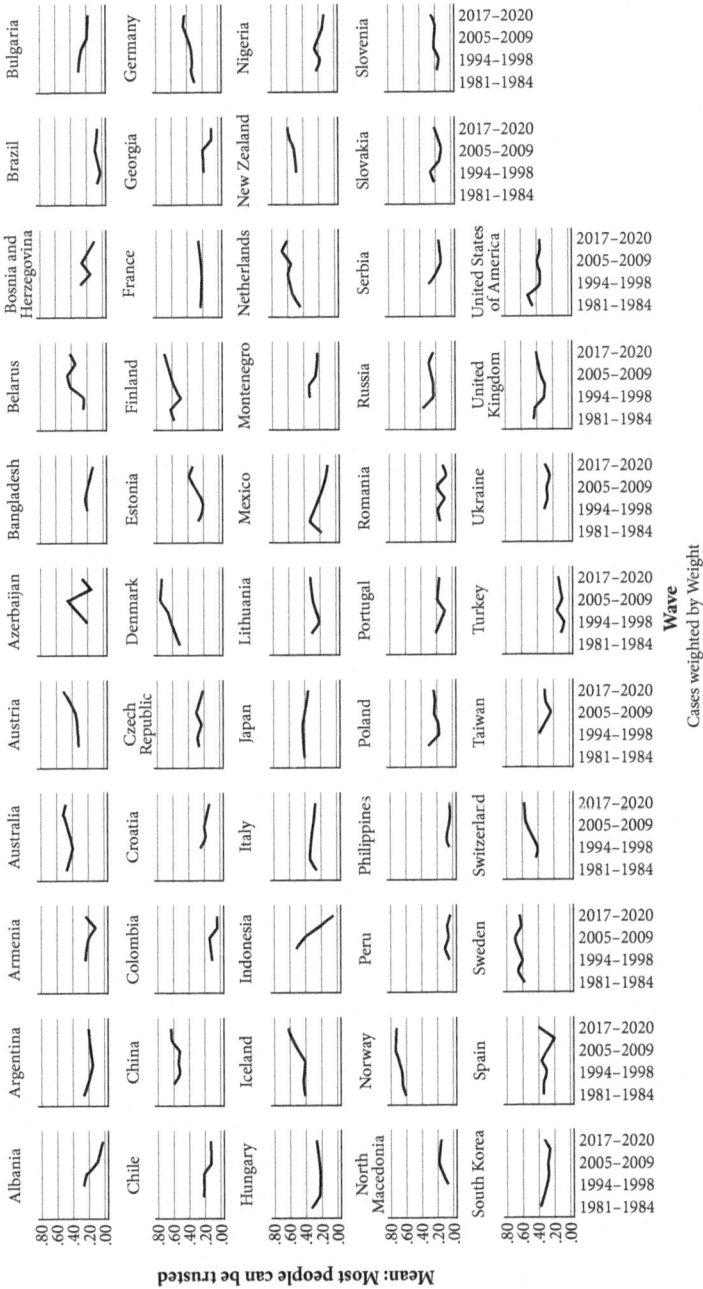

Figure 4.1. Trends in social trust.

Note: Q: "Most people can be trusted (1) or you can't be too careful in dealing with people? (0)." The table presents the proportion responding positively that "most people can be trusted."

Source: European Values Survey/World Values Survey County Pooled Dataset Waves 1–7 (1981–2021) in 53 societies.

societies characterized by well-functioning systems of democratic governance, rule of law, power-sharing constitutions, and lack of corruption, according to international indices. Most people living in these states have
grown up under comfortable conditions of security, peace, and prosperity,
in highly educated and affluent societies where existential life-threatening
risks are mitigated for most citizens by egalitarian social policies and cradle-
to-grave welfare states. These typical characteristics are often thought to encourage social and political trust.[70] Subsequent chapters will examine how
well the observed trends reflect performance theories which suggest that the
role of the state, and in particular the quality of fair and impartial processes
of democratic governance, play a critical role strengthening generalized trust
as a moral orientation.[71] Nevertheless, any links between generalized (social) trust and political trust could run through multiple pathways, which
are often not sufficiently clarified in many studies.[72] In addition, establishing
the direction of causality linking political institutions and processes of governance with citizens' feelings of generalized trust remains difficult to dis-
entangle without longitudinal panel survey data, since theoretically the
association may be regarded as reciprocal.[73]

In addition, rather than performance, many other historical cultural legacies and social characteristics shared among Scandinavian and Northern
European societies could potentially provide alternative explanations of
contemporary absolute levels of social trust in these regions. For centuries,
until recently, societies in these regions have been inhabited by relatively
homogeneous white Protestant populations, with relatively few foreign-
born immigrants or ethnic minorities drawn from other regions around the
world. Ethnic homogeneity has often been found to strengthen feelings of
solidarity, tolerance, and trust.[74] Comparative studies of the sociology of religion also point toward the historical legacies of shared Protestant cultures
and Lutheran churches in the region. Religious organizations in all faiths
with forms with collective worship are thought to play an important role
in the formation of social capital.[75] Mainline Protestant churches in the
United States—Methodists, Presbyterians, Episcopalians, and Lutherans—
have long been regarded as central to the lives of their local communities.[76] Religious organizations are believed to strengthen social capital by
providing places for people to meet, fostering informal social networks of
friends and neighbors, developing leadership skills in religious organizations and church committees, informing people about public affairs, delivering welfare services, providing a community meeting place, drawing

together people from diverse social and ethnic backgrounds, and encouraging active involvement in associational groups concerned with education, youth development, and human services. Active membership in religious organizations in Protestant churches can thereby foster egalitarian horizontal social connections and feelings of in-group trust within faith-based communities, with spill-over effects for civic attitudes and engagement.[77] By contrast, religious institutions may function differently for social capital under the more hierarchical forms of spiritual authority and religious organizations found in Catholic churches, in Orthodox basilicas, and in Islamic mosques. For all these reasons, performance theories may provide one plausible explanation of the observed persistent contrasts in national levels of social trust, and volatility over time, but further systematic scrutiny is needed in subsequent chapters, since many other cultural factors may also play an important role.[78]

Unfortunately, the standard survey item measuring social trust refers to "most people" but it does not differentiate by the radius of trust, such as toward close friends or more distant acquaintances, nor does it make any distinction between generalized and particularized trust.[79] Figure 4.2 allows us to observe the relationship between social trust toward in-groups (acquaintances like close-knit family, neighbors, and friends) and out-groups (more distant and weaker relationships toward people from different faiths or places), using the composite scales from items listed in Table 3.3. Arguably, trust in outsiders is most important for strengthening tolerance and cooperation in diverse multicultural societies, although accurate evaluations of unfamiliar group members are also potentially riskier and more demanding than judgments about close personal relationships, which may extend over years or even a lifetime. Data using these in-group and out-group scales are unavailable for previous waves of the survey, but comparisons can be made for the fifty-eight countries where these questions were included in the seventh wave of the WVS (2017–2021). The scattergram identifies several societies with high levels of both in-group and out-group trust, located in the top right quadrant. This includes many smaller welfare states in Scandinavia and Northern Europe which were commonly observed as high-trust societies in the previous table using the standard measure, led by Denmark, Norway, Sweden, the Netherlands, and Finland. Some other affluent postindustrial societies also ranked highly on both dimensions, such as the United Kingdom, Spain, and Switzerland in Western Europe, along with Anglo-American democracies, such as Canada and New Zealand. Overall,

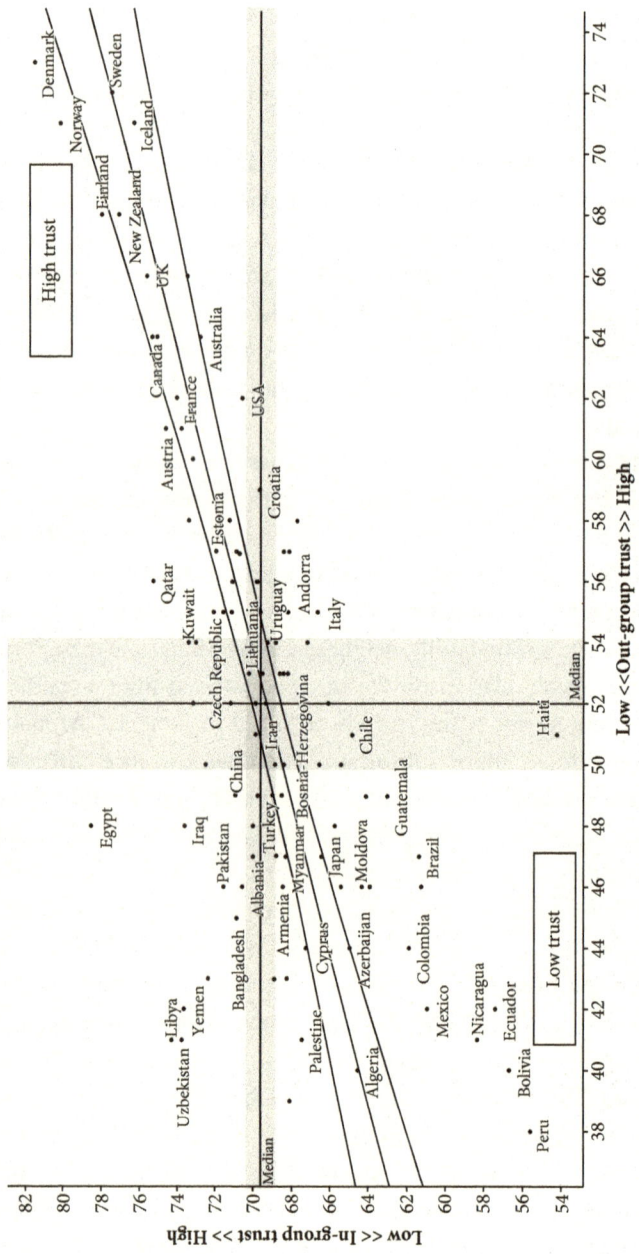

Figure 4.2. Worldwide distribution in types of social trust.

Notes: For the composition of the 100-point standardized scales, see Table 3.3. In-group trust is trust in your family, neighborhood, and people you know personally. Outgroup trust is trust in people of another nationality or religion, people you meet for the first time, agreement that most people can be trusted.

Source: European Values Survey/World Values Survey 5–7 (2000–2021) 115 societies (N. 49,328).

the measures of in-group and out-group trust were strongly correlated at the societal level (R = 0.588).

Many diverse types of countries can be observed to be clustered in the top-left quadrant of the distribution, expressing greater in-group trust toward immediate friends and neighbors than toward outsiders drawn from different religions and nations. This was notably the case in several poorer developing societies with Muslim religious cultures in the Middle East and North Africa (MENA) region, like Egypt, Libya, Yemen, and Iraq, as well as in South Asian cases such as Bangladesh and Pakistan, in East and Southeast Asian states as diverse as China, Malaysia, and Thailand, along with several societies in post-Communist Europe, such as Russia, Albania, Georgia, and Slovenia. Interestingly, a few cases display a more complex radius of trust, with more trust toward out-groups than in-groups, thus falling below the regression line, as exemplified by both the United States and Italy.

By contrast, several societies located in the bottom left quadrant were observed to mistrust out-groups as well as in-groups, according to both these measures, proving wary of both friends and strangers alike. This culture is exemplified by the Latin American cases of Ecuador, Peru, Bolivia, Colombia, and Mexico. Theories seeking to explain these observed societal-level patterns will be analyzed in subsequent chapters, but the updated comparison appears generally consistent with the result of several previous cross-national studies. This includes Delhey and Newton's observation that the most trusting societies are generally correlated with the characteristics of ethnic homogeneity, Protestant religious traditions, good government, affluence, and income equality.[80]

Civil Society Agencies: The Media and Churches

Public confidence in accuracy, truth, and credibility in the legacy or mainstream news media and online digital media platforms is also widely believed to be under growing challenge in many parts of the world, with important consequences for civic engagement and political behavior.[81] In the United States, annual Gallup polls report declining media trust since the 1970s, decades which have seen plummeting newspaper sales, and the explosive growth of digital media supplanting time spent watching television.[82] This decline has been linked with growing party polarization in the United States, as Democrats and Republicans differ sharply today in their trust of television channels such as Fox and CNN, as well as in their confidence in major newspapers.[83] The rise of online misinformation and disinformation, reflecting older traditions of propaganda intending to mislead, is thought to have exacerbated mistrust of the media, especially the credibility of online information from social platforms.[84]

Yet some studies suggest that claims of steadily falling trust in the media are exaggerated.[85] It may well be problematic to generalize from the US case; for example, a 2021 YouGov poll online survey of news consumers in forty-four countries, conducted for the Reuters Institute for the Study of Journalism, found that overall trust in the news varied substantially across societies, but only 29% said that they trusted the news in the United States, the lowest proportion of all countries in the study, compared with the highest level of trust (65%) in Finland.[86] Gallup global annual surveys also document varied levels of trust in journalists in over 144 countries, with less confidence generally found in open societies with greater freedom of expression and more diverse sources of news.[87] Generic measures of trust and confidence in "journalism" or "the media" are also highly abstract, given variations in evaluations of the multiple actors and agencies playing a role in communication systems. Measurement has become more complicated following the proliferation of sources, including fragmentation among radio and television broadcasters, legacy and digital newspapers, and the diverse array of digital platforms.[88] The criteria used to judge the trustworthiness of the media are theorized in this book as similar to those underlying judgments of other actors and agencies, including expectations about their integrity (such as the honesty of journalists), competency (their capacity to report without undue pressures or restriction), and impartiality (or the fairness of the media and their lack of bias).

To broaden the comparison, Figure 4.3 describes the trends and comparisons of absolute levels of trust in the press in the EVS/WVS data set across fifty-three diverse societies. The picture suggests that, once again, generalizations are complex and trends about declining trust in the media, widely discussed in the United States, prove somewhat atypical. Thus, trust is relatively low in several Anglo-American cases such as Australia, the United Kingdom, and New Zealand, while being higher in some Asian societies such as South Korea, China, and Japan. Several post-Communist states in Central Europe and the Baltics do see eroding trust in the media, notably a strong decline in Hungary, Estonia, the Czech Republic, Georgia, Slovenia, Poland, and Bulgaria, as well as in Latin American societies like Brazil and

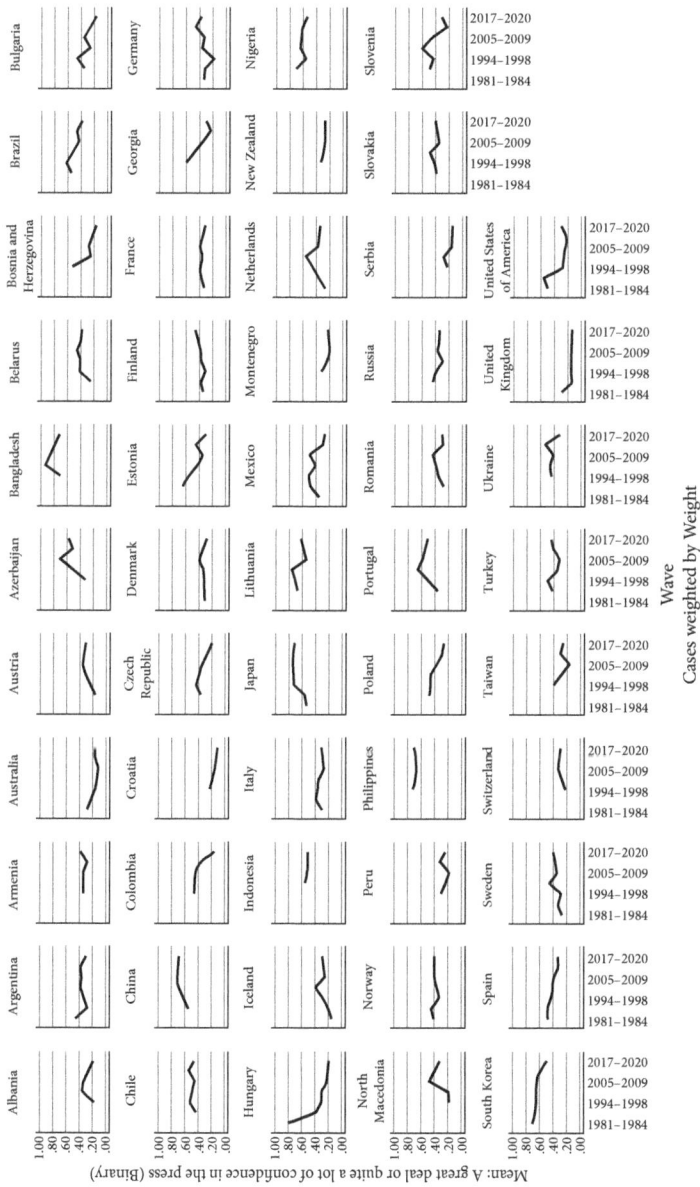

Figure 4.3. Trends in confidence in the press.

Notes: Q: "I am going to name a number of organizations. For each one, could you tell me how much confidence you have in them: is it a great deal of confidence, quite a lot of confidence, not very much confidence, or none at all?" Total % responding "a great deal" or "quite a lot" of confidence in the press.

Source: European Values Survey/World Values Survey County Pooled Dataset Waves 1–7 (1981–2021) in 53 societies.

Colombia, and in Spain. But several other societies, such as France, Italy, and Norway, show stability during these decades or trendless fluctuations with minimal net change.

Are similar cross-national contrasts evident concerning confidence in other civil society agencies, including new social movements, NGOs, and traditional non-state agencies, such as religious organizations, trade unions, banks, and major corporations? It is important to monitor public confidence in varied types of agencies since theories of social capital suggest that associational membership and generalized trust are closely related in a reciprocal connection.[89] Putnam argues that belonging to community groups like local sports clubs, arts organizations, churches, and neighborhood associations in the United States strengthens both in-group *and* out-group social trust through building face-to-face interpersonal networks, reinforcing group norms and social sanctions. At the same time, however, Putnam acknowledges that both positive and negative consequences for social trust toward out-groups like foreigners or people of different faith or race and ethnicity can clearly flow from associational membership, contingent upon their type, for example white supremacy, homophobic, and misogynist groups seek to stoke intolerance and hatred. Much theorizing treats the relationship as flowing from joining to trusting, but the causal direction in this assumption is also difficult to establish, even with longitudinal panel studies, since obviously there can be much reciprocity involved, where trusting people are also more likely to join local groups.[90]

Beyond the consequences for social trust, it is also important to understand confidence in these sorts of civil society organizations, as they serve as vital intermediaries connecting citizens and the state, expanding opportunities for expression, engagement, and participation in democratic societies, as exemplified by the role of the Catholic Church in mobilizing support for Christian Democratic parties on the center-right, and the role of environmental groups and activists on climate change fulfilling a similar function for Green parties. Systematic cross-national time-series data that monitor grassroots voluntary involvement in civic society are difficult to assemble on a consistent basis across diverse countries, however, given the sheer diversity of groups, issues, and organizations engaged in this subfield and the informal nature of much activity. Nevertheless, modernization theories suggest that new social movements seeking to raise public awareness, lobby policymakers, and catalyze direct action in local communities have proliferated and flourished in recent decades, especially in many affluent postindustrial societies around progressive issues such as LGBTQ and women's rights, social justice, economic development and poverty alleviation, and climate change.[91] At the same time, however, there is also widespread concern that voluntary engagement in traditional interest groups and membership in nonprofit associations has weakened, as exemplified by behavioral indicators such as shrinking membership of trade unions as a proportion of the working-age population, declining involvement in older charitable and philanthropic voluntary organizations, and falling church attendance, as well as by attitudinal indicators.[92]

The traditional core of many civil society activities concerns religious organizations, where churches, temples, mosques, and synagogues bring together the faithful for collective services, developing bridging social networks. Putnam argues that religious organizations, particularly Protestant churches, are uniquely important for American civic society: "Faith communities in which people worship together are arguably the single most important repository of social capital in America."[93] Religious involvement is seen by Putnam as building communities, with faith-based organizations serving civic life directly by providing social support for members and voluntary services to the local area, as well as indirectly, by nurturing local connections, organizational skills, inculcating moral values, and encouraging altruism. Elsewhere in the world, religious organizations in multiple faiths with collective religious services can serve similar social functions beyond the purely spiritual. At the same time, processes of secularization have been eroding attendance at religious services in postindustrial societies, weakening feelings of religiosity and the authority of religious leaders and institutions.[94]

To examine the longitudinal evidence for trust in religious organizations, Figure 4.4 displays trends concerning trust in religious organizations since the early 1980s. The comparison of societies demonstrates substantial cross-national contrasts, with far more confidence in religious institutions in poorer and less secure places, which tend to be highly religious in their cultural attitudes, such as Bangladesh, the Philippines, Indonesia, and Nigeria, rather than in more secular and affluent postindustrial societies, such as Japan, Switzerland, and the United Kingdom. The longitudinal data suggest some modest net changes can be observed during these three decades, with more net losses than gains, but the direction of these shifts varies cross-nationally. Thus, confidence in religious agencies is observed to grow following the post-Communist dissolution of the Republic of Yugoslavia and conflict in the Balkans heightening ethno-religious and ethno-nationalistic

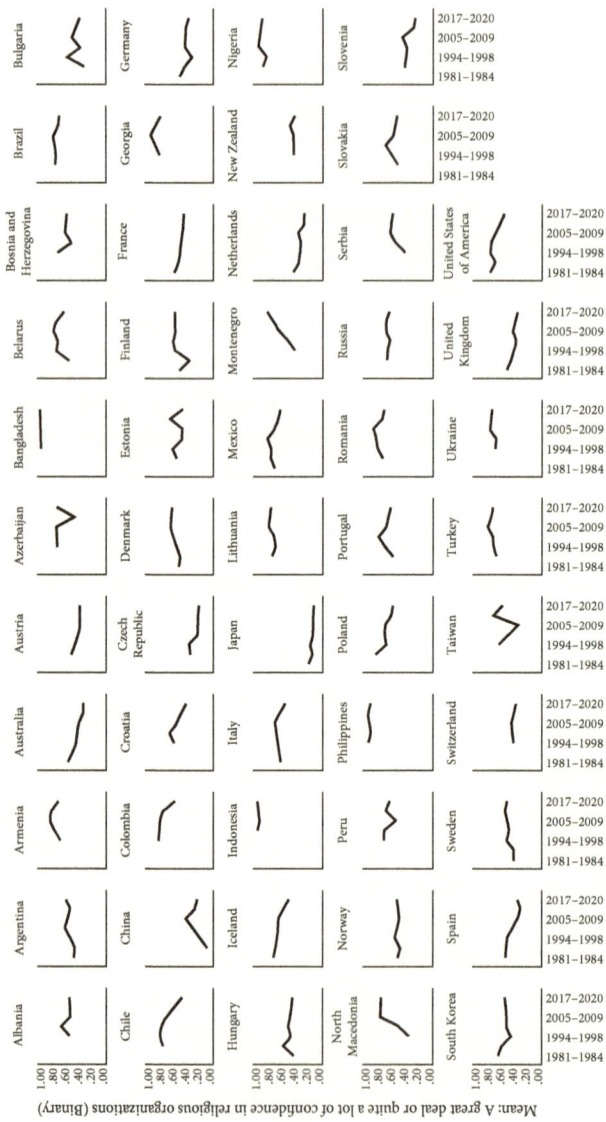

Figure 4.4. Trends in confidence in religious organizations.

Notes: Q: "I am going to name a number of organizations. For each one, could you tell me how much confidence you have in them: is it a great deal of confidence, quite a lot of confidence, not very much confidence, or none at all?" Total % responding "a great deal" or "quite a lot" of confidence in religious organizations.

Source: European Values Survey/World Values Survey County Pooled Dataset Waves 1–7 (1981–2021) in 53 societies.

identities, such as in Montenegro, Serbia, and North Macedonia, while trust falls during the same period in countries such as Australia, Spain, Chile, and Iceland—as well as the United States. And some other countries see minimal net change over time.

State Security Agencies

The factor analysis presented earlier in Table 3.3 suggests that public confidence in the armed forces, the police, and the justice system emerged as a separate dimension, reflecting attitudes toward state security agencies. The drivers of trust in these institutions can be expected to prove distinct from confidence in civil society NGOs, for example if older generations of social conservatives prove more likely to favor the military and police, while younger liberal progressives express greater trust in social movements promoting issues like the environment and human rights.

Figure 4.5 describes levels of confidence in these agencies, showing that some post-Communist societies such as Estonia, Lithuania, Azerbaijan, and Georgia have seen growing trust following the fall of the Berlin Wall and liberalization in these states, a similar pattern to some established liberal democracies such as Portugal, Austria, Finland, and Germany. Yet by contrast, several other nations see relatively low and falling trust in the security services during these decades, notably in several middle-income states in Southeastern Europe (Albania, Bulgaria, Croatia, Montenegro, and Bosnia-Herzegovina), with ex-Eastern Bloc countries in the Balkan region destabilized during the transition toward free market societies by government corruption and ethno-religious conflicts following the dissolution of Yugoslavia. Similar patterns of low and eroding trust can be observed in several Latin American states where stability has come under challenge from corruption scandals and violent internal conflict, like Colombia, Peru, and Mexico.

Governance Agencies of the Nation-State

As well as anxiety about the loss of trust in civic organizations and in social trust, there has been widespread and long-standing concern about the potential loss of confidence in the core agencies of the nation-state. As

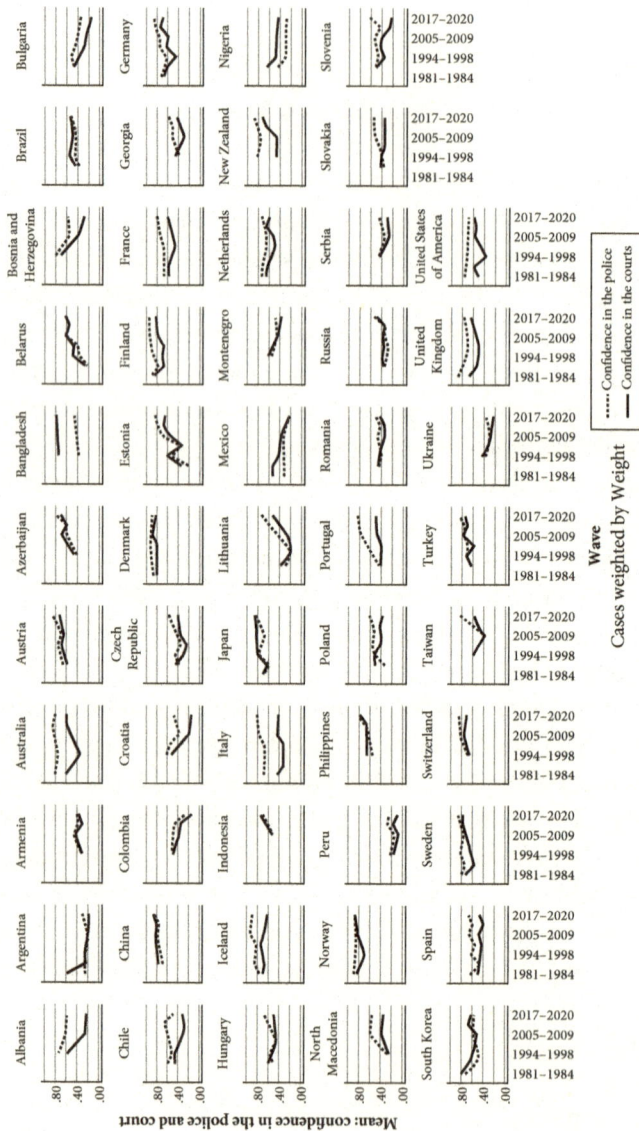

Figure 4.5. Trends in confidence in the police and courts.

Notes: Q: "I am going to name a number of organizations. For each one, could you tell me how much confidence you have in them: is it a great deal of confidence, quite a lot of confidence, not very much confidence, or none at all?" Total % responding "a great deal" or "quite a lot" of confidence in the police/the courts.

Source: European Values Survey/World Values Survey County Pooled Dataset Waves 2–7 (1990–2021) in 53 societies.

discussed earlier, numerous observers have commonly detected signs of contemporary political discontent even in long-standing European democracies and affluent postindustrial societies.[95] Most concern has focused on any signs of growing disaffection with political parties, governments, the media, and parliaments.[96] Yet at the same time, divergent patterns have often been observed, even among relatively similar European societies. For example, the 2018 Eurobarometer survey reports that citizens in many Mediterranean European states and in the Balkans express widespread mistrust in their national parliaments, with only 15% of Greeks and Spaniards saying that they trust their national parliament, although by contrast two-thirds or more of the public in Nordic nations expressed similar sentiments.[97] Even before Brexit, according to the British Social Attitudes survey, trust in government in the United Kingdom halved since the early 1980s.[98] Trends have been measured in the EVS/WVS since the 1990s, and the items can be compared using a standardized scale combining trust in four agencies—the national parliament, civil service, political parties, and the government. All these institutions play a vital role in the policymaking process within the nation-state. As Table 3.3 illustrates, trust in governance agencies within the nation-state formed a consistent and distinct dimension which was separate from the others considered so far.

Figure 4.6 shows the absolute levels of trust in political parties in fifty-three diverse societies from the early 1990s until today. Net change is calculated as the difference between the earliest and latest decade. The comparisons confirm the picture observed earlier regarding other dimensions of trust; in a few diverse countries, far from eroding, in fact net political trust in parties increases, including in Turkey, New Zealand, and Belarus. Some other countries, like Switzerland and Australia, display either relatively stable levels of political trust or trendless fluctuations around the mean, while conversely the remainder see either steady or sudden sharp declines in confidence during these eras, especially in Latin American societies like Chile, Brazil, and Mexico, as well as in several other post-Communist societies, such as Bulgaria, Slovenia, the Czech Republic, Albania, and Croatia. Most strikingly, trust in parties is particularly high in Communist China, for reasons explored in later chapters.

Figure 4.7 looks at parallel trajectories in confidence in government, confirming very similar but not identical patterns. Thus, public confidence rises in diverse places like Indonesia, New Zealand, Russia, Turkey, and South Korea, while steadily falling in Ukraine, Chile, Brazil, and the Czech

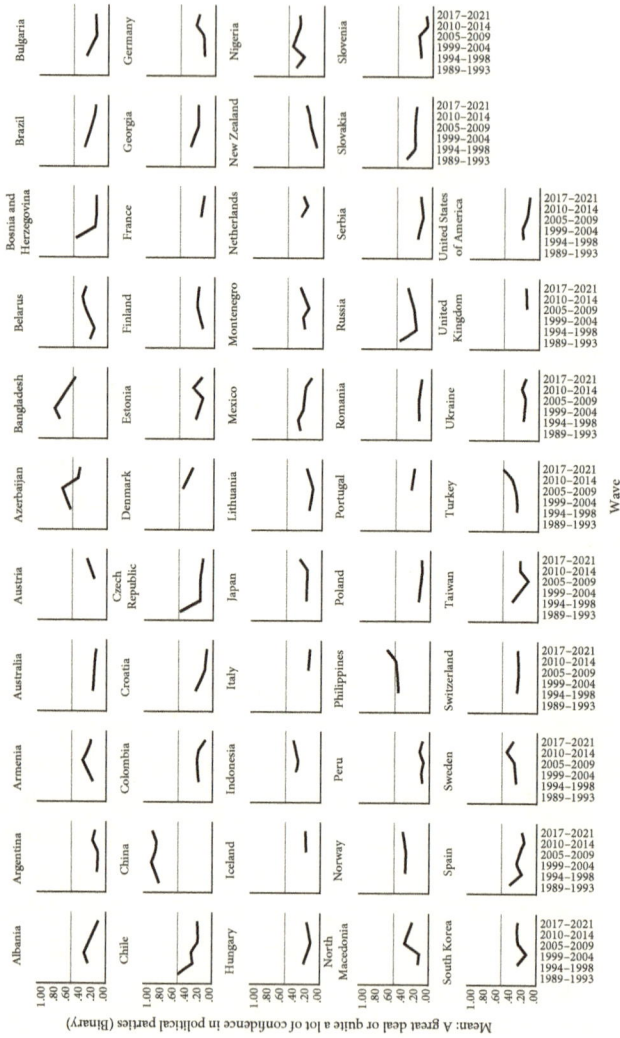

Figure 4.6. Trends in confidence in political parties.

Notes: Q: "I am going to name a number of organizations. For each one, could you tell me how much confidence you have in them: is it a great deal of confidence, quite a lot of confidence, not very much confidence, or none at all?" Total % responding "a great deal" or "quite a lot" of confidence in political parties.

Source: European Values Survey/World Values Survey County Pooled Dataset, Waves 2–7 (1989–2021) in 53 societies.

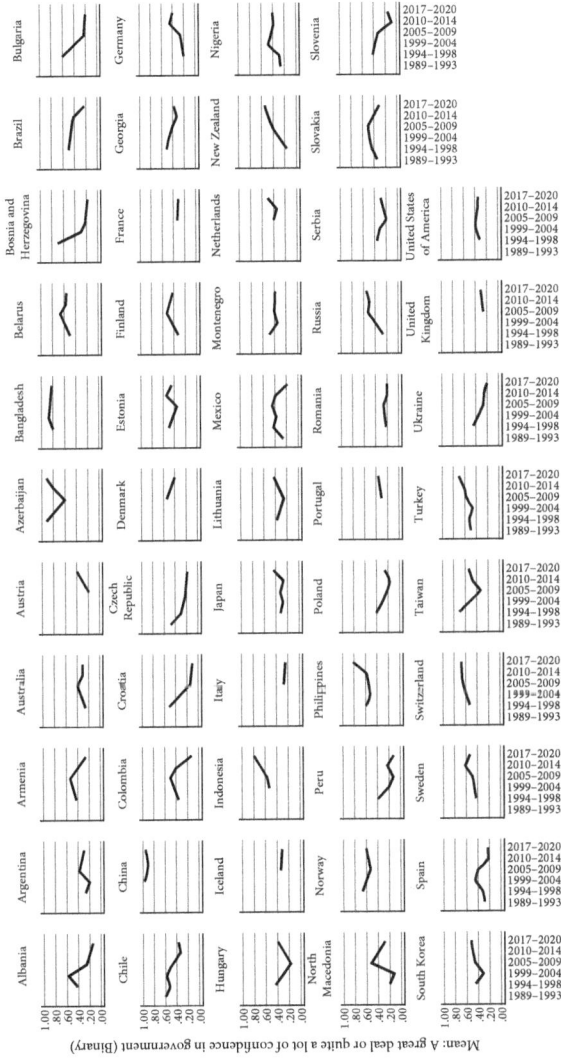

Figure 4.7. Trends in confidence in government.

Notes: Q: "I am going to name a number of organizations. For each one, could you tell me how much confidence you have in them: is it a great deal of confidence, quite a lot of confidence, not very much confidence, or none at all?" Total % responding "a great deal" or "quite a lot" of confidence in the national government.

Source: European Values Survey/World Values Survey County Pooled Dataset Waves 2–7 (1989–2021) in 53 societies.

Republic. Moreover, trust in government is remarkably high in China and Bangladesh, while being low in Italy, the United States, and the United Kingdom. What this diversity suggests is that oversimple generalizations based on cherry-picking a few cases to claim an inexorable fall in public trust should be avoided, as a broader comparison reveals a far more complex picture of changes in political trust worldwide. Subsequent chapters focus on trust in political institutions to see how far these variations can be explained by the performance of governments in each country, both in terms of delivering public goods and services, as well as the quality of government.

International Agencies of Global Governance

What are the worldwide patterns of confidence and trust in the agencies of global governance? A growing body of literature has developed to understand the legitimacy of multilateral institutions of global governance, including trust and confidence in the United Nations and the European Union.[99] Many agencies are included in the seventh wave of the EVS/WVS, but unfortunately here the EVS/WVS time-series data remain limited. It is possible to compare longitudinal trends in confidence in the United Nations, the most familiar agency of global governance. Figure 4.8 shows relatively high levels of trust in the United Nations in most countries—and an overall picture of considerable stability. Approval is highest in developing countries dependent upon international aid and assistance, such as Bangladesh and the Philippines, but public trust is also stable and strong in leading donor nations such as Norway, the Netherlands, Japan, and Sweden.

Finally, how do confidence and trust vary across agents and agencies in the pooled sample of all the countries in the most recent (seventh wave) survey? Figure 4.9 illustrates the contrasts, with trust strongest in family, friends, and neighbors, close circles of familiar people that people interact with on a daily basis. Confidence is also relatively high in several agencies, such as universities, the armed forces and the police, religious, charitable, and women's organizations. By contrast, the institutions where the public expresses least confidence involve politics and the media, including the government, labor unions, television and the press, parliament, and political parties, with the latter rated as marginally worse than trust in strangers. As we have already observed, however, these patterns vary considerably across societies, so the rank order of agencies and agents in the pooled sample needs to be

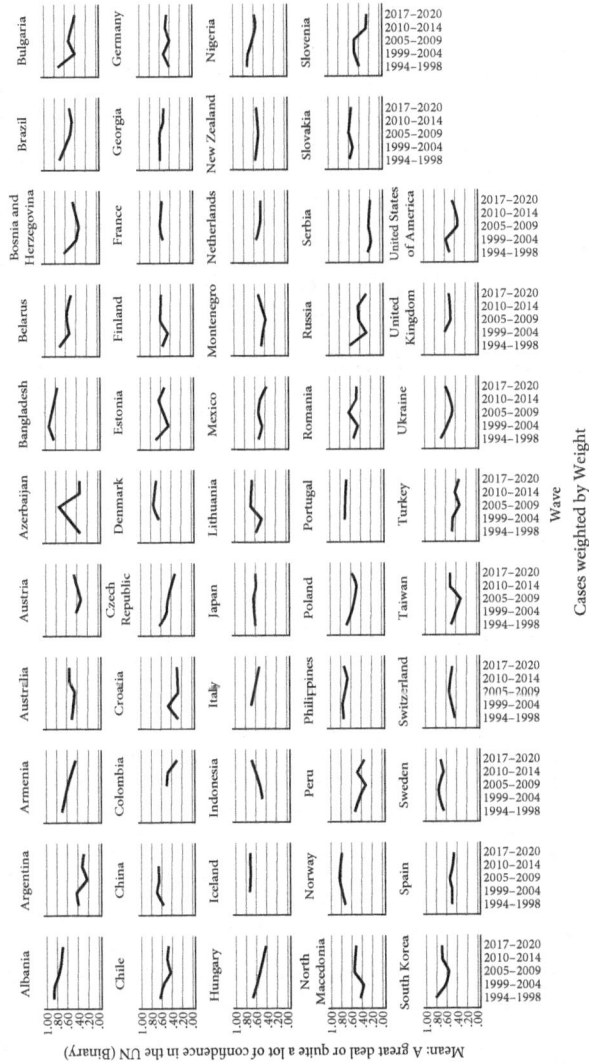

Figure 4.8. Trends in confidence in the United Nations.

Notes: Q: "I am going to name a number of organizations. For each one, could you tell me how much confidence you have in them: is it a great deal of confidence, quite a lot of confidence, not very much confidence, or none at all?" Total % responding "a great deal" or "quite a lot" of confidence in the United Nations.

Source: European Values Survey/World Values Survey County Pooled Dataset Waves 3–7 (1994–2021) in 53 societies.

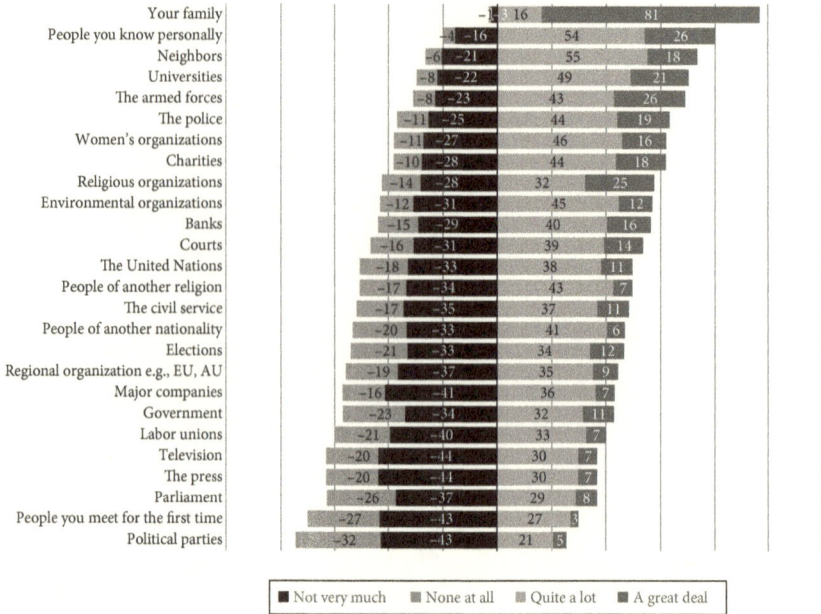

Figure 4.9. Trust and confidence in agents and agencies.

Source: European Values Survey/World Values Survey County Pooled Dataset Wave 7 (2017–2021) in 80 societies.

disaggregated more fully to understand the underlying reason for these sorts of contrast.

III. Social and Demographic Characteristics Associated with Trust

The map of societal patterns and trends is a critical foundation for understanding longitudinal and cross-national developments. But what are the individual-level characteristics most closely linked with the six dimensions of trust identified in Table 3.3, such as whether significant contrasts are observed by sex, age, and income? To address this question, regression models can be run for each type of trust using the seventh wave of the EVS/WVS (2017–2021) pooled across all societies. The models examine the association of trust with of sex (male = 1, female = 0); age (in years); educational attainment (coded into three categories of completing lower secondary school [low], higher secondary school [moderate], and tertiary education

[high]); the household income (10-point scale from low to high); frequency of news media use scale (including newspapers, TV news, radio news); and social media use scale (including the internet, social media, mobile phone, email). Table 4.1 shows the standardized beta coefficients to compare the strength of any relationship and their statistical significance.

Previous studies based on surveys and experiments have often reported differences between women and men in social (generalized) trust.[100] These may be due to mobilizing networks for men and women, such as informal social ties among neighbors, friends, and colleagues, which are generally thought to strengthen interpersonal trust by involving people in community groups, voluntary organizations, and professional associations. In particular, women with primary childcare responsibilities may be less involved in these informal social networks and therefore less likely to develop social trust. The analysis in Figure 3.2 confirms that a modest gender gap continues to endure, with men usually more trusting than women, across these dimensions, with the exception of confidence in global governance agencies, where the gender gap was reversed.

There are also ongoing debates about the relationship between different dimensions of trust, trustworthiness, and age. For example, Inglehart argues that processes of incremental generational change have steadily eroded political trust in postindustrial societies as the interwar and baby boomer cohorts are gradually replaced by successive generations of Gen Z and millennials, especially younger college-educated activists at the forefront of protest politics and progressive social movements critical of the established political system.[101] In a comparison of survey data in ten established democracies, Dalton reports that members of the younger generation display the greatest cynicism toward politician and political institutions, with population turnover reinforcing downward pressures over time.[102] Putnam emphasizes that generational contrasts have had profound consequences for social capital in America, with the interwar cohort far more likely to express social trust and to be engaged in voluntary organizations and associational networks than their children and grandchildren.[103] Based on experimental research, Sutter and Kocher suggest that social trust strengthens during the formative years from early childhood to early adulthood and then stabilizes across successive birth cohorts.[104]

To re-examine and update this relationship across diverse societies, the results of the analysis presented in Table 4.1 show that age-related patterns differ depending upon the dimension of trust under comparison. Thus, older

Table 4.1 The Social and Demographic Characteristics Associated with Six Dimensions of Trust

	Global Governance		National Government		Security Services		Civil Society		Out-group		In-group	
	Beta	Sig. (P)	Beta	Sig. (P)	Beta	Sig. (P)	Beta	Sig. (P)	Beta	Sig. (P)	Beta	Sig. (P)
Sex (male)	-0.25	***	0.00	N/s	0.01	*	0.00	N/s	0.03	***	0.04	***
Age	-0.08	***	0.00	N/s	0.08	***	-0.03	***	0.13	***	0.12	***
Education (low to high)	-1.28	***	-0.12	***	-0.08	***	-0.11	***	0.09	***	0.04	***
Income (low to high)	0.39	***	0.05	***	0.04	***	0.03	***	0.05	***	0.06	***
News media use	0.68	***	0.04	***	0.01	**	0.11	***	0.03	***	-0.01	***
Social media use	0.07	***	-0.02	***	0.03	***	0.01	N/s	0.11	***	0.02	***
(Constant)	2.27		59.02		61.20		58.79		35.22		70.33	
Number of respondents	52,080		72,499		73,315		68,291		74,326		77,298	
Adjusted R2	0.02		0.02		0.01		0.02		0.05		0.02	

Note: For the dimensions of trust and the composite scales, see Table 3.2.

Source: European Values Survey/World Values Survey County Pooled Data set, Waves 1–7 (1981–2021).

citizens express greater confidence in the traditional security services, such as the military, courts, and police, and also have more trust in both out-groups such as peoples of other religions and nationalities, and ingroups such as friends and family. By contrast, younger respondents express the most trust in the United Nations and related agencies of global governance, such as the WHO, IMF, and World Bank, a pattern which has been attributed to support for cosmopolitan over nationalist values.[105] Perhaps not surprisingly, given patterns of activism, Table 4.1 shows that the young also have greater trust in civil society agencies such as new social movements concerned with women's rights, environmental protection, and humanitarian organizations.

The impact of economic characteristics on trust is explored in more depth in subsequent chapters, but the results observed here suggest that people living in more affluent and financially secure households were usually consistently more trusting across all the dimensions under comparison than poorer sectors of society.

Finally, researchers and policymakers continue to debate the positive or negative effects on trust associated with regular use of legacy news sources like the television and newspapers, as well as from digital online information platforms, like Facebook and Twitter. Hence in the 1970s, theories of video-malaise by Michael Robinson claimed that extensive exposure to typical television entertainment and news was the root cause of a "mean world" effect, weakening trust in other people and in government and generating a broader sense of political malaise.[106] The typical negative slant of news coverage, especially "gotcha" journalism focusing upon personal scandals, policy failures, and public-sector waste, has been blamed for damaging the image of government.[107] A steady diet of negative news is thought to encourage a rising tide of political disenchantment.[108] Putnam also blamed the time-displacement effect of watching television for the decline of social capital in America. Capella and Jamieson argued that the media's heavy focus on the game of politics, rather than on its substance, starts a spiral of cynicism that directly causes an erosion of citizen interest and, ultimately, citizen participation.[109] Recent years have seen an avalanche of concern about the role of disinformation and misinformation intended to mislead, especially conspiracy theories reaching millions through social media platforms, talk radio, and cable television.[110] These theories have been revived by the recent wave of concern about the impact of misinformation and disinformation campaigns ("fake news") propagated by foreign and domestic actors through channels such as Twitter, Facebook, YouTube, and Instagram, and attacks on the free press.[111]

This general perspective has come under challenge from the "virtuous circle" counterargument, theorizing that repeated exposure to the news media leads to positive reinforcement of civic attitudes over time, by increasing political awareness of processes, institutions, and actors, thereby encouraging greater knowledge and trust in the political system.[112] Many studies of the empirical survey evidence in long-established Western democratic societies have generated findings which run counter to the media malaise thesis, as least with the role of the legacy media, where habitual use of newspapers and television news has commonly been associated with more political trust, knowledge, and civic engagement, not less.[113]

Debate about these issues remains, in part because of the difficulty of disentangling long-term processes of learning from media exposure from selection effects in the choice to pay attention to news media. Moreover, as explored in subsequent chapters, the broader information environment in open and closed societies and the positive or negative contents of media messages are likely to prove more important for dimensions of trust than the degree of regular exposure and attention. Given the limitations of cross-national survey data, some studies across or within societies have observed that the consumption of legacy and online news media is usually associated with higher political trust, but these findings have been challenged by others finding either decreased political trust or no effects.[114] The results of the models in Table 4.1 suggest that regular use of the legacy news media is generally positively associated with greater trust across all dimensions except for attitudes toward ingroups like friends and neighbors, which is likely to be more closely related to direct experience than mediated information. And the correlation between trust and use of the digital media platforms as sources of information is also observed to be positive across dimensions, except for a weak negative association with confidence in the government.

IV. Conclusions

To summarize, since the 1960s, periodic eras have seen revived waves of concern about the health of civic cultures in liberal democracies. Many accounts have claimed that ties of interpersonal trust and voluntary cooperation in society have steadily deteriorated, accompanied by a rising tide of political cynicism and disaffection with the core institutions of representative democracy. Angst is nothing new, but it has sharply intensified and deepened during the past decade, following the disruptive rise of populist forces and evidence of growing authoritarian practices undermining democratic norms and eroding constitutional checks and balances on executive powers in many democracies.[115] Nevertheless, the claim that Western publics have generally become more cynical about politics in recent years has been countered by other scholars who argue that this has become a widely popular yet unsubstantiated myth. European studies report that social surveys display a pattern of trendless fluctuations in political trust over time, and persistent cross-cultural differences observed in different societies, as well as clear contrasts between widespread public faith in democratic ideals and yet pervasive criticism of how democracy works in practice.[116] Similar debate continues about evidence for the state of social trust. Robert Putnam's seminal work on social capital in Italy and the United States catalyzed an extensive scholarly literature lamenting the loss of norms of reciprocity and civic networks across Western postindustrial societies.[117] Yet the narrative of a fraying social fabric has also come under strong challenge; for example, the more sweeping general claims have been criticized as "inaccurate, exceptional, one-sided or irrelevant."[118]

Building upon the literature, in light of the continuing debate, this chapter has described evidence documenting cross-national patterns and trends over time in absolute levels of trust, thereby updating previous research, drawing upon a rich body of data derived from the EV/WV Surveys of public opinion. This can help to detect whether a pattern of trendless fluctuations in several dimensions of trust can be observed across a range of relatively similar societies, or else, as often assumed in popular discussion, whether a systematic decay of trust has occurred. Descriptive analysis can expand our understanding of alternative theories about this phenomenon, examined further in subsequent chapters.

To summarize the key findings from this chapter, there is no simple support for claims of the steady erosion of trust across all the dimensions and countries under comparison. Instead, a more varied and complex picture emerges, with growing confidence in certain agencies in some places during recent decades, while the same years saw falling trust in others. This suggests that it would be wise to be skeptical about oversimple generalizations from sociological theories which attribute trajectories of value change to long-term processes of societal modernization and human development, as well as casting doubt on social psychological arguments that cultural patterns rooted in historical traditions or religious legacies are largely fixed and stable.

Moreover, despite heated debate about the role of generational change, and popular commentary blaming the mass and social media for any erosion of trust, overall the individual-level models suggest that, by themselves, demographic and socioeconomic characteristics can account for a strictly limited degree of variance in trust. These factors are observed to be significantly associated with trust, so they are included as standard controls in micro-level models in subsequent chapters, but they do not have the capacity to provide comprehensive explanations of this phenomenon.

If we accept that patterns of trendless fluctuations over time can be widely observed, rather than a steady net decline in trust, one puzzle concerns why popular assumptions of growing social distrust, political disenchantment, and cynicism appear so impervious to survey evidence. The myth may possibly reflect several factors more than substantial shifts in mass public opinion—such as the well-known bias toward highlighting negative news in the media, popular nostalgia for the politics of earlier eras, anti-establishment rhetoric among challenger parties, and concern commonly expressed in liberal elite discourse as the rationale justifying political reforms. It may also arise from the inadequacy of the standard survey measures used to capture popular disaffection. Some classic survey indicators have been used for decades now, such as the "trust in government" scales in the ANES and the "satisfaction with democracy" question in the Eurobarometer. Nevertheless, a long-standing debate about their meaning and measurement remains unresolved.[119]

Another reason could be that commentators also commonly infer attitudes from behavior—and from elite politics. For example, waning electoral turnout, falling party membership, and rising engagement in protest politics and online social movements are often seen as symptoms of an underlying deeper malaise in liberal democracies. Yet behavioral developments may reflect the changing structure of opportunities for political activism, rather than a crisis of political trust and legitimacy per se.[120] Similarly, many commentators have pointed to the rise in votes and seats won by populist parties as evidence of growing democratic disaffection in the mass electorate. Yet "supply-side" explanations suggest alternative factors are a major part of this phenomenon, including elite strategies of party competition through their rhetorical and issue appeals, the institutional rules of the game (especially types of electoral systems), and the role of the news and social media. Feelings of political disaffection and mistrust of traditional institutions do help to predict voting support for populist leaders and parties. But the reverse is not necessarily the case.[121]

This chapter has presented data generating grounds for skepticism for several accounts in the literature, including psychological and sociological accounts emphasizing the stability of trust—but we are still left with the puzzle of establishing plausible support for the alternative performance theory. To build upon this foundation, Chapter 5 goes on to explore evidence which could throw further insight into these explanations of trust and trustworthiness.

5

Competency

The concept of trustworthiness can be understood to involve an informal social contract where principals authorize others to act on their behalf in the expectation that the agent will fulfill their responsibilities, despite conditions of risk and uncertainty.[1] Performance in the agent-principal social contract is conceptualized as involving competency, so that agents or agencies fulfill specific responsibilities to their clients, while procedural mechanisms concerning standards of integrity and impartiality hold agents accountable for any general failures to do so. Hence citizens are widely believed to have more confidence in governments which have established a positive reputation for delivering national prosperity, social welfare, and peace, such as by improving the economy, schools, and healthcare. In principle, any lessons about the importance of government competency for trust should also provide broader insights into alternative types of principal-agent relationships beyond politics, such as trust in friends and strangers, in civil society organizations like the news media, environmental movement, and multinational companies, as well as in the agencies of global governance like the United Nations and the World Health Organization.

An extensive body of empirical studies in multiple societies has sought to compare public trust against the government's record of competency when delivering public goods and services. "Competency" means the ability to do something efficiently and well. For governments, this has commonly been measured using standard policy outcome benchmarks of macroeconomic management in achieving widely agreed-upon goals on valance issues, such as rising prosperity and full employment.[2] If governments meet targets and prove adept at steering the economy, and more generally effective in delivering a broader basket of public goods and services like improved healthcare, better education, and stronger national security, this is widely expected to bolster public confidence. The logic is straightforward. This argument has influenced many attempts to restore political trust through improving public-sector management and modernizing service delivery.[3] Yet the results of many previous empirical studies by scholars of public-sector management testing these claims have proved inconsistent and particularly sensitive to the choice of objective and subjective indices, comparative frameworks, and methods, as well as facing challenges of determining the direction of causality in complex reciprocal relationships.[4] Building on this foundation, this chapter seeks to re-examine and update the empirical evidence on the government policy competency thesis by using a broader comparative framework and new data.

Section I summarizes the thinking guiding the empirical analysis. Section II seeks to explore this issue in more depth, using individual-level survey data to establish how far a range of indicators about the pocketbook household economy predict trust in political authorities, and to determine whether this relationship varies in both open and closed societies. Information used to evaluate whether the government is trustworthy and competent based on their performance in managing the state of the national economy or societal problems, such as rates of violent crime, levels of healthcare, or lack of development, is largely indirect and heavily dependent upon media headlines. But citizens' views of the state of the economy can also be guided by their direct "pocketbook" experiences of real-world living conditions and the household budget. The previous chapter established that people living in high-income households were significantly and consistently more trusting across all types of agents and agencies, from social trust in friends and neighbors to confidence in institutions of global governance. Individual-level models in this chapter demonstrate that confidence in government is associated with direct experience of living in poorer households with financial insecurity, lack of savings, declining living standards, and problems of social deprivation, such as inadequate access to food or shelter. The results demonstrate that the role of the pocketbook economy on political trust is remarkably similar in both open and closed societies. This suggests that judgments of trust in the authorities are derived in part from direct experience of economic conditions, independent of the broader societal, political, and information environment. Poorer sectors of society typically lack the reservoir of financial assets common in middle-class households, such as rainy-day savings, investments, wealth, and property, as well as secure careers with professional salaries and benefits like private pensions or subsidized healthcare. Greater affluence mitigates many (not all) types of risks in decisions involving trust.

This book focuses on understanding principal-agent relationships of trust-worthiness, however, rather than the drivers of trust per se. Section III goes on to compare cross-national evidence at the macro level in around eighty nations worldwide to test whether the public's judgments of political trust-worthiness are consistently related to *objective* indicators of the government's policy performance on valance issues where there is widespread agreement about the goals, like improving national levels of economic growth, educa-tional attainment, healthcare, and income equality—and whether this re-lationship varies in open and closed societies. The results demonstrate that in open societies, public trust in government is usually (not always) sig-nificantly associated with seven out of ten objective policy performance indicators. Citizens living in open societies have access to multiple sources of alternative information, improving their capacity to arrive at accurate and informed judgments about economic and social challenges facing their country, and how far political leaders in office should be praised or blamed in their handling of these issues. In this type of society, the evidence suggests that public confidence in government is significantly related both positively and negatively to many objective indicators of economic prosperity and human development, suggesting more skeptical and informed assessments of trustworthiness, confirming performance theories.

But by contrast, in closed information environments, macro levels of po-litical trust in each society are not systematically and consistently related to almost all the objective indicators of economic prosperity or human devel-opment selected for comparison. Unlike the pocketbook economy, public perceptions of the government's handling of the national economy and social problems are heavily reliant upon indirect sources of information, which are open to political manipulation. In open societies, self-selection into "media bubbles" may limit exposure to two-sided commentary and balanced sources of information, if individuals rely heavily upon partisan news slanted to be either heavily pro- or anti-government. This can be particularly problematic in open societies like the United States where the news media increasingly comes to reflect extreme party polarization, reducing the common public spaces for deliberation. Nevertheless, even in deeply polarized media sys-tems, open societies provide greater opportunities for incidental exposure to diverse ideological viewpoints from two-sided or balanced news, dissem-inated by both critics and supporters of the government's record in office. In closed societies, however, public criticism of the authorities is far more restricted, and pro-state coverage dominates the media, limiting the public's access to balanced sources of alternative viewpoints which are needed to judge government performance accurately. This type of information environment exacerbates credulous judgments of trustworthiness, where people come to believe the positive messages about their leaders disseminated by the media. Or, alternatively, it can be associated with excessively cynical judgment, in cultures where most people learn to reject even genuinely positive reports about the government's competent performance, since they believe media sources to be manipulated "fake" news.

The conclusion in Section IV summarizes the overall results and considers their broader implications and the next steps in the process.

I. Performance Theories of Trust and Trustworthiness

The core argument developed in this book, summarized earlier in Figure 2.1, theorizes that decisions by principals about the trustworthiness of diverse agents can be understood as skeptical (implying that these involve a deliberative, informed, and thoughtful process) if people weigh the potential risks and benefits of delegating authority based on retrospective evaluations of the agent's or agencies' past record of competency when fulfilling their responsibilities, as well as the strength of accountability mechanisms protecting against future failures to do so.

The body of work in political economy and public administration examining empirical evidence for performance theories of trustworthiness has focused on confidence in government, parliaments, parties, and the civil service, as the key state institutions responsible for managing the delivery of public goods and services. Citizens are thought more likely to have more confidence in governments in the future if they perceive that political leaders running the country have established a reputation for competency when handling major economic, social, and international issues. Commonly used indices of effective policy outcomes are exemplified by official national statistics monitoring rates of GDP growth and unemployment for the economy, levels of carbon emissions as a proxy for environmental protection, cases and fatalities from Covid-19, or rates of longevity and infant and maternal mortality for health policy, all standardized for the relevant population and international definitions.

Studies of political economy suggest that governments are commonly held responsible by voters either for the perceived state of the household economy ("ego-tropic" judgments) and/or for the performance of the national economy ("socio-tropic" judgments).[5] Levels of national economic prosperity and rates of unemployment are usually found to be closely related to subsequent short-term fluctuations in government popularity, with voters using the ballot box to reward or punish the incumbent party or parties in executive office for the state of the national economy.[6] Following a similar logic, a large body of literature has tested how far public confidence in government is related to standard macroeconomic policy outcomes indices, exemplified by rates of economic growth, inflation, and unemployment.[7] Reliable annual or quarterly series of official national economic statistics are widely available for cross-national and longitudinal analysis. These are regarded as suitable indicators of government competency since monthly surveys monitoring the most important problems facing each country commonly report that the public usually prioritizes material economic issues such as unemployment and inflation, poverty and inequality, and standards of living, as well as national growth and development.[8]

Despite the plausibility of the argument, the overall results of the series of macroeconomic studies using these techniques have generally failed to demonstrate robust and consistent confirmation of the performance-trust thesis. Hence several scholars report that certain selected aggregate indicators of the state of the national economy (notably rates of growth and unemployment) do indeed correlate significantly with survey measures of political trust in each country. But others have failed to detect any significant relationships.[9] One reason is methodological. In assessing public services, it matters exactly what is being measured and compared, with differences between policy outputs (like laws, executive orders, and administrative regulations) and policy outcomes (like the societal impacts of these interventions). The roles and most suitable performance indices for specific agencies also differ, like the standards used to assess the efficiency of the civil service, the fairness and impartiality of the courts, and the responsiveness of parliament, or indeed the policy performance of the government in general.[10] Lack of robust findings across separate studies in the extensive body of literature suggests that research designs may be sensitive to technical and methodological issues, including the choice of specific performance benchmarks, the comparison of different countries and time periods, and the model specification and selection of controls.

Mediating Conditions in the Performance-Trust Theory

Another explanation for inconsistent findings is that studies examining the direct links between public confidence in government and the performance of the national economy often fail to control for mediating conditions. The attribution of praise or blame toward the government when steering the economy can be expected to be influenced by several factors, however, notably the availability of diverse sources of alternative information and freedom of the media in society, the legacy imprint of enduring cultural attitudes in each society, and citizens' cognitive skills, knowledge, and interest.

Open and Closed Societies

One important condition concerns freedom of the press and the availability of alternative sources of information about government performance. Monitoring agencies report that in recent years repressive states like China, Iran, Russia, and Turkey have aggressively restricted public access to negative news about the regime and its leaders, harshly penalizing independent journalists, publishers, bloggers, and media outlets, while simultaneously promoting positive commentary about the authorities. Reports from Reporters without Borders, the Committee to Protect Journalists, Amnesty International, and Freedom House document how autocracies use multiple techniques to control information flowing within and across their borders, including state censorship, control over broadcasting and publication licenses, coercion against dissidents, and legal constraints on independent journalism.[11] Attacks on press freedom and independent journalism, and the dissemination of misinformation through legacy and online media, have also become more common in electoral and liberal democracies, an especially common practice among authoritarian-populist leaders and parties.

In open information societies, it is believed that practices of journalistic balance, reflecting norms of internal diversity, have been undermined by the diminishing viewership for network news and growing partisanship in cable television news. There is concern that individuals get a lot of their information from social media "echo chambers" or "media bubbles" that provide information reinforcing their prior ideological and partisan beliefs.[12] This process could lead to deep disagreement about basic facts, like the existence of electoral fraud in the 2020 US election, or the role of Trump supporters in the January 6 Capitol insurrection, fueling polarization and conflict. Nevertheless, it remains unclear whether the use of social media has actually reinforced ideological views, or whether incidental exposure to diverse contents and heterogeneous viewpoints has been encouraged by the proliferation of online information across the political spectrum, the wider availability of digital platforms like Twitter streams, Facebook groups, and YouTube videos, as well as the diversity of cable channels, blogs, and radio channels.[13] Even if selection filters in use of the media reinforce ideological opinions, across society as a whole, citizens' judgments of political trustworthiness can be expected to be informed by greater exposure to "two-sided" perspectives in open than closed societies, thereby correlating more accurately (although not perfectly) with the actual government macroeconomic record.

Where there are limits on free expression, argument, association, debate, and discussion, and rights of access to information, the news media are unable to serve their functions effectively as watchdogs to the abuse of power, holding the authorities to account for their actions, as agenda setters calling attention to social problems, nor as gatekeepers disseminating a range of diverse political perspectives and viewpoints.[14] For those living in these societies, even well-educated and attentive citizens typically lack sufficient sources of "two-sided" information flows which facilitate more accurate and reliable judgments of the government's policy performance.[15] State control is likely to generate an asymmetrical bias, where citizens are predicted to be more trusting of the authorities than is warranted by the objective evidence of their performance. This positive skew is also expected to be greater in evaluations depending upon indirect sources of media information which are open to manipulation, such as public judgments about the state of the national economy. It is less likely to affect assessments of government performance drawing more heavily upon real-world conditions, such as direct experience of unemployment or poverty. In open societies, where rights to freedom of opinion and expression are protected by law and respected by informal democratic norms, the free press can fulfill their core functions more successfully. Under these conditions, a stronger correlation should be observed between government performance indicators and public trust. But even here, there are still limits on communication channels in the digital age, especially where people living in open societies choose to rely heavily on sources of misinformation, conspiracy theories, and fake news, a process exacerbated by cultural polarization and partisan media bubbles which restrict exposure to alternative viewpoints.[16]

Legacy Cultural Attitudes

Performance theories suggest that the public evaluates whether parties and leaders in governments have delivered public goods and services in the medium to short term, for example in the period between national elections, or even in the twelve months immediately prior to polling day. Yet theories of issue ownership suggest that the public is likely to form stable cultural attitudes based on cumulative evaluations of the overall reputation of governments for competent economic management over a long series of elections, especially when parties demonstrate a sustained record over successive periods in office.[17] Public perceptions of government competency, and how far judgments of trustworthiness match contemporary performance indicators, are therefore likely to reflect residual biases arising from legacy cultural values in each society, for example if center-left parties are seen as generally more effective in managing welfare and social policies, while center-right parties are usually regarded as better in achieving lower taxes and public spending. In this regard, trusting attitudes can be understood to reflect a sort of running tally of the accumulated reputation of political leaders and governing parties over successive administrations— or even decades. Cultural attitudes, beliefs, and values are likely to reflect sticky path-dependent phenomena which evolve slowly over time in each society. Even in information-rich open societies, therefore, judgments of government competency are likely to be colored by enduring cultural values, like partisan cues and individualistic or collectivistic attitudes toward the appropriate role of the state, without updating performance evaluations.

In this regard, the theoretical perspectives from the disciplines of social psychology and cultural sociology discussed in Chapter 2 can be integrated, rather than treating these artificially as alternative rival accounts. Psychological theories explain habitual trusting orientations primarily as personality traits; the repeated propensity toward gullible judgments may occur for these reasons, for example, where citizens learn to emphasize conformity with social norms, agreeableness, and deference to governing authorities and party leaders, leading toward faith in untrustworthy scams or misinformation.[18] Similarly, studies in cultural sociology emphasize that the social and cultural context of formative experiences in childhood and adolescence is important for the acquisition and persistence of trusting attitudes in adulthood, such as whether people grow up in secure and affluent societies, universalistic welfare states, and stable liberal democracies like Sweden,

Norway, and Switzerland, where the widespread view among the public is one trusting government, or whether, alternatively, people grow up to acquire cynical political views when living in weak states with cultures shaped by a long series of incompetent political leaders, corruption scandals in politics, and frequent economic or political crises.[19]

Therefore, orientations arising from legacy societal cultures and individual personality traits are likely to influence contemporary attitudes about government, irrespective of their actual performance. These prior attitudes and beliefs are likely to generate either *cynical* judgments (where the public expresses relatively less trust than would be warranted by the objective indicators of contemporary performance) or else *credulous* assessments (where the public expresses relatively high trust, despite low scores on current performance). Observing similar evaluations toward government trustworthiness among societies within global regions with shared cultural values and historical legacies, like Latin America or post-Communist Europe, despite important variations in the contemporary performance of the economy in these regions, would lend support to the thesis, suggesting that these patterns reflect long-standing values and beliefs enduring from earlier eras.

Cognitive Skills and Education

Finally, among mediating conditions, the performance-trust thesis is expected to fit best among college-educated sectors, especially those living in open societies, affluent postindustrial states, and liberal democracies, where access to higher education is widely available and multiple sources of news provide alternative assessments of the government's performance when steering the economy. Education provides cognitive skills, literacy and numeracy, and knowledge, which facilitate information processing, interest, and political engagement.[20] These characteristics strengthen the capacity to sort out valid and reliable views in making complex judgments. But, as discussed earlier, the performance-trust theory may not fit so well among populations with low levels of education, literacy, and numeracy, especially common in low-income developing societies, especially in closed societies where states use repression to limit press freedom, to deter criticism of the regime, and to control the flow of favorable news about political leaders. Judgments of government competency are therefore theorized to be mediated by the information environment, by legacy cultural attitudes and values, and by educational levels within each nation.

II. Trust and the Pocketbook Economy

Oversimple "black box" models based solely on macroeconomic indicators assume that policy outcomes and procedures have the capacity to exert a *direct* impact on public judgments of government trustworthiness, without investigating intervening stages in this sequential process. The core model illustrated schematically in Figure 2.1, however, suggests that there is an essential middle step which needs analyzing, namely public perceptions of agency performance and direct experience of household "pocketbook" economic and social conditions, requiring individual- or micro-level survey data. Ideally, both aggregate and individual-level analyses should be compared; if the results point in the same direction, this increases confidence in the interpretation of the results. Studies of economic voting, for example, report that the findings of aggregate and individual-level analyses are often highly correlated.[21] The literature on voting suggests that ordinary citizens usually have relatively informed views about the overall state of the national economy, allowing them to attribute praise or blame to the party or parties in government when they decide how to vote at the ballot box, even if they lack awareness of many specific economic facts, like current rates of unemployment, or the size of the national debt.

At the same time, however, this issue needs to be examined in the context of trust judgments, since for many decades a wealth of research in cognitive psychology and political behavior has long suggested that the public is often unaware of many basic facts taken for granted by educated elites, such as those about constitutional procedures, political institutions, and public policies.[22] Achen and Bartels argue that even basic perceptions of personal and household economic well-being are powerfully shaped by partisan biases, rationalization, and randomness.[23] The contemporary era of misinformation is widely believed to have exacerbated these issues. Lack of information and uncertainty can generate flawed retrospective estimates of government competency, such as mistaking national rates of crime, unemployment, or immigration. The public's grasp of highly technical economic issues, like the size of the national debt or the amount of the budget spent on overseas aid, is likely to prove even more tenuous. Debates continue about what constitutes political knowledge and what level of civic awareness is needed to cast informed ballots.[24] Much research has examined these issues in terms of rational retrospective economic voting. But similar arguments can be made about the knowledge required for making informed judgments of political trustworthiness. It is therefore important to unpack the evidence of public perceptions of government performance more directly, testing whether the results are robust and consistent using both macro- and micro-level evidence.

The most consistent confirmation of the performance-trust thesis, based on cross-national survey data, has demonstrated that political trust is often related to socio-tropic evaluations, such as citizens' *subjective* feelings of satisfaction or approval of the government's handling of the macroeconomy.[25] Yet rationalizations are very likely to color such judgments, such as common cognitive biases arising from motivated reasoning, affective cues, and habitual partisan loyalties.[26] Loyal supporters of the party in power are far more likely to approve of their performance in office. Panel surveys involving repeated interviews with the same respondents over time, monitoring changes in their subjective perceptions of the performance of the economy and subsequent changes in their political trust, provide one way to overcome these problems within specific national studies, but suitable panel survey data are unavailable for this purpose cross-nationally. Another way to circumvent this problem using EVS/WVS cross-national survey data is to monitor how far judgments of political trust correlate with direct experience of the pocketbook economy in a wide variety of open and closed societies. Experiential measures can be gauged by the household economic resources and levels of financial security reported by respondents, such as their wages and standard of living, experience of lived poverty, unemployment, and socioeconomic deprivation, dependency on welfare benefits, and level of savings or debt. This chapter measures the direct experience of the pocketbook (ego-tropic) household economy by a series of questions in the EVS/WVS survey, including reported levels of household income, experience of "lived" poverty (such as experience of going without enough food to eat, medicine or medical treatment, cash income, and safe shelter), the level of household savings or borrowing, satisfaction with the household's financial situation, as well as how far respondents feel that their standard of living is better or worse off compared with that of their parents at the same age. The regression model in Table 5.1 compares the results of the analysis in open and closed societies controlling for standard socio-demographic factors, identified as related to trust in Chapter 4, including sex (male), age (in years), education (on a 3-category scale), and attention to the legacy news media and digital social media.

The results presented in Table 5.1 demonstrate that the pocketbook household economy tells a remarkably similar story in both open and closed

Table 5.1 Citizens' Pocketbook Economy and Trust in Government

		OPEN SOCIETIES				CLOSED SOCIETIES			
		B	SE	Beta	Sig.	B	SE	Beta	Sig.
POCKETBOOK	Income scale (low to high)	-0.12	0.05	-0.01	*	-0.20	0.06	-0.02	***
ECONOMY	Currently unemployed (0/1)	-1.14	0.37	-0.02	***	-0.74	0.38	-0.01	*
	Lived poverty Index (low to high)	0.05	0.01	0.04	***	-0.05	0.01	-0.04	***
	Feel financially secure (low to high)	5.34	0.12	0.25	***	4.25	0.13	0.16	***
	Household financial security (low to high)	0.61	0.11	0.03	***	1.16	0.13	0.05	***
	Satisfaction with financial situation (low to high)	0.62	0.05	0.08	***	0.65	0.05	0.08	***
	Standard of living compared with your parents (worse/better)	0.81	0.13	0.04	***	3.92	0.15	0.14	***
CONTROLS	Sex (male)	-0.72	0.19	-0.02	***	-0.54	0.21	-0.01	**
	Age (years)	0.04	0.01	0.04	***	-0.04	0.01	-0.03	***
	Education (Low to high scale)	-1.15	0.15	-0.05	***	-3.52	0.14	-0.14	***
	News media use (newspapers, TV news, radio news)	0.17	0.03	0.03	***	0.57	0.04	0.09	***
	Social media use (internet, FB/Twitter, mobile phone, email)	0.10	0.02	0.03	***	-0.27	0.02	-0.07	***
	(Constant)	26.73	0.87			41.81	0.96		
	N. respondents	31,560				36,699			
	N. Societies	42				38			
	Adjusted R2	0.09				0.11			

Notes: The model uses Ordinary Least Squared (OLS) regression with individual-level survey data in 80 societies where the dependent variable is the Trust in Government standardized scale (including government, parliament, parties, and the civil service). The table presents the beta coefficients (B), standard errors (SE), standardized beta coefficients (Beta), and their significance (Sig.). Open and closed societies were categorized by the V-Dem Freedom of Expression Index. All models were tested and found to be free of problems of multicollinearity. P. $\star$ = .05; $\star\star$ = .01; $\star\star\star$ = .001. N/s = not significant

Source: European Values Survey/World Values Survey Wave 7 (2017–2021).

societies. Mistrust of government was indeed usually greater in low-income households and among the currently unemployed, while conversely, political trust was greater among the more affluent, including those reporting being financially secure, expressing greater satisfaction with their household finances, and with a better standard of living than their parents. Therefore, at the individual level, direct experience of economic security and household prosperity was significantly related to more confidence in government. The only significant difference observed between open and closed societies emerged over the Lived Poverty Index, which may reflect the existential risks of severe poverty experienced in developing societies. The demographic and social controls show that in general, once the models control for the pocket-book economy, the less educated were usually more trusting toward government, especially in closed societies where many citizens have lower levels of schooling, literacy, and numeracy. Political trust was also stronger in both open and closed societies among those most attentive to legacy news media, including newspapers, television news, and radio news, confirming the "virtuous circle" thesis observed many decades ago.[27] Those choosing to follow the news most closely tend to be more politically interested, knowledgeable, and trusting than those who tune out. Societies varied, however, in the effects of using digital social media platforms, Information and communication technologies (ICTs), and interpersonal communications networks like Facebook, Twitter, email, mobile phones, and the Internet. Users of digital media expressed less trust in government than average in closed societies, suggesting that online platforms and digital networks may provide opportunities for the expression of political dissent despite attempts by authoritarian states to censor internet content and limit access to independent blogs and critical political commentary. But regular users of digital media reported greater than average political trust in open societies, where online users have potential access to multiple online platforms, social networks, and diverse viewpoints.

III. Government Competency and Trustworthiness

The primary focus of the book, however, is less on the factors associated with trust, than on the capacity of principals to make accurate and informed judgments of agency trustworthiness, or else for such decisions to be erroneous if skewed by either credulous or cynical biases. Several methods are available to test the performance-trust relationship. Some studies have analyzed whether political confidence by ordinary citizens is correlated with sub-national variations in local government service delivery within a single country, such as comparing the performance of municipalities or states, counties, and provinces in China or Norway.[28] The most common strategy in comparative research, however, has been cross-national studies comparing aggregate indicators of the government's economic record with levels of trust. Regional comparisons among relatively similar nations within a global cultural region or level of development thereby control for many confounding conditions, although this approach is commonly confronted by the dilemma of identifying too many potential variables but too few cases. These studies usually treat macroeconomic conditions as endogenous to trust, although this assumption also raises challenges when interpreting the direction of causality involved in any observed correlation.[29] In practice, some recursive processes may be at work, if markets and governments function better, as theorized, in high-trust societies.[30] Equally serious challenges in determining causality arise from survey-based micro-level studies using subjective perceptions as the primary independent measure of government policy performance, such as satisfaction with the state of the nation's economy. It is unclear from such studies whether citizens lack political trust because the government actually fails to deliver on their policy promises, or whether citizens regard the delivery of public goods and services poorly because their image of government is generally negative due to their partisan identities.[31] Longitudinal studies incorporating time-series data within a country or region, lagging objective performance indicators against ensuing levels of trust, partially help to identify issues of reciprocity in the relationship.[32] Panel studies of the same respondents over time have the advantage of monitoring the period effects of previous major "shocks" on subsequent medium- and short-term changes in public opinion, like the "rally-round-the flag" effects on trust commonly observed in the aftermath of the events of 9/11 and the outbreak of the Covid-19 pandemic.[33] Many studies have examined whether the 2007–2008 banking and financial crisis in the eurozone, and the ensuing sharp uptick in unemployment, catalyzed an ensuing loss of European trust of national parliaments and governments in subsequent months and years, eroding confidence in the European Union Commission and European Parliament, and deepening dissatisfaction with democracy.[34]

What empirical evidence would allow us to re-examine policy performance theories of trust? Figure 3.2, presented earlier, illustrates the main types of societal-level and individual-level benchmarks used for cross-national comparison in this book, including those measuring competency in the delivery of public goods and services, and those monitoring integrity and impartiality in governance procedures. A wide range of policy performance indicators are available from diverse sources of official statistics, expert estimates, and social surveys.[35] Selecting appropriate benchmarks raises challenges, however, not least in identifying valid and reliable indices which are equally applicable across a wide range of countries and time periods, because citizens living in different societies are likely to differ in their cultural values, expectations of the state's roles and responsibilities, and views about the priority issues on the policy agenda.[36] The most commonly used performance benchmarks of government policy outcomes involve objective indicators of "valence" issues, meaning widely agreed-upon goals like shared prosperity, better healthcare, and improved education. On these types of issues, there is likely to be the broadest agreement among citizens and political elites about desirable policy goals, even if heated debate may surround the most effective policy interventions designed to manage these objectives.[37]

To test the empirical evidence, this chapter expands the cross-national comparisons to include diverse contexts around the world. Using the seventh wave of the EVS/WVS survey, based on fieldwork conducted during 2017–2021, the data compares up to eighty societies worldwide, including a wide range of open and closed societies. The dependent variable is the Trust in Government Index described earlier, the standardized scale combining measures of public confidence in government, parliament, political parties, and civil service. This scale provides a more reliable measure of public assessments of the trustworthiness of the main agencies of state responsible for policymaking and implementation, rather than focusing solely upon confidence in the party or parties in government, which is more open to partisan skews. For the measures of policy performance, the bivariate analysis in Table 5.2 looks at how far selected World Bank Development Indicators are generally correlated with the Trust in Government Index in open and closed societies. The macroeconomic indices for each country are lagged and averaged across the period 2015–2020, to examine performance in the medium to short term and to reduce noise from any random volatility or shocks occurring during specific years. The chosen indices include several standard measures widely used to monitor the state of the macroeconomy, including: (i) rates of per capita growth in GDP; (ii) levels of economic development by per capita GDP in purchasing power parity; (iii) rates

Table 5.2 Developmental Indicators and Trust in Government

Indices	OPEN SOCIETIES		CLOSED SOCIETIES		Definitions
	Correlation (R)	Significance (P)	Correlation (R)	Significance (P)	
ECONOMIC INDICATORS					
Economic growth	.287	*	.233	N/s	Mean annual % change in GDP per capita in purchasing power parity (PPP; current international $)
Economic development	.686	***	.112	N/s	GDP per capita, PPP (constant 2017 international $)
Unemployment	−.293	*	−.498	***	The total unemployed as a % of the total labor force
Inflation	−.152	N/s	.094	N/s	Mean annual % change in consumer prices
Income share for highest 20%	−.490	***	−.021	N/s	Income share held by highest 20%
Income share for lowest 20%	.445	**	.331	N/s	Income share held by lowest 20%
SOCIAL INDICATORS					
Secondary education attainment	.583	***	−.188	N/s	Educational attainment, at least completed lower secondary, population 25+, total (%) (cumulative)
Homicide rate	−.599	***	−.153	N/s	Intentional homicides (per 100,000 people)
Longevity rate	.259	N/s	−.108	N/s	Life expectancy at birth, total (years)
Maternal mortality rate	−.005	N/s	.118	N/s	Maternal mortality ratio (modeled estimate, per 100,000 live births)
Number of societies	25–43		18–39		
Number of respondents	29,432		31,380		

Notes: The table presents the simple bivariate correlation coefficients between the mean Trust in Government 100-point standardized index (including government, parliament, parties, and the civil service) for each society, from the EVS/WVS, and macro-level socioeconomic indicators, lagged mean for 2016–2019, from the World Development Indicators. Open and closed societies were categorized by the V-Dem Freedom of Expression Index (dichotomized). Sig.* = .05; ** = .01; *** = .001. N/s = not significant.

Sources: European Values Survey/World Values Survey Wave 7 (2017–2021); World Development Indicators (World Bank).

of unemployment as a percentage of the total labor force; (iv) rates of inflation based on annual changes in the consumer price index; (vi) the income
share for the highest 20%; and (vii) the income share for the lowest 20% (to
measure economic inequality).[38] In addition, to compare a broader range of
social indices monitoring human development, the analysis also includes
measures of (viii) secondary school attainment; (ix) the homicide rate (as a
measure of safe and secure societies); (x) the longevity rate (life expectancy
at birth, in years); and (xi) the maternal mortality rate (as a measure of the
quality of healthcare). This covers a wide range of standard indices commonly associated with economic and human development where reliable international data are available for the societies under comparison.

The results presented in Table 5.2 confirm that, in the open societies, as
predicted, *greater trust in government was consistently associated with better
quality performance across all the selected socioeconomic indices.* The correlation coefficient was strong and also statistically significant in seven of the
ten performance indices. In other words, people usually expressed greater
political trust in more open societies with higher economic growth and development, economic equality, education, and longevity, as well as lower
rates of unemployment, inflation, and insecurity. In open societies, where
multiple sources of alternative information are widely available to assess the
record of government institutions, judgments of political trustworthiness
generally reflect levels of prosperity and development fairly accurately. By
contrast, in closed societies, the direction of the correlations linking levels
of trust with policy outcome indices for rates of economic growth, development, and income inequality were consistent with the performance theory,
but the correlations were weak in strength and failed to reach the conventional threshold of statistical significance. Several of the social indicators, like
rates of education and longevity, also point in the contrary direction to that
predicted by performance theories. The only indicator which proved a strong
and significant predictor of greater mistrust in closed societies was the rate
of unemployment. Therefore, in countries with greater freedom of expression, independent media, government transparency, and plural information
sources, trust in government was more consistently associated with a range
of socioeconomic development indicators. Absolute *levels* of economic development (per capita GDP), in particular, were confirmed as strong and significant predictors of trust in government in open societies, as performance
theories predict. But similar relationships were not usually observed consistently in closed societies, where citizens had fewer opportunities to access

accurate, reliable, and balanced information about the state of the national economy, and voices critical of the government's record were silenced by state authorities through censorship, repression of free speech, and control of the primary channels of mass communications. The macro-level model is therefore consistent with the claim that governments earn public judgments of trustworthiness through a establishing a record of competency in delivering public goods and services—but the association is strongly conditioned by the type of information society.

Do cognitive skills, civic awareness, literacy and numeracy capacities, and reasoning capacities reinforce these patterns in open societies, strengthening informed assessments of trustworthiness, as theorized? These qualities cannot be measured directly from the available macro-level data, but as a proxy the United Nations Development Programme (UNDP) Index of Education can be used to classify the general population in open and closed societies. This standardized index is measured by combining average adult years of schooling with expected years of schooling for students under the age of twenty-five, each receiving 50% weighting. The Index was dichotomized around the mean to categorize the formal level of education among the population living in low and highly educated societies. Table 5.3 displays how far trust is correlated with the range of selected policy performance indices, breaking down the results by the educated populations in each type of society. The number of cases under observation in each category remains limited, due to data limitations, but the results do not provide consistent support for the role of education, after controlling for the information environment. Thus, in open societies with highly educated populations, economic development, unemployment, and longevity are significantly and strongly related to trust in government in the predicted direction. But in open societies, unemployment and growth are also significant and strongly associated with trust. In the limited number of closed societies, none of the correlation coefficients approaches statistical significance.

Economic Growth

To look at these patterns in more detail, and to identify outlying cases of cynical mistrust and credulous trust, scatter graphs illustrate how these relationships compare when disaggregated in a wide range of around eighty open and closed societies. Figure 5.1 compares rates of economic growth

Table 5.3 Developmental Indicators and Trust in Government, with Levels of Education

	OPEN SOCIETIES				CLOSED SOCIETIES			
	Low Education		High Education		Low Education		High Education	
	Correlation (R)	Sig. (P)	Correlation (R)	Sig. (P)	Correlation (R)	Sig. (P)	Correlation (R)	Sig. (P)
ECONOMIC INDICATORS								
Economic growth	0.55	**	0.08	N/s	0.29	N/s	−0.45	N/s
Economic development	−0.10	N/s	0.67	**	0.14	N/s	0.55	N/s
Unemployment	−0.56	**	−0.45	*	0.09	N/s	−0.14	N/s
Inflation	0.08	N/s	−0.16	N/s	0.41	N/s	0.18	N/s
Income share for highest 20%	−0.09	N/s	−0.19	N/s	−0.67	N/s	−0.38	N/s
Income share for lowest 20%	0.26	N/s	0.17	N/s	0.73	N/s	0.64	N/s
SOCIAL INDICATORS								
Secondary education attainment	−0.04	N/s	0.40	N/s	−0.82	N/s	−0.16	N/s
Homicide rate	−0.24	N/s	−0.31	N/s	−0.49	N/s	0.20	N/s
Longevity rate	−0.20	N/s	0.42	*	−0.52	N/s	0.20	N/s
Maternal mortality rate	0.08	N/s	−0.32	N/s	0.49	N/s	0.21	N/s
Number of societies	27		30		9		8	

Notes: The table presents the simple bivariate correlation coefficients between the mean Trust in Government 100-point standardized index (including government, parliament, parties, and the civil service) for each society, from the EVS/WVS, and macro-level socioeconomic indicators, lagged mean for 2016–2019, from the World Development Indicators. Societal education is categorized by the UNDP Education Index dichotomized around the mean. Open and Closed societies were categorized by the V-Dem Freedom of Expression Index (dichotomized). Sig.* = .05; ** = .01; *** = .001. N/s = not significant.

Sources: European Values Survey/World Values Survey Wave 7 (2017–2021); World Development Indicators (World Bank).

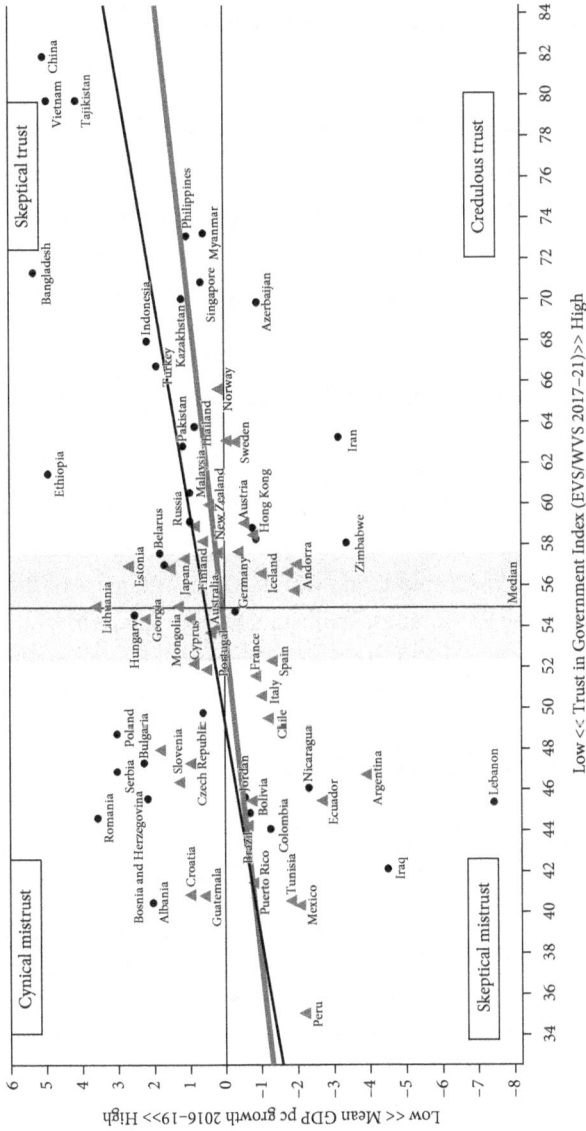

Figure 5.1. Economic growth and trust in government.

Notes: The horizontal axis is the EVS/WVS Trust in Government standardized scale (including government, parliament, parties, and the civil service). The vertical axis shows annual rates of growth in per capita GDP averaged during 2016–2020 as derived from the World Development Indicators (World Bank). Open Societies (Gray) and Closed Societies (Black) are categorized by the V-Dem Freedom of Expression Index (dichotomized).

Source: European Values Survey/World Values Survey Wave 7 in 76 societies (2017–2021).

against macro-levels of political trust in each society. The figure identifies many congruent cases which fit the line in both types of society, where public trust in political leaders and government institutions closely reflects national economic conditions.

Thus, confidence in government can be observed to be relatively high in several booming East Asian economies and closed societies governed by authoritarian states located in the top right quadrant, exemplified by the cases of China, Vietnam, and Tajikistan. This confirms previous detailed studies which have reported that the remarkable local economic growth rates achieved in China are strongly related not just to trust in the president, but also in the security forces, the Chinese Communist Party, and village councils.[39] The structural changes and industrialization in the booming Chinese economy during the early twenty-first century mean that it is now comparable in size and global impact only to the United States, with GDP of US$14.7 trillion in 2020, compared with US$20.94 trillion in the United States. Many other Southeast Asian developing societies started from a low-income base and enjoyed remarkably successful economic growth of 5% or more during these years. Export-led economies, generated by the rapid expansion of manufacturing industry and fast-growing domestic consumer markets, have radically transformed living standards in urban areas, lifting millions out of poverty. The Philippines, Tajikistan, and Bangladesh, with relatively high levels of growth, were also cases of developing countries which fell into this quadrant. Rising GDP in these states has been accompanied by increased school enrollment and life expectancy, and lower poverty rates.[40] In these low- and middle-income societies, rapid gains in material prosperity, lifting lifestyles and standards of living, provide instrumental reasons for ordinary people to express considerable faith in the competence of their state's management of the economy. Direct experience provides reason to trust the competency of the state. At the same time, however, closed societies in this quadrant, exemplified by China, also exert a tight grip over channels of political communications, so that its citizens are presented with positive news of the government's economic performance, while dissent and criticism of the authorities are strongly suppressed. Reporters without Borders reports that China is one of the world's biggest jailors of defenders of press freedom, and the country gets the 173rd lowest score in their 2021 World Press Freedom Index.[41]

Societies located in the bottom left-hand quadrant are also congruent cases, but these represent the reverse pattern of countries with stalled

economic growth and minimal trust in government, exemplified by
Lebanon, Iraq, and Jordan in the Middle East, as well as Argentina, Mexico,
and Nicaragua in Latin America. Among established democracies, Italy,
France, and Spain are less extreme cases, but they also fall into this category. In this group, many citizens are *skeptical mistrusters* toward the state,
evaluating their governments' competency poorly when based on the record of their economic performance alone. In Lebanon, for example, the
economy has been weakened by a failing banking system, high levels of inequality, and public services crippled by massive levels of government debt,
leading to what the World Bank estimates to be the country's worst economic meltdown in more than a century.[42] By the fall of 2021, the Lebanese
pound had lost 90 percent of its value since 2019, and annual inflation was
84.9 percent in 2020. Lebanon's GDP plummeted from about US$55 bil-
lion in 2018 to a projected US$20.5 billion in 2021, while real GDP per
capita fell by 37.1%. Political unrest and financial turmoil generated crisis
conditions. The survey data on trust reflect real-world events. In recent
years, the country has seen a series of public protests directed against
the government, catalyzing political instability, following accusations of
widespread public-sector corruption, failure to respond adequately to the
Covid-19 pandemic, shortages of basic fuel, medicine, and electricity services, the fallout from the devastating Beirut port explosion, and the refugee
crisis from neighboring Syria.[43]

As well as cases which fit the performance-trust thesis, the figure also identifies important outliers. In these cases, enduring cultural values seem to outweigh current evaluations of the economy. The top left quadrant in Figure 5.1
illustrates societies characterized by cynical political mistrust, especially
common in post-Communist Europe and the Balkans, as exemplified by
Romania, Armenia, Bulgaria, Bosnia-Herzegovina, Croatia, and the Czech
Republic. Citizens expressed little confidence in their state institutions, although these economies experienced above-average growth during these
years, following the liberalization of their markets and the initial disruptive
shocks experienced by the privatization of state-owned industries and cuts
in the welfare state during the 1990s, after the death of the Soviet Union. The
2019 Global Attitudes Survey reports that citizens in many of these societies
perceived that the economic situation had improved for most people since
the end of Communism.[44] The expression of cynical trust toward the state in
the region is therefore likely to reflect a residual cultural legacy, stamped by
long memories of the state-managed economy during the Communist era

that have not been updated to reflect judgments of the contemporary positive record of economic growth in recent years. Mishler and Rose document
how lack of trust toward the state persisted for years in the region well after
the fall of the Berlin Wall.[45]

Moreover, some other societies are located in the lower right-hand
quadrant of Figure 5.1, classified as cases of *credulous trust*, which display
considerable confidence in government despite relatively low or even negative economic growth. This category includes strikingly diverse states and
regimes. Some are open societies and long-established liberal democracies with universalistic welfare states and media pluralism, as well as being
highly affluent postindustrialized societies with well-educated populations,
such as Sweden, Norway, and Switzerland. Accounts using comparative historical sociology suggest that Scandinavian societies have established a long
track record of peace, prosperity, and social harmony over many centuries,
which is likely to encourage feelings of generalized competence and integrity in the state today.[46] Trust is understood in cultural theories as reflecting
accumulated reputations over many decades, or even centuries, as much as
a response to contemporary performance. These countries have developed
a deep cultural reservoir of faith in government competency which appears
to persist through medium- and short-term upticks and downturns in the
economy.

By contrast, this category in the comparison also includes several emerging Asian economies and closed societies which have experienced low
or negative growth over recent years, but which are governed by diverse
types of authoritarian states which repress free speech and public criticism
of the regime, and with less educated populations. The category includes
Azerbaijan, a Muslim state where power and resources have been concen-
trated in the hands of President Ilham Aliyev and his extended family since
2003, when the country achieved independence from Soviet rule.[47] Studies
analyzing Caucasus Barometer survey data report that deference toward political leaders is more clearly related to cultural legacies than to evaluations
of the contemporary record of state performance.[48] Similarly, in Iran, despite some periods of liberalization, power remains highly centralized in
the Guardian Council and vested in the country's supreme leader, Ayatollah
Ali Khamenei.[49] As we will explore further in the next chapter, one factor
likely to maintain public expressions of support for autocratic leaders is that
freedom of expression and media independence are severely restricted, with
regimes suppressing popular dissent and critical commentary of the leader,

and with strict state control of broadcast news. For example, in assessing press freedom, the 2021 World Press Freedom Index ranked Iran 174th- and Azerbaijan 167th-worst out of 179 nations worldwide.[50] In Iran, the regime has constructed a sophisticated censorship network and has used information and communication technologies to proliferate propaganda and control cyber-protest.[51] In repressive states, public expressions of trust in the leader are likely to reflect the institutional context of closed societies, preventing overt criticism and encouraging practices of self-censorship, along with feelings that citizens are unable to hold authoritarian leaders to account for systematic failure in delivering public services.

Unemployment

What of other economic indices? Figure 5.2 demonstrates that similar patterns in open and closed societies can also be observed concerning rates of unemployment. This scattergram displays several cases characterized by skeptical mistrust, located in the bottom-left quadrant, as exemplified by Balkan states such as Greece, Bosnia-Herzegovina, North Macedonia, and Armenia. This quadrant also includes several Middle Eastern and North African Muslim societies, like Iraq, Tunisia, and Jordan, a region with exceptionally high official rates of unemployment and widespread mistrust of the state.[52]

There are also many diverse congruent nations observed in the top-right quadrant displaying skeptical trust, where low levels of unemployment are combined with considerable trust in government authorities. This includes affluent Western democracies and open societies such as Norway, Switzerland, Germany, and the Netherlands, but also, in contrast, several developing economies and closed societies, such as Myanmar, the Philippines, Bangladesh, and Kazakhstan, which reported relatively low rates of official unemployment in the period under comparison. In addition, a few cases fall clearly into the category of credulous trust, where the public expresses confidence in government despite relatively high rates of unemployment, notably in Iran and Turkey, both closed societies governed by repressive regimes where citizens have good reason to fear expressing overt criticism of the authorities, and where independent media have been under attack, journalists jailed, and social media censored.[53] There are also many societies which can be categorized as cases of cynical mistrust, if based on the rates

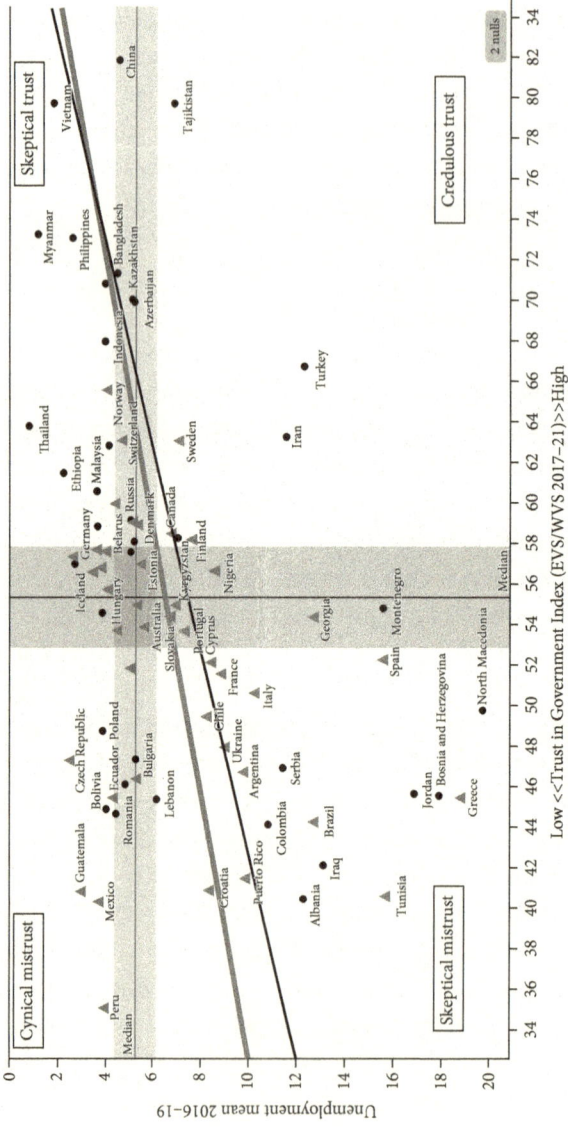

Figure 5.2. Unemployment and trust in government.

Notes: The horizontal axis is the mean EVS/WVS Trust in Government standardized scale (including government, parliament, parties, and the civil service) for each society. The vertical axis is the mean national annual rate of unemployment as a % of the total workforce averaged during 2016–2919, estimated by the ILO, and derived from the World Development Indicators (World Bank). Open and closed societies are categorized by the V-Dem Freedom of Expression Index (dichotomized).

Source: European Values Survey/World Values Survey Wave 7 (2017–2021).

of unemployment alone, including post-Communist states such as Poland, Romania, and the Czech Republic, as well as several Latin American states such as Peru, Mexico, and Guatemala. Although less extreme than several others in the Americas, the United States also falls into this group.

By contrast, Figures 5.3, 5.4, and 5.5 show alternative socioeconomic indicators where the trust-performance relationship diverges sharply in open and closed societies. In many open societies, a strong and significant correlation can be observed where political trust rises and falls consistently with each country's levels of economic development (measured by level of per capita GDP) and economic equality (gauged by the income share of the richest 20%). Equally striking patterns are displayed for the role of education in open societies, where higher attainment of secondary education in society is strongly associated with greater trust in government. But, by contrast, no such positive relationships can be seen in these figures for closed societies, where confidence in the state is not significantly linked with economic and social performance. In open societies, the share of the adult population completing secondary education is strongly correlated with greater political trust—but this relationship is negative in closed societies.

Overall, therefore, the data expand comparisons of a range of macroeconomic and developmental performance indicators well beyond Western states to compare varied rich and poor countries, and open and closed information societies, in all major regions around the globe. The analysis confirms that in open societies, where citizens have widespread access to the plural sources of information and news media commentary, the socioeconomic measures of government policy performance are consistently related to political trust across almost all the selected indicators. Nevertheless, even in these types of societies, there are country outliers, both those commonly shown in post-Communist Europe and Latin America, where citizens are relatively cynical of the state capacity to deliver despite a positive record of economic management and prosperity in recent years, and those cases where citizens are relatively credulous, expressing more trust in their government than seems warranted if judged by current economic indicators alone. The residual cultural legacy of trust in political institutions observed for decades in these global regions seem to persist, so that the public's evaluations of government's trustworthiness are not updated by medium- and short-term economic indices. In closed societies, the performance-trust relationship is generally weaker in strength, statistically insignificant, and inconsistent across indices.

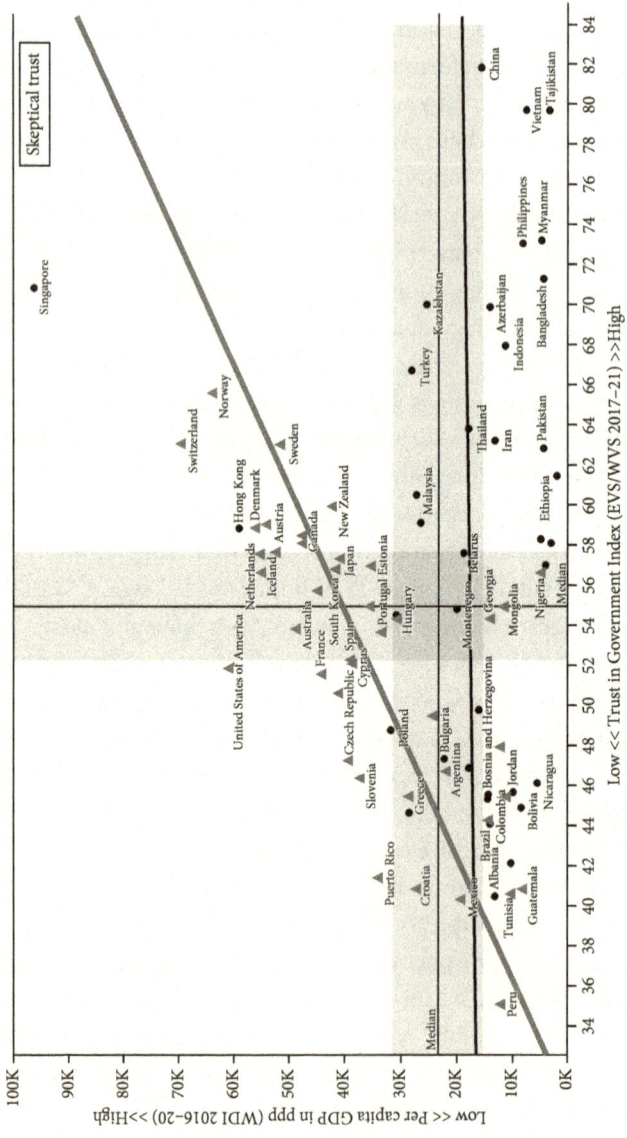

Figure 5.3. Development and trust in government.

Notes: The horizontal axis is the mean EVS/WVS Trust in Government standardized scale (including government, parliament, parties, and the civil service) for each society. The vertical axis is the mean level of development (per capita GDP in ppp) derived from the World Development Indicators (World Bank). Open and closed societies are categorized by the V-Dem Freedom of Expression Index (dichotomized).

Source: European Values Survey/World Values Survey Wave 7 (2017–2021).

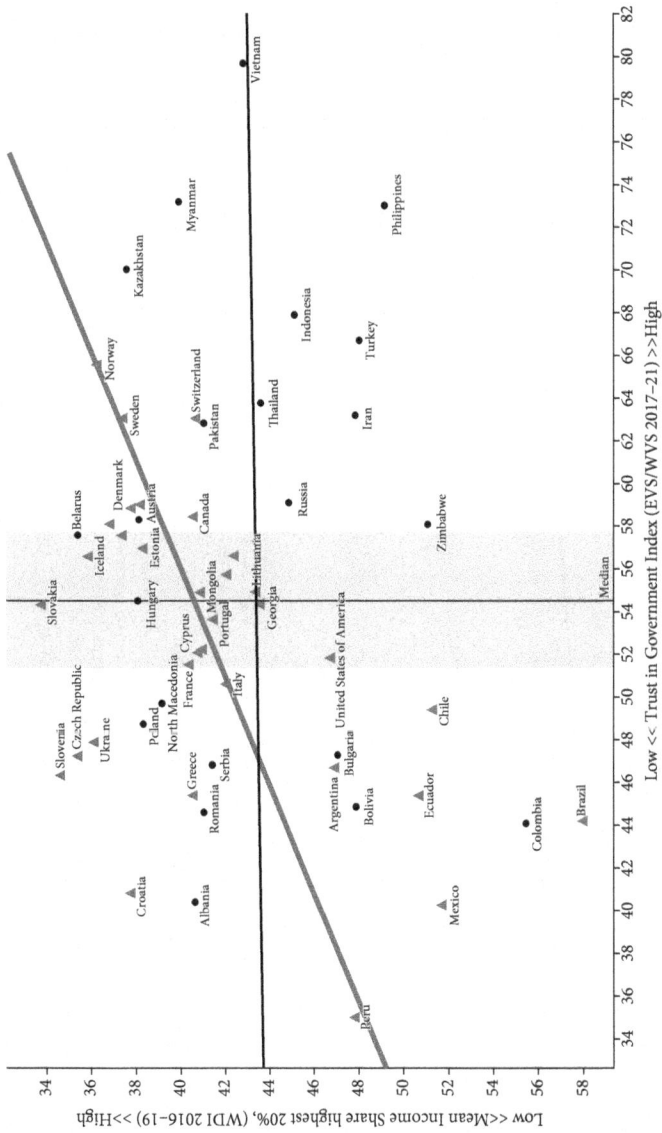

Figure 5.4. Economic equality and trust in government.

Notes: The horizontal axis is the mean EVS/WVS Trust in Government standardized scale (including government, parliament, parties, and the civil service) for each society. The vertical axis is the mean income share for the top 20% (reversed), derived from the World Development Indicators (World Bank). Open and closed societies are categorized by the V-Dem Freedom of Expression Index (dichotomized).

Source: European Values Survey/World Values Survey Wave 7 (2017–2021).

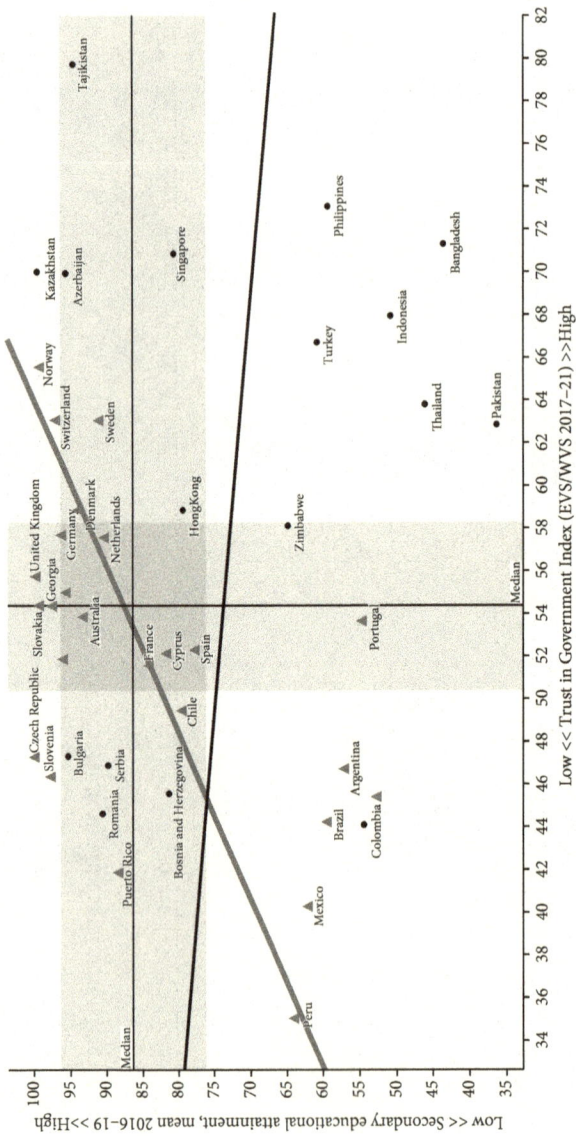

Figure 5.5. Education and trust in government.

Notes: The horizontal axis is the mean EVS/WVS Trust in Government standardized scale (including government, parliament, parties, and the civil service) for each society. The vertical axis is the lagged mean educational attainment, the % at least completed lower secondary school, among the population 25+, derived from the World Development Indicators (World Bank). Open and closed societies are categorized by the V-Dem Freedom of Expression Index (dichotomized).

Source: European Values Survey/World Values Survey Wave 7 (2017–2021).

At the same time, these macro-level tests of the performance-trust thesis are limited in important regards. In particular, citizens are likely to evaluate their government to deliver on far more issues than their capacity to steer the economy. When asked about the most important problem facing each country, economic issues often prove highly salient in many surveys, but other concerns can prove important. Since 1945, Gallup surveys have regularly monitored the "most important problem facing America today," using open-ended questions. The series suggests that trends in the issue agenda are dynamic. In the longer term, issues can gradually rise or fall in importance due to changing cultural and political cleavages in the electorate and processes of generational turnover, such as growing concern about environmentalism, gender equality, multiculturalism, and LGBTQ rights among younger citizens.[54] The salience of issues can also change in the short term, in a model of punctuated equilibrium, following major events such as the financial crisis of 2007–2008, which placed the economy at the center of US attention, the September 11, 2001, attacks in the United States, which brought terrorism to the forefront of the political agenda, and the Covid-19 pandemic, highlighting healthcare.[55]

The biannual series of Eurobarometer surveys document similar short-term shifts in the most important problem among the public in twenty-seven member states, such as the rising importance of climate change in 2021 following European experience of environmental disasters like floods in Germany and wildfires in Greece, and anxiety about the influx of immigration in Southern Europe and the Balkans at the height of the European refugee crisis in 2015–2016.[56] Agenda-setting theories suggest that public concerns respond to headline coverage by the news media, policy debates among political elites, and lived experience of real-world events.[57] Hence a monthly survey by Ipsos comparing the public in twenty-eight nations found that Covid-19 was rated highest in concern in September 2021, when pandemic cases and fatalities were surging, but the following month this declined, and the issues of poverty and unemployment were identified by the public as the most worrying concerns.[58] The world faces multiple non-economic problems which polls report rising or falling as issues of public concern in different societies, reflecting media coverage and real-world events, such as addressing the Covid-19 pandemic, climate change, responding to population migration and refugees, eradicating financial and political corruption, coping with natural and humanitarian disasters, improving healthcare and schools, and protecting against risks of crime, violence, and threats to national security. Beyond the macroeconomy, therefore, the public may be expected to trust government based on their reputation for handling multiple critical challenges facing each society, reflecting judgments of generalized government competency.[59]

IV. Conclusions and Discussion

The theory at the heart of this book suggests that skeptics judge agents and agencies as trustworthy based on relatively accurate and informed assessments of their reputation when delivering on their contractual promises and fulfilling their responsibilities with competency, as well as with integrity and impartiality. Skeptical thinking implies a deliberative decision-making process to trust someone or something based on conscious choices, logical reasoning, and careful weighing of the available information, rather than relying upon affective biases, cultural feelings, gut instincts, or habitual loyalties. The logic explored in this chapter suggests that the more closely the public's evaluations of trustworthiness are correlated with objective macro-level indicators of competent economic management by governments, and with the pocketbook economy, ipso facto, the more accurate the skeptical judgments. By contrast, the record of governments in managing the nation's economy may be systematically underestimated in some societies, due to enduring cultural legacies—and overestimated by the public elsewhere, if they express confidence in the authorities despite their incompetent performance. At the same time, the information environment is theorized to mediate the links connecting political trust with evaluations of the governments' management of the national economy—but not with direct experience of the household economy.

The individual-level evidence suggests that direct experience of the household or "pocketbook" economy is related to political trust. In particular, in both open and closed societies, people living in economically insecure households expressed significantly less trust in their government, including the unemployed, poor and low income, and those with declining social mobility. People can extrapolate to the real world from their direct experience of the pocketbook economy within their own household, to make firsthand judgments of whether the government has generally proved trustworthy through proving competent and being responsive to their everyday economic situation. Citizens know whether there have been improvements in their material standards of living, without reliance upon mediated information.

But judgments about the performance of the national economy are far more dependent upon mediated sources of information, which may or may not be accurate and reliable guides to government competency. The analysis of the macro-level evidence suggests that in a wide range of open societies, public trust in the authorities is often significantly associated with several standard national economic and social policy indicators, including per capita rates of growth in GDP and rates of unemployment in each society.[60] In this context, independent news media provide critical scrutiny of the government's record, and alternative sources of information about the state of the nation's economy are available to citizens. Where plural media provide multiple sources of alternative information, therefore, public judgments of government trustworthiness fairly accurately correlate with their actual success or failure in managing public goods and services. By contrast, in closed societies, almost all the macroeconomic performance indices failed to predict public confidence in state authorities. In this context, repressive regimes commonly use many techniques to suppress negative news about the government, restricting criticism of the authorities and actively repressing public dissent, limiting independent journalism and censoring access to online blogs and political commentary, while promoting positive news about its leaders. In an information environment and media system with one-sided messages about the authorities, citizens appear to respond either through expressing attitudes of credulous trust in the authorities, where deferential citizens in authoritarian cultures come to believe state misinformation and propaganda about the competence of their leaders—or else they react with cynical disbelief and mistrust, which is likely to occur if the mediated messages about the government's record come into conflict with direct personal experiences and also legacy cultural attitudes toward the state.

Overall, the evidence in this chapter provides additional grounds of support for the trust-as-performance thesis. When it comes to evaluating the pocketbook household economy, across a range of measures, those individuals living in more prosperous and secure conditions are more likely to trust their government. When it comes to judging the state of the national macroeconomy, objective economic and developmental performance indices also predict trust in government for citizens living in open information societies—but this relationship was not observed in closed societies. The most plausible explanation lies in the harsh repression of voices critical of the authorities in these countries, and the dissemination of state propaganda emphasizing the positive and effective role leaders running the economy. As already observed, response bias in the survey may also play a role here; citizens in authoritarian states may be reluctant to admit in public that they mistrust the government, even if they remain deeply dissatisfied with the performance of the macroeconomy.

But are judgments of trustworthiness also influenced by processes and procedures in how agents work, notably the existence of strong and effective institutional safeguards which can deter betrayals in informal social contracts? If so, the public is likely to care about accountability mechanisms which strengthen integrity and impartiality, measured by objective macro-level indices gauging the overall quality of government and democracy, as well as more public perceptions of the performance of their government and public-sector corruption.[61] To build upon these insights, the book goes on to consider alternative versions of performance theories which claim that political trust is more strongly related to the general quality of government integrity and impartiality, rather than their competence at managing policy outcomes. Evidence for this claim can be compared from expert indicators like the World Bank's measures of "good governance," Transparency International's Corruption Perception Index, and the Varieties of Democracy index of Liberal Democracy.[62] Accordingly, the next chapter goes on to consider this argument.

6

Integrity and Impartiality

Above and beyond the competent delivery of specific policy outcomes, procedural indicators of performance are expected to be even more important for trustworthy principal-agent relationships, representing the "input" and "throughput" side of the policymaking process.[1] When evaluating the work of national governance institutions, judgments of trustworthiness are expected to reflect the quality of how these agencies work, especially the principles of impartiality and integrity. Accountability mechanisms are designed to deter abuses of power by elected politicians, ministers, and departments of state, so that they serve the public interest. Safeguards are exemplified by independent electoral commissions safeguarding the integrity of elections, watchdogs monitoring public-sector malfeasance, the oversight role of committee hearings by independent legislatures scrutinizing executive orders, and civil service bodies monitoring the truthfulness, ethics, and probity of public sector officials. The empirical evidence supporting the general theory deserves critical scrutiny. The chapter examines three issues: (1) how far subjective views about the quality of governance, like perceptions of corruption, are consistently associated with attitudes of political trust; (2) more importantly, whether objective indices of the performance of democracy and good governance in each society predict public judgments of trustworthiness; and finally, (3) whether these relationships vary in open and closed information societies.

To explore these issues, Section I summarizes the theoretical argument. To identify the drivers of trust, Section II examines individual-level data to analyze how far confidence in political institutions is strengthened by *subjective* perceptions about the quality of governance. Models examine these relationships, controlling for the sociodemographic and economic characteristics which previous chapters demonstrated are associated with political trust, as well as the type of information society. The results of the analysis confirm that citizens' trust in government is indeed strongly linked with general satisfaction about the workings of the political system and the performance of democracy in their country, as well as with views about problems of corruption in the public sector. The more positively individuals regard the quality of their governance, especially its competency and integrity, the greater their trust in state authorities. These associations are very similar in both open and closed societies, suggesting that citizens associate these qualities with feelings of trust irrespective of the broader environment. But are these attitudes the genuine reasons driving political trust—or are they simply rationalizations concerning prior preferences, reflecting processes of motivated reasoning? Unfortunately, the direction of causality in this recursive relationship cannot be determined from the individual-level analysis of cross-sectional surveys alone. For example, in a series of Gallup polls, around one-third of Americans, and a majority of Republicans, said they believe former President Trump to be honest and trustworthy.[2] This belief persisted, and even rose slightly over time, despite his record of continuous mendacity and outrageous lies. Fact checkers estimate that during his term in office, President Trump made over 30,000 false or misleading claims.[3] This may reflect genuine but mistaken assessment of his character and verisimilitude by those who subsequently decided to vote for Trump. Or it could reflect their prior affective partisan loyalties, where loyal Republican voters and MAGA activists project this quality upon their party leader.

For a more rigorous test of the core theory, Section III compares objective performance indicators to see how far independent measures of the quality of government by monitoring agencies predict public judgments of the trustworthiness of core political institutions—and how far such relationships are conditioned by the type of information society and the predominant societal culture. Indicators based on expert evaluations are selected from the Varieties of Democracy (V-Dem) project's liberal democracy index and the World Bank Institute measures of six dimension of good governance.[4] The results of the analysis suggest striking contrasts in these relationships by the type of information environment, as theorized. In the open societies, trust in government is significantly correlated with objective indicators of the quality of government, such as control of corruption, government effectiveness, rule of law, and liberal democracy. The better the quality of government, in these societies, the stronger the trustworthiness of the institutions. But no such relationship is observed in closed societies, where states limit independent media, repress critical voices, censor digital communications, and promote domestic news coverage favorable of the regime. Controlling for the type of open or closed societies, education also makes a significant difference, with objective indicators of the quality of good governance more weakly correlated with trust in government in less-educated societies, as expected. In this context, ordinary citizens lack the necessary information and cognitive skills that facilitate accurate assessments of the quality of government. Section IV illustrates the existential risks of excessive credulous public trust in untrustworthy leaders with a case study of the performance of countries in the Covid-19 pandemic. The conclusions in Section V highlight the key findings and consider their broader implications for trust and trustworthiness.

I. Why Agency Accountability Matters

The previous chapter observed that objective indicators monitoring the delivery of public goods and services were linked with public trust in government. Yet at the same time, political leaders may fail to deliver prosperity and growth for multiple reasons beyond their control, such as the headwinds of global markets, rates of bilateral trade and international investment, the productivity and capacity of the workforce, the occurrence of specific "shock" events like Covid-19 or natural disasters, and numerous contingent factors, as much as the government's skills in steering the macroeconomy. When evaluating government performance, judgments of trustworthiness can also be expected to reflect the quality of underlying procedures and institutions which strengthen accountability.[5] In particular, researchers in organizational studies have theorized that trust is generally related to three judgment criteria which can apply across all types of agents and agencies, namely their reputation for competency (their capacity to deliver consistently according to expectations), integrity (their honesty and transparency), and impartiality (avoiding conflicts of interest).[6] This is exemplified by processes in democratic governance safeguarding party competition and electoral integrity, which have been found to strengthen voter confidence through allowing citizens to kick out incompetent, corrupt, or scandal-ridden governments through the ballot box.[7] Similarly, political trust can be expected to be strengthened by the general quality of democratic governance, including through effective institutions undergirding rule of law, legislative scrutiny and oversight of executive actions, and transparency mechanisms monitoring the truthfulness, ethics, and probity of public officials.[8] In liberal democratic states, institutions providing effective checks and balances produce safeguards against the abuse of power by any branch of government, especially the executive.[9]

By contrast, if incumbent politicians, judges, civil servants, or governments usually prove demonstrably corrupt, inept, or self-serving, or are seen to be so, and if they can't be easily removed from office or held accountable through regular processes such as elections, sackings, or impeachment, then citizens can be expected to conclude that they are likely to continue to abuse their office in the future. Accountability implies that agents have to give reasons justifying their conduct, and any shortcomings are subject to formal or informal sanctions.[10] This approach theorizes that the public will regard the regime and its agencies as more trustworthy where citizens express approval of the underlying fairness of the procedures governing the state. The procedural accountability argument goes beyond discontent with specific policy outcomes or administrative decisions in particular cases to tap more deep-rooted perceptions about how government institutions usually work and what generally protects against their failure to maintain ethical standards in public office. Even if I lack confidence in the past decisions or economic record of any individual political leader, for example, I may still have faith in the electoral mechanisms and the constitutional and legal procedures which constrain the abuse of power. If sufficient citizens lack faith in both their leaders and these institutions, however, then this raises risks of a major legitimacy crisis.

Previous empirical cross-national research lends at least partial support for procedural theories of trust. In particular, several studies observe that levels of public-sector corruption in a country are strongly linked with both social and political trust, in a reciprocal relationship.[11] Others have emphasized that political trust is strengthened by related qualities associated with good governance, including procedural fairness, transparency, and honesty.[12] One of the most comprehensive arguments by Bo Rothstein suggests that trust in government is widespread within the Nordic region because these are safe and secure societies characterized by universal access to comprehensive cradle-to-grave public services and welfare benefits, as well as having open societies and well-functioning systems of democratic governance, minimal problems of corruption, and professional standards of administration in the public sector.[13] In the United Kingdom and the United States, as well, studies report that scandals involving lawmakers have damaged trust in parliament and the political process.[14]

For all these reasons, trust judgments can be expected to go beyond the specific record of competency demonstrated by individual agents and particular agencies, like their record of economic management, to reflect broader assessments about the effectiveness of accountability safeguards more generally. This chapter examines the individual-level links between trust and subjective perceptions of how government works, such as satisfaction with democracy and the political system, and perceptions of corruption, using data from the European Values Survey/World Values Survey (EVS/WVS).

More rigorous tests come from correlating citizens' judgments of political trustworthiness with objective indicators of the quality of good governance and liberal democracy in a wide range of countries and types of regimes around the world. In general, estimates of trustworthiness in politics should be observed to be correlated with objective indices of the performance of democracy and good governance which strengthen accountability, integrity, and impartiality, such as measures of judicial independence and rule of law, control of corruption, government transparency, and the overall quality of public-sector management.[15] By contrast, in general, mistrust is predicted to be far stronger in states where rulers manipulate elections, employ coercion against dissent, abuse human rights, profit from endemic corruption and crony capitalism, and fail to respect rule of law and constitutional constraints. But public perceptions are expected to differ in open and closed societies, as the information about good governance that is available to citizens differs. To update and review evidence concerning these arguments, this chapter compares political trust among the general public with expert estimates of the quality of governance and strength of accountability institutions in each country. These measures are derived from sources such as the V-Dem project and the World Governance Indicators which compile expert data from multiple sources to estimate annual levels of political corruption, government effectiveness, and rule of law in nation-states worldwide.[16] As argued in Chapter 2, skeptical orientations—the capacity of citizens to make informed and accurate judgments of the trustworthiness of government—are expected to be strengthened at the individual level by educational qualifications and the cognitive and information-processing skills derived from formal schooling, as well as by government transparency, freedom of expression, and media pluralism in society. By contrast, both credulous trust (or gullibility) and cynical mistrust (blanket suspicion) are cultural biases expected to flourish under repressive regimes controlling information in closed societies through official censorship of the news media and internet, limits on independent journalism and public commentary critical of the authorities, and the existence of widespread misinformation and disinformation. Therefore, micro-level models control for individual levels of education, while macro-level models of political trust in this chapter control for freedom of information and expression and whether societies are open or closed, which are predicted to mediate the links connecting public trust with the quality of government.

II. Subjective Perceptions of the Quality of Government and Trust

As already observed in Chapter 4, different dimensions of trust display enduring contrasts in levels and trajectories even among relatively similar post-industrial societies and liberal democracies in Europe, such as political trust observed in Sweden and Denmark compared with Italy and Greece—and the global disparities in the performance of the state and types of regimes in power are even more substantial. Evidence for the theory in this book can be tested more effectively where public trust in government is compared across a broad range of societies worldwide, to maximize contrasts among diverse types of open and closed information environments and regimes, as well as tracing fluctuations in political trust and government performance over time within societies. Micro-level analysis also provides leverage into understanding the "black-box" cognitive processes which ordinary people use to arrive at trust judgments, such as where they get their information, how this is sifted and weighed, what thinking skills, prior knowledge, values, and heuristic shortcuts they employ, how they use intuition or reason to decide on trustworthiness, how groups and sectors differ in their evaluations, and so on.[17]

To explore how far subjective perceptions of the quality of government are related to trust in government, the models in Table 6.1 use data from the seventh wave of the EVS/WVS and enter satisfaction with the political system and the performance of democracy in each country, perceptions of corruption in the country, the involvement of corruption of state and local authorities as well as the civil service, and the frequency with which ordinary people are thought to pay a bribe. The models control for the economic characteristics such as household income and financial security, and the socio-demographic factors like sex and age, which were found to be importantly related to trust in previous chapter. The dependent variable remains the

Table 6.1 Perceived Quality of Governance and Political Trust

	OPEN SOCIETIES				CLOSED SOCIETIES			
	B	SE	Beta	Sig.	B	SE	Beta	Sig.
PERCEIVED QUALITY OF GOVERNANCE								
Satisfaction with the political system (low to high)	1.50	0.04	0.22	***	2.02	0.05	0.28	***
How democratically this country is being governed today	0.67	0.04	0.09	***	0.67	0.05	0.09	***
Perceptions of corruption in the country (low to high)	-0.85	0.04	-0.11	***	-1.15	0.04	-0.14	***
Involved in corruption: State authorities (low to high)	-2.84	0.15	-0.12	***	-4.58	0.16	-0.18	***
Involved in corruption: Local authorities (low to high)	-1.80	0.16	-0.08	***	-1.60	0.17	-0.06	***
Involved in corruption: Civil service (low to high)	-1.36	0.15	-0.06	***	-0.61	0.16	-0.02	***
Frequency ordinary people pay a bribe (low to high)	-1.54	0.11	-0.08	***	1.09	0.11	0.05	***
ECONOMIC CHARACTERISTICS								
Income scale (low to high)	-0.30	0.05	-0.04	***	-0.44	0.05	-0.04	***
Currently unemployed (0/1)	-0.76	0.33	-0.01	*	-0.46	0.35	-0.01	N/s
Lived poverty Index (low to high)	0.09	0.01	0.08	***	-0.04	0.01	-0.03	***
Feel financially secure (low to high)	3.27	0.11	0.15	***	1.19	0.12	0.05	***
Household financial security (low to high)	0.35	0.10	0.02	***	0.78	0.11	0.03	***
Satisfaction with financial situation (low to high)	0.24	0.04	0.03	***	0.10	0.04	0.01	*
Standard of living compared with your parents (worse/better)	0.66	0.12	0.03	***	2.10	0.13	0.08	***

Continued

Table 6.1 *Continued*

	OPEN SOCIETIES				CLOSED SOCIETIES			
	B	SE	Beta	Sig.	B	SE	Beta	Sig.
CONTROLS Sex (male)	-0.13	0.17	0.00	N/s	0.17	0.19	0.00	N/s
Age (years)	-0.02	0.01	-0.02	***	-0.04	0.01	-0.03	***
Education (low to high scale)	-1.41	0.13	-0.06	***	-2.35	0.13	-0.09	***
News media use (newspapers, TV news, radio news)	0.07	0.03	0.01	**	0.27	0.03	0.04	***
Social media use (internet, FB/Twitter, mobile phone, email)	0.10	0.02	0.03	***	-0.17	0.02	-0.05	***
(Constant)	51.30	0.97			66.50	1.04		
Number of respondents	29,432				31,380			
Number of Societies	42				38			
Adjusted R²	0.31				0.37			

Note: The model uses OLS regression with individual–level survey data in 80 societies where the dependent variable is the EVS/WVS Trust in Government standardized index (including government, parliament, parties, and the civil service). The table presents the beta (B), standard error (SE), standardized beta coefficients (Beta), and their significance (Sig.). All models were tested and found to be free of problems of multicollinearity. P: * = .05; ** = .01; *** = .001. N/s = not significant.

Source: European Values Survey/World Values Survey Wave 7 (2017–2021).

summary Trust in Government Index, summed from trust in government, parliament, parties, and the civil service. The models are analyzed for both open and closed societies.

The results demonstrate that a remarkably similar range of attitudes toward the quality of government are linked with political trust for citizens living in both open and closed societies. Thus, not surprisingly perhaps, satisfaction with the political system and with the performance of democracy in their country were positively associated with greater political trust, while perceptions of widespread corruption were significantly related to lower confidence in government. Of these factors, satisfaction with the political system was most closely related to trust—and indeed this proved to be the single strongest predictor in the models, based on comparing the size of all the standardized beta coefficients. The controls in the models did not change substantially so that the basic relationship between political trust and the pocketbook economy, demographic characteristics, and media use remain as discussed earlier.

To explore the basis of trust judgments in closed society in more detail, the seventh wave EVS/WVS data included a special battery of questions which were designed to monitor trust and assessments of the qualities of competency, integrity, and impartiality in the performance of parliaments, governments, and the United Nations. These batteries were included in the standard questionnaire in selected cases of closed societies and autocratic states, as described earlier in Chapter 3. The national surveys include Kyrgyzstan, Tajikistan, Philippines, Myanmar, Vietnam, Nicaragua, Zimbabwe, Kenya, Ethiopia, and Iran. Individual-level regression models examine the impact of perceptions of integrity, competency and impartiality in each agency on trust in parliaments, governments, and the United Nations. Models control for the standard socio-demographic variables associated with trust in previous tables, including sex and age, as well as cognitive skills from education, use of news and social media, and household income.

The results in Table 6.2 show that trust in each of these bodies was indeed strongly correlated with perceptions of their competency and efficiency, impartiality, and freedom from corruption. Overall, all these factors proved to be strong and significant predictors of trust, explaining a high level of variance in trust in these institutions. Perceptions of corruption were confirmed as strong predictors of trust, as many other previous studies have reported, but citizens living in these societies prioritized competence and impartiality even more highly as criteria associated with trust. Therefore, even in closed

Table 6.2 Criteria Associated with Trust in Closed Societies

	Parliament				Government				United Nations			
	B	SE	Beta	Sig.	B	SE	Beta	Sig.	B	SE	Beta	Sig.
COMPETENCY: The agency is usually competent and efficient	0.31	0.01	0.36	***	0.29	0.01	0.33	***	0.26	0.01	0.29	***
IMPARTIALITY: The agency usually wants to serve the country/world	0.19	0.01	0.22	***	0.22	0.01	0.25	***	0.22	0.01	0.24	***
INTEGRITY: The agency is usually free of corruption	0.11	0.01	0.13	***	0.08	0.01	0.10	***	0.08	0.01	0.10	***
Sex (male)	-0.01	0.02	0.00	N/s	-0.01	0.02	0.00	N/s	0.00	0.02	0.00	N/s
Age (years)	0.00	0.00	0.05	***	0.00	0.00	0.05	***	0.00	0.00	0.02	*
Education 3 categories (low to high)	0.00	0.01	0.00	N/s	-0.03	0.01	-0.02	***	0.00	0.01	0.00	N/s
Income 10-pt scale (low to high)	0.00	0.00	0.01	N/s	0.01	0.00	0.03	***	0.01	0.00	0.01	N/s
Use of news media	0.01	0.00	0.04	***	0.02	0.00	0.06	***	0.02	0.00	0.06	***
Use of social media	0.00	0.00	-0.01	*	0.00	0.00	-0.02	N/s	0.01	0.00	0.05	***
Constant	0.40	0.05			0.51	0.05			0.44	0.05		
Adjusted R2	0.38				0.37				0.29			
N.	11,089				11,626				10,403			

Note: The model uses OLS regression with individual-level survey data in 10 societies where the dependent variable is the EVS/WVS Trust in each agency, i.e., the national parliament, national government, and the United Nations (*). The table presents the beta (B), standard error (SE), standardized beta coefficients (Beta), and their significance (Sig.). All coefficients were checked to be free of problems of multicollinearity. P.* = .05; ** = .01; *** = .001. N/s = not significant. The TrustGov battery was included in surveys in 10 closed societies (Ethiopia, Iran, Kenya, Kyrgyzstan, Myanmar, Nicaragua, Philippines, Tajikistan, Vietnam, and Zimbabwe).

Source: World Values Survey 7, TrustGov surveys (2017–2021).

societies, many ordinary people offer plausible reasons for their trust in these agencies, suggesting internal consistency in their deliberative thinking. People living under strikingly different types of regimes around the world seem to desire much the same qualities in how their governments work.

III. Objective Indicators of Trustworthy Governance

Unfortunately, however, the analysis of cross-sectional survey data alone is unable to determine the direction of causality in any of these relationships, and complex reciprocal processes are likely to influence subjective attitudes. Do ordinary people consider the government's record of integrity and competency—whether there have been major financial and bribery scandals about kickbacks for cronies or leaders tainting the administration, whether public services like schools and clinics have improved, whether the economy has grown—and then subsequently decide on this basis to trust those in authority? Or do citizens have confidence in the government for many other reasons, like affective partisan identification, the personal qualities of particular leaders, habitual predispositions toward state authorities, or deep-rooted social identities—and evaluate the performance and integrity of political institutions accordingly through these cultural filters? Observing that people who are generally satisfied by the way their political system works are also more likely to trust political authorities is hardly unexpected.

But are public perceptions about the quality of government informed and accurate, reflecting independent evidence of real-world conditions, or are these judgments erroneous by being either too negative (and cynical) or too positive (and thus credulous) compared with reality? To explore this further, public trust in political institutions needs to be compared against objective indicators of the quality of the institutions of democratic governance. Here we can take advantage of the contemporary proliferation of independent measures of so-called good government and/or democratic governance, derived from either official statistics, expert surveys, or international monitoring NGOs.[18] This is exemplified by global data on public sector corruption, electoral integrity, rule of law, the independence of the judiciary, parliamentary effectiveness, transparency, accountability, media censorship, and so on. In particular, the World Bank Institute, the Quality of Government project, and the Varieties of Democracy (V-Dem 11.0, January 2020) data sets provide many macro-level indices widely used for ranking regime institutions, countries, and regions in the world.[19] The study selected measures of government integrity, impartiality, and competence which are widely used in the research and policy communities, as well as analyzing some new indices. Many previous empirical studies have been limited to comparing countries in specific regions of the world or to states with liberal democratic regimes. The procedural thesis can be tested most effectively, however, where public trust is compared across a broad range of open and closed societies, national cultures, and global regions, thereby maximizing variance in historical experiences of democracy and autocracy, the imprint of cultural legacies, as well as tracing political trust over time during periods of regime transitions within countries.

Mean levels of political trust in each society and wave are estimated using the pooled EVS/WVS Trust in Government 100-point standardized index (for parliaments, governments, political parties, and the civil service). This index can be estimated and compared most consistently in surveys contained in most recent (seventh) wave of the pooled EVS/WVS data set (2017–2021). As in previous chapters, "open" and "closed" societies are classified based on the dichotomized V-Dem Freedom of Expression and Alternative Sources of Information Index which is matched to the year of the survey fieldwork. The mean EVS/WVS Trust in Government Index for each nation is compared with the six World Bank Good Governance indices, as well as a summary Good Governance Index compiled from these, and the Liberal Democracy index from V-Dem.

Table 6.3 shows the results of the simple correlations at macro-level in all the open and closed societies. In the forty-three open societies, all the relationships are positive, moderately strong, and significant. In other words, it seems that irrespective of the indicators of good governance and liberal democracy which are selected for comparison, public confidence in political institutions is consistently linked with procedural performance in this context. This confirms the importance of control of corruption for political trust, as reported in many previous studies.[20] But it also adds other standards of good governance, such as government effectiveness (competency), rule of law (integrity), and liberal democracy (accountability), which function as equally strong predictors of political trust. By contrast, in the thirty-five closed societies under comparison, public trust is not significantly related with any of the six World Bank indices monitoring good governance. And the indices measuring voice and accountability and liberal democracy are significant and strong, but *negatively* linked with political trust in closed

Table 6.3 Quality of Governance and Societal-Level Trust in Government

	Open Societies		Closed Societies	
	Correlation (R)	Significance (P)	Correlation (R)	Significance (P)
Good Governance Index (WB)	0.558	***	−0.147	N/s
Control of corruption (WB)	0.581	***	−0.013	N/s
Government effectiveness (WB)	0.589	***	0.046	N/s
Political stability (WB)	0.398	**	−0.059	N/s
Rule of law (WB)	0.579	***	0.004	N/s
Regulatory quality (WB)	0.514	***	−0.140	N/s
Voice and accountability (WB)	0.520	***	−0.603	***
Liberal democracy index (V-Dem)	0.365	**	−0.639	***
Number of societies	43		35	
Number of respondents	29,432		31,380	

Notes: Simple correlations between the EVS/WVS Trust in Government 100-point standardized index (for parliaments, government, political parties and the civil service) and macro-level objective indices of good governance in each society, matched to the year of the survey. R = Correlation coefficient. P *** Coefficient is significant at the 0.001 level (2-tailed). ** Correlation coefficient is significant at the 0.01 level (2-tailed). Open and closed societies are categorized based on the V-Dem Freedom of Expression and Alternative Sources of Information index (dichotomized around the mean).

Sources: European Values Survey/World Values Survey Wave 7 (2017–2021); WB: World Bank Institute Worldwide Governance Indicators; V-Dem: Varieties of Democracy (V-Dem 11.0).

societies. Most strikingly, the more autocratic the regime, the more the public expresses trust.

Do cognitive skills, civic awareness, and reasoning capacities reinforce these patterns, as theorized? These cannot be measured directly from the available macro-level data, but as a proxy the UNDP Index of Education can be used to classify the general population in open and closed societies. This standardized index is measured by combining average adult years of schooling with expected years of schooling for students under the age of twenty-five, each receiving 50% weighting. The Index was dichotomized around the mean to categorize the formal level of education among the population living in low and highly educated societies. Table 6.4 displays how far trust is correlated with the quality of governance indices, breaking down the results by the average levels of educated populations in each society. The results show that in the closed societies, the coefficients are insignificant, as already observed, except for the link connecting the liberal democracy index

Table 6.4 Quality of Governance and Societal-Level Trust in Government, with Levels of Education

| | OPEN SOCIETIES | | | | CLOSED SOCIETIES | | | |
| | Low education | | High education | | Low education | | High education | |
	Correlation (R)	Significance (P)	Correlation (R)	Significance (P)	Correlation (R)	Significance (P)	Correlation (R)	Significance (P)
Good governance index	-0.95	***	0.78	***	0.14	N/s	-0.60	N/s
Control of corruption	-0.56		0.77	***	0.14	N/s	-0.11	N/s
Government effectiveness	-0.88	**	0.76	***	0.36	N/s	-0.05	N/s
Political stability	-0.77		0.46	**	-0.03	N/s	-0.24	N/s
Rule of law	-0.50		0.75	***	0.23	N/s	-0.13	N/s
Regulatory quality	-0.79		0.76	***	-0.01	N/s	-0.08	N/s
Voice and accountability	-0.76		0.72	***	-0.47	N/s	-0.67	N/s
Liberal democracy index	-0.10		0.54	***	-0.58	***	-0.56	N/s
N. respondents	41,169		22,965		20,104		52253	
N. societies	9		31		26		10	

Notes: Simple correlations between the EVS/WVS Trust in Government 100-point standardized index (for parliaments, government, political parties, and the civil service) and macro-level objective indices of good governance in each society, matched to the year of the survey. Societal education is categorized by the UNDP Education Index dichotomized around the mean. R = Correlation coefficient. P *** Coefficient is significant at the 0.001 level (2-tailed). ** Correlation coefficient is significant at the 0.01 level (2-tailed). Open and closed societies are categorized based on the V-Dem Freedom of Expression and Alternative Sources of Information index (dichotomized around the mean).

Sources: European Values Survey/World Values Survey Wave 7 (2017–2021); WB: World Bank Institute Worldwide Governance Indicators; V-Dem: Varieties of Democracy (V-Dem 11.0).

negatively with trust in government among the low-educated societies. In open societies, coefficients are stronger—and these are consistently both significant and positive among open societies with more educated populations. The only correlations which are significant in open societies with lower levels of education are negative—for the good governance index and government effectiveness. The evidence therefore confirms the argument that open societies (with freedom of expression and alternative sources of information) provide an environment facilitating public evaluations of trustworthiness to be more closely related to the actual quality of good governance. This process is further reinforced in countries with more educated populations (and thus the cognitive skills, literacy, numeracy, and general knowledge derived from formal schooling).

To look further at these relationships, and identify patterns and outliers, Figure 6.1 illustrates how the composite Good Governance Index from the World Bank Institute, compiled from expert estimates, compares with the Trust in Government Index in 80 societies from the most recent (seventh) wave of the EVS/WVS. The closed societies are nearly all scattered across the bottom two quadrants, summarized by a relatively flat best-fit line, characterized by relatively poor-quality governance according to the WBI estimates but sharply divergent public trust in the authorities, ranging from exceptionally low trust in Mexico, Lebanon, and Brazil to exceptionally high confidence expressed by respondents in China, Vietnam, and Tajikistan. The main exception is affluent Singapore, dominated by the center-right ruling People's Action Party in power since independence in 1965, but governed by pragmatic leaders and an effective public-sector bureaucracy, generating stability and growth, with minimal corruption.[21] The residual imprint of regional cultural legacies can also be observed, with Latin America and Central European nations often skeptical mistrusters, but Central and Southeast Asian countries far more trusting. Among open societies, however, there is a significant correlation where better quality governance according to the objective indices is closely associated with greater public trust. Thus, among the open societies and long-established liberal democracies, the evidence confirms the familiar contrasts, with Mediterranean European nations exemplified by Italy and Spain far lower in both good governance and political trust than Nordic Europe, as shown by the location of Norway, Sweden, and Denmark.

The contrasts in attitudes toward government authorities and political institutions between open and closed societies is even sharper when compared using the V-Dem liberal democracy index. As Figure 6.2 illustrates,

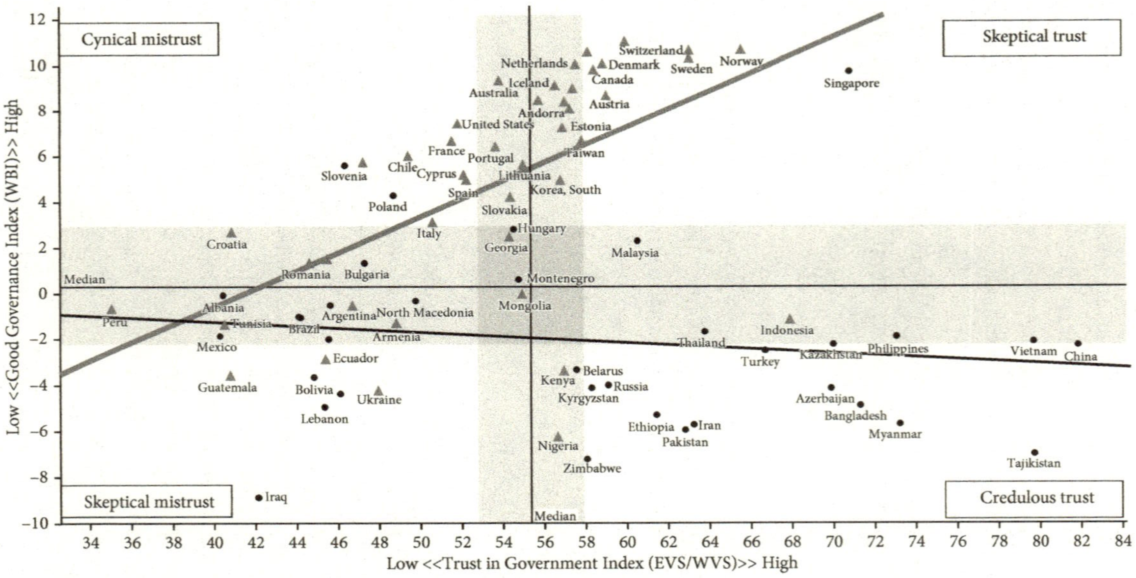

Figure 6.1. Good governance and trust in government.

Notes: The horizontal axis is the EVS/WVS Trust in Government standardized scale (including government, parliament, parties, and the civil service). The vertical axis shows the Good Governance Index as derived from the six World Governance Indicators (World Bank Institute). Open societies (Gray) and closed societies (Black) are categorized by the V-Dem Freedom of Expression Index (dichotomized).

Source: European Values Survey/World Values Survey Wave 7 in 80 societies (2017–2021); https://info.worldbank.org/governance/wgi/.

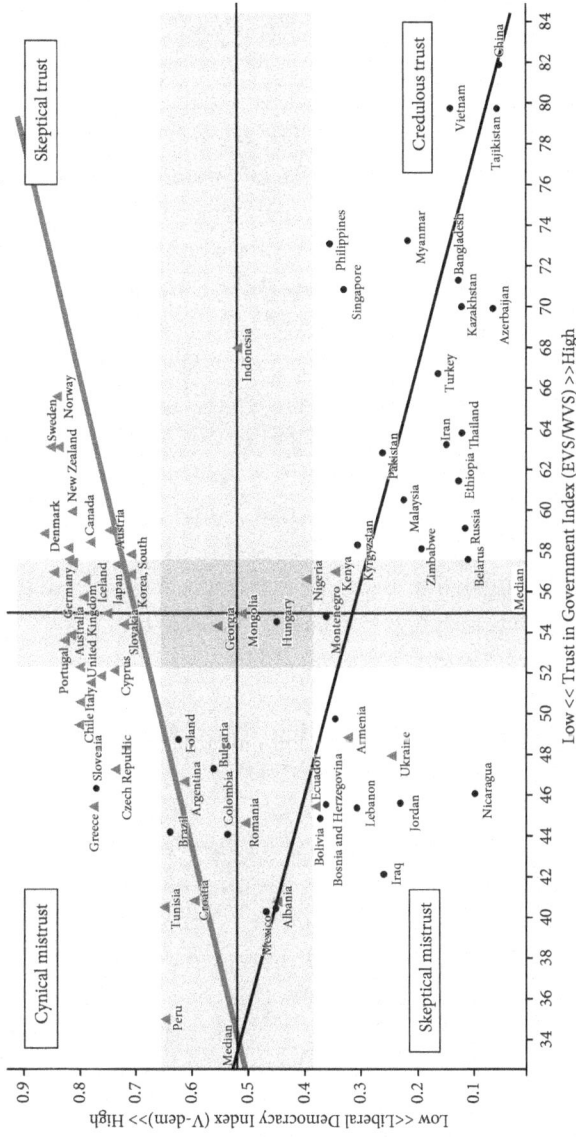

Figure 6.2. Liberal democracy and trust in government.

Notes: The horizontal axis is the EVS/WVS Trust in Government standardized scale (including government, parliament, parties, and the civil service). The vertical axis shows the Liberal Democracy Index as derived from the Varieties of Democracy project (V-Dem-11). Open societies (Gray) and closed societies (Black) are categorized by the V-Dem Freedom of Expression Index (dichotomized).

Source: European Values Survey/World Values Survey Wave 7 in 80 societies (2017–2021): https://www.v-dem.net/en/.

political trust steadily rises with more democratic open societies—
illustrating the differences between low-trust/poorer-quality newer democracies in Tunisia (during the time of the survey, prior to the presidential
invocation of emergency powers and suspension of parliament), Croatia,
and Peru compared with the high-trust/long-established democracies including New Zealand, Canada, and Germany. Among the closed societies,
however, the reverse pattern can be observed, where the public expression
of political confidence in the state grows with more *repressive* autocratic
regimes with the worst record of human rights and political freedoms. This
includes China where power has been increasingly consolidated in the hands
of President Xi Jinping, Myanmar where the military junta retook control of
the state in February 2021 before imprisoning Aung San Suu Kyi and other
democratically elected leaders, and Turkey, which has experienced backsliding in media freedom and academic freedom following the attempted
coup in 2016 against President Erdogan. Other cases in this category include
Iran under the hardline rule of President Ebrahim Raisi and the supreme
leader Ayatollah Alio Khamenei, Thailand which suspended elections after
the 2014 military coup d'état, Tajikistan governed since 1994 by President
Emimali Rahmon, Russia under Vladimir Putin, and Ethiopia where communal tensions and fighting in the north threaten civil war between the government, led by Abiy, and the Tigray People's Liberation Army.

IV. Why Credulous *and* Cynical Trust Matters: The Case of Covid-19

Why does misplaced trust matter? The case of the Covid-19 pandemic
illustrates these issues. Popular commentary has often blamed vaccine hes-
itancy, resistance to wearing masks, and failure to follow lockdowns and
to socially distance in the United States and Europe on a crisis of trust in
the public health guidelines provided by authorities and government, with
doubts over medical science fueling these attitudes and behaviors, generating
fatal consequences for individuals dying every month because they did not
get inoculated, as well as overcrowded hospitals and lack of herd immunity
for local communities. Some survey evidence confirms these claims; for example, the US Covid States Project estimates that only 71% of the vaccinated
say they trust hospitals and doctors "a lot," compared with 39% of the unvaccinated.[22] Massive differences were also observed between the vaccinated

and unvaccinated in their trust in different people and institutions. Many of the unvaccinated said that they did not trust what government told them, scientific knowledge about the potential risks and side effects of getting inoculated, and the information disseminated by the pharmaceutical companies, the White House, and the news media. Nevertheless, as with other decisions about trustworthiness, problems arise not just from undue cynicism, but also from excessive credulity in trusting the word of incompetent leaders or misleading authorities.

The Covid-19 pandemic provides a classic case study illustrating these issues. During the spring of 2020, the initial emergence of the global threat triggered a double-digit surge in public approval of many government leaders.[23]This reflects the "rally-round-the-flag" reaction in presidential popularity which has typically been observed at the outbreak of other major national crisis, like the outbreak of wars and terrorist incidents, when people look to government for protection.[24] But, the twenty-eight-nation 2002 Edelman Trust Barometer reported that this short-lived trust bubble subsequently deflated for government, returning to the status quo ante.[25] With the benefits of hindsight, should citizens have initially had faith and confidence in the capacity of their leaders to protect their well-being, health, and lives? Or was this misplaced?

Attempts to curb the pandemic have triggered divergent responses by governments around the globe. After the first two years, with new variants emerging and no end yet in sight, it is apparent that during this period some authorities have proved far more competent and effective than others in deploying strategies of containment, mitigation, and recovery, thereby protecting lives and livelihoods.

The contagion initially emerged in Wuhan city in China on December 8, 2019.[26] China first alerted the World Health Organization (WHO) about this cluster of cases on December 31, 2019, with these patients identified a week later as caused by human-to-human transmission of the novel coronavirus (SARS-CoV-2), soon known as Covid-19.[27] During January 2020, the WHO investigated these cases, consulted experts, published guidance, and shared knowledge of the outbreak. Initially, scientists were uncertain whether the virus could be transmitted by asymptomatic persons, without showing any signs of illness, thereby heightening risks of contagion. The Chinese government implemented a strict stay-at-home policy for all residents in the region. Quarantine of suspected cases and their close contacts sought to stop household and community transmission. By the end of the month, however, problems had already been detected in other Asian countries—including Thailand, Japan, South Korea, Vietnam, and Taiwan.

On January 31, 2020, the WHO issued a Global Health Emergency, alerting the world to the gravity of the risks from Covid-19. By this time the virus has spread to Europe, with the first two patients diagnosed in northern Italy. Within two weeks, the surge of Italian cases quickly threatened to overwhelm hospitals and morgues, leading Prime Minister Giuseppe Conte to order a nationwide lockdown. On March 11, 2020, the WHO director general declared Covid-19 a global pandemic. European countries overtook Asia to become the new hotspots; by March 25, all EU member states and 150 nations worldwide had cases. European governments implemented a multipronged set of pragmatic non-pharmaceutical steps designed to contain transmission, from closing schools and workplaces to testing and contact tracing, restricting travel, and canceling public events.[28] During the spring of 2020, rates of contagion and fatalities varied widely across EU member states. By mid-summer, the number of European cases had fallen, and countries cautiously started reopening their economies from lockdown, before being hit by a resurgence of cases again in the fall.

Across the pond, during the spring of 2020, the virus spiraled out of control in the United States as federal and state authorities did too little, too late. The responsible US agency, the Centers for Disease Control and Prevention (CDC), first warned the US National Security Council about the emerging coronavirus threat in China as early as January 2, with the message relayed to the White House the next day. Alarms should have started to flash crimson, but for a month the Trump administration, perhaps distracted by impeachment, was asleep at the wheel.[29] The first confirmed US case, in Washington State, was announced on January 20. Travel bans for flights from China were issued in around forty countries, and on January 31, President Trump followed suit. The administration restricted foreign nationals (but not Americans) from entering the United States if they had been in China during the prior two weeks and they were arriving on direct flights. Airports also implemented some desultory health screening of arrivals.[30] These actions probably delayed the onset of the virus, but they were insufficient to contain or prevent the global threat.[31] By March 10, the Covid Tracking Project recorded over 1,000 American coronavirus cases, with the first deaths reported in New York and Washington.

In response, President Trump repeatedly tried to downplay the pandemic, telling Americans to "just stay calm, it will go away."[32] The United

States was thought to have been well prepared for dealing with just such a dangerous health crisis, ranking first worldwide in the 2019 Health Security Index.[33] Under prior presidents from both parties, the United States had developed detailed contingency plans for just such a medical emergency, gathering experts, stockpiling equipment, and developing know-how. But the advance planning was discarded by the Trump White House. The Covid-19 Taskforce issued mixed public health messages. Above all, the federal government failed to take responsibility for coordinating an effective nationwide response to the crisis, leaving states scrambling to compete for scarce protective and testing supplies.[34] By late April, when cases had ratcheted up to almost one million Americans and over 4,000 fatalities, President Trump mused in the White House briefing room that ingesting a disinfectant like bleach could possibly "clean" the body of the virus, triggering a spike in calls to poison control centers. The president repeatedly advised people to take hydroxychloroquine ("What the hell do you have to lose?"), contrary to the US CDC warnings about potentially fatal side effects of cardiac seizures.[35] Over-the-counter sales of the drug surged by 260% compared with typical demand, to reach almost a million prescriptions.[36] The president mocked the use of masks, one of the few simple pragmatic steps which limit contagion, and he held rallies repeatedly without any social distancing. He also continued to assert falsely on numerous occasions that the United States record per capita rates of cases and deaths only looked disastrous compared with equivalent advanced industrial nations, like South Korea and Germany, because the United States did more tests.

Despite the lessons during early spring from Europe and then New York, Republican governors in sunbelt states like Georgia, Arizona, Colorado, Texas, and Florida closed down late and then initially attempted to reopen businesses like bars, gyms, and restaurants in July, without requiring masks to be worn. Disastrous consequences followed in a mid-summer second wave, including surges in local cases, positive test rates, ICU hospitalizations, and eventual deaths, triggering partial policy reversals. The megaphone of Fox News and Twitter amplified the president's falsehoods and promoted conspiratorial beliefs, leading their users to believe that vitamin C was a possible remedy, China created the virus in a lab, and medical experts exaggerated the risks of "the flu."[37] By early July, the United States, with around 4% of the world's population, had 3 million cases and more than 127,000 deaths, according to the Johns Hopkins database, one-quarter of the Covid fatalities around the globe.[38] By mid-summer, after a steady decline of the pandemic, Europe started cautiously reopening. But the United States saw another resurgence as new cases soared. Press briefings by the federal Task Force fell silent, and leading scientific members were forbidden by the White House to go on the media. President Trump golfed and continued to fantasize aloud that the virus would "sort of just disappear." Taking their cues from their leaders, partisanship consistently proved one of the strongest predictors of whether ordinary Americans practiced routine safety measures like wearing masks, physical distancing, and vaccinating themselves and their families.[39] A series of polls by different companies taken from early spring onward reported that, after an initial rally effect, President Trump's approval rating, already historically low among Democrats, dropped steadily among Independents.[40] Even as the effects of the virus spread from Democratic-controlled states in the Northeast to Republican-held states in the sunbelt, President Trump was hospitalized and the White House became a hot spot, and American Covid-19-related deaths topped 218,000, a series of polls reported that Trump supporters' faith in their leader was undimmed. By the November 2020 US elections, over 80% of Republicans approved of President Trump's handling of the coronavirus crisis. By contrast, only 39% of Republicans expressed confidence in Dr. Fauci, America's leading epidemiologist who had advised a half dozen presidents for more than three decades.[41]

When President Biden's administration took over in January 2021, the new team worked with states to implement the vaccine roll-out and US cases and fatalities gradually fell until the White House held a party on July 4, 2021, to celebrate the "return to normal," touting progress under the new administration, only to find that cases resurged in the fall. The proportion of Americans vaccinated proved stubbornly resistant to mask mandates by employers, financial incentives to get inoculated, and even rising deaths. Eight Republican governors in states such as Florida, Oklahoma, and Texas have not only rejected CDC-recommended school mask mandates, but also fought with local school boards to ban this practice. Two years after the initial outbreak, by the close of 2021, despite the US discovering and manufacturing billions of doses, only 60% of Americans were fully vaccinated with two shots, more than 50 million Covid cases had been recorded in the nation, and almost 800,000 US fatalities had occurred.[42] Despite the grim toll left by the pandemic, millions of Americans continued to reject scientific and medical advice to protect themselves through free vaccines. Surveys report that Republicans constituted 60% of the unvaccinated, with partisanship a stronger predictor of this status than social factors such as age, race, or education.[43] The majority of Republicans in these polls believed that the threat from the coronavirus is exaggerated, getting vaccinated is a personal choice, and they were not worried by getting sick from Covid. Trust in misinformation and conspiracy theories disseminated by the former president, by many federal and state Republican officials, and by right-wing online platforms and cable news channels proved deadly. In October 2021, Kaiser Vaccine Monitor polls found that 90% of Republicans surveyed endorsed or were unsure of at least one false statement about Covid-19, such as believing that vaccines damage fertility or contain microchips, that Ivermectin was a safe remedy, or that the number of Covid-19 deaths was inflated by the government.[44] The poll found that misinformation was strongly related to trust in right-wing cable TV such as Fox News, One America News, and Newsmax, as well as social media. The partisan gap in rates of vaccinations and Covid-related deaths continued to widen after vaccines became widely available in May 2021, so that by October 2021, after controlling for age, US counties which had voted heavily for President Trump in the 2020 election had death rates six times higher than those that went for President Biden.[45]

Nor is the United States an isolated case of misplaced faith in political leaders. In the United Kingdom, the first two cases of Covid-19 were detected on January 31, 2020. By mid-March, Prime Minister Boris Johnson continued to dilly-dally in announcing the UK government's response, despite the European Union becoming the new center of the epidemic, and the WHO's pandemic warning. Recommending "business as usual," Johnson continued shaking hands with coronavirus patients, and the Cabinet debated a laissez-faire policy encouraging "herd immunity." Westminster legislated to give the government emergency powers to implement a lockdown and quarantine on March 25. At this stage, YouGov polls suggest that almost three-quarters of respondents believed that the government was handling the crisis well. Yet public confidence subsequently plummeted as the government oversaw multiple failures, including providing inadequate protective gear for medical staff, organizing an ineffective tracing system, and proving incapable of protecting the elderly. By the end of April 2021, the United Kingdom had an estimated excess death count double the average in the previous five years, attributed to the effects of Covid-19, reflecting one of the worst fatality rates both in Europe and worldwide.[46] Compared with non-populists, government leaders such as Trump, Bosonaro, and Johnson initially implemented fewer health measures against the virus during the onset of the crisis in February 2020, and fewer mobility restrictions the following month, delays that proved fatal against an exponentially surging enemy.[47]

Elsewhere around the world, as warnings first emerged after the Wuhan outbreak in December 2019, many other leaders initially failed to grasp the scale of the unfolding disaster and the urgent need for containment. In Russia, for example, President Putin insisted during mid-March 2020 that the pandemic was under control. Two months later, the country had the third highest number of reported cases in the world. By August, Putin announced approval of the first Covid-19 vaccine, despite incomplete clinical trials. Next door in Belarus, President Lukashenko recommended drinking vodka as a cure. In Brazil, for months after the initial outbreak, President Jair Bolsonaro continued to downplay the coronavirus crisis, claiming that it was nothing more than a "little flu" to which Brazilians had a natural immunity, even participating in anti-lockdown protests. The government ordered vast quantities of hydroxychloroquine, an unproven treatment for Covid-19 with potentially dangerous side effects on heart rhythms. By mid-summer 2020, Brazil saw a massive surge in deaths, estimated to be 38% higher than usual, recording one of the highest numbers of confirmed infections of any country worldwide.[48] By early July 2020, President Bolsonaro tested positive. In the fall of 2021 a Brazilian Senate investigation recommended indicting officials, including President Bolsonaro, over negligence in handling of the pandemic, including delays in purchasing vaccines, disseminating dubious treatments, and attacking public health information.[49]

And in Sweden, a country long admired as a world leader by standard indices of good governance and healthcare, the Social Democratic/Green parties in a minority government led by Stefan Löfven initially rejected the lockdown strategy used throughout Europe. Swedish bars, gyms, and restaurants stayed open, following advice from their chief epidemiologist, Anders Tegnell, that this unorthodox strategy would gradually encourage "mitigation," while protecting vulnerable populations in nursing homes. Deaths in Sweden were eight times higher than in Denmark and nineteen times higher than in Norway, even though Sweden is only double each neighbors' size.[50] Estimates suggest that Swedish mortality rates would have halved from March to July 2020 had the country adopted Danish strategies.[51] As fatalities mounted, Tegnell eventually acknowledged that Sweden had been too laissez-faire in its approach, and a special commission was appointed in July 2020 to investigate the government's response to the pandemic. The official report concluded that Sweden acted far too slowly as the pandemic swept the country.[52]

These countries were far from alone. By contrast, however, where comparable data is available, estimates suggest that several other comparable societies had a far lower per capita excess death rate during 2020, even controlling for age group, with their government's management of the Covid-19 crisis widely hailed as successful by both experts and the general public.[53] This includes several high-income economies led by governments on the left and right, such as New Zealand under Prime Minister Jacinda Ardern's leadership, South Korea under President Moon Jae-in, Canada under Prime Minister Pierre Trudeau, Germany under Chancellor Angela Merkle, and Denmark under Prime Minister Mette Frederiksen. The course of the pandemic fluctuated as the pandemic continued to unfold, so that some cases like Germany, which had been relatively successful in limiting cases during the initial outbreak, subsequently experienced later surges, in part due to minimal herd immunity and low vaccine rates.

What has been the role of trust in this process? On the one hand, public confidence in scientific healthcare advice from authorities such as elected leaders, medical professionals, and epidemiologists should benefit individuals and the broader community, by encouraging social norms of voluntary compliance with official guidelines for physical distancing, washing hands, and wearing facemasks, practices proven to reduce contagion.[54] By contrast, lack of faith in scientific recommendations can be deeply problematic; mistrust of public health experts and belief in conspiratorial rumors can encourage behaviors which limit effective protection, for instance deterring the deployment of vaccines against contagious diseases.[55] Today many people don't trust medical advice, limiting the potential effectiveness of any fix for society.[56] Confidence in state authorities (specifically, the police, courts, and the government) is linked with *fewer* Covid-19 related deaths in a society.[57] By contrast, more social trust has been associated with higher death rates, possibly due to behavioral contagion and social interactions. Previous studies of the SARS and H1N1 pandemics reported similar findings.[58] Trust in the authorities can also play a critical role during other related types of national emergencies, including in cases of humanitarian and natural disasters, by providing official warnings and guidance to the general public on everything from the risks of the weather or the location of shelters. Public compliance with accurate technical information and proven scientific advice has the capacity to save lives.

What is less commonly recognized, however, is that during the pandemic crisis, as in many other cases, trust has two faces. Too much credulous trust in the authorities, in media misinformation, and in QAnon conspiracy theories, whether based on affective feelings like partisan identities, cues from group loyalties, media habits, or social networks, can have dangerous consequences, even proving deadly during pandemics where presidents, prime ministers, and ministers are themselves part of the problem, rather than part of the solution. The Covid-19 pandemic vividly illustrates this lesson in cases where incompetent leaders or malign demagogues have used official platforms, social media, and campaign rallies to spread misinformation capable of harming the public. The pandemic is not an isolated example; many other cases illustrate the risks of misplacing trust and confidence in malevolent actors, whether trusting Facebook posts spreading Russian disinformation during US campaigns, the folly of investing in the Ponzi scheme when believing the word of financial swindlers like Bernie Madoff, reliance on police in cases where they crack down violently on peaceful demonstrators, giving credence to Q-Anon claims of a cabal of Democratic Satanic worshippers running global pedophile rings, or following President Trump's repeated recommendations to take hydroxychloroquine for Covid-19. Or even, in the most extreme cases, following Jim Jones–like cults by drinking the grape Kool-Aid.

V. Conclusions and Discussion

The chapter suggests several key findings. First, at the micro level, citizens' subjective perceptions of the quality of governance are usually closely associated with political trust—and this relationship proved similar in both open and closed societies. Expressions of confidence in parliament, government, and the United Nations were consistently associated in the minds of respondents with whether they met the criteria of competency, impartiality, and integrity, serving as proxy evidence suggesting underlying processes of deliberative thinking. The more internally consistent the reasons associated with trust in each of these institutions, the more this can be understood to reflect genuine beliefs. The fact that many people say that they trust agencies which they also regard as more competent and efficient, or honest and impartial, is far from surprising, however, and the analysis of subjective perceptions alone is unable to sort out authentic reasons for trust from post-hoc rationalizations.

For more convincing evidence, the chapter has compared *objective* performance indicators in a wide range of countries to see how far public judgments of the trustworthiness of core political institutions were correlated with independent measures of the quality of government—and compared how far such relationships are conditioned by the type of information society and the predominant societal culture. Indicators based on the expert evaluations were selected from the V-Dem project and related World Bank Institute measures of six dimensions of good governance.[59] The results of the analysis confirm the striking contrasts observed by the type of information environment, as theorized. In the open societies, trust in government was indeed significantly correlated with objective indicators of the quality of government, such as control of corruption, government effectiveness, rule of law, and liberal democracy. The better the actual quality of government in these societies, according to independent estimates, the stronger the perceived trustworthiness of the institutions. But in closed societies, no such significant relationship linking trust with good governance indices can be observed, with political trust proving stronger in more authoritarian states, not more democratic countries.

What explains the observed mismatch between performance and trust—generating either overly cynical or overly credulous judgments? Several alternative explanations can be proposed, including cultural value preferences about what constitutes an effective policy performance or good governance, the role of response bias on sensitive questions carried in social surveys, and the impact of the information environment.

One possible argument suggests that many people living in absolute authoritarian states like China, Thailand, and Vietnam, and citizens in electoral autocracies such as Russia, Ethiopia, and Egypt, may express relatively high political trust in their regime if this reflects their underlying authoritarian values and authentic preference for how their country should be governed. For example, citizens in unstable states like Afghanistan, Haiti, and Myanmar, with recent experience of deadly political violence, deeply disruptive economic crisis, humanitarian disasters, or armed conflict, may prefer being governed by strongman leaders if they believe that this will lead to conditions of greater security, economic development, and social order, while rejecting the instability and turmoil associated with flawed and stalled transitions to electoral democracy. The desire for material growth and prosperity in developing societies may outweigh public preferences for democracy and freedom. This view suggests that the expressions of trust toward leaders observed in authoritarian states and closed societies like China and

Vietnam may therefore reflect authentic public preferences in these political cultures. This raises complex issues when interpreting evidence about
the legitimacy of authoritarian regimes, and the relationship between culture
and institutions, which deserve fuller attention in future research but which
cannot be fully unpacked in this volume.[60] On the other hand, the evidence
in this chapter does demonstrate that the desirable values associated with
political trust among citizens living in repressive states like China and Russia
were very similar to those found in open societies and liberal democracies
like Sweden and Canada; in both contexts, governments were regarded by
citizens as more trustworthy if they were *perceived* as competent, honest, and
impartial. Similarly, subjective trust in government was found to be strengthened among citizens with direct experience of economic prosperity and security. These appear from this evidence to be certain shared values about
what people want from their leaders in many societies around the world, irrespective of the types of regime in power.

Another potential explanation suggests that response bias in surveys
could be at least partially to blame for the non-congruent cases and thus the
apparent errors in judgments. People living in repressive authoritarian states
may express relatively high confidence in the state and political authorities
in response to direct survey questions, despite being ruled in practice by
corrupt and incompetent government leaders, if respondents disguise their
genuine mistrust of those in power, for fear of retribution should any public
criticism come to the attention of the authorities. The list count experiments
documented in Chapter 3 certainly suggest that support for political leaders
is often considerably inflated by using direct questions in repressive societies.
Substantial disparities were apparent between the direct expression of trust
in their leader and the estimated levels of trust using the indirect question
format. Citizens living in the world's most repressive states lacking freedom
of expression, such as in Iran, China, and Myanmar, may therefore report
that they trust the authorities in response to survey questions, as they are
hesitant to express honest criticism of their government in a public record.
Given this evidence, response bias is therefore likely to be *part* of the answer,
with self-censorship generating inauthentic answers in surveys containing
politically sensitive questions about trust in the authorities.

The final argument suggests that subjective beliefs about trustworthiness
are poorly correlated with objective evidence of actual government performance due to the broader information environment. People living in closed
societies like China and Vietnam may express relatively high trust in their

government and leaders because they receive one-sided misinformation, including state propaganda lauding the positive achievements and record of the authorities while silencing criticism. These messages are bolstered by the population's actual experience of remarkably rapid economic growth in these societies. By contrast, media coverage of governments in liberal democracies and open societies provides two-sided information from both supporters and critics of the authorities. In closed societies, the public is likely to regard the government as trustworthy, even where this conflicts with the objective record of corruption and incompetence, after long exposure to state propaganda, disinformation, and misinformation presenting a positive image of the authorities, as conveyed through the main channels of mass and social communications.

Like general macroeconomic performance indices, therefore, judgments of the quality of governance are also consistently mediated by the type of open or closed information society. In other words, citizens everywhere seem to generally trust leaders more if they *believe* them to be competent, honest, and disinterested, as theorized. In information environments with plural media and freedom of expression, citizen's judgments correlate more closely with *objective* measures estimating the actual quality of political institutions, suggesting the public in this context has the capacity to make relatively informed and knowledgeable evaluations of their leaders. In states lacking freedom of speech and the press, citizens also trust governments more if the authorities are *believed* to have similar qualities of competency, integrity, and impartiality. But these subjective perceptions turn out to be relatively poorly correlated with objective indicators of the quality of governance.

Overall, therefore, the results confirm the thesis that in authoritarian states lacking a free press and freedom to dissent, citizens are more likely to be misled when evaluating untrustworthy leaders, or else they are self-censoring in their public expressions of dissent. In this context, citizens are more susceptible to either credulous or cynical errors of judgment, depending upon the legacy of the predominant societal culture. But what are the broader implications of these findings, and what practical steps could be taken to strengthen judgments of trust by principals and trustworthiness by agents? The next chapter goes on to summarize the key conclusions from the study and to consider their broader consequences.

PART III
CONCLUSIONS

7

In Praise of Skepticism

To summarize, the understanding of trust and trustworthiness developed throughout this book seeks to challenge many conventional normative suppositions dominating much social-psychological and cultural research, as well as assumptions pervasive in popular narratives and media commentary. A Greek chorus has decried the supposed erosion of social trust, confidence in government, and international trust, sparking endless discussions of what can be done to restore faith. From the perspective of agents, this is understandable. Trust induces voluntary compliance with the authorities. From the perspective of ordinary citizens, however, trust is Janus-faced and its consequences may be beneficial or harmful. The book has sought to restore a more balanced understanding which acknowledges the risks of compliant trust in a world full of seductive demagogues playing on our insecurities, lying swindlers exploiting our greed, and silver-tongued conspiracy theorists manipulating our darkest fears. Sorting out truth from falsehoods is far from straightforward—especially in media echo chambers where people are constantly bombarded by misinformation reinforcing cultural biases. To consider these issues, Section 1 in this chapter revisits some of the leading scholarship in the extensive literature emphasizing the positive consequences of trust—including the benefits thought to flow from generalized trust among people, confidence in political institutions, and trust among countries. Section II summarizes the alternative theory presented throughout this book, where it is suggested that what matters normatively is not whether trust is rising or falling, but rather the quality of skeptical forms of trustworthy judgments which accurately mirror performance by agents, avoiding undue cynicism and blind credulity. Section III summarizes the main findings from the empirical evidence covering more than one hundred diverse societies and considers their broader implications, including for democratic backsliding and the legitimacy crisis facing liberal democracies.

I. Conventional Views about the Benefits of Trust

Social Trust in Local Communities

Concern about trust has revived in periodic waves. The era of the mid-1990s, following the fall of the Berlin Wall and the end of the Cold War, saw an outpouring of heady optimism about the capacity of social (generalized) trust to facilitate the inexorable spread of liberal democracy, free markets, and global trade. Several influential books, published by leading social theorists during this era, celebrated the value of social and political trust and warned about signs of its decline, catalyzing widespread debate about these issues in policy-making circles well beyond academia.

The most widely cited theory of social capital during this period was developed by Robert Putnam, first in *Making Democracy Work: Civic Traditions in Modern Italy* (1993), and then as the best-selling book *Bowling Alone* (2000), expounding the challenges of social disconnection and civic disengagement thought to be afflicting America.[1] A growing number of sociologists, political scientists, and economists adopted the concept of social capital as a way to understand social relations and cooperation, informing studies in fields as diverse as education, public health, economic growth, and community life.[2] Putnam drew on social surveys of Americans to document a growing disconnect among friends and families, neighborhoods, and local communities in the United States. The loss of civic organizations, local clubs, and voluntary societies, Putnam theorized, eroded the reservoir of interpersonal or "horizontal" trust among friends, neighbors, and fellow citizens, and the bonds of civic engagement which help to overcome collective action problems within local communities.[3] Attenuated social connections and norms of generalized reciprocity have important consequences for individuals and for the quality of life in local areas, he argued, ranging from rates of crime, suicide, and healthcare to education, mortality, and political participation. Putnam acknowledged the dangers of "bonding" forms of social capital, in social bubbles of people "like us." The risks are exemplified most dramatically by Gambetta's study of the deep ties of loyal trust among members of the Sicilian La Cosa Nostra, which profits by selling private protection to its clients, but generates ruthless extortion and violent crime as negative externalities for society as a whole.[4] But theories of social capital generally celebrate the myriad benefits claimed to arise from "bridging" forms of trust, connecting people in diverse groups. "Trustworthiness lubricates social life," Putnam wrote, "Frequent interactions among a diverse set of people tends to produce a norm of generalized reciprocity. Civic engagement and social capital entail mutual obligation and responsibility for action . . . incentives for opportunism and malfeasance are reduced."[5]

These ideas coincided with publication of another equally influential book in 1995, *Trust: The Social Virtues and the Creation of Prosperity*, where Frances Fukuyama argued that informal relationships, the handshake rather than written contract, strengthen opportunities for economic cooperation, investment, and growth, facilitating well-functioning markets even in the societies lacking formal property rights and rule of law.[6] Social norms of trust among people, corporations, and states, he emphasized, lubricate interactions and reduce transaction costs, without the need for legal enforcement through the palaver of third-party lawyers and courts. Such cooperation is vital, Fukuyama argues, particularly for flexible forms of social collaboration and mutually productive market exchanges fueling growth in a globalized world, where the allure of rigid state economic planning had faded. "By contrast, people who do not trust one another will end up cooperating only under a system of formal rules and regulations, which have to be negotiated, agreed to, litigated, and enforced, sometimes by coercive means. This legal apparatus, serving as a substitute for trust, entails what economists call 'transaction costs.' Widespread distrust in a society, in other words, imposes a kind of tax on all forms of economic activity, a tax that high-trust societies do not have to pay."[7] This account celebrated free market exchanges and fitted the zeitgeist of its era, after the deregulation of state ownership of industry and the bonfire of national economic regulation associated with the spread of neoliberalism and liberal democracy from Europe to Latin America and Asia. Like Putnam, however, while emphasizing the positive virtues of trust, Fukuyama also expressed concern about a breakdown of older community ties, like neighborhoods, churches, and workplaces, and a rising tide of distrust and individualism that increasingly atomized societies.

These positive perspectives were reinforced through a wealth of social psychological research. Eric Uslaner presented the case in *The Moral Foundations of Trust* (2020) that "generalized" social trust (meaning, toward people different from ourselves, like strangers) underlies a wide range of positive human interactions, from charitable giving and voluntary work to social tolerance and support for government. Generalized trust is regarded in this account as a moral orientation rooted in an optimistic worldview, inherited psychologically as a stable personality trait from our parents which is reinforced by early childhood socialization.[8] "Cities, regions and countries with more trusting people are likely to have better working democracy, to have more open economies, greater economic growth and less crime and corruption. Both at the individual and societal levels, many things that are normatively desirable seem connected to social trust."[9]

The revival of interest in social trust generated a resurgent literature, one of the growth stocks in the social sciences in the 1990s, as scholars debated the empirical measurement and longitudinal evidence, and the causes of any erosion of social trust, as well as advocating alternative ways to overcome any decline. But the positive value of trust was more rarely questioned—after all, who could be against the Girl Scouts, Parent-Teacher Associations, or charitable organizations—while the dark side of trust was largely glossed over.[10] Along related lines to the Putnam view, for example, William Tov and Ed Diener report that cooperative and trusting relationships carry a wide range of benefits by heightening people's feelings of subjective well-being, happiness, life satisfaction, sociability, and community involvement.[11] Organizational studies rediscovered trust as the basis for effective collaboration, open communications, and successful management.[12] In the private sector as well, small businesses and multinational corporations regard consumer trust in their brands as a strategic asset, scrambling to restore confidence among customers, clients, stakeholders, and employees after a product recall. Research in business studies and computer science identifies effective security measures designed to strengthen confidence in the integrity and authenticity of technology, online networks, and electronic commerce websites.[13] It follows, in the standard view, that the more we feel that other people are trustworthy, honest, and altruistic, the more likely we are to cooperate socially for the common good. During the Covid-19 pandemic, for example, social trust and confidence in scientific and medical authorities have been found to encourage people to follow the recommendations of public health officials, such as maintaining physical distancing, getting vaccinated, and wearing masks to protect friends, colleagues, and neighbors in local communities.[14] By contrast, following the onset of the Covid-19 pandemic, plummeting trust in public health agencies among Republicans, blamed on President Trump's rhetoric and its amplification by conservative media, has stoked rejection of science-based mitigation efforts, generating a deep divide in vaccination rates in Red and Blue states as the virus resurged again.[15]

Political Cynicism about National Governments

Similarly, in the public sphere, public confidence in political institutions and "vertical" trust—linking citizens with political parties, parliaments, and governments—has long been widely celebrated as vital for civic cultures, political engagement, and solving the nation's problems—forming one of the core pillars of stable liberal democracies. Gabriel Almond and Sidney Verba's *Civic Culture* depicted confidence and trust in the legitimacy of the formal rules of the political game, rule of law, and the unwritten democratic norms as providing a common framework about how to resolve societal disagreements, which is especially valuable in polarized societies. Trust facilitates bargaining, collaboration, and consensus, overcoming partisan fragmentation, and bridging deep divisions both within elites, and among elites and the public.[16] If the electoral process is regarded as legitimate, Anderson et al. suggest, both winners *and* losers are more likely to comply with the outcome.[17]

Moreover, trust in the rules of the game in liberal democracies is thought to oil the wheels of legislative bargaining by promising give-and-take compromise over time, rather than incentivizing zero-sum games and lopsided winner-take-all outcomes. For example, Marc Hetherington and Thomas Rudolph argue that in the US Congress, deep mistrust of the other party weakens prospects of bipartisan compromise, exacerbating polarization and legislative gridlock so that Washington no longer works.[18] Hetherington warns that wariness of "big government" undermines the United States' capacity to deliver the sort of social welfare safety-net common in other affluent Western societies, exemplified by universal healthcare.[19] A "rally-round-the-flag" reaction is often observed to boost confidence in the authorities during periods of crisis, such as the 9/11 terrorist attacks.[20] In the Edelman Trust Index, for example, diverse countries such as Canada, Germany, the United Kingdom, India, Mexico, and China saw a record short-term resurgence in public confidence in government during the spring of 2020, following outbreaks of the coronavirus pandemic, before divergent trends in government trust emerged, reflecting varied performance in handling the crisis.[21] Confidence in government and in scientific authorities has been found to help mitigate the COVID-19 crisis by encouraging voluntary public compliance with official guidelines, public health advice, and laws, like those concerning social distancing and wearing masks inside public places.[22]

In the most extreme cases, a dearth of public faith in political institutions among both elites and the general public has been blamed for partisan polarization and disenchantment with the performance of liberal democracy.[23] Steve Levitsky and Daniel Ziblatt caution that the erosion of liberal norms and growing distrust of the core institutions checking executive abuse of power, including parliaments, the courts, and the media, is one of the conditions under which "democracies die," as exemplified by contemporary backsliding in societies such as Turkey, Venezuela, Brazil, Russia, and Hungary.[24] The claim that democracies are most likely to persist when built upon a foundation of popular legitimacy draws upon classic ideas developed by Max Weber,[25] expanded in Almond and Verba's (1963) seminal thesis on the *Civic Culture*. Building upon this tradition, Seymour Martin Lipset argued that legitimacy can be understood as "the capacity of a political system to engender and maintain the belief that existing political institutions are the most appropriate and proper ones for the society."[26] Empirical explorations of this phenomenon investigate whether an agent is thought to exercise authority appropriately, so that officeholders are recognized as having the right to exercise power. Legitimacy is not equivalent to trust; people can obey a regime for many reasons, such as respecting the outcome of an election, the succession process in hereditary monarchies, or expecting material rewards in exchange for support, without necessarily trusting rulers. But a deep reservoir of trust is also commonly associated with legitimacy, especially in democracies. Tom Tyler argues that trust of the authorities makes democratic regimes work more effectively through reinforcing citizens' voluntary obedience with laws and regulations, in good times and bad, without governments resorting to control mechanisms, such as the deployment of coercion and force, or the material incentives associated with clientelism and corruption.[27]

International Trust among Countries

Internationally, as well, trust across national borders among peoples and states, liberal theories suggest, provides the foundation for enduring international alliances, effective treaties, and peaceful collaboration, strengthening confidence in the legitimacy of the Bretton Woods architecture of global governance, a rules-based world order, and universal human rights.[28] Where international agencies are regarded as legitimate, this promotes the belief that they exercise appropriate and rightful authority, making member states more willing to pool resources, comply with multilateral agreements, and cooperate peacefully on a voluntary basis to address common concerns, like achievement of the United Nations' Sustainable Development Goals.[29] By contrast, lack of legitimacy in international organizations like the United Nations and its agencies such as the World Health Organization, or the European Commission and Parliament in the European Union, can undermine the capacity of member states to achieve collective goods beyond their borders, such as through multilateral agreements designed to broker peace, mitigate the effects of deadly epidemics, secure justice against war criminals, protect cybersecurity against hackers, or coordinate policies seeking to mitigate global risks of climate change.[30] Cosmopolitanism, binding together people living within diverse communities and nation-states, reflecting trust across state borders, is thought to function as a building-block for international peace and support for multilateral solutions to global policy problems.[31] By contrast, fears that cooperation with other countries threatens national interests can encourage isolationism, restricting the free flow of peoples, goods, information, and services, escalating interstate hostility and weakening alliances, preventing effective cooperation in response to global disasters such as pandemics with no respect for national borders, and in the worst-case scenarios, even catalyzing deadly wars.[32]

Contemporary waves of anxiety about a "crisis of trust" are cyclical, as exemplified by the turbulent outbreak of protest politics during the mid-1960s and early 1970s, catalyzing angst about political mistrust and government malaise.[33] The mid-1990s saw another revival of concern surrounding popular debate about the loss of social capital and fears of eroding community engagement in the post–World War II generation.[34] And the last decade has seen intensified anxiety following the rise of authoritarian-populism parties and leaders in the early twenty-first century, associated with the retreat from globalization, liberal backsliding in democracy and human rights, and an erosion of the post–World War II Bretton Woods architecture for multilateral cooperation. Populism is a style of rhetoric which questions pluralist beliefs about the rightful location of power and authority, and thus trust in establishment elites, while claiming that the only legitimate source of political and moral authority in a democracy rests with the people.[35] In particular, parties, leaders, and social movements that combine populist rhetoric with authoritarian values are thought to threaten the basic fabric of live-and-let-live social tolerance, the core norms of liberal democracy, and the rules-based world order.[36] The links between authoritarian-populism and democratic backsliding is clearest in countries like Hungary, Poland, Venezuela, India, and the Philippines. But even long-established democracies, like the United States and the United Kingdom, have proved far from immune from these developments.[37] Populism can be regarded as both the consequence, as well as the cause, of growing public discontent with the core institutions of liberal democracy and with multilateral bodies like the European Union.[38]

The contemporary view is reflected in the words of David Brooks, the *New York Times* columnist: "Distrust is a cancer eating away at our society. It magnifies enmity, stifles cooperation and fuels conspiracy thinking. So the question is, how do you rebuild trust?"[39] If trust is believed to be good for individuals, organizations, liberal democracies, and societies, it is almost unquestioningly assumed that additional trust must be better.

II. The Revised Conceptual and Theoretical Framework

Given the strength of these arguments, for all these reasons, the predominant assumption in the wealth of empirical social scientific research from diverse disciplines, as well as popular commentary, has emphasized that trust is intrinsically beneficial, with positive instrumental consequences capable of enhancing a wide range of private and public goods. A minority of contrarian naysayers have sporadically warned about the dark side of trust.[40] During recent decades, several political theorists have also increasingly recognized the ambivalent nature of trust—how it can function as both a blessing and a curse—and have acknowledged its complex relationship with "trustworthiness."[41] Unfortunately, in the extensive body of empirical research in the social sciences, as well as the unreflective Greek chorus seeking "fixes" among commentary disseminated by think tanks and research centers, polling companies, and popular media, a more nuanced understanding of the two faces of trust has been heavily outweighed by the conventional view.[42] The perspective developed in this book suggests that one of the most serious challenges facing contemporary societies is not an erosion of trust per se. Rather, it concerns the accuracy and reliability of public judgments of trustworthy agents to avoid the risks of either excessive cynicism (like anti-vaxxers rejecting sound medical advice and peer-reviewed scientific evidence) or of naïve lemming-like compliance with untrustworthy actors (like

Q-Anon followers believing misinformation about electoral fraud and conspiracy theories of a shadowy cabal of Democratic pedophiles).

It is important to think more critically about why trust is valued—and valuable. The first two chapters of this book unpacked the conceptual and theoretical foundations. Confidence can be understood as the probabilistic belief that certain future outcomes will obtain. The related notion of "trustworthiness" is conceptualized as an informal social contract where principals authorize agents to act on their behalf in the expectation that the agent will fulfill their responsibilities with competency, integrity, and impartiality, despite conditions of risk and uncertainty. The relationship is understood as vesting authority in specific institutions (agencies) or individuals (agents) responsible for acting on behalf of principals such as clients (for lawyers), customers (for companies), or citizens (for elected representatives). Trust is therefore best understood not as an individual attribute or trait, but rather as a delegative principal-agent relationship. In this regard, principals expect agents will probably act on their behalf to achieve certain desired objectives. Decisions that agents are trustworthy typically operate within an environment of imperfect information and vulnerability to uncertainty. If there are cast-iron guarantees that certain outcomes will always prevail, as night follows day, then trust becomes irrelevant.

To expand this notion, we cannot avoid making decisions about whether many types of agents or agencies are trustworthy. These may involve other individuals (should I trust a lawyer's advice, or my doctor's prescription?). Or judgments may involve broader social groups (such as whether communities of color trust the police or whether citizens have faith in politicians' promises). Collective agencies may be involved (such as the public's trust in their government, parliament, and the courts). And they may engage transnational relationships among people (whether Americans trust Mexicans), nation-states (such as confidence in US-Canadian trade agreements), and agencies of global governance (such as faith in findings on global warming by the UN Intergovernmental Panel on Climate Change or Covid-19 guidelines by the World Health Organization). Vertical trust relationships connect principals with less power (such as ordinary voters and party activists) and elites authorized to act on their behalf (such as politicians). Horizontal trust connects principals and agents with more equal powers (such as among Democratic and Republican Senators). The simple antithesis of these notions are mistrust and untrustworthiness, an alternative delegative relationship where principals expect that agents will probably not act on their behalf to achieve certain outcomes, for example, where agents lack competence to deliver, where there are ethical lapses, few effective sanctions for misconduct and lack of integrity, or where the agent's self-interests take priority over the interests of the principal they are designated to serve.

Several alternative theoretical frameworks seeking to explain the drivers of trust have predominated in the literature, including *psychological* theories that trust has innate or biological roots or that it derives from intuitive cognitive heuristics, *sociological* arguments about changes in societal modernization and cultural values, and *communication* studies emphasizing the role of negative news in influencing attitudes. All these factors may indeed potentially shape trust relationships—and thus predict affective feelings of social, political, and international trust. Heuristic shortcuts may help us to decide, in a complex and uncertain world—but they can also provide misleading cues about the *actual* trustworthiness of agents. Errors can arise if decisions do not involve prudent and informed evidence-based reasoned judgments based on the agent's past performance or the effectiveness of institutional safeguards. Affective trust arising for any reason—as an enduring personality trait or an acquired habit, a cognitive shortcut, an ingrained cultural bias, or the product of media misinformation—may certainly encourage compliance toward authorities. But affective trust in untrustworthy agents can also have potentially damaging consequences, failing to safeguard the interests of the principal, as well as ultimately proving dysfunctional for the collective good of society and for democratic governance.

The book's general theory in Chapter 2 argues that skeptical judgments of agents, based on reason rather than emotion, can be expected to arise from three standards which Mayer et al. suggest reflect a deliberative process in decisions of trustworthiness.[43] This includes retrospective evaluations of the agent's *competency* to deliver, so that their performance is thought likely to meet expectations. There is little reason to have faith in an agent if they lack the ability, qualifications, technical know-how, and the resources to meet their responsibilities. An agent's *impartiality* is also likely to be important, so that they are willing to set aside their own self-interest and serve their client. And finally, standards of *integrity* are also expected to matter, so that agents behave in ways which are ethical, honest, and truthful.[44]

Drawing upon these notions, the book suggests that skeptical and informed judgments are evident empirically where trust correlates with performance, as measured by subjective and objective indicators of the reputation of agencies or agents for meeting standards of competence (promises are actually fulfilled), impartiality (the client's interests are served), and integrity (honesty, fairness, and transparency prevail). Skeptical trust judgments also assess the effectiveness of broader institutional accountability mechanisms, mitigating the risks of agency failure to meet these standards. Where principals make positive evaluations of trustworthiness, they decide to enter informal social contracts with agents or agencies, delegating authority to them over certain actions or decisions. Lawyers, for example, are authorized to act on behalf of clients. Parents, children. Physicians, patients. Police, community. Company directors, shareholders. Elected representatives, constituents. Scientific advisers, governments. The United Nations General Assembly, member states. Trust reflects the calculus that decisions will turn out as anticipated where principals are utility maximizers, calculating how best to expand their expected gains and minimize their anticipated losses. Principals will only see their calculations fulfilled, however, if the agent does act on their behalf to achieve the principal's desired objectives. In turn, only agents who develop a reputation for reliably serving clients over successive transactions will gain the benefits of being trusted in the future and thereby achieving their longer-term goals. Companies build brand loyalty and profits. Scientists fund research and build labs. Political leaders return to office. Nation-states secure trade deals. And so on and so forth.

At the heart of this relationship, trustworthy agents are those in any relationship which are authorized to act in ways that principals *expect* are likely to achieve certain goals. Principals calculate probabilistic judgments about the future actions of any agent and their likely consequences if they delegate decisions. Social psychological accounts suggest that these evaluations are often based on affective feelings—such as gut instincts, habitual loyalties, and trusting predispositions. Or they may engage in skeptical and informed assessments, such as by reviewing systematic evidence about past performance and using logical reasoning to calculate the odds for future actions. Getting these judgments right is challenging, especially where high-stakes risks are involved in making decisions in low-information contexts. This is the classic dilemma whenever parents warn their children to be wary of strangers. If principals and agents share the same interests, then this is conducive to having confidence in the agent's motivation—but not necessarily in their capacity to deliver. If interests differ, trust judgments become more challenging. If I need someone to look after my kids, I may need to ask for help from a reliable neighbor. If I am being prosecuted, I am likely to consult the services of an experienced law firm. If I need a heart operation, I must select a skilled surgeon. If robbed or mugged, I must trust the police to protect me. If retired, citizens rely upon government authorities to protect social security programs. If a NATO state is attacked, member states depend upon allies for their mutual defense. If the community is hit by coronavirus, it requires trust for all sides to cooperate on preventive measures such as wearing masks and social distancing. And so on. All of these relationships involve diverse principals and agents, as well as different dimensions, types, and levels of trust.

This argument leads to the core fourfold typology of trust judgments presented in this book. In the framework, trust by principals toward agents can be depicted heuristically as ideal types depicted simply as either high or low. And the performance of agents, when acting on their behalf to achieve certain outcomes, can be perceived as either positive or negative. Skeptical mistrust and skeptical trust are both categories where trust by principals matches agency performance with some degree of reliability, based on relatively well-informed judgments which prove reasonably accurate. Thus, confidence is rewarded by trust for future transactions, while people also learn to mistrust and to be wary of the promises and actions of the world's charlatans, demagogues, and thieves. The other two categories of cynical and credulous evaluations both involve erroneous judgments—but these differ in important ways. They are both problematic estimates because they involve miscalculations which fail to maximize the interests and goals of principals. The most widely recognized risk arises from *cynical* mistrust, where people are doubtful that agents will not serve their interests—for example, where parents are suspicious of proven vaccines for their children—even though the agent is actually benevolent, competent, and ethical. The opposite danger, less widely acknowledged in popular commentary and scientific research but equally important, arises from *credulous* trust, where people hold misplaced confidence in malevolent leaders, such as supporting demagogues and corrupt leaders who fail to deliver upon lofty campaign promises. The key challenge arising from this schematic for empirical research is to establish the distributions of each of these forms of trust relationships, to understand what drives each type, and to identify how best to strengthen more prudent, informed, and accurate judgments.

In a world of imperfect information, differing interests, and risky jeopardies, when principals have to place their interests in someone else's hands, do they have the capacity to make rational, prudent, and informed judgments calculating the trustworthiness of the individual agent or collective agency to act on their behalf? For decades, numerous scholars of public opinion have expressed serious doubts about the ability of ordinary people to make reasoned judgments based on evidence and logic, whether in society, the marketplace, or the public sphere.[45] Estimating the likely future actions of agents is challenging, especially where people lack firsthand familiarity over an extended period of time, such as when judging whether to have confidence in strangers, public officials, or new political parties, still less to predict the trustworthiness of technical agencies of global governance like the European Union or the United Nations. Agents also actively seek to foster confidence, such as companies seeking to strengthen customer loyalty toward brands, parties hoping to mobilize voters, or leaders seeking to bolster their popularity.

Cautious and shrewdly reasoned decisions based on deliberative processes reflect the notion of *skeptical trust*, the concept at the core of this book. The notion of "skepticism" generally implies an open-minded suspension of belief, doubting the truth, agnostic questioning of common dogma, and challenging articles of faith. Skeptics try to set aside emotional biases and group stereotypes, learned habits and ingrained loyalties, ideological dogma, and social identity cues. Skeptical trust is thus conceptualized to reflect forms of prudent reasoning, a running tally judgment estimating whether the future performance of agents will protect the interests of principals. These types of judgments are a tally because they are open to correction and updating through gathering new information, rather than being a fixed psychological orientation evident from birth, or being rooted in learned habits of the heart from a person's formative years growing up in each society, or else affective feelings acquired uncritically from absorbing media messages. Of course, when taken to the extreme, nothing about the future can be known with absolute certainly, and even perceptions from one's own senses can be doubted. But for more pragmatic skeptics, estimates of trustworthiness reflect different degrees of certainty.

Consideration in Skeptical Judgments of Trustworthiness

The general theory suggests that the reasoning behind calculations of an agent's trustworthiness are likely to be determined by two primary considerations: (i) information about the *reputation* of the particular agent or agency, based on their past performance and competencies, providing a rough-and-ready guide to their future conduct, and, at more diffuse level, (ii) awareness about the effectiveness of *structural guardrails*—institutional arrangements and formal rules and informal procedures designed to reinforce trustworthy behavior and limit the risks of authorizing unreliable agents who generally fail to serve the interests of their clients.

Reputation

In terms of reputation, skeptical trust is best understood as reflecting a cumulative judgment of the performance of particular agents or agencies, which is constantly updated in a running tally by new information and reinforced through repeated positive or negative experiences. Cumulative interactions provide more information about the agent's competencies and behavior which thicken habitual feelings of trust or mistrust. Has a bank established a solid reputation of safely protecting customers over many years? Does a familiar brand of goods usually work well for consumers? Do Amazon online consumer reviews say that specific products work? Do vaccinations prevent common childhood illnesses? Do the police protect the public in ethnic minority communities? Has the governing party generally delivered on most of its manifesto promises? Have corporate executives been free of scandal and graft? Has a state generally honored their commitments in international treaties? Have all sides in a civil war respected a cease-fire agreement? All these types of retrospective cues, where we trust the information source, can be expected to frame the cumulative evidence and the running tally available for us to judge the past performance of agents, reducing the risks of uncertainty associated with predicting their future actions. The reputation of agents is therefore normally expected to change incrementally, based on lagged judgments derived from accumulated past experiences and their previous record, but also to respond periodically to new information, rather than being either a permanent personality trait, or else largely stable over an adult's lifetime, as culturally derived. In this regard, reputational trust can be seen as like notions of party identification functioning as a running tally of retrospective evaluations of party promises and performance.[46]

Guardrails

By focusing upon the agent's record of past actions as a guide to their future performance, reputational judgments of trustworthiness reflect the "output" side of any trust relationships. Some decisions about whether individual and collective agents are trustworthy are relatively simple and clear-cut, based on long personal experience extended over many years or even decades—trusting the medical treatment recommended by a family doctor, the financial advice of a long-standing business partner, or the quality of an established drug. But other judgments are often far from straightforward. In a world of imperfect information and uncertain consequences, these sorts of complex calculations about whether to trust strangers are more likely to prove erroneous. Under these sorts of constraints, with risky decisions, do individuals have to decide whether to trust someone else based on gut instincts, ingrained loyalties, and irrational emotions, more or less like tossing a coin or picking from a random page of the Yellow Pages? Not necessarily. In the absence of direct personal experience, and reliable sources of reputational information about past performance, confidence in agents may be strengthened by awareness of effective guardrails—reflecting informal social norms, formal institutions, and legal rules regulating the future conduct of agents and sanctioning any misconduct. Will physicians get struck off the medical register if found guilty of breaking professional ethics? Will police officers be successfully disbarred and prosecuted in cases of the unjustifiable use of force? Will politicians and parties be thrown out of office if failing to honor their manifesto pledges? Will civil servants and policy advisors be sacked if proving corrupt and incompetent? Will states be isolated and subject to sanctions by the international community if violating basic human rights, such as instigating armed conflict?

Structural guardrails, formal procedures, legal institutions, and informal social norms represent the "input" side of any trust relationship. These function as fail-safe mechanisms which can serve to guide our decision-making calculus and ensure accountability for trustworthy behavior in the future, even if individual agents have proved undependable in the past. Others have referred to these as "enforceable trust," where the legal system will assure that the agent acts in a desired manner.[47] Even if I mistrust the motivation of a used car salesperson, I may still rely upon the legal warranty. Even if the local police force has a reputation for racially motivated brutality, oversight bodies ensure that citizens' complaints are handled fairly and transparently. Even if I doubt the past veracity of a particular political leader, I may still have faith in constitutional checks and balances designed to constrain their future conduct. Even though a state has a poor human rights record, I may still believe that the UN Security Council will enforce their subsequent compliance with international law. Structural guardrails are therefore also likely to prove important considerations in trust calculations. At the same time, where doubts about the reputation of specific agents extend more broadly to a lack of faith and confidence in the guardians and protective mechanisms, at a more diffuse level, for example if officials are corrupt, police racially biased, and the media unreliable, then these constraints may also fail.

This argument can be applied to any dimension of trust, although it draws heavily upon classical liberal theories of government which have long emphasized that vigilant civil societies and power-sharing constitutions, incorporating multiple checks and balances, function to strengthen oversight and mutual accountability, protecting citizens against undesirable conduct, the abuse of office, and unethical acts. Formal structures are also open to legal and administrative reform. However, even the best-designed constitutional protections can often prove ineffective in practice, of course, especially where founded upon unwritten conventions and tacit social norms of behavior. Heated debate continues about the most suitable mechanisms. But where principals have confidence in the processes and the mechanisms which have prevented deviant behaviors in the past, this can serve as a cognitive or heuristic shortcut used to estimate the future trustworthiness of any particular agent. For these reasons, a variety of insurance mechanisms are expected to reduce uncertainty and strengthen confidence in judgments of trustworthiness, exemplified by those which strengthen processes of accreditation, transparency, impartiality, integrity, accountability, and enforcement, providing alternative fail-safe layers of procedural protections.

III. Empirical Findings

Chapter 3 set out the research design and evidence. The first step in the research design concerns establishing the capacities of the *principal*, notably how far, and under what conditions, ordinary people have the necessary cognitive skills, information, and knowledge to make sound and knowledgeable trust judgments about the future likely actions of agents. Trust judgments involve challenging calculations given inherent risks, information asymmetries, and uncertainties in any such relationship. It is a complex matter to make optimal decisions about trustworthiness. Accurate judgments are likely to be based upon sifting alternative sources of information, evaluations of the track records of agents, and conscious calculations of risks and returns.

But far from following these steps, people may rely instead more upon affective feelings, embedded in individual personality traits and gut emotions, socially acquired cultural values, and/or media messages. Establishing trust judgments requires understanding the goals and values which principals seek to advance and their perceptions of agency trustworthiness, typically such as trust in courts, elected leaders, and the news media.

Building upon this foundation, the second step in the research design involves monitoring how far public trust correlates with *agency performance.* Often actors face multiple constraints in seeking to meet the expectations of their clients, whether arising from limited competences and resources, imperfect information, or conflicting demands. For example, it is challenging for even the best-intentioned scientists with most informed epidemiological models to predict the rate of Covid fatalities, and the effects of mitigating strategies, even without government leaders failing to act in timely fashion on expert advice. Managing the economic recovery after the pandemic subsides is also a complex issue, balancing the need to get people back to work while minimizing risks of further outbreaks. The book therefore sought to determine how far, and under what conditions, agents are generally perceived to have the capacity, impartiality, and integrity to act in a manner which serves the interests of the principal and meets their goals. The study does so by comparing public judgments of political trustworthiness against subjective perceptions of government performance, as well as varied objective performance indicators, monitoring both the policy and the procedural performance of governments.

Finally, it is also important to understand the wider societal and institutional contexts which condition trust relationships. This includes the broader information environment, conditioning knowledge about the actions of agents. Most research on trust has examined affluent Western societies and long-established democracies, especially in the United States and Europe, not least for the pragmatic reason that these societies contain a wealth of longitudinal and cross-national survey data. Comparative analysis using these resources has focused on determining levels of public trust in different agencies, such as political parties, the courts, and parliament, as well as monitoring trends over time across nations. In postindustrial societies and established liberal democracies, it has usually been commonly assumed, at least implicitly, that well-functioning governments will generally work to serve the public interest and, if not, that those in executive office will probably face an electoral penalty and lose office, or else will be constrained by other constitutional checks and balances, like the courts and legislature. In open societies, well-educated citizens have access to varied sources of information from independent media channels, facilitating informed public judgments of trustworthiness.

But these conditions may prove ineffective, and they do not apply in many parts of the world. Broadening the comparative framework worldwide allows us to compare skeptical trust across open societies and long-established democracies, updating and extending the standard time-series analysis, but also comparing varied closed societies, under authoritarian regimes, which restrict the free press and public dissent. The pooled European Values Survey/ World Values Survey (EVS/WVS) data set includes open liberal democracies like Sweden and Britain, but also a diverse range of closed societies governed by autocracies, some suffering from endemic corruption or deep-rooted conflict, in places where endemic malpractices undermine political accountability, and where press freedom and rule of law are weak or nonexistent. In closed societies, with limited information, judgments fall back on preexisting cultural biases, so that the public are expected to prove far more trusting or more critical of the authorities than performance suggests is actually warranted. This is a problem; optimal levels of trust for principals involve a careful balance which avoids both trusting agents too *little* (which limits delegation and weakens the benefits of cooperation) and too *much* (which leaves people vulnerable to exploitation).[48]

Chapter 4 compared the main cross-national patterns and the trends over successive decades. In the standard story, based largely on evidence gathered in the context of open societies and liberal democracies, trust is usually uncritically regarded as an intrinsic "good," and conversely, distrust as "bad." It follows that any significant decline of trust is conventionally lamented by observers as signaling a threat to social order and tolerance within local communities, reflecting a legitimacy "crisis" for the governing regime and its actors, heightening risks of global breakdown in the rules-based world order. The problem is that trust has two faces and both overly cynical *and* unduly compliant biases commonly skew evaluations of how well agents perform. From the perspective of the agent, public trust is a valuable commodity, irrespective of whether it is based on informed or erroneous grounds, because it encourages compliance. For the principal, only accurate judgments of trustworthiness are valuable, and mistaken judgments are risky—with potentially life-threatening consequences, like the false fears and common myths about being vaccinated. The accuracy of the public's judgments of agency trustworthiness seems to be conditioned by individual cognitive skills (facilitating information processing), the broader information environment in open and closed societies (providing few or many alternative viewpoints), and the legacy of prior cultural values (reflecting past beliefs about trustworthiness which may not be updated to reflect contemporary performance).

For all the reasons already discussed, excessive cynicism toward trustworthy agents serving the public good may indeed prove detrimental to societal relationships, political legitimacy, and international cooperation. *If* any steep erosion of trust in the national government has indeed metastasized in recent decades, as numerous commentators repeatedly suggest, this could point toward deeper civic ills. The root causes could potentially be attributed to an erosion in agency performance, such as the "government overload" thesis, or the notion that the autonomy and power of democratic institutions within the national state are increasingly constrained by the forces of globalization.[49] Or it could be explained by rising public expectations, for example, where irresponsible populists compete for votes by promising magical unicorns which fail to materialize.[50] Similarly, any major erosion of generalized social trust in strangers and people of other faiths and countries may heighten intolerance of refugees and asylum seekers, as well as weakening a sense of community solidarity to cope with collective risks. And mistrust of foreign allies can unravel alliances and the bonds of international cooperation at the heart of the rules-based world order.

Unfortunately for all these arguments, Chapter 4 demonstrated that far from a steady long-term erosion of many dimensions of trust over successive decades, as is often claimed in popular commentary, in fact the trends and cross-national patterns registered in successive waves of in the EVS/WVS survey evidence are far more complex. Trajectories suggest either noise in measurement (trendless fluctuations), or else short-term changes associated with major events, like the impact of economic downturns on confidence in markets and then their subsequent recovery, or the role of other country specific or global shocks—the fall of the Soviet Union, the aftermath of 9/11, the eurozone financial crisis, the sudden flood of Syrian refugees and Libyan migrants into the European Union, the outbreak and spread of the Covid-19 pandemic, and so on. Some contrasts observed among countries are relatively stable and predictable, suggesting the impact of legacy cultural values on trust in world regions, but others prove more variable even among relatively similar societies.

Despite widespread concern about steadily declining social (generalized) trust, in fact variable trajectories are observable across more than fifty societies where longitudinal data are available. In Northern Europe and Scandinavia, countries are not only relatively high in absolute levels of social trust—net growth in trust has occurred during the last four decades, contrary to widespread expectations. In many other nations under comparison, observed absolute levels of social trust usually display either a pattern of trendless fluctuations around the mean, or else fairly stable but relatively low levels of social trust. Public confidence in accuracy, truth, and credibility in the mainstream news media and online digital media platforms are also widely believed to be eroding in many parts of the world. The picture from the EVS/WVS data suggests that generalizations are complex, and declining trust in the media observed in the United States proves somewhat atypical. Thus, trust in the media is relatively low in several Anglo-American cases such as Australia, the United Kingdom, and New Zealand, but higher in Asian societies such as South Korea, China, and Japan. Other agencies in civil society display equally complex trends. Parallel trajectories can be observed in confidence in government, confirming very similar patterns. Thus, public confidence in government rises in diverse places like Indonesia, New Zealand, Russia, Turkey, and South Korea, while steadily falling in Ukraine, Chile, Brazil, and the Czech Republic. Moreover, trust in government is remarkably high in China and Bangladesh, while being relatively low in Italy, the United States, and the United Kingdom. What this diversity suggests is that oversimple generalizations based on cherry-picking a few cases to bolster claims of an inexorable fall in public trust should be avoided. The broader comparison reveals a far more complex picture of changes in trust worldwide.

To start to explain these cross-national contrasts, Chapter 5 examined how far experience of the pocketbook economy colored trust in government. Theories of pocketbook voting suggest that citizens may have a hard time in assessing how well parties and leaders are responsible for the state of the national macroeconomy, like understanding technical indicators monitoring quarterly trends in rates of unemployment or inflation. But they can judge the competency of government authorities more directly by whether they feel better-off or worse-off in their own and their family's lives. Do they have secure, well-paid careers? Does the family have rainy-day savings for unexpected emergencies—or do they have to try to get a bank loan? Do they feel that their family's lifestyle is more comfortable and secure than their parents at the same stage of life? Or do they and their family experience real poverty, such as occasionally going without adequate food or lacking a secure shelter at night? Many factors may be blamed for financial insecurity—the loss of the main breadwinner, shuttered factories in a global economic downturn, the effects of Covid lockdowns on the hospitality industry, and so on. In general, however, just as the pocketbook economy is expected to influence voting decisions, the better-off middle-class sectors of society are more likely to trust how well the government works compared with those living in poorer households.

Direct experience of living in more prosperous and financially secure households was confirmed to be consistently linked to greater trust in government, and the results were largely similar irrespective of the type of open or closed societies. Yet issues of reciprocity make this relationship difficult to interpret. To go further, public trust was compared with objective evidence of the performance of government in strengthening the macroeconomy and improving human development on issues which all people care about, like living longer, having better healthcare, and improved schools. Chapter 5 uses bivariate correlations to compare political trust with a range of ten standard developmental objective indicators of policy outcomes, derived from official statistics, like national rates of growth, longevity, and crime. In open societies, trust in government was significantly correlated, and in the expected direction, with seven out of ten indicators. Several of the bivariate relationships were also strong—such as those linking trust with economic development, secondary school attainment, and rates of homicide. In short, government which displayed a competent performance. In closed societies, however, where citizens receive a steady diet of positive news about the authorities and critical voices are silenced, there is usually no relationship between levels of public trust in government with policy performance indicators. The information environment, in the broadest sense, conditions whether public judgments of government trustworthiness accurately reflect economic performance. Once controlling for the type of information environment, the mediating effects of education (as a proxy for cognitive and knowledge) proved fairly modest.

But, of course, many economic problems can be blamed on factors outside the government's control—such as claiming that the cost of gas at the pumps is the fault of spikes in OPEC oil prices, supply-chain delivery problems fuel inflation for imported goods from China, and the pandemic has encouraged the Great Resignation and labor shortages. These claims are not without merit in a global economy. But the quality of democratic governance is more directly the responsibility of state authorities, especially the party or parties holding the reins of power. If there are major scandals of money-in-politics, corrupt contracts, or public-sector malfeasance which involve elected politicians, ministers, or civil servants, or if there are fraudulent or unfair elections, misconduct by the security forces, or failures of rule of law, then this is clearly a matter where the government has to take prime responsibility.

Accordingly, Chapter 6 first examined the links at the micro level connecting political trust with subjective evaluations of the quality of governance, including satisfaction with the political system and with how democracy works in each society, as well as perceptions of corruption in the public sector. The results of the multivariate analysis confirmed the strong and significant correlations in open societies; not surprisingly, perhaps, satisfaction with the political system and democracy were associated with greater trust, while perceptions of corruption were linked with greater mistrust of government. Most of the relationships were observed to be remarkably similar in closed societies, suggesting that most ordinary citizens are in broad agreement about the criteria they associate with government trustworthiness, irrespective of whether they live in Sweden and Switzerland or Myanmar and China. The more detailed multivariate analysis of public opinion in the ten selected cases of closed societies and authoritarian states confirmed that competency, impartiality, and integrity were important considerations associated with trust in parliament, government, and the United Nations.

The more rigorous test of how far political trust relates to the quality of governance requires us to turn from subjective to objective macro-level indicators, such as independent estimates of the control of corruption, government effectiveness, and rule of law in each country, as well as the state of liberal democracy. The bivariate correlations observed in Chapter 6 suggest that in open societies, these measures of the quality of governance were strongly and significantly associated with public trust in open societies—but not in closed societies lacking freedom of expression and alternative sources of information. Response bias is another factor, explored through list experiments in Chapter 3, which may plausibly limit how far survey respondents are willing to express criticism of the authorities in the world's most repressive states. In this context, practices of self-censorship in survey interviews are likely to produce inflated estimates of political trust.[51] In addition, however, where citizens lack an information environment with viewpoint diversity, including a robust and vibrant free press and transparent and accountable governments, they have real difficulties in making accurate assessments of the way that the regime works. Ordinary people cannot make informed judgments about the quality of governance in their own country in authoritarian states lacking civil liberties and political rights, where powerful state security agencies prevent media outlets, journalists, and digital platforms from publishing unfavorable coverage, and where civil society activists such as human rights monitors, investigative journalists, international reporters, newspaper commentators, local bloggers, and social media platforms are unable to disseminate public criticism of the authorities. Challenges also exist to a lesser degree in open societies where party politics are deeply polarized, where coverage of public affairs by partisan news media and social media networks reflects these divisions, and where citizens live in echo chambers reinforcing their prior values and beliefs, but not providing viewpoint diversity. In these media environments, however, in open society, citizens are still more likely to encounter sources of alternative information, even accidentally, compared with repressive regimes which tightly control the airwaves and independent press.

IV. Implications for Liberal Democracy

What are the broader normative implications arising from this study? The two faces of trust are important during any era, but are even more valuable today in a "post-truth" age of misinformation, replete with a jungle of hackers and trolls, kompromat and *dezinformatsiya*, where reason is under attack by forces propagating "alternative facts," dark conspiracy theories, and, yes, fake news.[52] Excessive deferential loyalty and blind faith accepting the rhetoric of populist-authoritarian leaders, accepting misinformation at face value without verification, can foster gullible trust, encourage compliant followers, advance unqualified acolytes, and thereby undermine accountable and responsible governance. As captured in the words of President Trump: "The polls, they say I have the most loyal people. Did you ever see that? I could stand in the middle of Fifth Avenue and shoot somebody, and I wouldn't lose any voters. It's like incredible."[53] Similarly, when he touted hydroxychloroquine as a cure for coronavirus, "one of the biggest game changers in the history of medicine," telling Americans "we ought to give it a try," this is not sufficient grounds to follow his advice.[54] There are sound reasons to be cautious about trusting mendacious demagogues, especially in societies where constitutional and legal protections prove ineffective constraints against the aggressive abuse of executive power, where doubts about the impartiality of the news media curtail the capacity of journalistic watchdogs to counter political spin, where bold-faced lies fuel the triumph of dogma over science, and where gut feelings ("trust me") trump facts. But the risks are not simply confined to this context; as the Covid death toll illustrates, citizens should question authorities, rather than complying automatically with official advice, even in high-trust, well-functioning liberal democracies like Sweden.

But equally it should be recognized from a global context that an overabundance of either cynical mistrust or compliant trust can prove problematic, not least by failing to protect the interests of principals, as well as the collective interests of society and democracy. The problem of "blind" confidence is particularly important today, including cult-like faith in leaders irrespective of their actions, whether arising from gut instinct, personality traits, cultural values, or affective heuristic shortcuts, rather than prudent and informed judgments of future expectations based on their past performance. The early twenty-first century is an age of rising authoritarian-populism, when many commentators warn that the Enlightenment notion of objective truth has come under frontal attack, scientific facts are doubted, mendacious demagogues have come to power, legacy journalistic watchdogs are no longer regarded as impartial, liberal democracy is under growing stress, and repressive forces are reviving.[55]

Figure 7.1 summarizes the curvilinear relationship linking public trust in government (from the EVS/WVS 7) with freedom of expression (from V-Dem 11). This vividly summarizes the core relationships at the heart of the book and suggests that trust relationships toward government can be observed to fall into three broad categories.

The strongest expression of political trust toward state authorities is observed in many of the world's closed information societies, serving to legitimize the rule of strongman leaders and dampen dissent in authoritarian regimes. The analysis of the results of the list experiments described in Chapter 3 suggests that the public in diverse repressive states are reluctant to express overt criticism of their leaders, thereby producing inflated estimates, even when participating in anonymous academic surveys, possibly for fear of the consequences. State authorities in traditional dictatorships strictly control the main domestic channels of political news, overriding human rights

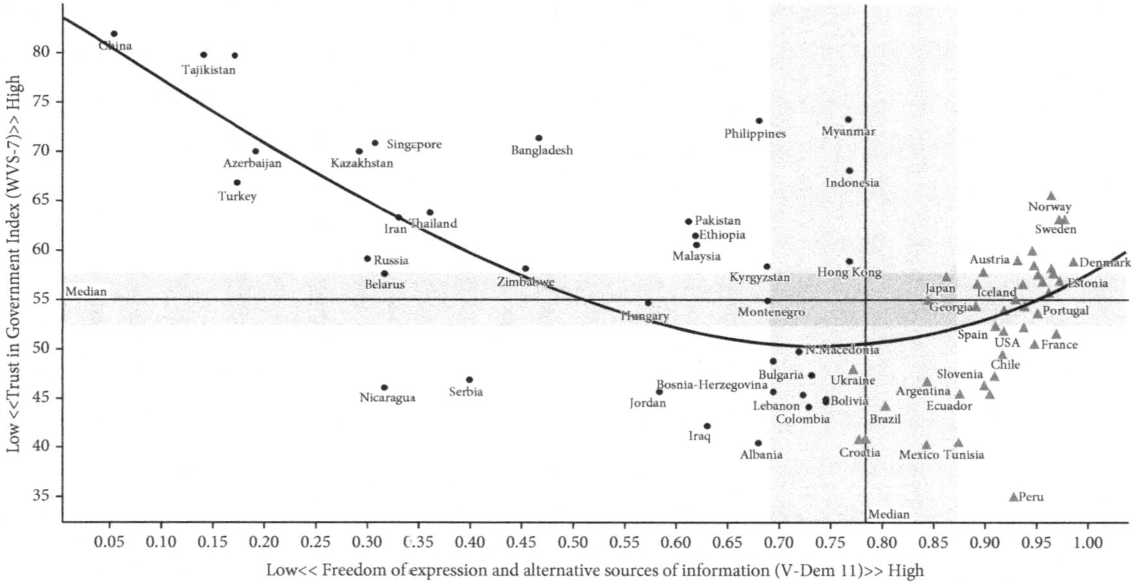

Figure 7.1. Freedom of information and trust in government.

Notes: The vertical axis is the EVS/WVS Trust in Government standardized scale (including government, parliament, parties, and the civil service). The horizontal axis shows the Freedom of Expression and alternative sources of information index as derived from the Varieties of Democracy project (V-Dem-11). Open societies (Gray) and closed societies (Black) are also categorized by the V-Dem Freedom of Expression Index (dichotomized).

Source: European Values Survey/World Values Survey Wave 7 in 80 societies (2017–2021); https://www.v-dem.net/en/.

by harshly repressing critics, opposition forces, and political dissidents. These techniques are deployed more subtly in electoral authoritarian regimes, but they are still evident through media manipulation and the dissemination of disinformation.[56] Closed information societies, especially in developing countries where the population has limited education, seek to foster attitudes of credulous political trust and voluntary compliance toward authorities among ordinary citizens.

By contrast, levels of trust in political leaders and institutions in liberal democracies and affluent postindustrial societies like Norway, Sweden, Switzerland, and New Zealand are relatively high in global comparison—although still lower than in the world's autocracies. This is a striking puzzle since these democracies repeatedly and consistently rank as some of the best in the world according to the standard objective indicators of the quality of government, whether measured by political rights and civil liberties, lack of corruption, effective and accountable governance, rule of law and access to justice, economic equality and the generous provision of universal welfare services, and inclusive processes of political representation and participation.[57] Citizens in liberal democratic societies with freedom of expression and plural media are exposed to two-sided information about their leaders and governments, including both supporters and critics. Partisan and media echo chambers exist even in open societies, a process exacerbated through the diversity of choices and processes of self-selection in the world of digital media. But freedom of expression generally means that citizens are more likely to encounter viewpoints and information dissonant from their own. In open societies, well-educated citizens have greater cognitive skills and opportunities to make skeptical assessments of the performance of those exercising power.

The distribution of states in Figure 7.1 follows a curvilinear trajectory. In the global comparison, the states located in the middle of the graph display a dispersed pattern but also some of the deepest political mistrust—as exemplified by the Latin American cases of Bolivia, Mexico, Brazil, as well as the post-Communist states of Ukraine and Croatia. During the initial transitions from authoritarian regimes, governments lost control of the flow of information and largely abandoned the techniques of overt state political propaganda and censorship of the airwaves. The liberalization of the mass media in newer democracies was accompanied by the explosion of access to digital media, more effective legal and constitutional rights protecting independent journalism and access to official information, and a plural media environment reflecting multiple political viewpoints.[58] Independent journalists and the news media have faced growing challenges in the last decade from democratic backsliding, including threats or use of violence attacking journalists.[59] Nevertheless, the Freedom of Expression index by V-Dem assesses contemporary levels of press freedom more favorably in these countries than in the world's most repressive states like China, Iran, and Russia. By contrast to long-established liberal democracies and affluent postindustrial democracies, however, in these countries the state's capacity to deliver basic public services like equitable growth, healthcare, housing, security, and jobs continues to be weakened by systemic corruption and crime, threats to political stability and national security, and ineffective institutions. Even where they have been more successful, governments in Latin American, Asia, and post-Communist Europe also inherit a deep-rooted historical culture of cynical political mistrust among their citizens which is difficult to overcome.

The notion that trust has two sides, not one, is far from novel. A long litany of classical liberal theorists from Hobbes and Locke to Bentham and John Stuart Mill have cautioned that trust has a dark side. After all, the British Victorian liberal prime minister, William Ewart Gladstone, once famously declared, "Liberalism is trust of the people tempered by prudence." Unwarranted, uninformed, or erroneous faith in incompetent, dishonest, or self-interested grifters, confidence tricksters, and swindlers, in any context, is likely to prove foolhardy and gullible, with harmful consequences for individuals and society. Recognition of the dark side of trust has gained growing attention among philosophers and theorists—but it has not yet become the mainstream interpretation. The extensive body of empirical research in sociology, social psychology, cultural studies, comparative politics, political behavior, and public opinion almost uniformly laments any erosion of trust.[60] Nor is it clear what level of skepticism is optimal, avoiding the extremes of foolish gullibility and corrosive cynicism, a situation like Goldilocks choosing among bowls of porridge.[61] Nor has it been established what individual and institutional characteristics determine healthy skepticism, still less how this can be strengthened to bolster informed opinions rather than blind faith.

Given complex information, considerable uncertainties, and limited attention spans, it is important to recognize that the process by which principals decide to trust agents may potentially draw upon multiple fast and frugal shortcuts. A substantial body of experimental research in behavioral economics, decision sciences, and cognitive psychology emphasizes that many heuristics are common in how even limited information is applied to make judgments.[62] Shortcuts in our thinking process compensate for modest attention, lack of information, and relatively shallow analysis. Thus, for example, prior partisan loyalties are likely to color voters' evaluations of the government's record and confidence in electoral integrity. Stereotypes will probably encourage trust in strangers with shared social identities and ideological values. Negative news about overseas terrorism, poverty, and conflict are likely to feed fear and mistrust of foreigners. But "fast" decisions, based purely on faith, hunch, gut feeling, or intuition, such as these, are more likely to be biased, erroneous, or fallible guides to making trust judgments. Governing parties promote their record in office, boasting about policy success but hiding failures. Stereotypes inject prejudice into our assessments of dissimilar strangers. Negative news headlines may distort our understanding of the world. And so on. Thus, skepticism in trust judgments helps principals to make more reliable predictions and reasonably informed calculations about the likely future behavior of agents.

Therefore, the optimal position, this book concludes, lies in *skepticism*, where faith and loyalty are open to modification in the light of new information. Of course, making accurate assessments which forecast the trustworthiness of another person, institution, or state is far from straightforward, and there are multiple ways to get this wrong. In this regard, we can learn from Tetlock's argument which defines a prudent and rational judgment as one rooted in *empirics* (that is, there is a match between the judgment and the evidence) and also one embedded in logic (or internally consistent thinking).[63] In any polity, ordinary citizens should ideally be skeptical and vigilant toward the authorities, making discriminating judgments about the future actions of political leaders based on weighing and sifting alternative sources of reliable evidence about their past reputation for competence, impartiality, and integrity, as well as evaluating the effectiveness of the insurance guardrails protecting against the abuse of power. This process helps to develop rational judgments which allow principals to trust those agents most likely to serve their interests, while avoiding the risks associated with placing confidence in those with a poor record for delivering upon their promises. The concept of skeptical citizens reflects the Russian saying, repeated by Ronald Reagan: trust but verify (Доверяй, но проверяй).

The normative framework adopted by this book therefore questions the predominant assumptions coloring conventional views. In particular, most of the empirical "crisis" literature implicitly or explicitly laments any supposed erosion of trust, which is thought to threaten many public goods, from societal cooperation to general feelings of well-being, economic development, democratic stability, peaceful cooperation across borders, and the legitimacy in international organizations. These views are widely held beyond academe; thus, many Western political leaders have echoed the idea of a pervasive crisis in representative democracy caused by declining public confidence and have pledged to restore trust in politics.[64] A dearth of trust can indeed be deplored, for these reasons. But this does not imply that all forms of trust should be valued equally—including those emotional reactions arising from innate psychological predispositions, learned cultural values in each society, or one-sided sources of media information. Indeed, an erosion of affective trust, compliant acceptance, and habitual loyalties over time can be regarded as a positive development, not a negative trend, especially when accompanied by critical thinking. The optimal balance of skeptical trust and mistrust among critical citizens serves to maximize public scrutiny and oversight of institutions and actors, while also encouraging a healthy questioning of authorities, rather than taking their word at face value. My previous work discussed the notion of "critical citizens," such as those who typically express faith in democratic principles but remain dissatisfied with how democracy works in practice.[65] This phenomenon has been widely recognized but still under-theorized in the empirical literature. Accordingly, this book has sought to build on the earlier work and advance our understanding of this orientation to a deeper level. Skeptics are those who avoid the Scylla of Type I errors (leading to excessive cynicism) and the Charybdis of Type II errors (leading to excessive gullibility).[66] The dividing line where healthy skepticism slides into outright cynicism, however, and where and why trust in agents is well-deserved or mistaken, remains a matter for debate.

What are the broader lessons for civic engagement, misinformation, and democratic backsliding? In political behavior, the conventional response decrying the supposed loss of trust in Western democracies is deeply permeated by liberal cosmopolitan values. Theories of social capital suggest that trust helps friends and neighbors overcome the tragedy of the commons, cooperating to achieve beneficial goals for local communities, like Parent-Teacher Associations raising funds for school sports or church members volunteering at foodbanks. Similarly, liberal values commonly underpin notions of political trust. It is often assumed that citizens should have confidence in democratic governments which generally serve the public interest, and, if not, the actions of elected leaders will be constrained by formal institutional checks and by informal social norms, so that officeholders remain periodically accountable to the electorate. If this is indeed the case, then trust in government can potentially generate many beneficial consequences for individuals and societies, as many scholars claim, such as by strengthening the willingness of all citizens to participate in civic affairs, to obey the law voluntarily, and to believe that elected officials exercise legitimate authority.[67] But what about many cases where many citizens believe the word of corrupt demagogues or assist illiberal strongman seeking to dismantle checks on executive powers? Liberal theories of international affairs, as well, emphasize mutual benefits accruing from cosmopolitan cooperation among states to resolve disputes, promote trade, and spread human rights. But, of course, such goals can also be perverted by collaboration across borders among drug cartels, terrorist groups, and authoritarian states.

The skewed and incomplete understanding of the problem fails to acknowledge that both overly cynical *and* unduly compliant biases commonly color evaluations of how well agents perform. The conventional narrative, arising in the context of open societies and liberal democracies, regards a culture of trust as an intrinsic "good," and conversely, distrust as "bad." It follows that any significant decline of trust has conventionally been lamented as signaling a threat to social order and tolerance within local communities, reflecting a legitimacy "crisis" for the governing regime and its actors, while heightening risks of global breakdown in the rules-based world order. For all the reasons already discussed, excessive cynicism toward trustworthy agents serving the public good may indeed be detrimental to societal relationships, political legitimacy, and international cooperation. *If* any steep erosion of trust in the national government has indeed metastasized in recent decades, as numerous observers suggest, this would point toward deeper political ills. The root causes could be faltering government effectiveness and/or rising public expectations, for example where irresponsible politicians casually promise unicorn policies but fail to deliver. Similarly, where it does occur, any loss of social trust in strangers and people of other faiths and nations may potentially heighten intolerance of refugees and asylum seekers, as well as weakening a sense of community and national solidarity to cope with collective risks. And mistrust of foreign allies can unravel alliances and the bonds of international cooperation. But misplaced cynicism is only one side of the trust relationship.

The perspective developed in this book argues that rosy normative claims about the intrinsic value of trust, implicitly permeating many expressions of concern about the supposed erosion of trust, deserve to be questioned more critically—or even abandoned, especially if and where agents lack competence, impartiality, and integrity. But pervasive cynicism and blanket mistrust of other people, governing authorities, and other countries are not the ideal answer either, since this also generates costs for society, democracy and alliances among nations.[68] Instead, in an age of scorpions replete with misinformation, democratic backsliding, and authoritarian resurgence, trust in authority functions as a double-edged sword. To understand this phenomenon, it may be useful to reverse the Russian adage: "verify and *then* trust." The notion is far from novel; it is the basis of our habitual warnings for children to be wary of strangers, for computer users to be suspicious of hackers, and for travelers to avoid pickpockets. Blind trust and habitual compliance can prove incautious, and potentially harmful to the individual and society, if the agent proves untrustworthy.

In many ways, the book's arguments return to ideas originally developed in Gabriel Almond and Sidney Verba's classic *The Civic Culture* (1963).[69] This suggested that some degree of trust in political institutions such as parties, interest groups, and leaders was essential for democratic governance to function, strengthening legitimacy. This lesson has been repeatedly echoed down the ages. By contrast, however, when memories of the rise of Communism and Fascism were still fresh, Almond and Verba emphasized that excessive and uncritical trust encourages citizens to be passive and deferential subjects toward the authorities governing any regime. This lesson has more often been forgotten. But it can prove dangerous to invest too much faith in deceitful and dishonest conmen in society, incompetent or corrupt politicians, or charlatans, faith healers, and quacks in science. The risks of deception have grown in a "post-truth" age where too often authoritarian populist leaders have risen to power in many countries based on mendacious claims, unicorn promises, and magical thinking untethered to factuality. Gullibility makes us all vulnerable to being duped, robbed, or worse.[70] Naïve lack of wary caution of authorities is risky anywhere. But it is a particularly imprudent and unwise strategy for those living in dangerous and crime-ridden societies—or those facing armed enemies in risky conflict zones, those living with fragile democratic institutions, or vulnerable populations in a pandemic. In general, the book sings in favor of a skeptical stance, a classical ideal of the Enlightenment era, reflecting open-minded questioning and cautious vigilance toward trustworthy relationships, guarding against misinformation and disinformation, separating reason from faith, and truth from emotions.[71]

Notes

Preface and Acknowledgments

1. https://www.worldvaluessurvey.org/
2. https://europeanvaluesstudy.eu/

Chapter 1

1. Robert E. Lazelere and Ted L. Huston. 1980. 'The dyadic trust scale: Towards understanding interpersonal trust in close relationships.' *Journal of Marriage and the Family* 42(3): 595–604; Robert D. Putnam. 1993. *Making Democracy Work: Civic Traditions in Modern Italy*. Princeton, NJ: Princeton University Press; Robert D. Putnam. 2000. *Bowling Alone?* New York: Simon and Schuster; Kenneth Arrow. 1972. 'Gifts and exchanges.' *Philosophy & Public Affairs* 1: 343–1018; Frances Fukuyama. 1995. *Trust: The Social Virtues and the Creation of Prosperity*. New York: Free Press; Marc J. Hetherington and Thomas Rudolph. 2015. *Why Washington Won't Work*. Chicago: University of Chicago Press; William Gamson. 1968. *Power and Discontent*. Homewood, IL: Dorsey Press; Roger C. Mayer, James H. Davis, and F. David Schoorman. 1995. 'An Integrative Model of Organizational Trust.' *The Academy of Management Review* 20(3): 709–734; Tom R. Tyler. 2006. *Why People Obey the Law*. New Haven, CT: Yale University Press; Bruce Russett. 1993. *Grasping the Democratic Peace*. Princeton, NJ: Princeton University Press.
2. Martin Gargiulo and Gokhan Ertug. 2006. 'The dark side of trust.' In Reinhard Bachmann and Akbar Zaheer (eds.), *Handbook of Trust Research*, pp. 165–186. Cheltenham, UK: Edward Elgar.
3. Charles S. Taber and Milton Lodge. 2006. 'Motivated skepticism in the evaluation of political beliefs.' *American Journal of Political Science* 50: 755–769. https://doi.org/10.1111/j.1540-5907.2006.00214.x; Charles S. Taber and Milton Lodge. 2013. *The Rationalizing Voter*. New York: Cambridge University Press; Jennifer Jerit and Yangzi Zhao. 2020. 'Political misinformation.' *Annual Review of Political Science* 23: 77–94.
4. Margaret Levi and Laura Stoker. 2000. 'Political trust and trustworthiness.' *Annual Review of Political Science* 3: 475–507.
5. Glynis Breakwell. 2014. *The Psychology of Risk*. 2nd ed. New York: Cambridge University Press.
6. R. H. Thaler and Cass Sunstein. 2008. *Nudge: Improving Decisions about Health, Wealth, and Happiness*. New Haven, CT: Yale University Press; Daniel Kahmann,

Olivier Sibony, and Cass Sunstein. 2021. *Noise: A Flaw in Human Judgment*. New York: Little, Brown.

7. M. Siegrist. 2021. 'Trust and risk perception: A critical review of the literature.' *Risk Analysis* 41: 480–490.

8. Roy J. Lewicki and Chad Bunker. 2015. 'Trust research: Measuring trust beliefs and behaviors.' In Fergus Lyon, Guido Mollering, and Mark N. K. Sanders (eds.), *Handbook of Research Methods on Trust*. Cheltenham, UK: Edward Elgar.

9. Glynis Breakwell. 2014. *The Psychology of Risk*. New York: Cambridge University Press. 2nd ed. Chapter 4.

10. Cailin O'Connor, and James Owen Weatherall. 2019. *The Misinformation Age*. Princeton, NJ: Yale University Press.

11. Federal Bureau of Investigation Internet Crime Complaint Center. 2020. *Internet Crime Report*. https://www.ic3.gov/Media/PDF/AnnualReport/2020_IC3Rep ort.pdf.

12. Leila Fadel. July 6, 2021. 'A ransomwares attack hit up to 1500 businesses.' *NPR*. https://www.npr.org/2021/07/06/1013266760/biden-is-pressured-to-take-action-after-latest-ransomware-attack.

13. Robert Griffin and Mayesha Quasem. 20201. 'The losers always doubt election results: That reached a dangerous level in 2020.' *Washington Post*. https://www.washingtonp ost.com/outlook/2021/06/24/polls-conservative-distrust-election-results/.

14. Dan Zak and Karen Heller. June 20, 2021. 'What were the Capitol rioters thinking on Jan. 6?' *Washington Post*. https://www.washingtonpost.com/lifestyle/style/capitol-riot-defense-trump-election/2021/07/19/e14f665e-d812-11eb-bb9e-70fda8c37057_story.html.

15. Centers for Disease Control and Prevention. Sept 17, 2021. 'Monitoring incidence of COVID-19 cases, hospitalizations, and deaths, by vaccination status.' https://www.cdc.gov/mmwr/volumes/70/wr/mm7037e1.htm.

16. S. Pagliaro, S. Sacchi, M. G. Pacilli, M. Brambilla, F. Lionetti, K. Bettache, et al. 2021. 'Trust predicts COVID-19 prescribed and discretionary behavioral intentions in 23 countries.' *PLoS ONE* 16(3): e0248334.

17. J. Roozenbeek, C. R. Schneider, S. Dryhurst, J. Kerr, A. L. J. Freeman, G. Recchia, A. M. van der Bles, and S. van der Linden. 2020. 'Susceptibility to misinformation about COVID-19 around the world.' *Royal Society Open Science* 7: 201199.

18. J. Zarocostas. 2020 'How to fight an infodemic.' *Lancet* 395: 676.

19. Kathy Frankovik. 2021. 'Why won't Americans get vaccinated?' *The Economist/YouGov* poll, July 10–13, 2021. https://today.yougov.com/topics/politics/articles-repo rts/2021/07/15/why-wont-americans-get-vaccinated-poll-data.

20. John Greco (ed.). 2008. *The Oxford Handbook of Skepticism*. New York: Oxford University Press.

21. For a discussion of ways of understanding the concept, see John Greco (ed.). 2008. *The Oxford Handbook of Skepticism*. Oxford: Oxford University Press.

22. Milton Lodge and C. S. Taber. 2013. *The Rationalizing Voter*. Cambridge, UK: Cambridge University Press.

23. For the Crime Index rating of cities, see https://www.numbeo.com/crime/ranki ngs.jsp.

24. John Greco (ed.). 2011. *The Oxford Handbook of Skepticism*. Oxford: Oxford University Press.

25. Kenneth Newton and Sonia Zmerli. 2011. 'Three forms of trust and their association.' *European Political Science Review* 3(2): 169–200; Kenneth Newton, Kenneth and Pippa Norris. 2000. 'Confidence in public institutions: Faith, culture or performance.' In Susan Pharr and Robert Putnam (eds.), *Disaffected Democracies: What's Troubling the Trilateral Countries?* Princeton, NJ: Princeton University Press.

26. For a good summary, see Tom Van der Meer. 2017. 'Dissecting the causal chain from quality of government to political support.' In Carolien Van Ham, Jacques Thomassen, Kaas Aarts, and Rudy Andeweg (eds.). 2017. *Myth and Reality of the Legitimacy Crisis.* Oxford: Oxford University Press. Chapter 8.

27. Fergus Lyon, Guido Mollering, and Mark N. K. Saunders (eds.). 2015. *Handbook on Research Methods on Trust.* 2nd ed. Cheltenham, UK: Edward Elgar.

28. For details, see www.worldvaluessurvey.org.

29. Jiayuan Li and Wim Van den Noortgate. 2022. 'A meta-analysis of the relative effectiveness of the item count technique compared to direct questioning.' *Sociological Methods and Research* 51(2): 760–799.

30. Ken Rotenberg (ed.). 2010. *Interpersonal Trust during Childhood and Adolescence.* New York: Cambridge University Press.

31. Ronald Inglehart. 1977. *The Silent Revolution: Changing Values and Political Styles among Western Publics.* Princeton, NJ: Princeton University Press; Ronald Inglehart. 1997. *Modernization and Postmodernization: Cultural, Economic and Political Change in 43 Societies.* Princeton, NJ: Princeton University Press; Ronald Inglehart and Christian Welzel. 2005. *Modernization, Cultural Change, and Democracy: The Human Development Sequence.* New York: Cambridge University Press.

32. Robert D. Putnam. 2000. *Bowling Alone?* New York: Simon and Schuster. For the impact of generational replacment, see also A. K. Clark. 2015. 'Rethinking the decline in social capital.' *American Politics Research* 43: 569–601 and P. Schwadel and M. Stout. 2012. 'Age, period and cohort effects on social capital.' *Social Forces* 91: 233–252.

33. Jan Delhey and Kenneth Newton. 2005. 'Predicting cross-national levels of social trust: Global patterns of Nordic exceptionalism?' *European Sociological Review* 21(4): 311–327.

34. Ibid.

35. Daniel Kahneman. 2011. *Thinking, Fast and Slow.* London: Penguin; Paul Sniderman, Richard Brady, and Philip Tetlock. 1991. *Reasoning and Choice.* New York: Cambridge University Press; Richard H. Thaler and Cass R. Sunstein. 2008. *Nudge: Improving Decisions about Health, Wealth, and Happiness.* New Haven, CT: Yale University Press.

36. [7] See Pippa Norris (ed.). 1999. *Critical Citizens.* New York: Oxford University Press.

37. Pippa Norris and Ron Inglehart. 2018. *Cultural Backlash.* New York: Cambridge University Press; Cas Mudde. 2007. *Populist Radical Right Parties in Europe.* New York: Cambridge University Press; Matthijs Rooduijn, Wouter Van Der Brug, and Sarah L. de Lange. 2016. 'Expressing or fueling discontent? The relationship between populist voting and political discontent.' *Electoral Studies* 43: 32–40.

38. Jan Van Deth, J. R. Montero, and Anders Westholm. 2007. *Citizenship and Involvement in European Democracies: A Comparative Analysis.* New York: Routledge.

39. Marc Hetherington. 1998. 'The political relevance of political trust.' *American Political Science Review* 92(4): 791–808; Marc Hetherington. 2005. *Why Trust Matters.* Princeton, NJ: Princeton University Press.

40. See, for example, annual reports by Freedom House, the Economist Democracy Index, Reporters without Borders, the Electoral Integrity Project, and the Varieties of Democracy Project.

41. See, for example, recommendations by the Democracy Project. June 2018. *Reversing a Crisis of Confidence.* https://www.bushcenter.org/publications/resources-reports/reports/the-democracy-project.html.

Chapter 2

1. Kenneth Newton and Pippa Norris. 2000. 'Confidence in public institutions: Faith, culture or performance.' In Susan Pharr and Robert Putnam (eds.), *Disaffected Democracies: What's Troubling the Trilateral Countries?* Princeton, NJ: Princeton University Press; Eunjung Choi and Jongseok Woo. 2016. 'The origins of political trust in East Asian Democracies: Psychological, cultural, and institutional arguments.' *Japanese Journal of Political Science* 17(3): 410–426. doi: 10.1017/S1468109916000165.

2. Ken Rotenberg (ed.). 2010. *Interpersonal Trust during Childhood and Adolescence.* New York: Cambridge University Press; Jeffrey Mondak. 2010. *Personality and the Foundations of Political Behavior.* New York: Cambridge University Press; Matthew Cawvey, Matthew Hayes, Damarys Canache, and Jeffery J. Mondak. 2018. 'Biological and psychological influences on interpersonal and political trust.' In Eris Uslaner (ed.), *Oxford Handbook of Social and Political Trust.* Oxford: Oxford University Press; Markus Freitaga and Paul C. Bauer. 2012. 'Personality traits and the propensity to trust friends and strangers.' *Social Science Journal* 53: 467–476.

3. P. Sturgis et al. 2010. 'A genetic basis for social trust?' *Political Behavior* 32: 205–230; Rotenberg (ed.). 2010. *Interpersonal Trust during Childhood and Adolescence*; Angelos Stamos, Efthymios Altsitsiadis, and Siegfried Dewitte. 2019. 'Investigating the effect of childhood socioeconomic background on interpersonal trust: Lower childhood socioeconomic status predicts lower levels of trust.' *Personality and Individual Differences* 145: 19–25; T. J. Bouchard Jr. 1997. 'The genetics of personality.' In K. Blum and E. P. Noble (eds.), *Handbook of Psychiatric Genetics*, pp. 273–296. Boca Raton, FL: CRC Press; Dietland Stolle and Laura Nishikawa. 2011. 'Trusting others: How parents shape the generalized trust of their children.' *Comparative Sociology* 10: 281–314.

4. P. Sturgis et al. 2010. 'A genetic basis for social trust?' *Political Behavior* 32: 205–230.

5. See Markus Freitaga and Paul C. Bauer. 2012. 'Personality traits and the propensity to trust friends and strangers.' *Social Science Journal* 53: 467–476.

6. Eric H. Erikson. 1950. *Childhood and Society.* New York: Norton; Gordon W. Allport. 1961. *Pattern and Growth in Personality.* New York: Holt, Rinehart and Winston; Raymond B. Cattell. 1965. *The Scientific Analysis of Personality.* Baltimore, MD: Penguin Books.

7. Morris Rosenberg. 1956. 'Misanthropy and political ideology.' *American Sociological Review* 21(6): 690–695.

8. P. Sturgis et al. 2010. 'A genetic basis for social trust?' *Political Behavior* 32: 205–230; Ken Rotenberg (ed.). 2010. *Interpersonal Trust during Childhood and Adolescence*. New York: Cambridge University Press; C. Dawson. 2019. 'How persistent is generalised trust?' *Sociology*, 53: 590–599.

9. Soloman Asch. 1956. 'Studies of independence and conformity.' *Psychological Monographs* 70(9): 1–70; Stanley Milgram. 1974. *Obedience to Authority*. New York: Harper & Row.

10. Ken Rotenberg (ed.). 2010. *Interpersonal Trust during Childhood and Adolescence*. New York: Cambridge University.

11. Eric M. Uslaner. 2002. *The Moral Foundations of Trust*. New York: Cambridge University Press.

12. Eric M. Uslaner. 2002. *The Moral Foundations of Trust*. New York: Cambridge University Press.

13. R. R. McCrae and P. T. Costa. 2003. *Personality in Adulthood: A Five-Factor Theory Perspective*. New York: Guilford Press. R. R. McCrae and P. T. Costa. 1997. 'Personality trait structure as a human universal.' *American Psychologist* 52(5): 509–516.

14. Markus Freitaga and Paul C. Bauer. 2012. 'Personality traits and the propensity to trust friends and strangers.' *Social Science Journal* 53: 467–476.

15. Toshio Yamagishi and Midori Yamagishi. 1994. 'Trust and commitment in the United States and Japan.' *Motivation and Emotion* 18(2): 129–166.

16. Jeff J. Mondak. 2010. *Personality and the Foundations of Political Behavior*. Cambridge, UK: Cambridge University Press; Jeff J. Mondak and David Halperin. 2008. 'A framework for the study of personality and political behaviour.' *British Journal of Political Science* 38(2): 335–362; Alan S. Gerber, Gregory A. Huber, David Doherty, and Conor M. Dowling. 2011. 'The Big Five personality traits in the political arena.' *Annual Review of Political Science* 14: 265–287.

17. Virginia A. Chanley. 2002. 'Trust in government in the aftermath of 9/11: Determinants and consequences.' *Political Psychology* 23(3): 469–483; Bruno Arpinio and Anastassia V. Obyden. 2020. 'Democracy and political trust before and after the Great Recession of 2008: The European Union and the United Nations.' *Social Indicators Research* 148: 395–415.

18. See, for example, Dietland Stolle and Laura Nishikawa. 2011. 'Trusting others: How parents shape the generalized trust of their children.' *Comparative Sociology* 10: 281–314; Angelos Stamos, Efthymios Altsitsiadis, and Siegfried Dewitte. 2019. 'Investigating the effect of childhood socioeconomic background on interpersonal trust: Lower childhood socioeconomic status predicts lower levels of trust.' *Personality and Individual Differences* 145: 19–25.

19. Markus Freitaga and Paul. C. Bauer. 2012. 'Personality traits and the propensity to trust friends and strangers.' *Social Science Journal* 53: 467–476.

20. Markus Freitaga and Paul. C. Bauer. 2012. 'Personality traits and the propensity to trust friends and strangers.' *Social Science Journal*. 53: 467–476.

21. Pippa Norris. 2011. *Democratic Deficit*. New York: Cambridge University Press, Chapter 4; Jan Delhey and Kenneth Newton. 2005. 'Predicting cross-national levels of

social trust: Global patterns of Nordic exceptionalism?' *European Sociological Review* 21(4): 311–327; A. Cavalli. 2001. 'Reflections on political culture and the "Italian National Character."' *Daedalus* 130(3): 119–137.

22. Daniel Lerner. 1958. *The Passing of Traditional Society*. New York: Glencoe; Gabriel A. Almond and Sydney Verba. 1963. *The Civic Culture*. Princeton, NJ: Princeton University Press.

23. Dietland Stolle and Laura Nishikawa. 2011. 'Trusting others: How parents shape the generalized trust of their children.' *Comparative Sociology* 10: 281–314.

24. Staffan Kumlin. 2004. *The Personal and the Political: How Personal Welfare State Experiences Affect Political Trust and Ideology*. London: Palgrave Macmillan; Staffan Kumlin and Bo Rothstein. 2005. 'Making and breaking social capital.' *Comparative Political Studies* 38(4): 339–365.

25. A. Bergh and R. Öhrvall. 2018. 'A sticky trait: Social trust among Swedish expatriates in countries with varying institutional quality.' *Journal of Comparative Economics* 46: 1146–1157.

26. Y. Algan and P. Cahuc. 2010. 'Inherited trust and growth.' *The American Economic Review* 100(5): 2060–2092.

27. Ronald Inglehart. 1977. *The Silent Revolution: Changing Values and Political Styles among Western Publics*. Princeton, NJ: Princeton University Press; Ronald Inglehart. 1997. *Modernization and Postmodernization: Cultural, Economic and Political Change in 43 Societies*. Princeton, NJ: Princeton University Press; Ronald Inglehart and Christian Welzel. 2005. *Modernization, Cultural Change, and Democracy: The Human Development Sequence*. New York: Cambridge University Press.

28. Hans-Dieter Klingemann and Dieter Fuchs. 1995. *Citizens and the State*. Oxford: Oxford University Press.

29. Ronald Inglehart. 1977. *The Silent Revolution: Changing Values and Political Styles among Western Publics*. Princeton, NJ: Princeton University Press; Ronald Inglehart. 1997. *Modernization and Postmodernization: Cultural, Economic and Political Change in 43 Societies*. Princeton, NJ: Princeton University Press; Ronald Inglehart and Christian Welzel. 2005. *Modernization, Cultural Change, and Democracy: The Human Development Sequence*. New York: Cambridge University Press.

30. Robert D. Putnam. 2000. *Bowling Alone?* New York: Simon and Schuster. For the impact of generational replacement, see also A. K. Clark. 2015. 'Rethinking the decline in social capital.' *American Politics Research* 43: 569–601 and P. Schwadel and M. Stout. 2012. 'Age, period and cohort effects on social capital.' *Social Forces* 91: 233–252.

31. Virginia A. Chanley. 2002. 'Trust in government in the aftermath of 9/11: Determinants and consequences.' *Political Psychology* 23(3): 469–483; Virginia A. Chanley, Thomas J. Rudolph, and Wendy Rahn. 2000. 'The origins and consequences of public trust in government: A time series analysis.' *Public Opinion Quarterly* 64(3): 239–256.

32. Michael Lewis-Beck. 1988. *Economics and Elections: The Major Western Democracies*. Ann Arbor: University of Michigan Press.

33. Stefan Dahlberg, Jonas Linde, and Soren Holmberg. 2015. 'Democratic discontent in old and new democracies: Assessing the importance of democratic input and governmental output.' *Political Studies* 63(1): 18–37.

34. Stephen E. Finke, Edward Muller, and Mitchell A. Seligson. 1987. 'Economic crisis, incumbent performance and regime support.' *British Journal of Political Science* 19: 329–351; Stephen M. Weatherford. 1987. 'How does government performance influence political support?' *Political Behavior* 9: 5–28; Kenneth Newton. 2006. 'Political support: Social capital, civil society and political and economic performance.' *Political Studies* 54(4): 846–864.

35. Donald F. Kettl. 2017. *Can Governments Earn Our Trust?* Cambridge, UK: Polity.

36. David Easton. 1975. 'Reassessment of the concept of political support.' *British Journal of Political Science* 5: 435–457; Vivienne Schmidt. 2013. 'Democracy and legitimacy in the European Union revisited: Input, output, *and* throughput.' *Political Studies* 61(1): 2–22.

37. Bo Rothstein and Jan Teorell. 2008. 'What is quality of government? A theory of impartial government institutions.' *Governance* 21(2): 165–190.

38. Mark Warren. 1999. *Democracy and Trust.* Cambridge, UK: Cambridge University Press.

39. See Tom Van der Meer and Armen Hakhverdian. 2016. 'Political trust as an evaluation of process and performance: A cross-national study of 42 European countries.' *Political Studies* 65(1): 81–102.

40. See, for example, Tom Van der Meer and Paul Dekker 2011. 'Trustworthy states, trusting citizens? A multilevel study into objective and subjective determinants of political trust.' In Sonia Zmerli and Marc Hooghe (eds.), *Political Trust: Why Context Matters*, pp. 95–116. Colchester: ECPR Press; Tom Van der Meer and Armen Hakhverdian. 2016. 'Political trust as an evaluation of process and performance: A cross-national study of 42 European countries.' *Political Studies* 65(1): 81–102; Christina Boswell. 2018. *Manufacturing Political Trust: Targets and Performance Management in Public Policy.* Cambridge, UK: Cambridge University Press.

41. Ibid.

42. See, for example, Tom Van der Meer and Paul Dekker 2011. 'Trustworthy states, trusting citizens? A multilevel study into objective and subjective determinants of political trust.' In Sonia Zmerli and Marc Hooghe (eds.), *Political Trust. Why Context Matters.* Colchester: ECPR Press; Tom Van der Meer and Armen Hakhverdian. 2016. 'Political trust as an evaluation of process and performance: A cross-national study of 42 European countries.' *Political Studies* 65(1): 81–102; Christina Boswell. 2018. *Manufacturing Political Trust: Targets and Performance Management in Public Policy.* Cambridge, UK: Cambridge University Press.

43. Pew Center 'Facttank,' January 30, 2017. https://www.pewresearch.org/fact-tank/2017/01/20/6-things-weve-learned-since-the-2016-election/.

44. Pew Center. https://www.pewresearch.org/fact-tank/2019/01/30/partisans-agree-political-leaders-should-be-honest-and-ethical-disagree-whether-trump-fits-the-bill/.

45. See Peter Thisted Dinesen and Kim Mannemar Sonderskov. 'Quality of govern-
ment and social trust.' In Andreas Bagenholm, Monika Bauhr, Marciua Grimes and
Bo Rothstein (eds.), *The Oxford Handbook of the Quality of Government*. New York:
Oxford University Press.

46. F. W. Scharpf. 1999. *Governing in Europe: Effective and Democratic?* New York:
Oxford University Press; Vivienne Schmidt. 2013. 'Democracy and legitimacy in the
European Union revisited: Input, output, *and* throughput.' *Political Studies* 61(1):
2–22.

47. Pippa Norris. 2011. *Democratic Deficit.* New York: Cambridge University Press,
Table 10.3; Tom Van der Meer and Armen Hakhverdian. 2016. 'Political trust as an
evaluation of process and performance: A cross-national study of 42 European countries.' *Political Studies* 65(1): 81–102.

48. Pippa Norris (ed.). 1999. *Critical Citizens.* New York: Oxford University Press.

49. F. W. Scharpf. 1999. *Governing in Europe: Effective and Democratic?* New York: Oxford
University Press; Tom Van der Meer. 2017. 'Dissecting the causal chain from quality
of government to political support.' In Carolien Van Ham, Jacques Thomassen, Kees
Aarts, and Rudy Andeweg (eds.), *Myth and Reality of the Legitimacy Crisis.* Oxford:
Oxford University Press.

50. Herbert Simon. 1956. 'Rational choice and the structure of the environment.'
Psychological Review 63: 129–138; Amos Tversky and D. Kahneman. 1974. 'Judgment
under uncertainty: Heuristics and biases.' *Science* 185: 1124–1131.

51. Hugo Mercier. 2020. *Not Born Yesterday: The Science of Who We Trust and What We
Believe.* Princeton, NJ: Princeton University Press.

52. See also Tom Van der Meer. 2017. 'Dissecting the causal chain from quality of government to political support.' In Carolien Van Ham, Jacques Thomassen, Kees Aarts,
and Rudy Andeweg (eds.), *Myth and Reality of the Legitimacy Crisis.* Oxford: Oxford
University Press.

53. Tom Van der Meer. 2017. 'Dissecting the causal chain from quality of government to
political support.' In Carolien Van Ham, Jacques Thomassen, Kees Aarts, and Rudy
Andeweg (eds.), *Myth and Reality of the Legitimacy Crisis.* Oxford: Oxford University
Press; Tom Van der Meer and Armen Hakhverdian. 2016. 'Political trust as an evalu-
ation of process and performance: A cross-national study of 42 European countries.'
Political Studies 65(1): 81–102..

54. Roger C. Mayer, James H. Davis, and F. David Schoorman. 1995. 'An integrative
model of organizational trust.' *The Academy of Management Review* 20(3): 709–734.

55. https://www.pewresearch.org/politics/2020/02/07/views-of-nations-economy-rem
ain-positive-sharply-divided-by-partisanship/.

56. Jennifer Hochschild and K. L. Einstein. 2015. *Do facts matter? Information and misinformation in American politics.* Oklahoma: University of Oklahoma Press.

57. See, for example, Tom Van der Meer and Paul Dekker 2011. 'Trustworthy states,
trusting citizens? A multilevel study into objective and subjective determinants of political trust.' In Sonia Zmerli and Marc Hooghe (eds.), *Political Trust: Why Context
Matters*, pp. 95–116. Colchester: ECPR Press.

58. E. J. Van Elsas. 2015. 'Political trust as a rational attitude: A comparison of the nature of political trust across different levels of education.' *Political Studies* 63(5): 1158–1178; Armen Hakhverdian and Quintin Mayne. 2012. 'Institutional trust, education, and corruption: A micro-macro interactive approach.' *Journal of Politics* 74(3): 739–750.

59. Robert D. Putnam. 2000. *Bowling Alone?* New York: Simon and Schuster; Erika J. Van Elsas. 2015. 'Political trust as a rational attitude: A comparison of the nature of political trust across different levels of education.' *Political Studies* 63(5): 1158–1178; Armen Hakhverdian and Quintin Mayne. 2012. 'Institutional trust, education, and corruption: A micro-macro interactive approach.' *Journal of Politics* 74(3): 739–750.; Marc Hooghe, Sofie Marien, and Thomas de Vroome. 2012. 'The cognitive basis of trust: The relation between education, cognitive ability, and generalized and political trust.' *Intelligence* 40(6): 604–613; J. Huang, H. M. van den Brink, and W. Groot. 2009. 'A meta-analysis of the effect of education on social capital.' *Economics of Education Review* 28(4): 454–464; Cecilia Güemes and Francisco Herreros. 2019. 'Education and trust: A tale of three continents.' *International Political Science Review* 40(5): 676–693; Nicholas Charron and Bo Rothstein. 2016. 'Does education lead to higher generalized trust? The importance of quality of government.' *International Journal of Educational Development* 50: 59–73; Morten Frederiksen, Christian A. Larsen, and Henrik L. Lolle. 2016. 'Education and trust: Exploring the association across social relationships and nations.' *Acta Sociologica* 59(3): 293–308.

60. Aidan Connaughton. 2020. 'Social trust in advanced economies is lower among young people and those with less education.' *Pew Research Center.* https://www.pewresearch.org/fact-tank/2020/12/03/social-trust-in-advanced-economies-is-lower-among-young-people-and-those-with-less-education/.

61. Daniel Kahneman. 2013. *Thinking Fast and Slow.* New York: Farrar, Straus and Giroux.

62. Toshio Yamagishi. 2001. 'Trust as a form of social intelligence.' In K. Cook (ed.), *Trust in Society.* New York: Russell Sage Foundation; Toshio Yamagishi, Masako Kikuchi, and Motoko Kosugi. 1999. 'Trust, gullibility and social intelligence.' *Asian Journal of Social Psychology* 2(1): 145–161.

63. Christopher J. Anderson and Yuliya V. Tverdova. 2003. 'Corruption, political allegiances, and attitudes toward government in contemporary democracies.' *American Journal of Political Science* 47(1): 91–109.

64. Valeriya Mechkova et al. 2017. 'How much democratic backsliding?' *Journal of Democracy* 28(4): 162–169; Stephan Haggard and Robert Kaufman. 2021. 'The anatomy of democratic backsliding.' *Journal of Democracy* 32(4): 27–41.

65. Steven Levitsky and Daniel Ziblatt. 2018. *How Democracies Die.* New York: Crown.

66. https://freedomhouse.org/report/freedom-and-media/2019/media-freedom-downward-spiral.

67. https://rsf.org/en/ranking.

Chapter 3

1. Fergus Lyon, Guido Mollering, and Mark N. K. Saunders (eds.). 2015. *Handbook on Research Methods on Trust*. 2nd ed. Cheltenham, UK: Edward Elgar.

2. J. E. Berg, J. W. Dickhaut, and K. McCabe. 1995. 'Trust, reciprocity, and social history.' *Games and Economic Behavior* 10: 122–142.

3. Edward Glaeser, David Laibson, Jose Scheinkman, and Christine Soutter. 2000. 'Measuring trust.' *Quarterly Journal of Economics* 115(3): 811–846.

4. N. D. Johnson and A. A. Mislin. 2011. 'Trust games: A meta-analysis.' *Journal of Economic Psychology* 32: 865–889.

5. J. N. Druckman, D. P. Green, J. H. Kuklinski, and A. Lupia (eds.). 2011. *Cambridge Handbook of Experimental Political Science* Cambridge: Cambridge University Press.

6. Diana Mutz and Byron Reeves. 2005. 'The new videomalaise: Effects of televised incivility on political trust.' *American Political Science Review* 99(1): 1–15.

7. Rose McDermott. 2002. 'Experimental methods in political science.' *Annual Review of Political Science* 5: 31–61.

8. Kyle Irwin, Laetitia Mulder, and Brent Simpson. 2014. 'The detrimental effects of sanctions on intragroup trust: Comparing punishments and rewards.' *Social Psychology Quarterly* 77(3): 253–272.

9. Deepak Malhotra and J. Keith Murnighan. 2002. 'The effects of contracts on interpersonal trust.' *Administrative Science Quarterly* 47(3): 534–559.

10. Paola Sapienza, Anna Toldra-Simats, and Luigi Zingales. 2013. 'Understanding trust.' *The Economic Journal* 123: 1313–1332.

11. Sonia Zmerli and Marc Hooghe (eds.). 2011. *Political Trust: Why Context Matters*. Colchester: ECPR Press.

12. Alain Cohn, Michel André Maréchal, David Tannenbaum, and Christian Lukas Zünd. 2019. 'Civic honesty around the globe.' *Science* 365: 70–73.

13. Diana C. Mutz. 2011. *Population-Based Survey Experiments*. Princeton, NJ: Princeton University Press.

14. For a discussion about the mismatch between experimental and survey measures of interpersonal trust, see Rick K. Wilson. 'Trust experiments, trust games and surveys.' In Eric Uslaner (ed.), *The Oxford Handbook of Social and Political Trust*. New York: Oxford University Press.

15. K. Gross, S. Aday, and Paul Brewer. 2004. 'A panel study of media effects on political and social trust after September 11, 2001.' *Harvard International Journal of Press-Politics* 9(4): 49–73.

16. Will Jennings. 2021. 'Trust, Brexit and beyond.' In Anand Menon (ed.), *Brexit and Beyond*. London: UK in a Changing Europe. https://ukandeu.ac.uk/wp-content/uploads/2021/01/Brexit-and-Beyond-report-compressed.pdf.

17. Marc Hooghe and Ruth Dassonneville. 2018. 'A spiral of distrust: A panel study on the relation between political distrust and protest voting in Belgium.' *Government and Opposition* 53(1): 104–130. doi:10.1017/gov.2016.18.

18. See Blaine G. Robbins. 2012. 'Institutional quality and generalized trust: A nonrecursive causal model.' *Social Indicators Research* 107(2): 235–258; Blaine G. Robbins.

2012. 'A blessing and a curse? Political institutions in the growth and decay of general-ized trust: A cross-national panel analysis, 1980–2009.' *PloS One* 7(4): e35120.

19. Adam Przeworski and H. Teune. 1970. *The Logic of Comparative Social Inquiry.* Oxford: Wiley Interscience; Arendt Lijphart. 1971. 'Comparative politics and the comparative methods.' *American Political Science Review* 65(3): 682–693.

20. Alain Cohn, Michel André Maréchal, David Tannenbaum, and Christian Lukas Zünd. 2019. 'Civic honesty around the globe.' *Science* 365: 70–73.

21. See www.worldvaluessurvey.org.

22. See, for example, Pippa Norris (ed.). *Public Sentinel.* Washington, DC: World Bank.

23. Pippa Norris and Ronald Inglehart. *Cosmopolitan Communications.* New York: Cambridge University Press.

24. Michael Robinson. 1976. 'Public affairs television and the growth of political malaise.' *American Political Science Review* 70: 409–432.

25. Thomas Patterson. 1993. *Out of Order.* New York: Knopf.

26. Suzanne Garment. 1991. *Scandal: The Crisis of Mistrust in American Politics.* New York: Random House; Gary Orren 1997. 'Fall from grace: The public's loss of faith in government.' In Joseph S. Nye, Jr., Philip D. Zelikow, and David C. King (eds.), *Why People Don't Trust Government.* Chicago: University of Chicago Press.

27. Pippa Norris. 2000. *A Virtuous Circle.* New York: Cambridge University Press; Claes H. De Vreese. 2005. 'The spiral of cynicism reconsidered.' *European Journal of Communication* 20(3): 283–301; Richard R. Lau and I. B. Rovner. 2009. 'Negative campaigning.' *Annual Review of Political Science* 12: 285–306; Nicholas A. Valentino. 2001. 'A spiral of cynicism for some: The contingent effects of campaign news frames on participation and confidence in government.' *Political Communication* 18: 347.

28. See the discussion in James M. Avery. 2009. 'Videomalaise or virtuous circle? The influence of the news media on political trust.' *International Journal of Press-Politics* 14(4): 410–433; Anna Brosius, Erika J. van Elsas, and Claes H. de Vreese. 2019. 'Trust in the European Union: Effects of the information environment.' *European Journal of Communication* 34(1): 57–73.

29. https://rsf.org/en/china.

30. https://rsf.org/en/tajikistan.

31. Freedom House. *Freedom in the World, 2021.* https://freedomhouse.org/reports/free dom-world/freedom-world-research-methodology.

32. Larry Diamond. 2002. 'Thinking about hybrid regimes.' *Journal of Democracy* 13(2): 21–35.

33. Adam Przeworski, Michael Alvarez, Jose Cheibub, and F. Limongi. 2000. *Democracy and Development: Political Institutions and Well-Being in the World, 1950–1990.* Cambridge: Cambridge University Press.

34. Anna Lührmann, Marcus Tannenberg, and Staffan I. Lindberg. 2018. 'Regimes of the World (RoW): Opening new avenues for the comparative study of political regimes.' *Politics and Governance* 6(1): 1–18.

35. See, for example, Eric M. Uslaner (ed.). 2018. *The Oxford Handbook of Social and Political Trust.* New York: Oxford University Press.

36. See, for example, Sergio Martini and Mario Quaranta. 2020. *Citizens and Democracy in Europe: Contexts, Changes and Political Support.* London: Palgrave Macmillan.

37. Andrew H. Kydd. 2007. *Trust and Mistrust in International Relations.* Princeton, NJ: Princeton University Press; Jonas Tallberg, Karin Backsterand, and Jan Aart Scholte (eds.). 2018. *Legitimacy in Global Governance.* Oxford: Oxford University Press.

38. Morris Rosenberg. 1956. 'Misanthropy and political ideology.' *American Sociological Review* 21(6): 690–695.

39. Jan Delhey, Kenneth Newton, and Chris Welzel. 2011. 'How general is trust in "most people"? Solving the radius of trust issue.' *American Sociological Review* 76: 786–807.

40. Edward Glaeser, David Laibson, Jose Scheinkman, and Christine Soutter. 2000. 'Measuring trust.' *Quarterly Journal of Economics* 115(3): 811–846.

41. Paola Sapienza, Anna Toldra-Simats, and Luigi Zingales. 2013. 'Understanding trust.' *The Economic Journal* 123: 1313–1332.

42. Andre Van Hoorn. 2014. 'Trust radius versus level.' *American Sociological Review* 79(6): 1256–1259.

43. F. Herreros and H. Criado. 2009. 'Social trust, social capital and perceptions of immigration.' *Political Studies* 57: 337–355.

44. Niklas Luhmann. 1979. *Trust and Power.* Cambridge: Polity Press.

45. It should be noted that the terms "trust" and "confidence" are used interchangeably in this book, following standard conventions and the way that both terms can be used to refer to expectations about the actions of the agent.

46. The factor analysis model was also tested using the pooled EVS/WVS 1990–2020, generating similar results, although the pooled survey questionnaires contained fewer of the items on international trust.

47. It is also worth noting that the simply binary item measuring social trust ("Most people can be trusted"), where we have the longest time-series, is correlated with the trust in out-groups rather than friends and family.

48. For the comparison of these items used in other established democracies, see Russell J. Dalton. 2004. *Democratic Challenges, Democratic Choices: The Erosion of Political Support in Advanced Industrial Democracies.* New York: Oxford University Press, Table 2.2.

49. The four standard ANES questions are: RIGHT: "How much of the time do you think you can trust the government in Washington to do what is right—just about always, most of the time or only some of the time?"; WASTE: "Do you think that people in the government waste a lot of money we pay in taxes, waste some of it, or don't waste very much of it?"; INTERESTS: "Would you say the government is pretty much run by a few big interests looking out for themselves or that it is run for the benefit of all the people?"; CROOKED: "Do you think that quite a few of the people running the government are (1958–1972: a little) crooked, not very many are, or do you think hardly any of them are crooked (1958–1972: at all)?" It should be noted that it is unclear who is the object of these questions as "the government," when American decision-making is divided horizontally among the executive, legislative, and judicial branches, as well as vertically among districts, states, and the federal levels.

50. Paul R. Abramson and Ada W. Finifter. 1981. 'On the meaning of political trust: New evidence from items introduced in 1978.' *American Journal of Political Science* 25(2): 297–307; Edward N. Muller and Thomas O. Jukam. 1977. 'On the meaning of political support.' *American Political Science Review* 71: 1561–1595.

51. Margaret Levi and Laura Stoker. 2000. 'Political trust and trustworthiness.' *Annual Review of Political Science* 3: 475–508.

52. Seymour Martin Lipset and William C. Schneider. 1983. *The Confidence Gap: Business, Labor, and Government in the Public Mind.* New York: Free Press; Ola Listhaug and Matti Wiberg. 1995. 'Confidence in political and private institutions.' In Hans-Dieter Klingemann and Dieter Fuchs (eds.), *Citizens and the State.* Oxford: Oxford University Press.

53. The NORC GSS questions remain somewhat ambiguous to interpret. The items ask about "the people running" these agencies, but this does not refer to any individual incumbents by name or office (such as "your Congressional representative," "the Chief Justice," or "your bank manager" or "your doctor"). Even the item concerning the executive branch is framed collectively, to include the White House, all departments, secretaries of state in cabinet, and federal bureaucrats, and it does not refer by name to individual presidents. As such, although the wording is imprecise, it seems most likely that people will usually respond with their general impressions of each institution, although these judgments may inevitably be colored by evaluations of specific incumbent officeholders.

54. See Seymour Martin Lipset and William C. Schneider. 1983. *The Confidence Gap: Business, Labor, and Government in the Public Mind.* New York: Free Press; Ola Listhaug and Matti Wiberg. 1995. 'Confidence in political and private institutions.' In Hans-Dieter Klingemann and Dieter Fuchs (eds.), *Citizens and the State.* Oxford: Oxford University Press.

55. William Mishler and Richard Rose. 2005. 'Trust, distrust and skepticism: Popular evaluations of civil and political institutions in post-communist societies.' *Journal of Politics* 59(2): 418–451.

56. Timothy E. Cook and Paul Gronke. 2005. 'The skeptical American: Revisiting the meanings of trust in government and confidence in institutions.' *Journal of Politics* 67(3): 784–803.

57. Cary Wu and Rima Wilkes. 2018. 'Finding critical trusters: A response pattern model of political trust.' *International Journal of Comparative Sociology* 59(2): 110–138.

58. For an earlier argument along these lines, see Pippa Norris (ed.). 1999. *Critical Citizens.* Oxford: Oxford University Press.

59. Eric M. Uslaner. 2002. *The Moral Foundations of Trust.* New York: Cambridge University Press; A. Bergh and R. Öhrvall. 2018. 'A sticky trait: Social trust among Swedish expatriates in countries with varying institutional quality.' *Journal of Comparative Economics* 46: 1146–1157.

60. Anning Hu and Chen Yin. 2021. 'Typology of political trustors in contemporary China: The relevance of authoritarian culture and perceived institutional performance.' *Journal of Chinese Political Science.* doi.org/10.1007/s11366-021-09751-6.

61. See, for example, Blaine G. Robbins. 2012. 'Institutional quality and generalized trust: A non-recursive causal model.' *Social Indicators Research* 107(2): 235–258; Blaine G. Robbins. 2012. 'A blessing and a curse? Political institutions in the growth and decay of generalized trust: A cross-national panel analysis, 1980–2009.' *PloS One* 7(4): e35120.

62. Alexander Cooley and Jack Snyder (eds.). 2015. *Ranking the World*. New York: Cambridge University Press.

63. Roger C. Mayer, James H. Davis, and F. David Schoorman. 1995 'An integrative model of organizational trust.' *Academy of Management Review* 20(3): 709–734.

64. Elisabeth Noelle-Neumann. 1974. 'The spiral of silence: A theory of public opinion.' *Journal of Communication* 24: 43–51; Elisabeth Noelle-Neumann. 1984. *The Spiral of Silence*. Chicago: University of Chicago Press.

65. Daniela Stockmann, Ashley Esarey, and Jie Zhang. 2018. 'Who is afraid of the Chinese state? Evidence calling into question political fear as an explanation for overreporting of political trust.' *Political Psychology* 39(5): 1105–1121.

66. Hugh J. Arnold and Daniel C. Feldman. 1981. 'Social desirability response bias in self-report choice situations.' *Academy of Management Journal* 24(2): 377–385; Timur Kuran. 1997. *Private Truths, Public Lies: The Social Consequences of Preference Falsification*. Cambridge, MA: Harvard University Press; Irena Schneider. 2017. 'Can we trust measures of political trust? Assessing measurement equivalence in diverse regime types.' *Social Indicators Research* 133: 963–984.

67. Daniel Corstange. 2009. 'Sensitive questions, truthful answers? Modeling the list experiment with LISTIT.' *Political Analysis* 17(1): 45–63; Kosuke Imai. 2011. 'Multivariate regression analysis for the item count technique.' *Journal of the American Statistical Association* 106(494): 407–416; Adam N. Glynn. 2013. 'What can we learn with statistical truth serum? Design analysis of the List Experiment.' *Public Opinion Quarterly* 77: 159–172; Junyan Jiang and Dali L Yang. 2016. 'Lying or believing? Measuring preference falsification from a political purge in China.' *Comparative Political Studies* 49(5): 600–634; Bryn Rosenfeld, Kosuke Imai, and Jacob N. Shapiro. 2016. 'An empirical validation study of popular survey methodologies for sensitive questions.' *American Journal of Political Science* 60(3): 783–802.

68. Jiayuan Li and Wim Van den Noortgate. 2019. 'A meta-analysis of the relative effectiveness of the item count technique compared to direct questioning.' *Sociological Methods and Research*. https://journals-sagepub-com.ezp-prod1.hul.harvard.edu/doi/full/10.1177/0049124119882468 .

69. Timothy Frye, Scott Gehlbach, Kyle L. Marquardt, and Ora John Reuter. 2017. 'Is Putin's popularity real?' *Post-Soviet Affairs* 33(1): 1–15.

70. Bryn Rosenfeld, Kosuke Imai, and Jacob N. Shapiro. 2016. 'An empirical validation study of popular survey methodologies for sensitive questions.' *American Journal of Political Science* 60(3): 783–802.

71. It should be noted that survey questions about leadership popularity could not be asked in several of the TrustGov authoritarian states due to official restrictions.

72. https://rsf.org/en/ranking.

73. Timothy Frye, Scott Gehlbach, Kyle L. Marquardt, and Ora John Reuter. 2017. 'Is Putin's popularity real?' *Post-Soviet Affairs* 33(1): 1–15.

74. Janelle Fetterolf and Nicholas Kent. June 11, 2021. 'Americans have less confidence in key world leaders than other global publics do.' Pew Research Center. https://www.pewresearch.org/fact-tank/2021/06/11/americans-have-less-confidence-in-key-world-leaders-including-biden-than-other-global-publics-do/.

75. Elisabeth Noelle-Neumann. 1974. 'The spiral of silence: A theory of public opinion.' *Journal of Communication* 24: 43–51; Elisabeth Noelle-Neumann. 1984. *The Spiral of Silence.* Chicago: University of Chicago Press.

76. Pippa Norris. 2021. 'Cancel culture? Myth or reality.' *Political Studies* (Online First 11 August 2021).

77. Robert D. Putnam. 2000. *Bowling Alone?* New York: Simon and Schuster.

78. Jonas Tallberg, Karin Backsterand, and Jan Aart Scholte (eds.). 2018. *Legitimacy in Global Governance.* Oxford: Oxford University Press.

79. John R. Hibbing and Elizabeth Theiss-Morse. 1995. *Congress as Public Enemy.* New York: Cambridge University Press.

80. See, for example, Markus Freitaga and Paul. C. Bauer. 2012. 'Personality traits and the propensity to trust friends and strangers.' *Social Science Journal.* 53: 467–476.

81. Lisa van der Werff and Finian Buckley. 2017. 'Getting to know you: A longitudinal examination of trust cues and trust development during socialization.' *Journal of Management* 43(3): 743–770.

82. Tom Van der Meer and Armen Hakhverdian. 2016. 'Political trust as an evaluation of process and performance: A cross-national study of 42 European countries.' *Political Studies* 65(1): 81–102; Marcia Grimes. 2006. 'Organizing consent: The role of procedural fairness in political trust and compliance.' *European Journal of Political Research* 45(2): 285–315.

83. Yann Algan, Sergei Guriev, Elias Papaioannou, and Evgenia Passari. 2017. 'The European trust crisis and the rise of populism.' *Brookings Papers on Economic Activity* 2: 309–400.

84. Rick Wilson and Catherine C. Eckel. 2017. 'Political trust in experimental designs.' In Sonja Zmerli and Tom Van der Meer (eds.), *Handbook on Political Trust.* New York: Edward Elgar.

85. Ronald Inglehart. 1997. *Modernization and Post-modernization: Cultural, Economic and Political Change in 43 Societies.* Princeton, NJ: Princeton University Press; Ronald Inglehart and Christopher Welzel. 2005. *Modernization, Cultural Change, and Democracy: The Human Development Sequence.* New York: Cambridge University Press.

86. Stephen Grimmelikhuijsen and Eva Kniew. 2017. 'Validating a scale for citizen trust in government organizations.' *International Review of Administrative Sciences* 83(3): 583–601.

87. William Mishler and Richard Rose. 2001. 'What are the origins of political trust? Testing institutional and cultural theories in post-Communist societies.' *Comparative Political Studies* 34(1): 30–62.

88. Michael Bratton and Robert Mattes. 2001. 'Support for democracy in Africa: Intrinsic or instrumental.' *British Journal of Political Science* 31(3): 447–474.

89. T. J. Shi. 2001. 'Cultural values and political trust: A comparison of the People's Republic of China and Taiwan.' *Comparative Politics* 33(4): 401–419; L. J. Li. 2004. 'Political trust in rural China.' *Modern China* 30(2): 228–258; Qing Yang and Wenfang Tang. 2010. 'Exploring the sources of institutional trust in China: Culture, mobilization, or performance?' *Asian Politics and Society* 2(3): 415–436; Deyong Ma and Feng Yang. 2014. 'Authoritarian orientations and political trust in East Asian societies.' *East Asia* 31(4): 323–341.

Chapter 4

1. Gabriel Almond and Sidney Verba. 1963. *The Civic Culture*. Princeton, NJ: Princeton University Press.

2. For details, see www.worldvaluessurvey.org.

3. Ronald Inglehart. 2018. *Cultural Evolution*. New York: Cambridge University Press.

4. G. Cordero and P. Simón. 2015. 'Economic crisis and support for democracy in Europe.' *West European Politics* 39(2): 305–325; Veronica Fagerland Kroknes, Tor Georg Jakobsen, and Lisa-Marie Grønning. 2016. 'Economic performance and political trust: The impact of the financial crisis on European citizens.' *European Societies* 17(5): 700–723; L. Kenworthy and L. A. Owens. 2011. 'The surprisingly weak effect of recessions on public opinion.' In D. B. Grusky, B. Western, and C. Wimer (eds.), *The Great Recession*. New York: Russell Sage Foundation.

5. Jack Citrin and Laura Stoker. 2018. 'Political trust in a cynical age.' *Annual Review of Political Science* 21(1): 49–70; Mark J. Hetherington. 2005. *Why Trust Matters*. Princeton, NJ: Princeton University Press; Pew Research Center. April 26, 2018. *The Public, the Political System and American Democracy*. https://www.people-press.org/2018/04/26/1-democracy-and-government-the-u-s-political-system-elected-offici als-and-governmental-institutions/.

6. Marie F. Lindholt, Frederick Jørgensen, Alexander Bor, and Michael B. Petersen. 2021. 'Public acceptance of COVID-19 vaccines: Cross-national evidence on levels and individual-level predictors using observational data.' *BMJ Open* 11(6). http://dx.doi.org/10.1136/bmjopen-2020-048172.

7. Mathias Rooduijn, Wouter Van Der Brug, and Sarah L. de Lange. 2016. 'Expressing or fuelling discontent? The relationship between populist voting and political discontent.' *Electoral Studies* 43: 32–40.

8. Michel Crozier, Samuel P. Huntington, and Joji Watanuki. 1975. *The Crisis of Democracy*. New York: Trilateral Commission.

9. Samuel Barnes and Max Kaase. 1979. *Political Action: Mass Participation in Five Western Democracies*. Cambridge: Cambridge University Press.

10. Pierre Bourdieu. 1986. 'The forms of capital.' In J. G. Richardson (ed.), *Handbook of Theory and Research for the Sociology of Education*, pp. 241–258. New York:

Greenwood Press; James Coleman. 1988. 'Social capital and the creation of human capital.' *American Journal of Sociology* 94: 95–120.

11. Robert Putnam. 1993. *Bowling Alone?* New York: Simon and Schuster; Susan J. Pharr and Robert D. Putnam (eds.). 2000. *Disaffected Democracies: What's Troubling the Trilateral Countries?* Princeton, NJ: Princeton University Press.

12. Robert D. Putnam, R. Leonardi, and R. Y. Nanetti. 1993. *Making Democracy Work: Civic Traditions in Modern Italy.* Princeton, NJ: Princeton University Press.

13. Gallup. 2019. *Trust in Government.* https://news.gallup.com/poll/5392/trust-gov ernment.aspx.

14. E. J. Dionne, Jr. 1991. *Why Americans Hate Politics.* New York: Simon and Schuster; Joseph S. Nye, Philip D. Zelikow, and David C. King (eds.). 1997. *Why People Don't Trust Government.* Cambridge, MA: Harvard University Press; John R. Hibbing and Elizabeth Theiss-Morse (eds.). 2001. *What Is It about Government That Americans Dislike?* Cambridge: Cambridge University Press.

15. Russell J. Dalton. 2004. *Democratic Challenges, Democratic Choices: The Erosion of Political Support in Advanced Industrial Democracies.* New York: Oxford University Press.

16. Philippe Schmitter and Alexander Trechsel. 2004. *The Future of Democracy in Europe.* Strasbourg: Council of Europe.

17. Mariano Torcal and Jose Ramon Montero (eds.). 2006. *Political Disaffection in Contemporary Democracies: Social Capital, Institutions, and Politics.* London: Routledge.

18. Susan J. Pharr and Robert D. Putnam (eds.). 2000. *Disaffected Democracies: What's Troubling the Trilateral Countries?* Princeton, NJ: Princeton University Press; Mattei Dogan (ed.). 2005. *Political Mistrust and the Discrediting of Politicians.* Leiden: Brill; Gerry Stoker. 2006. *Why Politics Matters: Making Democracy Work.* London: Palgrave/Macmillan, Ch. 2; Mariano Torcal and José R. Montero (eds.). 2006. *Political Disaffection in Contemporary Democracies: Social Capital, Institutions, and Politics.* London: Routledge; Colin Hay. 2007. *Why We Hate Politics.* Cambridge: Polity Press; Russell J. Dalton. 2004. *Democratic Challenges, Democratic Choices: The Erosion of Political Support in Advanced Industrial Democracies.* New York: Oxford University Press.

19. Mattei Dogan (ed.). 2005. *Political Mistrust and the Discrediting of Politicians.* Leiden: Brill, p. 12.

20. Freedom in the World, 2019. https://freedomhouse.org/report/freedom-world/free dom-world-2019.

21. Hans-Dieter Klingemann and Dieter Fuchs (eds.). 1994. *Citizens and the State.* Oxford: Oxford University Press.

22. Sergio Martini and Mario Quaranta. 2020. *Citizens and Democracy in Europe: Contexts, Changes and Political Support.* London: Palgrave Macmillan; Sofie Marien. 2013. 'Measuring political trust across time and space.' In Donja Zimerli and Marc Hooghe (eds.), *Political Trust: Why Context Matters.* Colchester: ECPR Press; Monica Ferrin and Hanspeter Kreisi (eds.). 2016. *How Europeans View and Evaluate Democracy.* New York: Oxford University Press.

23. Rudy B. Andeweg and Kees Aarts. 2017. 'Studying political legitimacy.' In Carolien van Ham, Jacques Thomassen, Kaas Aarts, and Rudy Andeweg (eds.), *Myth and Reality of the Legitimacy Crisis*, Ch. 11, p. 202. Oxford: Oxford University Press.

24. Carolien Van Ham, Jacques Thomassen, Kees Aarts, and Rudy Andeweg (eds.). 2017. *Myth and Reality of the Legitimacy Crisis.* Oxford: Oxford University Press.

25. Edelman Trust Barometer, 2021. https://www.edelman.com/trust/2021-trust-barometer.

26. David Brooks. October 5, 2020. 'America is having a moral convulsion.' *The Atlantic.* https://www.theatlantic.com/ideas/archive/2020/10/collapsing-levels-trust-are-deva stating-america/616581/.

27. Carolien Van Ham, Jacques Thomassen, Kees Aarts, and Rudy Andeweg (eds.). 2017. *Myth and Reality of the Legitimacy Crisis.* Oxford: Oxford University Press. For similar conclusions, see also Russell J. Dalton. 2004. *Democratic Challenges, Democratic Choices: The Erosion of Political Support in Advanced Industrial Democracies.* New York: Oxford University Press; Pippa Norris. 2011. *Democratic Deficit.* New York: Cambridge University Press; Christian Schnaudt. 2018. *Political Confidence and Democracy in Europe.* New York: Springer.

28. Seymour Martin Lipset. 1987. *The Confidence Gap.* 2nd ed. Baltimore, MD: Johns Hopkins University Press; John R. Hibbing and Elizabeth Theiss-Morse (eds.). 2001. *What Is It about Government That Americans Dislike?* Cambridge: Cambridge University Press. For debates over the meaning of the ANES battery of questions on trust in government, see Jack Citrin. 1974. 'Comment: The political relevance of trust in government.' *American Political Science Review* 68: 973–988; Arthur Miller. 1974. 'Political issues and trust in government, 1964–1970.' *American Political Science Review* 68: 951–972.

29. For contemporary trends, see the Pew Research Center. December 2019. *Public Trust in Government: 1958–2019.* https://www.people-press.org/2019/04/11/public-trust-in-government-1958-2019/.

30. Gallup: Q: "Now I am going to read you a list of institutions in American society. Please tell me how much confidence you, yourself, have in each one—a great deal, a fair amount, not very much or none at all? Congress." Gallup 2019. *Trust in Government.* https://news.gallup.com/poll/5392/trust-government.aspx.

31. Concern about this development has generated an extensive American literature; cf. Stephen Craig. 1993. *The Malevolent Leaders: Popular Discontent in America.* Boulder, CO: Westview Press; John R. Hibbing and E. Theiss-Morse (eds.). 2001. *What Is It about Government That Americans Dislike?* Cambridge: Cambridge University Press.

32. Roberto Stephen Foa and Yasha Mounk. 2016. 'The dangers of deconsolidation: The democratic disconnect.' *Journal of Democracy* 27: 5–17; Roberto Stephen Foa and Yasha Mounk. 2017. 'The signs of deconsolidation.' *Journal of Democracy* 28(1): 5–15. For critiques, however, see Ronald Inglehart. 2016. 'The danger of deconsolidation: How much should we worry?' *Journal of Democracy* 27; Erik Voeten. December 5, 2016. 'That viral graph about millennials' declining support for democracy? It's very misleading.' *Washington Post/Monkey Cage*; Erik Voeten. December 14, 2016. 'It's actually older people who have become more cynical about U.S. democracy.'

Washington Post/Monkey Cage; Jan Zilansky. 'Democratic deconsolidation: revisited: Young Europeans are not dissatisfied with democracy.' *Research & Politics* 6(1): 1–8.

33. Cas Mudde and C. R. Kaltwasser (eds.). 2012. *Populism in Europe and the Americas: Threat or Corrective for Democracy?* New York: Cambridge University Press; Pippa Norris and Ron Inglehart. 2018. *Cultural Backlash*. New York: Cambridge University Press.

34. Pippa Norris and Ronald Inglehart. 2019. *Cultural Backlash*. New York: Cambridge University Press.

35. Pippa Norris. 2005. *Radical Right: Voters and Parties in the Electoral Market*. New York: Cambridge University Press.

36. Jan-Werner Muller. 2016. *What is Populism?* Philadelphia: University of Pennsylvania Press; Benjamin Moffitt. 2016. *The Global Rise of Populism: Performance, Political Style and Representation*. Palo Alto, CA: Stanford University Press.

37. Margaret Canovan. 1999. 'Trust the people! Populism and the two faces of democracy.' *Political Studies* XLVII: 2–16.

38. Mark Potok. 2017. *The Year in Hate and Extremism*. Montgomery, AL: Southern Poverty Law Center. https://www.splcenter.org/fighting-hate/intelligence-report/2017/year-hate-and-extremism.

39. Eric Kaufmann. 2019. *Whiteshift: Populism, Immigration, and the Future of White Majorities*. New York: Abrams; Kathleen Belew. 2019. *Bring the War Home: The White Power Movement and Paramilitary America*. Cambridge, MA: Harvard University Press.

40. J. Eric Oliver and Wendy M. Rahn. 2016. 'Rise of the Trumpenvolk: Populism in the 2016 election.' *Annals of the American Academy of Political and Social Science* 667(1): 189–206; Steven W. Webster. 2018. 'Anger and declining trust in the American electorate.' *Political Behavior* 40: 933–964.

41. Cas Mudde. 2007. *Populist Radical Right Parties in Europe*. New York: Cambridge University Press.

42. Allan R. Brewer-Carías. 2010. *Dismantling Democracy in Venezuela: The Chávez Authoritarian Experiment*. Cambridge: Cambridge University Press.

43. Gerry Stoker. 2006. *Why Politics Matters: Making Democracy Work*. London: Palgrave/Macmillan; Colin Hay. 2007. *Why We Hate Politics*. Cambridge: Polity Press.

44. Will Jennings, Nick Clarke, Jonathan Moss, and Gerry Stoker. 2017. 'The decline in diffuse support for national politics: The long view on political discontent in Britain.' *Public Opinion Quarterly* 81(3): 748–758.

45. Stephan Haggard and Robert Kaufman. 2021. *Backsliding: Democratic Regress in the Contemporary World*. Cambridge: Cambridge University Press.

46. V. Mechkova, Anna Luhrmann, and Staffan Lindberg. 2017. 'How much democratic backsliding?' *Journal of Democracy* 28: 162–169; D. Waldner and Ellen Lust. 2018. 'Unwelcome change.' *Annual Review of Political Science* 21: 93–113.

47. Freedom House. 2022. *Freedom in the World, 2021*. https://freedomhouse.org/report/freedom-world/2021/democracy-under-siege.

48. Larry Diamond and Marc Plattner (eds.). 2015. *Democracy in Decline?* Baltimore, MD: Johns Hopkins University Press; J. Kurlantzick. 2014. *Democracy in Retreat*.

New Haven, CT: Yale University Press; Larry Diamond, Marc Plattner, and Caroline Walker. 2016. *Authoritarianism Goes Global.* Baltimore, MD: Johns Hopkins University Press; E. Luce. 2017. *The Retreat of Western Liberalism.* New York: Little Brown; Brian Klass. 2017. *The Despot's Apprentice.* New York: Hot Books; Yasha Mounk. 2018. *The People vs. Democracy.* Cambridge, MA: Harvard University Press; Steven Levitsky and Daniel Ziblatt. 2018. *How Democracies Die.* New York: Crown; Cass R. Sunstein (ed.). 2018. *Can it Happen Here?* New York: HarperCollins.

49. International IDEA. 2021. *The Global State of Democracy 2021.* Stockholm: Sweden. https://www.idea.int/gsod/.

50. Pippa Norris and Ronald Inglehart. 2019. *Cultural Backlash.* New York: Cambridge University Press.

51. Matthijs Rooduijn, Wouter Van Der Brug, and Sarah L. de Lange. 2016. 'Expressing or fueling discontent? The relationship between populist voting and political discontent.' *Electoral Studies* 43: 32–40.

52. Cas Mudde and Cristóbal Rovira Kaltwasser (eds.). 2012. *Populism in Europe and the Americas: Threat or Corrective for Democracy?* New York: Cambridge University Press; Jasper Muis and Tim Immerzeel. 2018. 'Causes and consequences of the rise of populist radical right parties and movements in Europe.' *Current Sociology* 65(6): 909–930.

53. Gallup. https://news.gallup.com/poll/1597/confidence-institutions.aspx.

54. See also, Pew Research Center. May 17, 2021. *Public trust in government: 1958–2021.* https://www.pewresearch.org/politics/2021/05/17/public-trust-in-government-1958-2021/.

55. https://gssdataexplorer.norc.org/.

56. Edward Glaeser, David I. Laibson, Jose A. Scheikman, and Christine Southtter. 2000. 'Measuring trust.' *The Quarterly Journal of Economics* 115(3): 811–846; Paul Bauer and Marcus Frietag. 2018. 'Measuring trust.' In Eric Uslaner (ed.), *Oxford Handbook of Social and Political Trust.* New York: Oxford University Press.

57. Dorian Schaap and Peer Scheepers. 2014. 'Comparing citizens' trust in police across European countries: An assessment of cross-country measurement equivalence.' *International Criminal Justice Review* 24(1), 82–98; Irena Schneider. 2017. 'Can we trust measures of political trust? Assessing measurement equivalence in diverse regime types.' *Social Indicators Research* 133: 963–984.

58. Eric M. Uslaner. 2002. *The Moral Foundations of Trust.* New York: Cambridge University Press.

59. See, for example, Jan Delhey and Kenneth Newton. 2005. 'Predicting cross-national levels of social trust: Global patterns of Nordic exceptionalism?' *European Sociological Review* 21(4): 311–327; A. Bergh and R. Öhrvall. 2018. 'A sticky trait: Social trust among Swedish expatriates in countries with varying institutional quality.' *Journal of Comparative Economics* 46: 1146–1157.

60. Ronald Inglehart. 1997. *Modernization and Postmodernization: Cultural, Economic and Political Change in 43 Societies.* Princeton, NJ: Princeton University Press.

61. Virginia A. Chanley, Thomas J. Rudolph, and Wendy Rahn. 2000. 'The origins and consequences of public trust in government: A time series analysis.' *Public Opinion Quarterly* 64(3): 239–256.

62. See, for example, Stephen E. Finke, Edward Muller, and Mitchell A. Seligson. 1987. 'Economic crisis, incumbent performance and regime support.' *British Journal of Political Science* 19: 329–351; G. M. Dotti Sani and B. Magistro. 2016. 'Increasingly unequal? The economic crisis, social inequalities and trust in the European Parliament in 20 European countries.' *European Journal of Political Research* 55(2): 246–264; Veronica Fagerland Kroknes, Tor Georg Jakobsen, and Lisa-Marie Grønning. 2016. 'Economic performance and political trust: The impact of the financial crisis on European citizens.' *European Societies* 17(5): 700–723; Chase Foster and Jeffry Frieden. 2017. 'Crisis of trust: Socioeconomic determinants of European confidence in government.' *European Union Politics* 18(4); Bruno Arpinio and Anastassia V. Obyden. 2020. 'Democracy and political trust before and after the Great Recession of 2008: The European Union and the United Nations.' *Social Indicators Research.* 148: 395–415.

63. Daniel Devine, Jennifer Gaskell, Will Jennings, and Gerry Stoker. 2020. 'Trust and the Coronavirus pandemic: What are the consequences of and for trust? An early review of the literature.' *Political Studies Review* 19(2): 274–285.

64. Virginia A. Chanley. 2002. 'Trust in government in the aftermath of 9/11: Determinants and consequences.' *Political Psychology* 23(3): 469–483.

65. Dhavan V. Shah, Mark D. Watts, David Domke, and David Fan. 2002. 'News framing and cueing of issue regimes: Explaining Clinton's public approval in spite of scandal.' *Public Opinion Quarterly* 66(3): 339–370; David J. Smyth and Susan Washburn Taylor. 2003. 'Presidential popularity: What matters most, macroeconomics or scandals?' *Applied Economics Letters* 10(9): 585–588.

66. G. Catterberg and Alejandro Moreno. 2006. 'The individual bases of political trust: Trends in new and established democracies.' *International Journal of Public Opinion Research* 18(1): 31–48.

67. Jan Delhey and Kenneth Newton. 2005. 'Predicting cross-national levels of social trust: Global patterns of Nordic exceptionalism?' *European Sociological Review* 21(4): 311–327.

68. See Kim Mannemar Sønderskov and Peter Thisted Dinesen. 2014. 'Danish exceptionalism: Explaining the unique increase in social trust over the past 30 years.' *European Sociological Review* 30(6): 782–795.

69. https://gssdataexplorer.norc.org/.

70. See Bo Rothstein. 2000. 'Social capital in the social democratic state.' In Robert D. Putnam (ed.), *Democracies in Flux.* Oxford: Oxford University Press.

71. Staffan Kumlin and Bo Rothstein. 2005. 'Making and breaking social capital.' *Comparative Political Studies* 38(4): 339–365; Staffan Kumlin. 2004. *The Personal and the Political: How Personal Welfare State Experiences Affect Political Trust and Ideology.* London: Palgrave Macmillan; Bo Rothstein. 2011. *The Quality of Government: Corruption, Social Trust and Inequality in International Perspective.* Chicago: University of Chicago Press; Bo Rothstein and Dieter Stolle. 2008. 'The state and social capital: An institutional theory of generalized trust.' *Comparative Politics* 33(4): 401–419.

72. Carles Boix and Daniel N. Posner. 1998. 'Social capital: Explaining its origins and effects on government performance.' *British Journal of Political Science* 28(4): 686–693.

73. See, however, Blaine G. Robbins. 2012. 'Institutional quality and generalized trust: A non-recursive causal model.' *Social Indicators Research* 107(2): 235–258; Blaine G. Robbins. 2012. 'A blessing and a curse? Political institutions in the growth and decay of generalized trust: A cross-national panel analysis, 1980–2009.' *PloS One* 7(4): e35120.

74. Robert D. Putnam. 2007. 'E pluribus unum: Diversity and community in the twenty-first century: The 2006 Johan Skytte Prize Lecture.' *Scandinavian Political Studies* 30(2): 137–174.

75. Pippa Norris and Ronald Inglehart. 2011. *Sacred and Secular.* 2nd ed. New York: Cambridge University Press, Ch 8.

76. Robert D. Putnam. 2000. *Bowling Alone: The Collapse and Revival of American Community.* New York: Simon and Schuster. P.66.

77. Richard Traunmüller. 2011. 'Moral communities? Religion as a source of social trust in a multilevel analysis of 97 German regions.' *European Sociological Review* 27(3): 346–363; Robert Putnam and David E. Campbell. 2010. *American Grace: How Religion Divides and Unites Us.* New York: Simon & Schuster; E. Dingemans and E. Van Ingen. 2015. 'Does religion breed trust? A cross-national study of the effects of religious involvement, religious faith, and religious context on social trust.' *Journal for the Scientific Study of Religion* 54: 739–755; Pippa Norris and Ronald Inglehart. 2011. *Sacred and Secular.* 2nd ed. New York: Cambridge University Press, Ch. 8.

78. For one approach trying to get over this issue using migration data, see, for example, Peter Nannestad, Gert T. Svendsen, Peter T. Dinesen, and Kim M. Sønderskov. 2014. 'Do institutions or culture determine the level of social trust? The natural experiment of migration from non-western to western countries.' *Journal of Ethnic and Migration Studies* 40(4): 544–565.

79. Andre Van Hoorn. 2014. 'Trust radius versus trust level: Trust radius as a distinct trust construct.' *American Sociological Review* 79(6): 1256–1259; Paul Bauer and Marcus Frietag. 2018. 'Measuring trust.' In Eric Uslaner (ed.), *Oxford Handbook of Social and Political Trust.* New York: Oxford University Press.

80. Jan Delhey and Kenneth Newton. 2005. 'Predicting cross-national levels of social trust: Global patterns of Nordic exceptionalism?' *European Sociological Review* 21(4): 311–327. See also Christian Bjornskov. 2007. 'Determinants of generalized trust: A cross-country comparison.' *Public Choice* 130(1–2): 1–21.

81. Stephen Earl Bennett, Stephen L. Rhine, R. S. Flickinger, and Lance Bennett. 1999. ' "Video Malaise" revisited: Public trust in the media and government.' *Harvard International Journal of Press/Politics* 4(4): 8–23; Pippa Norris. 1999. *A Virtuous Circle.* New York: Cambridge University Press; James M. Avery. 2009. 'Videomalaise or virtuous circle? The influence of the news media on political trust.' *International Journal of Press-Politics* 14(4): 410–433.

82. Megan Brenan. 2020. 'Americans Remain Distrustful of Mass Media.' *Gallup Polls,* https://news.gallup.com/poll/321116/americans-remain-distrustful-mass-media.aspx; Michael Schudson. 2019. 'The fall, rise and fall of media trust.' *Columbia Journalism Review.* https://www.cjr.org/special_report/the-fall-rise-and-fall-of-media-trust.php.

83. Jeffrey Gottfried et al. 2019. 'Trusting the news media in the Trump era.' Pew Research Center.   https://www.journalism.org/2019/12/12/trusting-the-news-media-in-the-trump-era/.

84. Yochasi Benkler, Robert Faris, and Hal Roberts. 2018. *Network Propaganda*. New York: Oxford University Press.

85. Thomas Hanitzsch, A. Van Dalen, and N. Steindl. 2018. 'Caught in the nexus: A comparative and longitudinal analysis of public trust in the press.' *International Journal of Press/Politics* 23(1): 3–23.

86. Nic Newman. 2021. *Reuters Institute Digital News Report 2021*, 10th ed. https://reute rsinstitute.politics.ox.ac.uk/digital-news-report/2021.

87. Zacc Ritter. 2019. 'How much does the world trust journalists?' *Gallup*, https://news.gallup.com/opinion/gallup/272999/world-trust-journalists.aspx.

88. A. Daniller, D. Allen, A. Tallevi, and D. Mutz. 2017. 'Measuring trust in the press in a changing media environment.' *Communication Methods and Measures* 11(1): 76–85; Katherine M. Engelke, Valerie Hase, and Florian Wintterlin. 2019. 'On measuring trust and distrust in journalism: Reflection of the status quo and suggestions for the road ahead.' *Journal of Trust Research* 9(1): 66–86.

89. Robert D. Putnam. 2000. *Bowling Alone: The Collapse and Revival of American Community*. New York: Simon & Schuster.

90. Pamela Paxton. 2007. 'Association memberships and generalized trust: A multilevel model across 31 countries.' *Social Forces* 86(1): 47–76.

91. Ronald Inglehart and W. E. Baker. 2000. 'Modernization, cultural change, and the persistence of traditional values.' *American Sociological Review* 65(1): 19–51.

92. Pippa Norris. 2003. *Democratic Phoenix*. New York: Cambridge University Press; Pippa Norris and Ronald Inglehart. 2011. *Sacred and Secular*. 2nd ed. New York: Cambridge University Press; J. E. Curtis, E. G. Grabb, and D. E. Baer. 1992. 'Voluntary association membership in fifteen countries: A comparative analysis.' *American Sociological Review* 57(2): 139–152, J. E. Curtis, D. E. Baer, and E. G. Grabb. 2001. 'Nations of joiners: Explaining voluntary association membership in democratic societies.' *American Sociological Review* 66(6): 783–805.

93. Robert D. Putnam. 2000. *Bowling Alone: The Collapse and Revival of American Community*. New York: Simon & Schuster, p. 66.

94. Pippa Norris and Ronald Inglehart. 2011. *Sacred and Secular*. 2nd ed. New York: Cambridge University Press; Ronald Inglehart. 2021. *Religion's Sudden Decline: What's Causing It, and What Comes Next?* New York: Oxford University Press.

95. Pippa Norris (ed.). 1999. *Critical Citizens: Global Support for Democratic Governance*. New York: Oxford University Press.

96. Susan Pharr and Robert D. Putnam (eds.). 2000. *Disaffected Democracies: What's Troubling the Trilateral Countries?* Princeton, NJ: Princeton University Press; Russell. J. Dalton. 2004. *Democratic Challenges, Democratic Choices: The Erosion of Political Support in Advanced Industrial Democracies*. New York: Oxford University Press.

97. European Commission 2018. http://ec.europa.eu/commfrontoffice/publicopinion/index.cfm.

98. Allison Park, C. Bryson, E. Clery, John Curtice, and Melanie Phillips (eds.). 2013. *British Social Attitudes: The 30th Report*. London: NatCen Social Research.

99. Jonas Tallberg, Karin Backsterand, and Jan Aart Scholte (eds.). 2018. *Legitimacy in Global Governance*. Oxford: Oxford University Press.

100. See, for example, Pippa Norris and Ronald Inglehart. 2006. 'Gendering social capital: Bowling in women's leagues?' In Brenda O'Neill and Elizabeth Gidengil (eds.), *Gender and Social Capital*. New York: Routledge; Shagata Mukherjee. 2020. 'What drives gender differences in trust and trustworthiness?' *Public Finance Review* 48(6): 778–805. doi:10.1177/1091142120960801.

101. Ronald Inglehart. 1997. *Modernization and Postmodernization: Cultural, Economic and Political Change in 43 Societies*. Princeton, NJ: Princeton University Press.

102. Russell J. Dalton. 2005. 'The social transformation of trust in government.' *International Review of Sociology* 15(1): 133–154.

103. Robert D. Putnam. 2000. *Bowling Alone: The Collapse and Revival of American Community*. New York: Simon & Schuster.

104. Matthias Sutter and Martin G. Kocher. 2007. 'Trust and trustworthiness across different age groups.' *Games and Economic Behavior* 59(2): 364–382,

105. Pippa Norris. 2009. 'Confidence in the United Nations: Cosmopolitan and nationalistic attitudes.' In Yilmaz Esmer and Thorleif Pettersson (eds.), *The International System, Democracy and Values*. Uppsala: Uppsala University Press.

106. Michael Robinson. 1976. 'Public affairs television and the growth of political malaise.' *American Political Science Review* 70: 409–432.

107. Thomas Patterson. 1993. *Out of Order*. New York: Knopf.

108. Suzanne Garment. 1991. *Scandal: The Crisis of Mistrust in American Politics*. New York: Random House; Gary Orren 1997. 'Fall from grace: The public's loss of faith in government.' In Joseph S. Nye, Jr., Philip D. Zelikow, and David C. King (eds.), *Why People Don't Trust Government*. Chicago: University of Chicago Press.

109. Joseph Capella and Kathleen Hall Jamieson. 1997. *Spiral of Cynicism*. New York: Oxford University Press.

110. Kathleen Hall Jamieson. 2018. *Cyberwar: How Russian Hackers and Trolls Helped Elect a President*. New York: Oxford University Press; Elad Klein and Joshua Robison. 2019. 'Like, post, and distrust? How social media use affects trust in government.' *Political Communication* 1–19; Russell Muirhead and Nancy Rosenbau. 2020. *A Lot of People Are Saying: The New Conspiracism and the Assault on Democracy*. Princeton, NJ: Princeton University Press.

111. Johannes Gerschewski. 2013. 'The three pillars of stability.' *Democratization* 20(1): 13–38; Johannes Gerschewski. 2018. 'Legitimacy in autocracies: Oxymoron or essential feature?' *Perspectives on Politics* 16(3): 652–665.

112. Pippa Norris. 2000. *A Virtuous Circle*. New York: Cambridge University Press; Claes H. De Vreese. 2005. 'The spiral of cynicism reconsidered.' *European Journal of Communication* 20(3): 283–301; Richard R. Lau and I. B. Rovner. 2009. 'Negative campaigning.' *Annual Review of Political Science* 12: 285–306; Nicholas A. Valentino. 2001. 'A spiral of cynicism for some: The contingent effects of campaign news frames on participation and confidence in government.' *Political Communication* 18: 347.

113. Earl Bennett, Stephen L. Rhine, R. S. Flickinger, and Lance Bennett. 1999. ' "Video Malaise" revisited: Public trust in the media and government.' *Harvard International Journal of Press/Politics* 4(4): 8–23; Claes H. De Vreese. 2005. 'The spiral of cynicism reconsidered.' *European Journal of Communication* 20(3): 283–301; Anna Brosius, Erika J. van Elsas, and Claes H. de Vreese. 2019. 'Trust in the European Union: Effects of the information environment.' *European Journal of Communication* 34(1): 57–73; James M. Avery. 2009. 'Videomalaise or virtuous circle? The influence of the news media on political trust.' *International Journal of Press-Politics* 14(4): 410–433.

114. See the discussion in James M. Avery. 2009. 'Videomalaise or virtuous circle? The influence of the news media on political trust.' *International Journal of Press-Politics* 14(4): 410–433; Anna Brosius, Erika J. van Elsas, and Claes H. de Vreese. 2019. 'Trust in the European Union: Effects of the information environment.' *European Journal of Communication* 34(1): 57–73.

115. Steven Levitsky and Daniel Ziblatt. 2018. *How Democracies Die*. New York: Crown; Stephan Haggard and Robert Kaufman. 2021. *Backsliding: Democratic Regress in the Contemporary World*. Cambridge: Cambridge University Press.

116. Carolien van Ham, Jacques Thomassen, Kaas Aarts, and Rudy Andeweg (eds.). 2018. *Myth and Reality of the Legitimacy Crisis*. Oxford: Oxford University Press.

117. Robert D. Putnam. 1993. *Making Democracy Work: Civic Traditions in Modern Italy*. Princeton, NJ: Princeton University Press; Robert D. Putnam. 1995. 'Bowling Alone: America's Declining Social Capital.' *Journal of Democracy* 6: 65–78; Robert D. Putnam. 2000. *Bowling Alone: The Collapse and Revival of American Community*. New York: Simon & Schuster; Robert Putnam (ed.). 2002. *Democracies in Flux: The Evolution of Social Capital in Contemporary Society*. Oxford: Oxford University Press; Susan Pharr and Robert Putnam (eds.). 2000. *Disaffected Democracies*. Princeton, NJ: Princeton University Press; Robert Putnam and Lewis Feldstein. 2003. *Better Together: Restoring the American Community*. New York: Simon & Schuster.

118. Dietlind Stolle and Marc Hooghe. 2005. 'Inaccurate, exceptional, one-sided or irrelevant? The debate about the decline of social capital and civic engagement in Western Societies.' *British Journal of Political Science* 35(1): 149–167; Everett C. Ladd. 1996. 'The data just don't show erosion of America's "social capital." ' *The Public Perspective* 5–22; Pippa Norris. *Democratic Phoenix*. 2002. New York: Cambridge University Press.

119. Jack Citrin. 1974. 'Comment: The political relevance of trust in government.' *American Political Science Review* 68: 973–988; Arthur H. Miller. 1974. 'Political issues and trust in government, 1964–1970.' *American Political Science Review* 68: 951–972; Jonas Linde and J. Ekman. 2003. 'Satisfaction with democracy: A note on a frequently used indicator in comparative politics.' *European Journal of Political Research* 42(3): 391–408; David Canache, Jeff J. Mondak, and Mitch A. Seligson. 2001. 'Meaning and measurement in cross-national research on satisfaction with democracy.' *Public Opinion Quarterly* 65(4): 506–528; Geert Bouckaert and Steven van de Walle. 2003. 'Comparing measures of citizen trust and user satisfaction as indicators of "good governance": Difficulties in linking trust and satisfaction

indicators.' *International Review of Administrative Sciences* 69(3): 329–343; Tom Reeskens and Marc Hooghe. 2008. 'Cross-cultural measurement equivalence of generalized trust: Evidence from the European Social Survey (2002 and 2004).' *Social Indicators Research* 85: 515–532.

120. Pippa Norris. 2002. *Democratic Phoenix*. New York: Cambridge University Press.
121. Pippa Norris and Ronald Inglehart. 2019. *Cultural Backlash*. New York: Cambridge University Press, Ch. 8 and 12; Mathias Rooduijn, Wouter Van Der Brug, and Sarah L. de Lange. 2016. 'Expressing or fuelling discontent? The relationship between populist voting and political discontent.' *Electoral Studies* 43: 32–40.

Chapter 5

1. See Jack Citrin and Laura Stoker. 2018. 'Political trust in a cynical age.' *Annual Review of Political Science* 21(1): 49–70.
2. For a thorough meta-analysis of over 70 studies published in the empirical literature, see Jiasheng Zhang, Hui Li, and Kaifeng Yang. 2021. 'A meta-analysis of the Government Performance-Trust link: Taking culture and methodological factors into account.' *Public Administration Review* 82: 39–58.
3. Alex Jingwei He and Liang Ma. 2021. 'Citizen participation, perceived public service performance, and trust in government: Evidence from health policy reforms in Hong Kong.' *Public Performance & Management Review* 44(3): 471–493; Rifat Mahmud. 2021. 'What explains citizen trust in public institutions? Quality of government, performance, social capital, or demography.' *Asia Pacific Journal of Public Administration* 43(2): 106–124.
4. Jiasheng Zhang, Hui Li, and Kaifeng Yang. 2021. 'A meta-analysis of the Government Performance-Trust link: Taking culture and methodological factors into account.' *Public Administration Review* 82: 39–58; Steven Van de Walle and Geert Bouckaert. 2003. 'Public service performance and trust in government: The problem of causality.' *International Journal of Public Administration* 26(8–9): 891–913; Patrick Weber, Holger Steinmetz, and Rüdiger Kabst. 2017. 'Trust in politicians and satisfaction with government: A reciprocal causation approach for European Countries.' *Journal of Civil Society* 13(4): 392–405.
5. Christopher Anderson. 1995. *Blaming the Government: Citizens and the Economy in Five European Democracies*. New York: M. E. Sharpe; Jane Green and Will Jennings. 2017. *The Politics of Competence*. Cambridge: Cambridge University Press, pp. 13–14.
6. Michael Lewis-Beck. 2019. 'Economic voting.' In Roger D. Congleton, Bernard Grofman, and Stefan Voigt (eds.), *The Oxford Handbook of Public Choice*. Oxford: Oxford University Press.
7. Tom Van der Meer and Armen Hakhverdian. 2016. 'Political trust as an evaluation of process and performance: A cross-national study of 42 European countries.' *Political Studies* 65(1): 81–102.

8. For example, see the series of Gallup polls: https://news.gallup.com/poll/1675/most-important-problem.aspx.

9. See, for example, Tom Van der Meer and Paul Dekker 2011. 'Trustworthy states, trusting citizens? A multilevel study into objective and subjective determinants of political trust.' In Sonia Zmerli and Marc Hooghe (eds.), *Political Trust: Why Context Matters*. Colchester: ECPR Press; Tom Van der Meer and Armen Hakhverdian. 2016. 'Political trust as an evaluation of process and performance: A cross-national study of 42 European countries.' *Political Studies* 65(1): 81–102; Christina Boswell. 2018. *Manufacturing Political Trust: Targets and Performance Management in Public Policy*. Cambridge: Cambridge University Press; Klaus Armingeon and B. Ceka. 2013. 'The loss of trust in the great recession since 2007: The role of heuristics from the national political system.' *European Union Politics* 15(1): 82–107; G. Cordero and P. Simón. 2015. 'Economic crisis and support for democracy in Europe.' *West European Politics* 39(2): 305–325.

10. Richard Cowell et al. 2012. 'Public confidence in public services: It matters what you measure.' *Policy and Politics* 40(1): 123–143.

11. See, for example, L. B. Becker, T. Vlad, and N. Nusser. 2007. 'An evaluation of press freedom indicators.' *International Communication Gazette* 69: 5–28.

12. G. Eady, J. Nagler, A. Guess, J. Zilinsky, and J. A. Tucker. 'How many people live in political bubbles on social media? Evidence From linked survey and twitter data.' *SAGE Open*. doi:10.1177/2158244019832705.

13. Y. Benkler. 2006. *The Wealth of Networks: How Social Production Transforms Markets and Freedom*. New Haven, CT: Yale University Press; R. Fletcher, and R. K. Nielsen. 2018. 'Are people incidentally exposed to news on social media? A comparative analysis.' *New Media & Society* 20: 2450–2468.

14. Pippa Norris (ed.). 2010. *Public Sentinel: News Media and the Governance Agenda*. Washington, DC: World Bank.

15. The concept and theory of "two-sided" information flows, with both dominant and countervailing messages, was developed by John Zaller. 2012. *The Nature and Origins of Mass Opinions*. New York: Cambridge University Press, Ch. 9.

16. Cailin O'Connor and James Owen Weatherall. 2019. *The Misinformation Age*. New Haven, CT: Yale University Press; Kembrew McLeod and Melissa Zimdars (eds.). 2020. *Fake News: Understanding Media and Misinformation in the Digital Age*. Cambridge, MA: MIT Press.

17. Jane Green and Will Jennings. 2017. *The Politics of Competence*. Cambridge: Cambridge University Press.

18. S. Greenspan. 2009. *Annals of Gullibility: Why We Get Duped and How to Avoid It*. Westport, CT: Praeger; J. Rotter. 1980. 'Interpersonal trust, trustworthiness, and gullibility.' *American Psychologist* 35: 1–7; P. Fischer, S. E. Lea, and K. M. Evans. 2013. 'Why do individuals respond to fraudulent scam communications and lose money? The psychological determinants of scam compliance.' *Journal of Applied Social Psychology* 43: 2060–2072; Alessandra K. Teunisse, Trevor I. Case, Julie Fitness, and Naoimi Swellere. 2019. 'I should have known better: Development of a self-report measurement of gullibility.' *Personality and Social Psychology Bulletin* 46(3): 408–423;

Joseph P. Forgas. 2019. 'Happy believers and sad skeptics? Affective influences on gul-libility.' *Current Directions in Psychological Science* 28(3): 306–313.

19. Hugo Mercier. 2020. *Not Born Yesterday: The Science of Who We Trust and What We Believe*. Princeton, NJ: Princeton University Press.

20. Pippa Norris. 2000. *A Virtuous Circle*. New York: Cambridge University Press; Jesper Stromback and Adam Shehata. 2010. 'Media malaise or a virtuous circle? Exploring the causal relationship between news media exposure, political news attention and political interest.' *European Journal of Political Research* 49: 575–597.

21. Michael Lewis-Beck. 2019. 'Economic voting.' In Roger D. Congleton, Bernard Grofman, and Stefan Voigt (eds.), *The Oxford Handbook of Public Choice*. Oxford: Oxford University Press.

22. Michael Delli Carpini and Scott Keeter. 1996. *What Americans Know about Politics and Why It Matters*. New Haven, CT: Yale University Press.

23. Christopher Achen and Larry Bartels. 2016. *Democracy for Realists*. Princeton, NJ: Princeton University Press, Ch. 4.

24. Michael Delli Carpini and Scott Keeter. 1996. *What Americans Know about Politics and Why It Matters*. New Haven, CT: Yale University Press; Arthur Lupia. 2016. *Uninformed: Why People Know So Little about Politics and What We Can Do about It*. New York: Oxford University Press.

25. Ian McAllister. 1999. 'The economic performance of governments.' In Pippa Norris (ed.), *Critical Citizens: Global Support for Democratic Governance*. New York: Oxford University Press.

26. See Jane Green and Will Jennings. 2017. *The Politics of Competence*. New York: Cambridge University Press. "We believe performance fluctuations reflect mean-ingful updating among those people who have partisan attachment. . . . Generalized competence assessments more commonly lead partisanship than vice versa" (p. 93).

27. Pippa Norris. 1999. *A Virtuous Circle*. New York: Cambridge University Press.

28. See, for example, James Downe et al. 2013. 'The determinants of public trust in English local government: How important is the ethical behavior or elected councilors?' *International Review of Administrative Sciences* 79(4): 597–617; L. Dong and D. Kübler. 2017. 'Sources of local political trust in rural China.' *Journal of Contemporary China* 27(110): 193–207; Lorenzo Eastra and Fraccisco Bastida. 2019. 'Effective trans-parency and institutional trust in Honduran municipal government.' *Administration and Society* 52(6): 890–926.

29. Tom Van der Meer and Armen Hakhverdian. 2016. 'Political trust as an evaluation of process and performance: A cross-national study of 42 European countries.' *Political Studies* 65(1): 81–102.

30. Frances Fukuyama. 1995. *Trust: The Social Virtues and The Creation of Prosperity*. New York: Free Press; Robert D. Putnam. 1993. *Making Democracy Work: Civic Traditions in Modern Italy*. Princeton, NJ: Princeton University Press; Robert D. Putnam. 2000. *Bowling Alone?* New York: Simon and Schuster; Steven Van de Walle and Geert Bouckaert. 2003. 'Public service performance and trust in government: The problem of causality.' *International Journal of Public Administration* 26(8–9): 891–913.

31. Steven Van De Walle and Geert Bouckaert. 2003. 'Public service performance and trust in government: The problem of causality.' *International Journal of Public Administration* 26(8–9): 891–913.

32. Blaine G. Robbins. 2012. 'Institutional quality and generalized trust: A non-recursive causal model.' *Social Indicators Research* 107(2): 235–258; Blaine G. Robbins. 2012. 'A blessing and a curse? Political institutions in the growth and decay of generalized trust: A cross-national panel analysis, 1980–2009.' *PLOS One* 7(4): e35120.

33. David Devine et al. 2020. 'Trust and the coronavirus pandemic: What are the consequences of and for trust? An early review of the literature.' *Political Studies Review.* https://doi.org/10.1177/1478929920948684.

34. G. Cordero and P. Simón. 2015. 'Economic crisis and support for democracy in Europe.' *West European Politics* 39(2): 305–325; Veronica Fagerland Kroknes, Tor Georg Jakobsen, and Lisa-Marie Grønning. 2016. 'Economic performance and political trust: The impact of the financial crisis on European citizens.' *European Societies* 17(5): 700–723; L. Kenworthy and L. A. Owens. 2011. 'The surprisingly weak effect of recessions on public opinion.' In D. B. Grusky, B. Western, and C. Wimer (eds.), *The Great Recession.* New York: Russell Sage Foundation; Patricia Van Erkel and Tom Van der Meer. 2016. 'Macroeconomic performance, political trust and the Great Recession: A multilevel analysis of the effects of within-country fluctuations in macroeconomic performance on political trust in 15 EU countries, 1999–2011.' *European Journal of Political Research* 55(1): 177–197; Mariano Torcal. 2014. 'The decline of political trust in Spain and Portugal: Economic performance or political responsiveness?' *American Behavioral Scientist* 58: 1542–1567; Sergio Martini and Mario Quaranta. 2020. *Citizens and Democracy in Europe: Contexts, Changes and Political Support.* London: Palgrave Macmillan.

35. Rhys Andrews, George A. Boyne, and Richard M. Walker. 2006. 'Subjective and objective measures of organizational performance.' In George A. Boyne, Kenneth J. Meier, Kenneth J. Meier, Laurence J. O'Toole Jr., and Richard M. Walker (eds.), *Public Service Performance: Perspectives on Measurement and Management*, pp. 14–34. Cambridge: Cambridge University Press.

36. Lotte Bøgh Andersen, Andreas Boesen, and Lene Holm Pedersen. 2016. 'Performance in public organizations: Clarifying the conceptual space.' *Public Administration Review* 76(6): 852–862.

37. Jane Green. 2016. 'When voters and parties agree: Valence issues and party competition.' *Political Studies* 55(3): 629–655.

38. World Bank. *World Development Indicators.* Consulted September 2021 https://databank.worldbank.org/source/world-development-indicators.

39. Qing Yang and Wenfang Tang. 2010. 'Exploring the sources of institutional trust in China: Culture, mobilization, or performance?' *Asian Politics and Society* 2(3): 415–436.

40. The World Bank database: https://databank.worldbank.org/source/world-development-indicators.

41. https://rsf.org/en/china.

42. The World Bank. October 2021. *Lebanon's Economic Update.* https://www.worldbank. org/en/country/lebanon/publication/economic-update-october-2021..

43. Mona Yacoubian. July 2021. *Lebanon: Assessing Political Paralysis, Economic Crisis and Challenges for U.S. Policy.* Testimony before the House Foreign Affairs Subcommittee on the Middle East, North Africa, and Global Counterterrorism. https://www.usip. org/publications/2021/07/lebanon-assessing-political-paralysis-economic-crisis- and-challenges-us-policy.

44. Pew Research Center. Oct 2019. *European Public Opinion Three Decades after the Fall of Communism.* https://www.pewresearch.org/global/2019/10/14/political-and- economic-changes-since-the-fall-of-communism/.

45. William Mishler and Richard Rose. 2001. 'What are the origins of political trust? Testing institutional and cultural theories in post-communist societies.' *Comparative Political Studies* 34(1): 30–62; William Mishler and Richard Rose. 2005. 'Trust, dis- trust and skepticism: Popular evaluations of civil and political institutions in post- communist societies.' *Journal of Politics* 59(2): 418–451.

46. O. P. Dahlen and H. Skirbekk. 2021. 'How trust was maintained in Scandinavia through the first crisis of modernity.' *Corporate Communications* 26(1): 23–39; Y. Algan and P. Cahuc. 2010. 'Inherited trust and growth.' *The American Economic Review* 100(5): 2060–2092; Bo Rothstein and Dieter Stolle. 2003. 'Introduction: Social capital in Scandinavia.' *Scandinavian Political Studies* 26(1): 1–26.

47. https://freedomhouse.org/country/azerbaijan.

48. Anar Valiyev, Axer Babayev, Hajar Huseynova, and Khalida Jafarova. 2017. 'Do citizens of the former Soviet Union trust state institutions and why: The case of Azerbaijan.' *Communist and Post-Communist Studies* 50(3): 221–231; S. O'Lear. 2007. 'Azerbaijan's resource curse: Political legitimacy and public opinion.' *Geographical Journal* 173: 207–223.

49. https://freedomhouse.org/country/iran.

50. Pavel Yakovlev and David Gilson. 2015. 'Public trust and press freedom.' *Economics Bulletin* 35(1): 214–219.

51. D. Baldino and J. Goold. 2014. 'Iran and the emergence of information and communi- cations technology: The emergence of revolution?' *Australian Journal of International Affairs* 68(1): 17–35.

52. Niels Spierings. 2017. 'Trust and tolerance across the Middle East and North Africa: A comparative perspective on the impact of the Arab uprisings. *Politics and Governance* 5(2): 4–15.

53. Human Rights Watch. 2020. *Turkey: Press Freedom under Attack.* https://www.hrw. org/news/2020/10/14/turkey-press-freedom-under-attack.

54. Ronald Inglehart. 2018. *Cultural Evolution.* New York: Cambridge University Press.

55. Frank R. Baumgartner and Bryan D. Jones. 1993. *Agendas and Instability in American Politics.* Chicago: University of Chicago Press; Chico Q. Camargo, Peter John, Helen Z. Margetts, Scott A. Hale. 2021. 'Measuring the volatility of the political agenda in public opinion and news media.' *Public Opinion Quarterly*; see also the series of Gallup polls: https://news.gallup.com/poll/1675/most-important-problem.aspx.

56. https://europa.eu/eurobarometer.

57. Frank Baumgartner, Brian Jones, and J. D. Wilkerson. 2002. 'Studying policy dynamics.' In Frank Baumgartner and B. D. Jones (eds.), *Policy Dynamics*, pp. 37–56. Chicago: University of Chicago Press. Frank Baumgartner, Brian Jones, and J. D. Wilkerson. 2011. 'Comparative studies of policy dynamics.' *Comparative Political Studies* 44(8): 947–972.

58. See, for example, Edelman Trust Barometer, 2021: https://www.edelman.com/trust/ 2021-trust-barometer.

59. Jane Green and Will Jennings. 2017. *The Politics of Competence*. New York: Cambridge University Press.

60. Marc J. Hetherington and Thomas Rudolph. 2008. 'Priming, performance, and the dynamics of political trust.' *Journal of Politics* 70(2): 498–512; Tom Van der Meer. 2018. 'Economic performance and political trust.' In Eric Uslaner (ed.), *The Oxford Handbook of Social and Political Trust* (pp. 599–616). New York; Oxford: Oxford University Press; Patrick Van Erkel and Tom Van der Meer. 2016. 'Macroeconomic performance, political trust and the Great Recession: A multilevel analysis of the effects of within-country fluctuations in macroeconomic performance on political trust in 15 EU countries, 1999–2011.' *European Journal of Political Research* 55(1): 177–197.

61. Stefan Dahlberg, Jonas Linde, and Soren Holmberg. 2015. 'Democratic discontent in old and new democracies: Assessing the importance of democratic input and governmental output.' *Political Studies* 63(1): 18–37.

62. See Tom Van der Meer and Armen Hakhverdian. 2016. 'Political trust as an evaluation of process and performance: A cross-national study of 42 European countries.' *Political Studies* 65(1): 81–102; and also Gregg Van Ryzin. 2011. 'Outcomes, process, and trust of civil servants.' *Public Performance and Management Review* 30(4): 521–535.

Chapter 6

1. Vivienne Schmidt. 2013. 'Democracy and legitimacy in the European Union revisited: Input, output, and throughput.' *Political Studies* 61(1): 2–22.

2. Gallup Polls. Presidential Ratings—Personal Characteristics. https://news.gallup. com/poll/1732/presidential-ratings-personal-characteristics.aspx.

3. Glenn Kessler. January 24, 2021. 'Trump's false or misleading claims total 30,573 over 4 years.' *Washington Post*. https://www.washingtonpost.com/politics/2021/01/24/tru mps-false-or-misleading-claims-total-30573-over-four-years/.

4. Varieties of Democracy: https://www.v-dem.net/en/; Worldwide Governance Indicators: https://info.worldbank.org/governance/wgi/.

5. Mark Bovens, Robert E. Goodin, and Thomas Schillemans (eds.). 2012. *The Oxford Handbook of Public Accountability*. Oxford: Oxford University Press.

6. Roger C. Mayer, James H. Davis, and F. David Schoorman. 1995. 'An integrative model of organizational trust.' *Academy of Management Review* 20(3): 709–734.

7. Pippa Norris. 2014. *Why Electoral Integrity Matters.* New York: Cambridge University Press.

8. H. A. Khan. 2016. 'The linkage between political trust and the quality of government: An analysis.' *International Journal of Public Administration* 39(9): 665–675.

9. Tom Van der Meer. 2017. 'Dissecting the causal chain from quality of government to political support.' In Carolien Van Ham, Jacques Thomassen, Kaas Aarts, and Rudy Andeweg (eds.), *Myth and Reality of the Legitimacy Crisis.* Oxford: Oxford University Press, Ch. 8.

10. Mark Bovens. 2007. 'Public accountability.' In Ewan Ferlie, Laurence Lynn, and Christopher Pollitt (eds.)., *The Oxford Handbook of Public Management.* Oxford: Oxford University Press.

11. Christopher J. Anderson and Yuliya V. Tverdova. 2003. 'Corruption, political allegiances, and attitudes toward government in contemporary democracies.' *American Journal of Political Science* 47(1): 91–109; Armen Hakhverdian and Quintin Mayne. 2012. 'Institutional trust, education, and corruption: A micro-macro interactive approach.' *Journal of Politics* 74(3): 739–750; Jong-sung You. 2018. 'Trust and corruption.' In Eric M. Uslaner (ed.), *The Oxford Handbook of Social and Political Trust* New York: Oxford University Press; S. Kang and J. Zhu. 2020. 'Do people trust the government more? Unpacking the distinct impacts of anti-corruption policies on political trust.' *Political Research Quarterly.* https://doi.org/10.1177/1065912920 91201.

12. Stephan Grimmelikhuijsen, Gregory Porumbescu, Boram Hong, and Tobin Im. 2013. 'The effect of transparency on trust in government: A cross-national comparative experiment.' *Public Administration Review* 73(4): 575–586; Kimmo Grönlund and Maija Setälä. 2012. 'In honest officials we trust: Institutional confidence in Europe.' *American Review of Public Administration* 42(5): 523–542; Christopher J. Anderson and Yuliya V. Tverdova. 2003. 'Corruption, political allegiances, and attitudes toward government in contemporary democracies.' *American Journal of Political Science* 47(1): 91–109; Ching-Hsing Wang. 2016. 'Government performance, corruption, and political trust in East Asia.' *Social Science Quarterly* 97(2): 211–231; Alexander I. Ruder and Neal D. Woods. 2020. 'Procedural fairness and the legitimacy of agency rulemaking.' *Journal of Public Administration Research and Theory* 30(3): 400–414.

13. Bo Rothstein. 2003. 'Social capital, economic growth and quality of government: The causal mechanism.' *New Political Economy* 8(1): 49–71; Bo Rothstein and Dieter Stolle. 2008. 'The state and social capital: An institutional theory of generalized trust.' *Comparative Politics* 33(4): 401–419; Bo Rothstein and Eric Uslaner. 2005. 'All for one: Equality, corruption, and social trust.' *World Politics* 58(1): 41–72. Bo Rothstein. 2011. *The Quality of Government: Corruption, Social Trust and Inequality in International Perspective.* Chicago: University of Chicago Press.

14. Shaun Bowler and Jeffrey Karp. 2004. 'Politicians, scandals, and trust in government.' *Political Behavior* 26(3): 271–287.

15. Christopher J. Anderson and Yuliya V. Tverdova. 2003. 'Corruption, political allegiances, and attitudes toward government in contemporary democracies.' *American Journal of Political Science* 47(1): 91–109.

16. Varieties of Democracy: https://www.v-dem.net/en/; Worldwide Governance Indicators: https://info.worldbank.org/governance/wgi/.

17. Tom Van der Meer. 2017. 'Dissecting the causal chain from quality of government to political support.' In Carolien Van Ham, Jacques Thomassen, Kees Aarts, and Rudy Andeweg (eds.), *Myth and Reality of the Legitimacy Crisis*. Oxford: Oxford University Press.

18. See Alexander Cooley and Jack Snyder (eds.). 2015. *Ranking the World*. New York: Cambridge University Press.

19. For details, see the Varieties of Democracy project: https://www.v-dem.net/en/. The World Bank Worldwide Governance Indicators: http://info.worldbank.org/governance/wgi/. The Quality of Government project: https://www.gu.se/en/quality-government.

20. Jong-sung You. 2018. 'Trust and corruption.' In Eric M. Uslaner (ed.), *The Oxford Handbook of Social and Political Trust*. New York: Oxford University Press.

21. J. S. T. Quah. 2018. 'Why Singapore works: Five secrets of Singapore's success.' *Public Administration and Policy: An Asia-Pacific Journal* 21(1): 5–21.

22. https://osf.io/fazup/.

23. Roge Karma. April 30, 2020. 'Many world leaders experience double-digit polling surges amid coronavirus. Trump isn't one of them.' *Vox*. https://www.vox.com/2020/4/30/21231217/trump-cuomo-whitmer-coronavirus-covid-19-approval-rating-polls-world-leaders-governors.

24. John E. Mueller. 1970. 'Presidential popularity from Truman to Johnson.' *American Political Science Review* 64(1): 18–34.

25. https://www.edelman.com/trust/2021-trust-barometer.

26. S. Muralidar, S. V. Ambi, S. Sekaran, and U. M. Krishnan. 2020. 'The emergence of COVID-19 as a global pandemic: Understanding the epidemiology, immune response and potential therapeutic targets of SARS-CoV-2.' *Biochimie* 179: 85–100.

27. https://coronavirus.jhu.edu/data/hubei-timeline.

28. Blavatnik School of Government, University of Oxford. *Coronavirus Government Response Tracker*: https://www.bsg.ox.ac.uk/research/research-projects/coronavirus-government-response-tracker.

29. https://www.politico.com/news/2020/04/14/what-trump-said-did-coronavirus-186464.

30. https://www.nytimes.com/2020/04/04/us/coronavirus-china-travel-restrictions.html.

31. https://nationalinterest.org/blog/buzz/why-travel-ban-won%E2%80%99t-stop-coronavirus-119681.

32. https://covidtracking.com/data/us-daily.

33. https://www.ghsindex.org/wp-content/uploads/2020/04/2019-Global-Health-Security-Index.pdf.

34. James Fallows. June 29, 2019. 'The three weeks which changed everything.' *The Atlantic*.

35. Tolouse Olorunnipa, Ariana Cha, and Laurie McGinley. May 15, 2020. Drug promoted by Trump coronavirus 'game changer increasingly linked to deaths.' *Washington Post*. https://www.washingtonpost.com/politics/drug-promoted-by-trump-as-coronavirus-game-changer-increasingly-linked-to-deaths/2020/05/15/85d024fe-96bd-11ea-9f5e-56d8239bf9ad_story.html.

36. Blake Ellis and Melanie Hicken. May 22, 2020. 'Sales of drug touted by Trump have soared.' CNN. https://www.cnn.com/2020/05/22/health/hydroxychloroquine-sales-covid-19-trump-invs/index.html.

37. Kathleen Hall Jamieson and Dolores Albarraci. 2020. 'The relation between media consumption and misinformation at the outset of the SARS-CoV-2 pandemic in the US.' *The Harvard Kennedy School Misinformation Review* 1.

38. https://coronavirus.jhu.edu/map.html.

39. A Gallup poll (June 29–July 5, 2020) reported that 61% of Democrats said they always used a mask outside their home, compared with 24% of Republicans. By contrast, 27% of Republicans said they never wore a mask, compared with 1% of Democrats. https://news.gallup.com/poll/315590/americans-face-mask-usage-varies-greatly-demographics.aspx.

40. https://projects.fivethirtyeight.com/coronavirus-polls/.

41. Economist/YouGov Poll, October 11–13, 2020. https://docs.cdn.yougov.com/1ace2lg idt/econTabReport.pdf. Real Clear Politics estimated that across a series of polls, on average 39% of Americans approved of President Trump's handling of the corona-virus. https://www.realclearpolitics.com/epolls/other/public_approval_of_presi-dent_trumps_handling_of_the_coronavirus-7088.html.

42. https://covid.cdc.gov/covid-data-tracker/#datatracker-home.

43. https://www.kff.org/coronavirus-covid-19/poll-finding/importance-of-partisans hip-predicting-vaccination-status/.

44. https://www.kff.org/coronavirus-covid-19/poll-finding/kff-covid-19-vaccine-moni tor-media-and-misinformation/.

45. https://www.npr.org/sections/health-shots/2021/12/05/1059828993/data-vaccine-misinformation-trump-counties-covid-death-rate.

46. "Excess deaths" is a term used in epidemiology and public health that refers to the number of deaths from all causes during a crisis above and beyond what we would have expected to see under "normal" conditions during the same period in previous years. See estimates by Charlie Giattino, Hannah Ritchie, Max Roser, Esteban Ortiz-Ospina, and Joe Hasell. October 15, 2020. 'Excess mortality during the Coronavirus pandemic (COVID-19). *Our World in Data.* https://ourworldindata.org/excess-mortality-covid.

47. Gaurav Chiplunkar and Sabyasachi Das. 2020. 'Political institutions and policy responses during a crisis.' SSRN. https://papers.ssrn.com/sol3/papers.cfm?abstract_id=3629397.

48. Siobhán O'Grady. May 22, 2020. 'Trump is not the only leader pushing unproven coronavirus remedies.' *Washington Post.* https://www.washingtonpost.com/world/2020/05/22/trump-is-not-only-leader-pushing-unproven-coronavirus-cures/.

49. https://www.thelancet.com/journals/lancet/article/PIIS0140-6736(21)02398-9/fulltext.

50. Cumulative deaths attributed to COVID-19 per million population. https://ig.ft.com/coronavirus-chart/?areas=swe&areas=nor&areasRegional=usny&areasRegional=usnj&cumulative=1&logScale=1&perMillion=1&values=deaths.

51. S. Mishra, J. A. Scott, and D. K. Laydon, et al. 2021. 'Comparing the responses of the UK, Sweden and Denmark to COVID-19 using counterfactual modelling.' *Scientific Reports* 11: 16342.

52. https://www.reuters.com/world/sweden-acted-too-slowly-pandemic-hit-commiss ion-finds-2021-10-29/.

53. Kat Devlin and Aidan Connaughton. August 27, 2020. 'Most approve of national response to COVID-19 in 14 advanced economies.' Washington, DC: Pew Research Center. https://www.pewresearch.org/global/2020/08/27/most-approve-of-national-response-to-covid-19-in-14-advanced-economies/.

54. D. K. Chu, E. A. Akl, S. Duda, et al. 2020. 'Physical distancing, face masks, and eye protection to prevent person-to-person transmission of SARS-CoV-2 and COVID-19: A systematic review and meta-analysis.' *Lancet* 396(10242): 1973–1987.

55. Heidi Larson. 2020. *Stuck: How Vaccine Rumors Start—and Why They Don't Go Away.* New York: Oxford University Press. Vaccine denialism is not simply confined to the extreme fringe, in the case of Covid-19, for example, an ABC News/Ipsos poll (May 6–7, 2020) reported that one-quarter of Americans said they would be unlikely to get vaccinated if a "safe and effective coronavirus vaccine is developed." https://www.ipsos.com/sites/default/files/ipsos-coronavirus-us-aggregate-topline-052020.pdf. Similar results were reported by the Pew Research Center. https://www.pewresearch.org/fact-tank/2020/05/21/most-americans-expect-a-covid-19-vaccine-within-a-year-72-say-they-would-get-vaccinated/.

56. Warren Cornwall. June 30, 2020. 'Just 50% of Americans plan to get a COVID-19 vaccine. Here's how to win over the rest.' *Science Magazine.* https://www.sciencemag.org/news/2020/06/just-50-americans-plan-get-covid-19-vacc ine-here-s-how-win-over-rest.

57. Frank J. Elgar, Anna Stefaniak, and Michael J. A. Woh. 2020. 'The trouble with trust: Time-series analysis of social capital, income inequality, and COVID-19 deaths in 84 countries.' *Social Science and Medicine* 263.

58. C. K. Cheung and J. W. Tse. 2008. 'Institutional trust as a determinant of anxiety during the SARS crisis in Hong Kong.' *Social Work in Public Health* 23: 41–54; V.S . Freimuth, D. Musa, K. Hilyard, S. C. Quinn, and K. Kim. 2014. 'Trust during the early stages of the 2009 H1N1 pandemic.' *Journal of Health Communication* 19: 321–339.

59. Varieties of Democracy: https://www.v-dem.net/en/; Worldwide Governance Indicators: https://info.worldbank.org/governance/wgi/.

60. See Johannes Gerschewski. 2013. 'The three pillars of stability.' *Democratization* 20(1): 13–38; Johannes Gerschewsk. 2018. 'Legitimacy in autocracies: Oxymoron or essential feature?' *Perspectives on Politics* 16(3): 652–665.

Chapter 7

1. Robert D. Putnam. 1993. *Making Democracy Work: Civic Traditions in Modern Italy.* Princeton, NJ: Princeton University Press; Robert D. Putnam. 2000. *Bowling Alone?* New York: Simon and Schuster.

2. Paul S. Adler and Seok-Woo Kwon. 2002. 'Social Capital: Prospects for a new concept.' *Academy of Management Review* 27(1): 17–40.

3. Robert D. Putnam. 2000. *Bowling Alone?* New York: Simon and Schuster.

4. Diego Gambetta. 1996. *The Sicilian Mafia: The Business of Private Protection.* Cambridge, MA: Harvard University Press.

5. Ibid., p. 21.

6. Francis Fukuyama. 1995. *Trust: The Social Virtues and the Creation of Prosperity.* New York: Free Press. See also Diego Gambetta. 2000. 'Can we trust trust?' In Diego Gambetta, *Trust: Making and Breaking Cooperative Relations*; Paul J. Zak and Stephen Knack. 2001. 'Trust and Growth.' *The Economic Journal* 111(470): 295–321.

7. Francis Fukuyama. 1995. *Trust: The Social Virtues and the Creation of Prosperity.* New York: Free Press.

8. Eric Uslaner. 2002. *The Moral Foundations of Trust.* New York: Cambridge University Press.

9. Bo Rothstein and Eric Uslaner. 2005. 'All for all: Equality, corruption and social trust.' *World Politics* 58(1): 41–72.

10. Denise Skinner, Graham Dietz, and Antoinette Weibel. 2013. 'The dark side of trust: When trust becomes a "poisoned chalice."' *Organization* 21: 206–224.

11. William Tov and Ed Diener. 2009. 'The wellbeing of nations: Linking together trust, cooperation and democracy.' In Ed Diener (ed.), *The Science of Well-Being*, pp. 155–173. Dordrecht: Springer.

12. Rodrick M. Kramer. 1999. 'Trust and distrust in organizations: Emerging perspectives, enduring questions.' *Annual Review of Psychology* 50: 590–598.

13. P. Cofta. 2007. *Trust, Complexity and Control: Confidence in a Convergent World.* New York: Wiley.

14. Marie F. Lindholt, Fredrik Jørgensen, Alexandor Bor, and Michael B. Petersen. 2021. 'Public acceptance of COVID-19 vaccines: Cross-national evidence on levels and individual-level predictors using observational data.' *BMJ Open* 11: e048172. doi:10.1136/bmjopen-2020-048172; Daniel Devine, Jennifer Gaskell, Will Jennings, and Gerry Stoker. 2020. 'Trust and the coronavirus pandemic: What are the consequences of and for trust? An early review of the literature.' *Political Studies Review* 19(2): 274–285; Lee Rainie and Andrew Perrin. April 6, 2020. 'The state of Americans' trust in each other amid the COVID-19 pandemic.' *Pew Research Center.* https://www.pewresearch.org/fact-tank/2020/04/06/the-state-of-americans-trust-in-each-other-amid-the-covid-19-pandemic/.

15. Lawrence Hamilton and Thomas Safford. 2021. 'Elite cues and the rapid decline in trust in science agencies on Covid-19.' *Sociological Perspectives* 64(5): 988–1011. doi:10.1177/07311214211022391.

16. Gabriel A. Almond and Sidney Verba. 1963. *The Civic Culture.* Princeton, NJ: Princeton University Press.

17. Christopher J. Anderson, Andre Blais, and Shaun Bowler. 2005. *Losers' Consent: Elections and Democratic Legitimacy.* Oxford: Oxford University Press.

18. Marc J. Hetherington and Thomas J. Rudolph. 2015. *Why Washington Won't Work.* Chicago: University of Chicago Press.

19. Marc Hetherington. 2005. *Why Trust Matters*. Princeton, NJ: Princeton University Press.
20. Virginia A. Chanley. 2002. 'Trust in government in the aftermath of 9/11: Determinants and consequences.' *Political Psychology* 23(3): 469–483.
21. Edelman Trust Barometer. 2020. *Spring Update: Trust and the Covid-19 pandemic.* https://www.edelman.com/sites/g/files/aatuss191/files/2020-05/2020%20Edel man%20Trust%20Barometer%20Spring%20Update.pdf.
22. C. Clark, A. Davila, M. Regis, and S. Kraus. 2020. 'Predictors of COVID-19 voluntary compliance behaviors: An international investigation.' *Global Transitions* 2: 76–82; Anton Pak et al. 2021. 'Does high public trust amplify compliance with stringent COVID-19 government health guidelines? A multi-country analysis using data from 102,627 individuals.' *Risk Management and Healthcare Policy* 14: 293–302.
23. Larry Diamond. 2019. *Ill Winds: Saving Democracy from Russian Rage, Chinese Ambition, and American Complacency.* New York: Penguin.
24. Steven Levitsky and Daniel Ziblatt. 2018. *How Democracies Die.* New York: Crown.
25. Max Weber. [1922] 1978. *Economy and Society.* Berkeley: University of California Press.
26. Seymour Martin Lipset. 1983. *Political Man: The Social Bases of Politics*, 2nd ed. London: Heinemann, p. 64. The concept of legitimacy is also discussed in Stephen M. Weatherford. 1992. 'Measuring political legitimacy.' *American Political Science Review* 86: 149–166; Bruce Gilley. 2006. 'The meaning and measure of state legitimacy: Results for 72 countries.' *European Journal of Political Research* 45: 499–525.
27. Tom R. Tyler. 2006. *Why People Obey the Law.* New Haven, CT: Yale University Press; S. Marien and Marc Hooghe. 2011. 'Does political trust matter? An empirical investigation into the relation between political trust and support for law compliance.' *European Journal of Political Research* 50(2): 267–291.
28. Paul Brewer, Kimberley Gross, Sean Aday, and Lars Willnat. 2004. 'International trust and public opinion about world affairs.' *American Journal of Political Science* 48(1): 93–109; Andrew H. Kydd. 2007. *Trust and Mistrust in International Relations.* Princeton, NJ: Princeton University Press; Jan Scholte. 2011. 'Towards greater legitimacy in global governance.' *Review of International Political Economy* 18(1): 110–120.
29. Jonas Tallberg, Karin Backsterand, and Jan Aart Scholte (eds.). 2018. *Legitimacy in Global Governance.* Oxford: Oxford University Press.
30. Steven Bernstein. 2011. 'Legitimacy in intergovernmental and nonstate global governance.' *Review of International Political Economy* 18(1): 17–51; Jonas Tallberg, Karin Backsterand, and Jan Aart Scholte (eds.). 2018. *Legitimacy in Global Governance.* Oxford: Oxford University Press.
31. For useful discussions of the concept, see Ulf Hannerz. 1990. 'Cosmopolitans and locals in world culture.' In Mike Featherstone (ed.), *Global Culture: Nationalism, Globalization and Modernity.* London: Sage; John Tomlinson. *Globalization and Culture.* Chicago: University of Chicago Press; Steven Vertovec and Robin Cohen (eds.). 2002. *Conceiving Cosmopolitanism: Theory, Context and Practice.* Oxford: Oxford University Press; Pippa Norris and Ronald Inglehart. 2009. *Cosmopolitan Communications.* New York: Cambridge University Press.
32. Andrew H. Kydd. 2007. *Trust and Mistrust in International Relations.* Princeton, NJ: Princeton University Press.

33. Michel Crozier, Samuel P. Huntington, and Joji Watanuki. 1975. *The Crisis of Democracy: Report on the Governability of Democracies to the Trilateral Commission.* New York: New York University Press.

34. Robert D. Putnam. 1993. *Making Democracy Work: Civic Traditions in Modern Italy.* Princeton, NJ: Princeton University Press; Robert D. Putnam. 2000. *Bowling Alone?* New York: Simon and Schuster; Susan Pharr and Robert D. Putnam (eds.). 2000. *Disaffected Democracies: What's Troubling the Trilateral Countries?* Princeton, NJ: Princeton University Press.

35. Pippa Norris and Ronald Inglehart. 2019. *Cultural Backlash.* New York: Cambridge University Press.

36. S. Rummens. 2017. 'Populism as a threat to liberal democracy.' In C. Rovira Kaltwasser, P. A. Taggart, P. O. Espejo, et al. (eds.), *The Oxford Handbook of Populism,* pp. 554–570. Oxford: Oxford University Press.

37. Steven Levitsky and Daniel Ziblatt. 2018. *How Democracies Die.* New York: Crown; Stephen Haggard and Robert Kaufman. 2021. *Backsliding.* New York: Cambridge University Press.

38. Catherine Fieschi and Paul Heywood. 2004. 'Trust, cynicism and populist anti-politics.' *Journal of Political Ideologies* 9(3): 289–309; Mathias Rooduijn, Wouter Van der Brug, and S. L. De Lange. 2016. 'Expressing or fueling discontent? The relationship between populist voting and political discontent.' *Electoral Studies* 43: 32–40; Mathias Rooduijn. 2018. 'What unites the voter bases of populist parties? Comparing the electorates of 15 populist parties.' *European Political Science Review* 10(3): 351–368; S. M. Van Hauwaert and S. Van Kessel. 2018. 'Beyond protest and discontent: A cross-national analysis of the effect of populist attitudes and issue positions on populist party support.' *European Journal of Political Research* 57(1): 68–92; Pippa Norris and Ronald Inglehart. 2019. *Cultural Backlash.* New York: Cambridge University Press, Ch. 8.

39. David Brooks. June 10 2021. 'How to build trust: A practical guide.' *New York Times.* https://www.nytimes.com/2021/06/10/opinion/distrust-respect-safety.html.

40. Denise Skinner, Graham Dietz, and Antoinette Weibel. 2013. 'The dark side of trust: When trust becomes a "poisoned chalice."' *Organization* 21: 206–224.

41. Margaret Levi and Laura Stoker. 2000. 'Political trust and trustworthiness.' *Annual Review of Political Science* 3: 475–507.

42. See, for example, Lee Tainie, Scott Keeter, and Andrew Perrin. 2019. 'Trust and distrust in America.' Washington, DC: Pew Research Center. https://www.pewresearch.org/politics/2019/07/22/trust-and-distrust-in-america/; 2020 Edelman Trust Barometer. https://www.edelman.com/trust/2020-trust-barometer.

43. Roger C. Mayer, James H. Davis, and F. David Schoorman. 1995. 'An integrative model of organizational trust.' *The Academy of Management Review* 20(3): 709–734.

44. Tom Van der Meer and Armen Hakhverdian. 2016. 'Political trust as an evaluation of process and performance: A cross-national study of 42 European countries.' *Political Studies* 65(1): 81–102.

45. For a discussion of this issue concerning the rationality of voting behavior, see Christopher H. Achen and Larry M. Bartels. 2016. *Democracy for Realists.* Princeton, NJ: Princeton University Press.

46. Morris Fiorina. 1981. *Retrospective Voting in American National Elections.* New Haven, CT: Yale University Press, p. 84.

47. A. Portes. 2010. *Economic Sociology: A Systematic Inquiry.* Princeton, NJ: Princeton University Press.

48. Valerie A. Braithwaite and Margaret Levi. 1998. *Trust and Governance.* New York: Russell Sage Foundation; Detlef Fetchenhauer and David Dunning. 2009. 'Do people trust too much or too little?' *Journal of Economic Psychology* 30(3): 263–276.

49. Colin Hay. 2007. *Why We Hate Politics.* Cambridge: Polity Press.

50. Russell J. Dalton. 2004. *Democratic Challenges, Democratic Choices: The Erosion of Political Support in Advanced Industrial Democracies.* New York: Oxford University Press.

51. Darrell Robinson and Marcus Tannenberg. 2019. 'Self-censorship of regime support in authoritarian states: Evidence from list experiments in China.' *Research and Politics* July: 1–9.

52. Kathleen Hall Jamieson. 20290. *Cyberwar.* New York: Oxford University Press; Lee McIntyre. 2018. *Post-Truth.* Cambridge, MA: MIT Press; William Davies. 2020. *Nervous States: Democracy and the Decline of Reason.* New York: W. W. Norton; Cailin O'Connor and James Owen Weatherall. 2018. *The Misinformation Age: How False Beliefs Spread.* New Haven, CT: Yale University Press; Nancy L. Rosenblum and Russell Muirhead. 2019. *A Lot of People Are Saying: The New Conspiracism and the Assault on Democracy.* Princeton, NJ: Princeton University Press.

53. President Trump. *Speech in Sioux City*, January 23, 2016. https://www.youtube.com/watch?v=ATuWvlYwdEY.

54. Charles Poller. March 26, 2020. ' "This is insane!" Many scientists lament Trump's embrace of risky malaria drug for conoravirus.' *Science.* https://www.sciencemag.org/news/2020/03/insane-many-scientists-lament-trump-s-embrace-risky-malaria-drugs coronavirus.

55. Lee McIntyre. 2018. *Post-Truth.* Cambridge, MA: MIT Press; William Davies. 2020. *Nervous States: Democracy and the Decline of Reason.* New York: W. W. Norton; Cailin O'Connor and James Owen Weatherall. 2018. *The Misinformation Age: How False Beliefs Spread.* New Haven, CT: Yale University Press; Nancy L. Rosenblum and Russell Muirhead. 2019. *A Lot of People Are Saying: The New Conspiracism and the Assault on Democracy.* Princeton, NJ: Princeton University Press.

56. Sergei Guriev and Daniel Treisman. 2022. *Spin Dictators: The Changing Face of Tyranny in the 21st Century.* Princeton, NJ: Princeton University Press.

57. Alexander Cooley and Jack Snyder (eds.). 2015. *Ranking the World: Grading States as Tools of Governance.* New York: Cambridge University Press; Bo Rothstein. 2011. *The Quality of Government: Corruption, Social Trust and Inequality in International Perspective.* Chicago: University of Chicago Press.

58. Pippa Norris (ed.). 2010. *Public Sentinel.* Washington, DC: World Bank.

59. See, for example, Louise Williams and Roland Rich (eds.). 2014. *Losing Control: Freedom of the Press in Asia.* Canberra: ANU Press.

60. See, for example, Patti T. Lenard. 2008. 'Trust your compatriots, but count your change: The roles of trust, mistrust and distrust in democracy.' *Political Studies* 36: 312–332; Patti T. Lenard. 2015. 'The political philosophy of trust and distrust in democracies

and beyond.' *Monist* 98(4): 353–359; C. A. Fulmer and M. J. Gelfand. 2012. 'At what level (and in whom) we trust: Trust across multiple organizational levels.' *Journal of Management* 38: 1167–1230; D. Skinner, G. Dietz, and A. Weibel. 2013. 'The dark side of trust: When trust becomes a "poisoned chalice."' *Organization* 21: 206–224; Pierre Rosanvallon. 2008. *Counter-Democracy: Politics in an Age of Distrust.* Cambridge: Cambridge University Press; Timothy E. Cook and Paul Gronke. 2005. 'The skeptical American: Revisiting the meanings of trust in government and confidence in institutions.' *Journal of Politics* 67(3): 784–803.

61. Detlef Fetchenhauer and David Dunning.2009. 'Do people trust too much or too little?' *Journal of Economic Psychology* 30(3): 263–276.

62. Daniel Kahneman. 2011. *Thinking, Fast and Slow.* London: Penguin; Paul Sniderman, Richard Brady, and Philip Tetlock. 1991. *Reasoning and Choice.* New York: Cambridge University Press; Richard H. Thaler and Cass R. Sunstein. 2008. *Nudge: Improving Decisions about Health, Wealth and Happiness.* New Haven, CT: Yale University Press.

63. Philip Tetlock. *Expert Political Judgement.* 2nd ed. New Haven, CT: Princeton University Press.

64. Tom W. G. van der Meer. 2017. 'Political trust and the "crisis of democracy."' In William Thompson (ed.), *Oxford Research Encyclopedia of Politics.* Oxford: Oxford University Press.

65. Pippa Norris (ed.). 1999. *Critical Citizens.* New York: Oxford University Press; Pippa Norris. 2010. *Democratic Deficit.* New York: Cambridge University Press.

66. See Cary Wu and Rima Wilkes. 2018. 'Finding critical trusters: A response pattern model of political trust.' *International Journal of Comparative Sociology* 59(2): 110–138.

67. Tom R. Tyler. 2002. *Trust in the Law.* New York: Russell-Sage Foundation; Tom R. Tyler. 2006. *Why People Obey the Law.* New Haven, CT: Yale University Press; Tom R. Tyler. 2011. *Why People Cooperate.* Princeton, NJ: Princeton University Press; Tom R. Tyler and Rick Trinkner. 2017. *Why Children Follow Rules.* Oxford: Oxford University Press.

68. For the thesis that a culture of widespread mistrust is healthy for democracy, see Matthew R. Cleary and Susan C. Stokes. 2006. *Democracy and the Culture of Skepticism: Political Trust in Argentina and Mexico.* New York: Russell Sage Foundation.

69. Gabriel Almond and Sydney Verba. 1963. *The Civic Culture.* Princeton, NJ: Princeton University Press.

70. Julien B. Rotter. 1980. 'Interpersonal trust, trustworthiness, and gullibility.' *American Psychologist* 35(1): 1–7.

71. Dan Sperber, Fabrice Clément, Christophe Heintz, Olivier Mascaro, Hugo Mercier, Gloria Origgi, and Deirdre Wilson. 2010. 'Epistemic vigilance.' *Mind & Language* 25(4): 359–393; Hugo Mercier. 2017. 'How gullible are we? A review of the evidence from psychology and social science.' *Review of General Psychology* 21(2): 103–122.

Select Bibliography

Algan, Yann, Sergei Guriev, Elias Papaioannou, and Evgenia Passari. 2017. 'The European trust crisis and the rise of populism.' *Brookings Papers on Economic Activity* 2: 309–400.

Almond, Gabriel A., and Sydney Verba. 1963. *The Civic Culture*. Princeton, NJ: Princeton University Press.

Anderson, Cameron D. 2009. 'Institutional change, economic conditions and confidence in government: Evidence from Belgium.' *Acta Politica* 44: 28–49.

Anderson, Christopher J. 1995. *Blaming the Government: Citizens and the Economy in Five European Democracies*. New York: M. E. Sharpe.

Anderson, Christopher J., Andre Blais, and Shaun Bowler. 2005. *Losers' Consent: Elections and Democratic Legitimacy*. Oxford: Oxford University Press.

Anderson, Christopher J., and Yuliya V. Tverdova. 2003. 'Corruption, political allegiances, and attitudes toward government in contemporary democracies.' *American Journal of Political Science* 47(1): 91–109.

Andrews, Rhys, Sebastian Jilke, and Steven Van de Walle. 2014. 'Economic strain and perceptions of social cohesion in Europe: Does institutional trust matter?' *European Journal of Political Research* 53(3): 559–579.

Anduiza, Eva, Marc Guinjoan, and Guillem Rico. 2019. 'Populism, participation, and political equality.' *European Political Science Review* 11(1): 109–124.

Armingeon, Klaus, and B. Ceka. 2014. 'The loss of trust in the European Union during the great recession since 2007: The role of heuristics from the national political system.' *European Union Politics* 15(1): 82–107.

Armingeon, Klaus, and kai guthmann. 2013. 'Democracy in crisis: The declining support for national democracy in European countries, 2007–2011.' *European Journal of Political Research* 53(3): 423–442.

Arpinio, Bruno, and Anastassia V. Obyden. 2020. 'Democracy and political trust before and after the Great Recession of 2008: The European Union and the United Nations.' *Social Indicators Research* 148: 395–415.

Avery, James M. 2009. 'Videomalaise or virtuous circle? The influence of the news media on political trust.' *International Journal of Press-Politics* 14(4): 410–433.

Bachmann, Reinhard. 2011. 'At the crossroads: Future directions in trust research.' *Journal of Trust Research* 1(2): 203–213.

Bahry, Donna, and Polina Kozyreva. 2017. 'Family socialization, trust and change: Evidence from Russia.' *Comparative Sociology* 17(3–4): 261–278.

Barnes, Samuel, and Max Kaase. 1979. *Political Action: Mass Participation in Five Western Democracies*. Cambridge: Cambridge University Press.

Bauer, Paul, and Marcus Frietag. 2018. 'Measuring trust.' In Eric Uslaner (ed.), *Oxford Handbook of Social and Political Trust*. New York: Oxford University Press.

Bauer, Paul, and Matthias Fatke. 2018. 'Direct democracy and political trust: Enhancing trust, initiating distrust—or both?' *Swiss Political Science Review* 20(1): 49–69.

Bauer, Paul. 2015. 'Negative experiences and trust: A causal analysis of the effects of vic-timization on generalized trust.' *European Sociology Review* 31: 397–417.

Bayram, A. Burcu. 2017. 'Aiding strangers: Generalized trust and the moral basis of public support for Foreign Development Aid.' *Foreign Policy Analysis* 13(1): 133–153.

Benvenisti, Eyal, 2018. 'Upholding democracy amid the challenges of new technology: What role for the law of global governance?' *European Journal of International Law* 29(1): 9–82.

Bergh, A., and R. Öhrvall. 2018. 'A sticky trait: Social trust among Swedish expatriates in countries with varying institutional quality.' *Journal of Comparative Economics* 46: 1146–1157.

Bernstein, Steven. 2011. 'Legitimacy in intergovernmental and non-state global govern-ance.' *Review of International Political Economy* 18(1): 17–51.

Binning, Kevin R. 2007. '"It's us against the world": How distrust in Americans versus people-in-general shapes competitive foreign policy preferences.' *Political Psychology* 28(6): 777–799.

Bishin, Benjamin G., Robert R. Barr, and Matthew J. Lebo. 2006. 'The impact of economic versus institutional factors in elite evaluation of presidential progress toward democ-racy in Latin America.' *Comparative Political Studies* 39(10): 1194–1219.

Bjørnskov, Christian, and Pierre-Guillaume Méon. 2013. 'Is trust the missing root of institutions, education, and development?' *Public Choice* 157(3–4): 641–669.

Bjornskov, Christian. 2007. 'Determinants of generalized trust: A cross-country compar-ison.' *Public Choice* 130(1–2): 1–21.

Bjørnskov, Christian. 2010. 'How does social trust lead to better governance? An attempt to separate electoral and bureaucratic mechanisms.' *Public Choice* 144(1–2): 323–346.

Boix, Carles, and Daniel N. Posner. 1998. 'Social capital: Explaining its origins and effects on government performance.' *British Journal of Political Science* 28(4): 686–693.

Boswell, Christina. 2018. *Manufacturing Political Trust: Targets and Performance Management in Public Policy*. Cambridge: Cambridge University Press.

Bouckaert, Geert, and Steven van de Walle. 2003. 'Comparing measures of citizen trust and user satisfaction as indicators of "good governance": Difficulties in linking trust and satisfaction indicators.' *International Review of Administrative Sciences* 69(3): 329–343.

Bouckaert, Geert, and S. Van der Walle. 2003. 'Public service performance and trust in government: The problem of causality.' *International Journal of Public Administration* 26(8–9): 891–913.

Boulianne, Shelley. 2019. 'Building faith in democracy: Deliberative events, political trust and efficacy.' *Political Studies* 67(1): 4–30.

Bovens, Mark, and Anchrit Wille. 2008. 'Deciphering the Dutch Drop: Ten explanations for decreasing political trust in the Netherlands.' *International Review of Administrative Sciences* 74(2): 283–305.

Bowler, Shaun, and Timothy Donovan. 2002. 'Democracy, institutions and attitudes about citizen influence on government.' *British Journal of Political Science* 32(2): 371–379.

Bowler, Shaun, and Jeffrey Karp. 2004. 'Politicians, scandals, and trust in government.' *Political Behavior* 26(3): 271–287.

Braithwaite, Valerie A., and Margaret Levi. 1998. *Trust and Governance*. New York: Russell Sage Foundation.

Brassett, James, and Eleni Tsingou. 2011. 'The politics of legitimate global governance.' *Review of International Political Economy* 18(1): 1–16.

Bratton, Michael, and Robert Mattes. 2001. 'Support for democracy in Africa: Intrinsic or instrumental.' *British Journal of Political Science* 31(3): 447–474.

Braun, Daniela, and Swen Hutter. 2016. 'Political trust, extra-representational participation and the openness of political systems.' *International Political Science Review* 37(2): 151–165.

Braun, Daniela, and Markus Tausendpfund. 2014. 'The impact of the euro crisis on citizens' support for the European Union.' *Journal of European Integration* 36(3): 231–245.

Brewer, Paul, Kimberley Gross, S. Aday, and Lars Willnat. 2004. 'International trust and public opinion about world affairs.' *American Journal of Political Science* 48(1): 93–109.

Brewer, Paul R., and M. Steenbergen. 2002. 'All against all: How beliefs about human nature shape foreign policy opinions.' *Political Psychology* 23: 39–58.

Brooks, D. J., and John G. Geer. 2007. 'Beyond negativity: The effects of incivility on the electorate.' *American Journal of Political Science* 51(1): 1–16.

Brosius, Anna, Erika J. van Elsas, and Claes H. de Vreese. 2019. 'Trust in the European Union: Effects of the information environment.' *European Journal of Communication* 34(1): 57–73.

Brownlee, Jason. 2007. *Authoritarianism in the Age of Democratization*. Cambridge: Cambridge University Press.

Brusca, Isabel, Francesca Manes Rossi, and Natalia Aversano. 2018. 'Accountability and transparency to fight against corruption: An international comparative analysis.' *Journal of Comparative Policy Analysis: Research and Practice* 20(5): 486–504.

Bustikova, Lenka, and Petera Guasti. 2017. 'The illiberal turn or swerve in Central Europe?' *Politics and Governance* 5(4): 166–176.

Campbell, W. R. 2004. 'The sources of institutional trust in East and West Germany: Civic culture or economic performance?' *German Politics* 13(3): 401–441.

Canache, Damarts, Jeffery Mondak, and Mitch A. Seligson. 2001. 'Meaning and measurement in cross-national research on satisfaction with democracy.' *Public Opinion Quarterly* 65(4): 506–528.

Cappella, Joseph A., and Kathleen Hall Jamieson. 1997. *Spiral of Cynicism*. New York: Oxford University Press.

Catterberg, G., and Alejandro Moreno. 2006. 'The individual bases of political trust: Trends in new and established democracies.' *International Journal of Public Opinion Research* 18(1): 31–48.

Ceron, Andrea, and Vincenzo Memoli. 2015. 'Trust in government and media slant: A cross-sectional analysis of media effects in twenty-seven European countries.' *International Journal of Press-Politics* 20(3): 339–359.

Chanley, Virginia A. 2002. 'Trust in government in the aftermath of 9/11: Determinants and consequences.' *Political Psychology* 23(3): 469–483.

Chanley, Virginia A., Thomas J. Rudolph, and Wendy Rahn. 2000. 'The origins and consequences of public trust in government: A time series analysis.' *Public Opinion Quarterly* 64(3): 239–256.

Charron, Nicholas, and Bo Rothstein. 2016. 'Does education lead to higher generalized trust? The importance of quality of government.' *International Journal of Educational Development* 50: 59–73.

Choi, Eunjung, and Jongseok Woo. 2016. 'The origins of political trust in East Asian Democracies: Psychological, cultural, and institutional arguments.' *Japanese Journal of Political Science* 17(3): 410–426. doi:10.1017/S1468109916000165.

Christensen, Tom, and Per Laegried. 2005. 'Trust in government: The relative importance of service satisfaction, political factors, and demography.' *Public Performance and Management Review* 28(4): 487–511.

Cinar, Kursat, and Meral Ugur-Cinar. 2018. 'The effects of executive constraints on political trust.' *Democratization* 25(8): 1519–1538.

Citrin, Jack. 1974. 'Comment: The political relevance of trust in government.' *American Political Science Review* 68: 973–988.

Citrin, Jack, and Laura Stoker. 2018. 'Political trust in a cynical age.' *Annual Review of Political Science* 21(1): 49–70.

Clark, A. K. 2015. 'Rethinking the decline in social capital.' *American Politics Research* 43: 569–601.

Clarke, Harold D., Nitish Dutt, and Alan Kornberg. 1993. 'The political economy of attitudes toward polity and society in Western European democracies.' *Journal of Politics* 55(4): 998–1021.

Clarke, Nick, Gerry Stoker, and Jonathan Moss, 2018. *The Good Politician.* New York: Cambridge University Press.

Cleary, Matthew R., and Susan C. Stokes. 2006. *Democracy and the Culture of Skepticism: Political Trust in Argentina and Mexico.* New York: Russell Sage Foundation.

Cole, Richard. 1973. 'Toward as model of political trust: A causal analysis.' *American Journal of Political Science* 17(4): 809–817.

Coleman, James S. 1990. *Foundations of Social Theory.* Cambridge, MA: Harvard University Press.

Cook, Karen (ed.). 2001. *Trust in Society.* New York: Russell Sage.

Cook, Karen (ed.). 2009. *Whom Can We Trust? How Groups, Networks, and Institutions Make Trust Possible.* New York: Russell Sage.

Cook, Timothy E., and Paul Gronke. 2005. 'The skeptical American: Revisiting the meanings of trust in government and confidence in institutions.' *Journal of Politics* 67(3): 784–803.

Cooley, Alexander, and Jack Snyder (eds.). 2015. *Ranking the World: Grading States as Tools of Governance.* New York: Cambridge University Press.

Cordero, G., and P. Simón. 2015. 'Economic crisis and support for democracy in Europe.' *West European Politics* 39(2): 305–325.

Córdova, A., and M. L. Layton. 2015. 'When is "delivering the goods" not good enough?' *World Politics* 68(1): 74–110.

Craig, Stephen. 1993. *The Malevolent Leaders: Popular Discontent in America.* Boulder, CO: Westview Press.

Cramer, Katherine J. 2016. *The Politics of Resentment: Rural Consciousness in Wisconsin and the Rise of Scott Walker.* Chicago: Chicago University Press.

Crozier, Michel, Samuel P. Huntington, and Joji Watanuki. 1975. *The Crisis of Democracy: Report on the Governability of Democracies to the Trilateral Commission.* New York: New York University Press.

Cusack, T. R. 1999. 'The shaping of popular satisfaction with government and regime performance in Germany.' *British Journal of Political Science* 29(4): 641–672.

Dahlberg, Stefan, Jonas Linde, and Soren Holmberg. 2015. 'Democratic discontent in old and new democracies: Assessing the importance of democratic input and governmental output.' *Political Studies* 63(1): 18–37.

Dalton, Russell. J. 2004. *Democratic Challenges, Democratic Choices: The Erosion of Political Support in Advanced Industrial Democracies.* New York: Oxford University Press.

Dalton, Russell J. 2005. 'The social transformation of trust in government.' *International Review of Sociology* 15(1): 133–154.

Dalton, Russell J., and Martin P. Wattenberg. 2000. *Parties without Partisans: Political Change in Advanced Industrial Democracies.* Oxford: Oxford University Press.

Dalton, Russell J., and Christian Welzel (eds.). 2018. *The Civic Culture Transformed.* New York: Cambridge University Press.

Damico, A., Margaret Conway, and S. Damico. 2000. 'Patterns of political trust and mistrust: Three moments in the lives of democratic citizens.' *Polity* 32(3): 377–400.

Dawson, C. 2019. 'How persistent is generalised trust?' *Sociology* 53: 590–599.

De Blok, Lisanne, Tom van der Meer, and Wouter Van der Brug. 2020. 'Policy area satisfaction, perceptions of responsibility, and political trust: A novel application of the REWB model to testing evaluation-based political trust.' *Journal of Elections Public Opinion and Parties.* doi 10.1080/17457289.2020.1780433.

De Vreese, Claes H. 2005. 'The spiral of cynicism reconsidered.' *European Journal of Communication* 20(3): 283–301.

Delhey, Jan. 2007. 'Do enlargements make the European Union less cohesive? An analysis of trust between EU nationalities.' *Journal of Common Market Studies* 45(2): 253–279.

Delhey, Jan, and Kenneth Newton. 2005. 'Predicting cross-national levels of social trust: Global patterns of Nordic exceptionalism?' *European Sociological Review* 21(4): 311–327.

Delhey, Jan, Kenneth Newton, and Chris Welzel. 2011. 'How general is trust in 'most people'? Solving the radius of trust issue.' *American Sociological Review* 76: 786–807.

Dellmuth, Lisa Maria, and Jonas Tallberg. 2015. 'The social legitimacy of international organisations: Interest representation, institutional performance, and confidence extrapolation in the United Nations.' *Review of International Studies* 41(3): 451–475.

Dellmuth, Lisa Maria, and Jonas Tallberg. 2020. 'Why national and international legitimacy beliefs are linked: Social trust as an antecedent factor.' *Review of International Organizations* 15: 311–337.

Devine, Daniel, Jennifer Gaskell, Will Jennings, and Gerry Stoker. 2020. 'Trust and the Coronavirus pandemic: What are the consequences of and for trust? An early review of the literature.' *Political Studies Review* 19(2): 274–285.

Deyong Ma and Feng Yang. 2014. 'Authoritarian orientations and political trust in East Asian societies.' *East Asia* 31(4): 323–341.

Di Mauro, Danilo, and Vincenzo Memoli. 2016. *Attitudes Towards Europe Beyond Euroscepticism: Supporting the European Union.* New York: Palgrave Macmillan.

Diamond, Larry, and Marc F. Plattner (eds.). 2015. *Democracy in Decline?* Baltimore, MD: Johns Hopkins University Press.

Diamond, Larry, Marc Plattner, and C. Walker. 2016. *Authoritarianism Goes Global.* Baltimore, MD: Johns Hopkins University Press.

Diamond, Larry. 2015. 'Facing up to the democratic recession.' *Journal of Democracy* 26(1): 141–155.

Dingemans, E., and E. Van Ingen. 2015. 'Does religion breed trust? A cross-national study of the effects of religious involvement, religious faith, and religious context on social trust.' *Journal for the Scientific Study of Religion* 54: 739–755.

Dionne, Eugene J., Jr. 1991. *Why Americans Hate Politics.* New York: Simon & Schuster.

Dogan, Mattei (ed.). 2005. *Political Mistrust and the Discrediting of Politicians.* Leiden: Brill.

Dotti Sani, G. M., and B. Magistro. 2016. 'Increasingly unequal? The economic crisis, social inequalities and trust in the European Parliament in 20 European countries.' *European Journal of Political Research* 55(2): 246–264.

Duncan, Grant. 2019. *The Problem of Political Trust: A Conceptual Reformulation.* London: Routledge.

Dunn, Kris. 2015. 'Voice, representation and trust in parliament.' *Acta Politica* 50(2): 171–192.

Dyck, Joshua. 2009. 'Initiated distrust: Direct democracy and trust in government.' *American Political Research* 37(4): 539–568.

Earl Bennett, S., Stephen L. Rhine, R. S. Flickinger, and Lance Bennett. 1999. '"Video Malaise" revisited: Public trust in the media and government.' *Harvard International Journal of Press/Politics* 4(4): 8–23.

Easton, David. 1965. *A framework for political analysis.* Englewood Cliffs, NJ: Prentice-Hall.

Easton, David. 1975. 'Reassessment of the concept of political support.' *British Journal of Political Science* 5: 435–457.

Edelman. 2019. *Edelman Trust Barometer.* https://www.edelman.com/trust-barometer.

Eder, Christina, Ingvill C. Mochmann, and Markus Quandt (eds.). 2015. *Political Trust and Disenchantment with Politics: International Perspectives.* Leiden: Brill.

Edwards, Martin S. 2009. 'Public support for the international economic organizations: Evidence from developing countries.' *Review of International Organizations* 4(2): 185–209.

Engler, Sarah. 2016. 'Corruption and electoral support for new political parties in Central and Eastern Europe.' *West European Politics* 39(2): 278–304.

Enos, Ryan. 2017. *The Space between Us: Social Geography and Politics.* Cambridge: Cambridge University Press.

Ercan, S. A., and J. P. Gagnon. 2014. The crisis of democracy: Which crisis? Which democracy? *Democratic Theory* 1(2): 1–10.

Erikson, Erik. 1964. *Childhood and Society.* New York: W. W. Norton.

Erman, Eva. 2018. 'The political legitimacy of global governance and the proper role of civil society actors.' *Res Publica* 24(1): 133–155.

Eurofund. 2018. *Societal Change and Trust in Institutions.* Luxembourg: Publications Office of the European Union.

European Commission. 2018. *Public Opinion.* http://ec.europa.eu/commfrontoffice/publicopinion/index.cfm.

Evans, Geoffrey, and Stephen Whitefield. 1995. 'The politics and economics of democratic commitment: Support for democracy in transition societies.' *British Journal of Political Science* 25(4): 485–513.

Fawzi, Nayla, et al. 2021. 'Concepts, causes and consequences of trust in news media – a literature review and framework.' *Annals of the International Communication Association,* doi:10.1080/23808985.2021.1960181.

Feldman, Stanley. 1983. 'The measurement and meaning of trust in government.' *Political Methodology* 9(3): 341–354.

Ferrin, Monica, and Hanpeter Kreisi (eds.). 2016. *How Europeans View and Evaluate Democracy.* New York: Oxford University Press.

Fetchenhauer, Detlef, and David Dunning. 2009. 'Do people trust too much or too little?' *Journal of Economic Psychology* 30(3): 263–276.

Finke, Stephen E., Edward Muller, and Mitchell A. Seligson. 1987. 'Economic crisis, incumbent performance and regime support.' *British Journal of Political Science* 19: 329–351.

Foa, Roberto S., and Yasha Mounk. 2016. 'The democratic disconnect.' *Journal of Democracy* 27(3): 5–17.

Foster, Chase, and Jeffry Frieden. 2017. 'Crisis of trust: Socioeconomic determinants of European confidence in government.' *European Union Politics* 18(4): 511–535.

Franklin, Mark N. 2004. *Voter Turnout and the Dynamics of Electoral Competition in Established Democracies since 1945*. New York: Cambridge University Press.

Frederiksen, Morten, Christian A. Larsen, and Henrik L. Lolle. 2016. 'Education and trust: Exploring the association across social relationships and nations.' *Acta Sociologica* 59(3): 293–308.

Freitag, Markus, and Richard Traunmüller. 2009. 'Spheres of trust: An empirical analysis of the foundations of particularised and generalised trust.' *European Journal of Political Research* 48: 782–788.

Freitaga, Markus, and Paul C. Bauer. 2012. 'Personality traits and the propensity to trust friends and strangers.' *Social Science Journal* 53: 467–476.

Frye, Timothy, Scott Gehlbach, Kyle Marquardt, and Ora John Reuter. 2017. 'Is Putin's popularity real?' *Post-Soviet Affairs* 33(1): 1–15.

Fukuyama, Francis. 1995. *Trust: The Social Virtues and the Creation of Prosperity*. New York: Free Press.

Fulmer, C. Ashley, and Michele J. Gelfand. 2012. 'At what level (and in whom) we trust: Trust across multiple organizational levels.' *Journal of Management* 38: 1167–1230.

Gallup. 2017. *Trust in Government*. https://news.gallup.com/poll/5392/trust-government.aspx.

Gambetta, Diego (ed.). 1988. *Trust: Making and Breaking Cooperative Relations*. Cambridge, MA: Basil Blackwell.

Gamson, William A. 1992. *Talking Politics*. Cambridge: Cambridge University Press.

Gargiulo, Martin, and Gokhan Ertug. 2006. 'The dark side of trust.' In Reinhard Bachmann and Akbar Zaheer (eds.), *Handbook of Trust Research*, pp. 165–186. Cheltenham, UK: Edward Elgar.

Garment, Suzanne. 1991. *Scandal: The Crisis of Mistrust in American Politics*. New York: Random House.

Geddes, Barbara, and John Zaller. 1989. 'Sources of popular support for authoritarian regimes.' *American Journal of Political Science* 33(2): 319–347.

Gerschewski, Johannes. 2013. 'The three pillars of stability.' *Democratization* 20(1): 13–38.

Gerschewski, Johannes. 2018. 'Legitimacy in autocracies: Oxymoron or essential feature?' *Perspectives on Politics* 16(3): 652–665.

Gershtenson, Joseph, Jeffrey Ladewig, and Dennis Plane. 2006. 'Parties, institutional control, and trust in government.' *Social Science Quarterly* 87(4): 882–902.

Gest, Justin, Tyler Reny, and Jeremy Mayer. 2017. 'Roots of the radical right: Nostalgic deprivation in the United States and Britain.' *Comparative Political Studies* 51(13): 1694–1719.

Glaeser, Edward, David I. Laibson, Jose A. Scheikman, and Christine Scoutter. 2000. 'Measuring trust.' *The Quarterly Journal of Economics* 115(3): 811–846.

Glanville, Jennifer L., and Pamela Paxton. 2007. 'How do we learn to trust? A confirmatory tetrad analysis of the sources of generalized trust.' *Social Psychology Quarterly* 70(3): 230–242.

González-Ocantos, Ezequiel, Chad Kiewiet de Jonge, and David W. Nickerson. 2015. 'Legitimacy buying: The dynamics of clientelism in the face of legitimacy challenges.' *Comparative Political Studies* 48(9): 1127–1158.

Greco, John (ed.). 2011. *The Oxford Handbook of Skepticism*. Oxford: Oxford University Press.

Griffiths, Ryan. 2016. *Age of Secession: The International and Domestic Determinants of State Birth*. New York: Cambridge University Press.

Grimes, Marcia. 2006. 'Organizing consent: The role of procedural fairness in political trust and compliance.' *European Journal of Political Research* 45(2): 285–315.

Grimmelikhuijsen, Stephen, and Eva Kniew. 2017. 'Validating a scale for citizen trust in government organizations.' *International Review of Administrative Sciences* 83(3): 583–601.

Güemes, Cecilia, and Francisco Herreros. 2019. 'Education and trust: A tale of three continents.' *International Political Science Review* 40(5): 676–693.

Haggard, Stephan, and Robert Kaufman. 2021. *Backsliding: Democratic Regress in the Contemporary World*. Cambridge: Cambridge University Press.

Hakhverdian, Armen, and Quintin Mayne. 2012. 'Institutional trust, education, and corruption: A micro-macro interactive approach.' *Journal of Politics* 74(3): 739–750.

Hale, Thomas. 2008. 'Transparency, accountability, and global governance.' *Global Governance* 14(1): 73–94.

Hamm, Joseph, Corwin Smidt, and Roger C. Mayer. 2019. 'Understanding the psychological nature of trust.' *PLOS One* 14(5): 1–20.

Hardin, Russell. 2004. *Trust and Trustworthiness*. New York: Polity/Russell Sage Foundation.

Hardin, Russell. 2006. *Trust*. Cambridge: Polity Press.

Hardin, Russell (ed.). 2009. *Distrust*. New York: Polity/Russell Sage Foundation.

Harteveld, Eelco, Tom van der Meer, and Catherine De Vries. 2013. 'In Europe we trust? Exploring three logics of trust in the European Union.' *European Union Politics* 14(4): 542–565.

Haugsgjerd, Atle, and S. Kumlin. 2019. 'Downbound spiral? Economic grievances, perceived social protection and political distrust.' *West European Politics* 43(4): 969–990.

Haugsgjerd, Atle. 2019. 'Moderation or radicalisation? How executive power affects right-wing populists' satisfaction with democracy.' *Electoral Studies* 57: 31–45.

Hay, Colin. 2007. *Why We Hate Politics*. Cambridge: Polity Press.

Hayo, Bernd, and Edith Neuenkirch. 2014. 'The German public and its trust in the ECB: The role of knowledge and information search.' *Journal of International Money and Finance* 47: 286–303.

Herreros, F., and H. Criado. 2009. 'Social trust, social capital and perceptions of immigration.' *Political Studies* 57: 337–355.

Hessami, Zohal. 2011. *What Determines Trust in International Organizations? An Empirical Analysis for the IMF, the World Bank, and the WTO*. Working Paper Series 2011-44.

Hetherington, Marc J. 1998. 'The political relevance of political trust.' *American Political Science Review* 92(4): 791–808.

Hetherington, Marc J. 2005. *Why Trust Matters*. Princeton, NJ: Princeton University Press.

Hetherington, Marc J., and Jason Husser. 2012. 'How trust matters: The changing political relevance of political trust.' *American Journal of Political Science* 56(2): 312–325.

Hetherington, Marc J., and Thomas Rudolph. 2008. 'Priming, performance, and the dynamics of political trust.' *Journal of Politics* 70(2): 498–512.

Hetherington, Marc J., and Thomas Rudolph. 2015. *Why Washington Won't Work*. Chicago: University of Chicago Press.

Hibbing, John R., and Elizabeth Theiss-Morse. 1995. *Congress as Public Enemy*. New York: Cambridge University Press.

Hibbing, John R., and Elizabeth Theiss-Morse (eds.). 2001. *What Is It about Government That Americans Dislike?* Cambridge: Cambridge University Press.

Hibbing, John R., and Elizabeth Theiss-Morse. 2002. *Stealth Democracy: Americans' Beliefs about How Government Should Work*. New York: Cambridge University Press.

Hicken, Allan. 2011. 'Clientelism.' *Annual Review of Political Science* 14: 289–310.

Hobolt, Sara B. 2012. 'Citizen satisfaction with democracy in the European Union.' *Journal of Common Market Studies* 50(1): 88–105.

Hobolt, Sara B., and James Tilley. 2014. *Blaming Europe? Responsibility without Accountability*. Oxford: Oxford University Press.

Hoffman, Aaron M. 2002. 'A conceptualization of trust in international relations.' *European Journal of International Relations* 8(3): 375–401.

Hooghe, Marc, Sofie Marien, and Thomas de Vroome. 2012. 'The cognitive basis of trust: The relation between education, cognitive ability, and generalized and political trust.' *Intelligence* 40(6): 604–613.

Hooghe, Liesbet, and Gary Marks. 2005. 'Calculation, community, and cues: Public opinion on European integration.' *European Union Politics* 6(4): 419–443.

Hooghe, Marc. 2011. 'Why there is basically only one form of political trust.' *British Journal of Politics and International Relations* 13(2): 269–275.

Hooghe, Marc, and Ruth Dassonneville. 2018. 'A spiral of distrust: A panel study on the relation between political distrust and protest voting in Belgium.' *Government and Opposition* 53(1): 104–130.

Hooghe, Marc, and Sonja Zmerli (eds.). 2011. *Political Trust: Why Context Matters*. Colchester, UK: ECPR Press.

Hopkins, D. 2017. *Red Fighting Blue: How Geography and Electoral Rules Polarize American Politics*. Cambridge: Cambridge University Press.

Hu, Anning, and Chen Yin. 2021. 'Typology of political trustors in contemporary China: The relevance of authoritarian culture and perceived institutional performance.' *Journal of Chinese Political Science*. doi.org/10.1007/s11366-021-09751-6.

Huang, J., H. M. van den Brink, and W. Groot. 2009. 'A meta-analysis of the effect of education on social capital.' *Economics of Education Review* 28(4): 454–464.

Huang, Kai-Ping, and Paul Schuler. 2018. 'A status quo theory of generalized trust.' *Comparative Politics* 51(1): 121–132.

Huang, M.-H., Y. Chang, and Y. Chu. 2008. 'Identifying sources of democratic legitimacy: A multilevel analysis.' *Electoral Studies* 27(1): 45–62.

Hudson, John. 2006. 'Institutional trust and subjective well-being across the EU.' *Kyklos* 59(1): 43–62.

Hutchens, Myiah, Jay Hmielowski, Bruce E. Pinkleton, and Michael Beam. 2016. 'A spiral of skepticism? The relationship between citizens' involvement with campaign information to their skepticism and political knowledge.' *Journalism and Mass Communication Quarterly* 93(4): 1073–1090.

Inglehart, Ronald. 1977. *The Silent Revolution: Changing Values and Political Styles among Western Publics*. Princeton, NJ: Princeton University Press.

Inglehart, Ronald. 1990. *Culture Shift in Advanced Industrial Society*. Princeton, NJ: Princeton University Press.

Inglehart, Ronald. 1997. *Modernization and Postmodernization: Cultural, Economic and Political Change in 43 Societies*. Princeton, NJ: Princeton University Press.

Inglehart, Ronald, and Pippa Norris. 2016. 'Trump, Brexit, and the rise of populism: Economic have-nots and cultural backlash.' *HKS Working Paper* No. RWP16-026.

Inglehart, Ronald, and Christopher Welzel. 2005. *Modernization, Cultural Change, and Democracy: The Human Development Sequence*. New York: Cambridge University Press.

Jacobs, A. M., and J. S. Matthews. 2012. 'Why do citizens discount the future? Public opinion and the timing of policy consequences.' *British Journal of Political Science* 42(4): 903–935.

Jagers, Jan, and Staffan Walgrave. 2007. 'Populism as political communication style: An empirical study of political parties' discourse in Belgium.' *European Journal of Political Research* 46(3): 319–345.

Jamal, Amaney. 2007. 'When is social trust a desirable outcome? Examining levels of trust in the Arab World.' *Comparative Political Studies* 40: 1–22.

Jamal, Amaney, and Irfan Nooruddin. 2010. 'The democratic utility of trust: A cross-national analysis.' *The Journal of Politics* 72(1): 45–59.

Jennings, Will, Gerry Stoker, and Joe Twyman. 2016. 'The dimensions and impact of political discontent in Britain.' *Parliamentary Affairs* 69(4): 876–900.

Jennings, Will, Nick Clarke, Jonathan Moss, and Gerry Stoker. 2017. 'The decline in diffuse support for national politics: The long view on political discontent in Britain.' *Public Opinion Quarterly* 81(3): 748–758.

Johnson, Irnya. 2005. 'Political trust in societies under transformation: A comparative analysis of Poland and Ukraine.' *International Journal of Sociology* 35(2): 63–84.

Jones, Karen. 1996. 'Trust as an affective attitude.' *Ethics* 10: 74–125.

Justwan, Florian, and Sarah K. Fisher. 2017. 'Generalized social trust and international dispute settlement.' *International Interactions* 43(5): 717–743.

Kaase, Max. 1999. 'Interpersonal trust, political trust and non-institutionalised political participation in Western Europe.' *West European Politics* 22(3): 1–21.

Kahneman, Daniel. 2013. *Thinking Fast and Slow*. New York: Farrar, Straus and Giroux.

Kaltenthaler, Karl, Christopher J. Anderson, and William J. Miller. 2010. 'Accountability and independent central banks: Europeans and distrust of the European Central Bank.' *Journal of Common Market Studies* 48(5): 1261–1281.

Kang, S., and J. Zhu. 2020. 'Do people trust the government more? Unpacking the distinct impacts of anti-corruption policies on political trust.' *Political Research Quarterly*. https://doi.org/10.1177/1065912920 91201.

Karakoç, Ekrem. 2016. 'Ethnicity and trust in national and international institutions: Kurdish Attitudes toward political institutions in Turkey.' *Political Psychology of Turkish Political Behavior* 3849: 92–114.

Karp, Jeffrey A., Susan Banducci, and Shaun Bowler. 2003. 'To know it is to love it? Satisfaction with democracy in the European Union.' *Comparative Political Studies* 36(3): 271–292.

Kavakli, Kerim Can. 2020. 'Did populist leaders respond to the COVID-19 pandemic more slowly? Evidence from a global sample.' https://kerimcan81.files.wordpress.com/.

Keele, Luke. 2007. 'Social capital and the dynamics of trust in government.' *American Journal of Political Science* 51: 241–254.

Keohane, Robert O. 2006. 'Accountability in world politics.' *Scandinavian Political Studies* 29(2): 75–87.

Kettl, Donald. 2017. *Can Governments Earn Our Trust?* Cambridge: Polity.

Khan, H. A. 2016. 'The linkage between political trust and the quality of government: An analysis.' *International Journal of Public Administration* 39(9): 665–675.

Kim, Soonhee. 2010. 'Public trust in government in Japan and South Korea: Does the rise of critical citizens matter?' *Public Administration Review* 70(5): 801–810.

Klass, Brian. 2017. *The Despot's Apprentice*. New York: Hot Books.

Klein, Elad, and Joshua Robison. 2019. 'Like, post, and distrust? How social media use affects trust in government.' *Political Communication* 37(1): 46–64.

Klingemann, Hans-Dieter. 1999. 'Mapping political support in the 1990s.' In Pippa Norris (ed.), *Critical Citizens: Global Support for Democratic Governance*. Oxford: Oxford University Press.

Klingemann, Hans-Dieter, and Dieter Fuchs. 1995. *Citizens and the State*. Oxford: Oxford University Press.

Kotze, Hennie, and Carlos-Rivero Garcia. 2017. 'Institutions, crises, and political confidence in seven contemporary democracies: An elite-mass analysis.' *Journal of Public Affairs* 17: 1–2.

Kotzian, Peter. 2011. 'Conditional trust: The role of individual and system-level features for trust and confidence in institutions.' *Zeitschrift fur Vergleichende Politikwissenschaft* 5(1): 25–49.

Kraft, Patrick W., Milton Lodge, and Charles S. Taber. 2016. 'Why people "don't trust the evidence": Motivated reasoning and scientific beliefs.' *Annals of The American Academy of Political and Social Science* 658(1): 121–133.

Kroknes, Veronica Fagerland, Tor Georg Jakobsen, and Lisa-Marie Grønning. 2016. 'Economic performance and political trust: The impact of the financial crisis on European citizens.' *European Societies* 17(5): 700–723.

Kumlin, Staffan, and Bo Rothstein. 2005. 'Making and breaking social capital.' *Comparative Political Studies* 38(4): 339–365.

Kumlin, Staffan. 2004. *The Personal and the Political: How Personal Welfare State Experiences Affect Political Trust and Ideology*. London: Palgrave Macmillan.

Kurlantzick, Joshua. 2014. *Democracy in Retreat*. New Haven, CT: Yale University Press.

Kydd, Andrew H. 2007. *Trust and Mistrust in International Relations*. Princeton, NJ: Princeton University Press.

Lamare, James. 2015. 'Electoral reform, situational forces, and political confidence: Results from a multi-wave panel.' *Electoral Studies* 40: 361–371.

Lau, Richard R. and Ivy Brown Rovner. 2009. 'Negative campaigning.' *Annual Review of Political Science* 12: 285–306.

Lawrence, Robert. 1997. 'Is it really the economy, stupid?' In Joseph Nye, Philip Zelikow, and David King (eds.), *Why People Don't Trust Government*. Cambridge, MA: Harvard University Press.

Lazarsfeld, P. F., and W. Thielens. 1958. *The Academic Mind*. New York: Free Press.

Lenard, Patti Tamara. 2008. 'Trust your compatriots but count your change: The roles of trust, mistrust and distrust in democracy.' *Political Studies* 56(2): 312–332.

Lenard, Patti Tamara. 2015. 'The political philosophy of trust and distrust in democracies and beyond.' *The Monist* 98(4): 353–359.

Levi, Margaret, and Laura Stoker. 2000. 'Political trust and trustworthiness.' *Annual Review of Political Science* 3: 475–507.

Levitsky, Steven, and Daniel Ziblatt. 2018. *How Democracies Die*. New York: Crown.

Lewis, J. David, and Andrew J. Weigert. 2012. 'The social dynamics of trust: Theoretical and empirical research, 1985–2012.' *Social Forces* 91(1): 25–31.

Li, Jiayuan, and Wim Van den Noortgate. 2019. 'A meta-analysis of the relative effectiveness of the item count technique compared to direct questioning.' *Sociological Methods and Research* 51(2): 760–799.

Li, L. J. 2004. 'Political trust in rural China.' *Modern China* 30(2): 228–258.

Li, Xiaojun, Jianwei Wang, and Dingding Chen. 2016. 'Chinese citizens' trust in Japan and South Korea: Findings from a four-city survey.' *International Studies Quarterly* 60(4): 778–789.

Lind, E. A., and T. R. Tyler. 1988. *The Social Psychology of Procedural Justice*. New York: Plenum Press.

Linde, Jonas, and Joakim Ekman. 2003. 'Satisfaction with democracy: A note on a frequently used indicator in comparative politics.' *European Journal of Political Research* 42(3): 391–408.

Lindholt, Marie F., Fredrik Jørgensen, Alexandor Bor, and Michael B. Petersen. 2021. 'Public acceptance of COVID-19 vaccines: Cross-national evidence on levels and individual-level predictors using observational data.' *BMJ Open* 11: e048172. doi:10.1136/bmjopen-2020-048172.

Lipset, Seymour Martin, and Stein Rokkan. 1967. *Party Systems and Voter Alignments: Cross-National Perspectives*. New York: Free Press.

Lipset, Seymour Martin. 1987. *The Confidence Gap*. 2nd ed. Baltimore, MD: Johns Hopkins University Press.

Listhaug, Ola Matti Wiberg. 1995. 'Confidence in political and private institutions.' In Dieter Fuchs and Hans-Dieter Klingemann (eds.), *Citizens and the State*, pp. 298–322. Oxford: Oxford University Press,.

Lodge, Milton, and Charles Tabor. 2013. *The Rationalizing Voter*. New York: Cambridge University Press.

Lofstedt, Ragnar. 2005. *Risk Management in Post-Trust Societies*. New York: Palgrave Macmillan.

Luce, Edward. 2017. *The Retreat of Western Liberalism*. London: Little Brown.

Luhmann, Niklas. 1979. *Trust and Power*. Cambridge: Polity Press.

Lührmann, Anna, Marcus Tannenberg, and Staffan I. Lindberg. 2018. 'Regimes of the World (RoW): Opening new avenues for the comparative study of political regimes.' *Politics and Governance* 6(1): 1–18.

Lupia, Arthur. 2016. *Uninformed: Why People Know So Little about Politics and What We Can Do about It*. New York: Oxford University Press.

Lyon, Fergus, Guido Mollering, and Mark N. K. Saunders (eds.). 2015. *Handbook on Research Methods on Trust*. 2nd ed. Cheltenham, UK: Edward Elgar.

Maciel, Gustavo, and Luis de Sousa. 2018. 'Legal corruption and dissatisfaction with democracy in the European Union.' *Social Indicators Research* 140(2): 653–674.

Magalhães, P. C. 2016. 'Economic evaluations, procedural fairness, and satisfaction with democracy.' *Political Research Quarterly* 69(3): 522–534.

Magaloni, Beatriz. 2006. *Voting for Autocracy*. Cambridge: Cambridge University Press.

Marien, Sofie. 2011. 'The effect of electoral outcomes on political trust: A multi-level analysis of 23 countries.' *Electoral Studies* 30(4): 712–726.

Marien, Sofie, and Marc Hooghe. 2011. 'Does political trust matter? An empirical investigation into the relation between political trust and support for law compliance.' *European Journal of Political Research* 50(2): 267–291.

Marien, Sofie, and Hannah Werner. 2019. 'Fair treatment, fair play? The relationship between fair treatment perceptions, political trust and compliant and cooperative attitudes cross nationally.' *European Journal of Political Research* 58: 72–95.

Martini, Sergio, and Mario Quaranta. 2020. *Citizens and Democracy in Europe: Contexts, Changes and Political Support*. London: Palgrave Macmillan.

Matthes, Jorg, Peter Maurer, and Florian Arendt. 2019. 'Consequences of politicians' perceptions of the news media.' *Journalism Studies* 20(3): 345–363.

Mayer, Roger C., James H. Davis, and F. David Schoorman. 1995. 'An integrative model of organizational trust.' *Academy of Management Review* 20(3): 709–734.

McAllister, Ian. 1999. 'The economic performance of governments.' In Pippa Norris (ed.), *Critical Citizens: Global Support for Democratic Governance*. New York: Oxford University Press.

McEvily, Bill, and Marco Tortoriello. 2011. 'Measuring trust in organisational research: Review and recommendations.' *Journal of Trust Research* 1(1): 23–63.

McKnight, D. Harrison, Vivek Choudhury, and Charles Kacmar. 2002. 'Developing and validating trust measures for e-commerce: An integrative typology.' *Information Systems Research* 13(3): 334–359.

McLaren, Lauren. 2012. 'The cultural divide in Europe: Migration, multiculturalism, and political trust.' *World Politics* 64(2): 199–241.

Mechkova, Valeriya, Anna Lührmann, and Staffan I. Lindberg. 2017. 'How much democratic backsliding?' *Journal of Democracy* 28: 162–169.

Mercier, Hugo. 2017. 'How gullible are we? A review of the evidence from psychology and social science.' *Review of General Psychology* 21(2): 103–122.

Mercier, Hugo. 2020. *Not Born Yesterday: The Science of Who We Trust and What We Believe*. Princeton, NJ: Princeton University Press.

Michel, Torsten. 2013. 'Time to get emotional: Reflections on the concept of trust in international relations.' *European Journal of International Relations* 19(4): 869–890.

Miller, Arthur H. 1974. 'Political issues and trust in government, 1964–1970.' *American Political Science Review* 68: 951–972.

Miller, Arthur H., and Ola Listhaug, 1999. 'Political performance and trust.' In Pippa Norris (ed.), *Critical Citizens: Global Support for Democratic Governance*. New York: Oxford University Press.

Miranti, Riyana, and Mark Evans. 2019. 'Trust, sense of community, and civic engagement: Lessons from Australia.' *Journal of Community Psychology* 47(2): 254–271.

Mishler, William, and Richard Rose. 2001. 'What are the origins of political trust? Testing institutional and cultural theories in post-communist societies.' *Comparative Political Studies* 34(1): 30–62.

Mishler, William, and Richard Rose. 2005. 'Trust, distrust and skepticism: Popular evaluations of civil and political institutions in post-communist societies.' *Journal of Politics* 59(2): 418–451.

Mishler, William, and Richard Rose. 2005. 'What are the political consequences of trust?' *Comparative Political Studies* 38(9): 1050–1078.

Moehler, Devra, and Staffan I. Lindberg. 2009. 'Narrowing the legitimacy gap: Turnovers as a cause of democratic consolidation.' *The Journal of Politics* 71(4): 1448–1466.

Mogensen, Kirsten. 2015. 'International trust and public diplomacy.' *International Communication Gazette* 77(4): 315–336.

Mondak, Jeffery J. 2010. *Personality and the Foundations of Political Behavior*. New York: Cambridge University Press.

Montero, Jose, Sonia Zmerli, and Kenneth Newton. 2008. 'Confianza social, confianza política y satisfacción con la democracia.' *Reis* 122: 11–54.

Mossberger, Karen, and Gerry Stoker. 2001. 'The evolution of urban regime theory: The challenge of conceptualization.' *Urban Affairs Review* 36: 810–835.

Mounk, Yasha. 2018. *The People vs. Democracy*. Cambridge, MA: Harvard University Press.

Moy, Patricia, and Michelle Pfau. 2000. *With Malice Toward All? The Media and Public Confidence in Democratic Institutions*. Westport, CT: Praeger.

Muñoz, J., M. Torcal, and E. Bonet. 2011. 'Trust in the European Parliament: From affective heuristics to rational cueing.' *European Union Politics* 12(4): 551–574.

Mutz, Diana C. 2011. *Population-Based Survey Experiments*. Princeton, NJ: Princeton University Press.

Mutz, Diana C., and B. Reeves. 2005. 'The new videomalaise: Effects of televised incivility on political trust.' *American Political Science Review* 99(1): 1–15.

Nannestad, Peter. 2008. 'What have we learned about generalized trust, if anything?' *Annual Review of Political Science* 11(1): 413–436.

Nannestad, Peter, Gert T. Svendsen, Peter T. Dinesen, and Kim M. Sønderskov. 2014. 'Do institutions or culture determine the level of social trust? The natural experiment of migration from non-western to western countries.' *Journal of Ethnic and Migration Studies* 40(4): 544–565.

Nanz, Patrizia, and Jens Steffek. 2004. 'Global governance, participation and the public sphere.' *Government and Opposition* 39(2): 314–335.

Newton, Kenneth. 2001. 'Trust, social capital, civil society, and democracy.' *International Political Science Review* 22(2): 201–214.

Newton, Kenneth. 2006. 'Political support: Social capital, civil society and political and economic performance.' *Political Studies* 54(4): 846–864.

Newton, Kenneth, and Pippa Norris. 2000. 'Confidence in public institutions: Faith, culture or performance.' In Susan Pharr and Robert Putnam (eds.), *Disaffected Democracies: What's Troubling the Trilateral Countries?* Princeton, NJ: Princeton University Press.

Newton, Kenneth, and Sonia Zmerli. 2011. 'Three forms of trust and their association.' *European Political Science Review* 3(2): 169–200.

Norris, Pippa. 1999. *A Virtuous Circle*. New York: Cambridge University Press.

Norris, Pippa. (ed.). 1999. *Critical Citizens: Global Support for Democratic Governance*. New York: Oxford University Press.

Norris, Pippa. 2000. 'Global governance and cosmopolitan citizens.' In Joseph Nye and John D. Donahue (eds.), *Governance in a Globalizing World*. Washington, DC: Brookings Institution Press.

Norris, Pippa. 2005. *Radical Right: Voters and Parties in the Electoral Market*. New York: Cambridge University Press.

Norris, Pippa. 2009. 'Confidence in the United Nations: Cosmopolitan and nationalistic attitudes.' In Yilmaz Esmer and Thorlief Pettersson (eds.), *The International System, Democracy and Values*. Uppsala: Acta Universitatis Upsaliensis.

Norris, Pippa (ed.). 2010. *Public Sentinel*. Washington, DC: World Bank.

Norris, Pippa. 2011. *Democratic Deficit*. New York: Cambridge University Press.

Norris, Pippa, John Curtice, David Sanders, Margaret Scammell, and Holli A. Semetko. 1999. *On Message: Communicating the Campaign*. London: Sage.

Norris, Pippa, and Ronald Inglehart. 2019. *Cultural Backlash*. New York: Cambridge University Press.

Nye, Joseph S., Philip D. Zelikow, and David C. King (eds.). 1997. *Why People Don't Trust Government*. Cambridge, MA: Harvard University Press.

O'Connor, Cailin, and James Owen Weatherall. 2019. *The Misinformation Age*. New Haven, CT: Yale University Press.

O'Neill, Onora. 2002. *A Question of Trust: The BBC Reith Lectures 2002*. Cambridge: Cambridge University Press.

Oliver, J. Erica, and Wendy M. Rahn. 2016. 'Rise of the Trumpenvolk: Populism in the 2016 election.' *The Annals of the American Academy of Political and Social Science* 667(1): 189–206.

Orren, Gary. 1997. 'Fall from grace: The public's loss of faith in government.' In Joseph S. Nye, Jr., Philip D. Zelikow, and David C. King (eds.), *Why People Don't Trust Government*. Chicago: University of Chicago Press.

Oskarsson, Sven. 2010. 'Generalized trust and political support: A cross-national investigation.' *Acta Politica* 45(4): 423–443.

Park, Alison, Caroline Bryson, Elizabeth Clery, John Curtice, and Miranda Phillips (eds.). 2013. *British social attitudes: The 30th Report*. London: NatCen Social Research.

Patterson, Thomas E. 1993. *Out of Order*. New York: Alfred A. Knopf.

Patterson, Thomas E. 2002. *The Vanishing Voter*. New York: Alfred A. Knopf.

Pew Research Center. December 2017. *Public Trust in Government: 1958–2017*. https://www.people-press.org/2017/12/14/public-trust-in-government-1958-2017/.

Pharr, Susan, and Robert Putnam (eds.). 2000. *Disaffected Democracies: What's Troubling the Trilateral Countries?* Princeton, NJ: Princeton University Press.

Pharr, Susan J., Robert Putnam, and Russell Dalton. 2000. 'A quarter century of declining confidence.' *Journal of Democracy* 11(2): 5–25.

Putnam, Robert D. 1993. *Making Democracy Work: Civic Traditions in Modern Italy*. Princeton, NJ: Princeton University Press.

Putnam, Robert D. 2000. *Bowling Alone?* New York: Simon and Schuster.

Putnam, Robert D. 2007. 'E pluribus unum: Diversity and community in the twenty-first century: The 2006 Johan Skytte Prize Lecture.' *Scandinavian Political Studies* 30(2): 137–174.

Putnam, Robert, and David E. Campbell. 2010. *American Grace: How Religion Divides and Unites Us*. New York: Simon & Schuster.

Pye, Lucien W., and M. W. Pye. 1985. *Asian Power and Politics: The Cultural Dimensions of Authority*. Cambridge, MA: Harvard University Press.

Rathbun, Brian C. 2011. 'The 'Magnificent Fraud': Trust, international cooperation, and the hidden domestic politics of American multilateralism after World War II.' *International Studies Quarterly* 55(1): 1–21.

Reeskens, Tim, and Marc Hooghe. 2008. 'Cross-cultural measurement equivalence of generalized trust: Evidence from the European Social Survey (2002 and 2004).' *Social Indicators Research* 85: 515–532.

Reulens, Anna, Bart Meuleman, and Ides Nicaise. 2019. 'Examining macroeconomic determinants of trust in parliament.' *Social Science Research* 75: 142–153.

Robbins, Blaine G. 2012. 'A blessing and a curse? Political institutions in the growth and decay of generalized trust: A cross-national panel analysis, 1980–2009.' *PLOS One* 7(4): e35120.

Robbins, Blaine G. 2012. 'Institutional quality and generalized trust: A non-recursive causal model.' *Social Indicators Research* 107(2): 235–258.

Robinson, Darrell, and Marcus Tannenberg. 2019. 'Self-censorship of regime support in authoritarian states: Evidence from list experiments in China.' *Research and Politics*: 1–9.

Robinson, Michael. 1976. 'Public affairs television and the growth of political malaise: The case of "The selling of the president."' *American Political Science Review* 70(3): 409–432.

Rodríguez-Pose, A. 2018. 'The revenge of the places that don't matter (and what to do about it).' *Cambridge Journal of Regions, Economy and Society* 11(3): 189–209.

Rooduijn, Mathias. 2018. 'What unites the voter bases of populist parties? Comparing the electorates of 15 populist parties.' *European Political Science Review* 10(3): 351–368.

Rooduijn, Mathias, Wouter Van Der Brug and Sarah L. de Lange. 2016. 'Expressing or fuelling discontent? The relationship between populist voting and political discontent.' *Electoral Studies* 43: 32–40.

Rosanvallon, Pierre. 2008. *Counter-Democracy: Politics in an Age of Distrust*. Cambridge: Cambridge University Press.

Rose, Richard, William Mishler, and Neil Munro. 2011. *Popular Support for an Undemocratic Regime*. New York: Cambridge University Press.

Rosenberg, Morris. 1956. 'Misanthropy and Political Ideology.' *American Sociological Review* 21(6): 690–695.

Rotenberg, Ken (ed.). 2010. *Interpersonal Trust during Childhood and Adolescence*. New York: Cambridge University Press.

Rothstein, Bo. 2003. 'Social capital, economic growth and quality of government: The causal mechanism.' *New Political Economy* 8(1): 49–71.

Rothstein, Bo. 2009. 'Creating political legitimacy: Electoral democracy versus quality of government.' *American Behavioral Scientist* 53(3): 311–330.

Rothstein, Bo. 2011. *The Quality of Government: Corruption, Social Trust and Inequality in International Perspective*. Chicago: University of Chicago Press.

Rothstein, Bo, Susan Rose-Ackerman, and J. Kornai (ed.). 2004. *Creating Social Trust in Post-Socialist Transition*. New York: Palgrave MacMillan.

Rothstein, Bo, and Dieter Stolle. 2008. 'The state and social capital: An institutional theory of generalized trust.' *Comparative Politics* 33(4): 401–419.

Rothstein, Bo, and Eric Uslaner. 2005. 'All for one: Equality, corruption, and social trust.' *World Politics* 58(1): 41–72.

Rotter, Julien B. 1980. 'Interpersonal trust, trustworthiness, and gullibility.' *American Psychologist* 35(1): 1–7.

Ruelens, Anna, Bart Meuleman, and Ides Nicaise. 2018. 'Examining measurement isomorphism of multilevel constructs: The case of political trust.' *Social Indicators Research* 140(3): 907–927.

Ruzicka, Jan, and Vincent Charles Keating. 2015. 'Going global: Trust research and international relations.' *Journal of Trust Research* 5(1): 8–26.

Sasaki, Masamichi, and Robert March (eds.). 2012. *Trust: Comparative Perspectives*. London: Brill.

Schaap, Dorian, and Peer Scheepers. 2014. 'Comparing citizens' trust in police across European countries: An assessment of cross-country measurement equivalence.' *International Criminal Justice Review* 24(1): 82–98.

Scharpf, F. W. 1999. *Governing in Europe: Effective and Democratic?* New York: Oxford University Press.

Schedler, Andreas. 2013. *The Politics of Uncertainty: Sustaining and Subverting Electoral Authoritarianism*. Oxford: Oxford University Press.

Schmidt, Vivienne. 2013. 'Democracy and legitimacy in the European Union revisited: Input, output, *and* throughput.' *Political Studies* 61(1): 2–22.

Schnaudt, Christian. 2018. *Political Confidence and Democracy in Europe*. Berlin: Springer.

Schneider, Irena. 2017. 'Can we trust measures of political trust? Assessing measurement equivalence in diverse regime types.' *Social Indicators Research* 133: 963–984.

Scholte, Jan. 2002. 'Civil society and democracy in global governance.' *Global Governance* 8(3): 281–304.

Scholte, Jan. 2011. 'Towards greater legitimacy in global governance.' *Review of International Political Economy* 18(1): 110–120.

Schwadel, P., and M. Stout. 2012. 'Age, period and cohort effects on social capital.' *Social Forces* 91: 233–252.

Seyd, Ben. 2015. 'How do citizens evaluate public officials? The role of performance and expectations on political trust.' *Political Studies* 63(1): 73–90.

Shah, Dhavan V., Mark D. Watts, David Domke, and David Fan. 2002. 'News framing and cueing of issue regimes: Explaining Clinton's public approval in spite of scandal.' *Public Opinion Quarterly* 66(3): 339–370.

Shi, T. J. 2001. 'Cultural values and political trust: A comparison of the People's Republic of China and Taiwan.' *Comparative Politics* 33(4): 401–419.

Skinner, Denise, Graham Dietz, and Antoinette Weibel. 2013. 'The dark side of trust: When trust becomes a "poisoned chalice."' *Organization* 21: 206–224.

Smyth, David J., and Susan Washburn Taylor. 2003. 'Presidential popularity: What matters most, macroeconomics or scandals?' *Applied Economics Letters* 10(9): 585–588.

Solt, F. 2012. 'The social origins of authoritarianism.' *Political Research Quarterly* 65(4): 703–713.

Sperber, Dan, Fabrice Clément, Christophe Heintz, Olivier Mascaro, Hugo Mercier, Gloria Origgi, and Deirdre Wilson. 2010. 'Epistemic vigilance.' *Mind & Language* 25(4): 359–393.

Stamos, Angelos, Efthymios Altsitsiadis, and Siegfried Dewitte. 2019. 'Investigating the effect of childhood socioeconomic background on interpersonal trust: Lower childhood socioeconomic status predicts lower levels of trust.' *Personality and Individual Differences* 145: 19–25.

Stockmann, Daniela, Ashley Esarey, and Jie Zhang. 2018. 'Who is afraid of the Chinese state? Evidence calling into question political fear as an explanation for overreporting of political trust.' *Political Psychology* 39(5): 1105–1121.

Stoker, Gerry. 2006. *Why Politics Matters: Making Democracy Work*. London: Palgrave/Macmillan.

Stoker, Gerry. 2019. 'Can the governance paradigm survive the rise of populism?' *Policy and Politics* 47(1): 3–18.

Stolle, Dieter. 1998. 'Bowling together, bowling alone: The development of generalized trust in voluntary associations.' *Political Psychology* 19(3): 497–525.

Stolle, Dieter, and Marc Hooghe. 2004. 'The roots of social capital: Attitudinal and network mechanisms in the relation between youth and adult indicators of social capital.' *ACTA Politica* 39: 422–441.

Stolle, Dietland and Laura Nishikawa. 2011. 'Trusting others: How parents shape the generalized trust of their children.' *Comparative Sociology* 10: 281–314.

Stoyan, Alissandra T., Sara Niedzwiecki, Jana Morgan, Jonathan Hartlyn, and Rosario Espinal. 2014. 'Trust in government institutions: The effects of performance and participation in the Dominican Republic and Haiti.' *International Political Science Review* 37(1): 1–18.

Sturgis P., et al. 2010. 'A genetic basis for social trust?' *Political Behavior* 32: 205–230.

Sunstein, Cass R. (ed.). 2018. *Can It Happen Here?* New York: HarperCollins.

Sztompka, Piotr. 1999. *Trust: A Sociological Theory*. Cambridge: Cambridge University Press.

Taber, Charles S., and Milton Lodge. 2006. 'Motivated skepticism in the evaluation of political beliefs.' *American Journal of Political Science* 50(3): 755–769.

Taber, Charles S., and Milton Lodge. 2016. 'The illusion of choice in democratic politics: The unconscious impact of motivated political reasoning.' *Political Psychology* 37(1): 61–85.

Tallberg, Jonas, Karin Backsterand, and Jan Aart Scholte (eds.). 2018. *Legitimacy in Global Governance*. Oxford: Oxford University Press.

Temmerman, Martina, Renee Moernaut, Roel Coesemans, and Jelle Mast. 2019. 'Post-truth and the political: Constructions and distortions in representing political facts.' *Discourse, Context and Media* 27: 1–6.

Thaler, Richard H., and Cass R. Sunstein. 2008. *Nudge*. New York: Penguin.

Thielmann, Isabel, and Benjamin E. Hilbig. 2015. 'Trust: An integrative review from a person–situation perspective.' *Review of General Psychology* 19(3): 249.

Thomson, Robert, and Heinz Brandenburg. 2019. 'Trust and citizens' evaluations of promise keeping by governing parties.' *Political Studies* 67(1): 249–266.

Tolchin, Susan J. 1996. *The Angry American: How Voter Rage Is Changing the Nation*. Boulder, CO: Westview Press.

Torcal, Mariano. 2014. 'The decline of political trust in Spain and Portugal: Economic performance or political responsiveness?' *American Behavioral Scientist* 58: 1542–1567.

Torcal, Mariano, and Jose Ramon Montero (eds.). 2006. *Political Disaffection in Contemporary Democracies: Social Capital, Institutions, and Politics*. London: Routledge.

Torgler, Benno. 2008. 'Trust in international organizations: An empirical investigation focusing on the United Nations.' *Review of International Organizations* 3: 65–93.

Traunmüller, Richard. 2011. 'Moral communities? Religion as a source of social trust in a multilevel analysis of 97 German regions.' *European Sociological Review* 27(3): 346–363.

Tsai, Ming Chang. 2017. 'Domestic politics, cultural conflict, and global exposure: Perceptions of intergovernmental organizations across Asia.' *Pacific Focus* 32(3): 319–350.

Tyler, Tom R. 2002. *Trust in the Law*. New York: Russell-Sage Foundation.

Tyler, Tom R. 2006. *Why People Obey the Law*. New Haven, CT: Yale University Press.

Tyler, Tom R. 2011. *Why People Cooperate*. Princeton, NJ: Princeton University Press.

Tyler, Tom R., and Rick Trinkner. 2017. *Why Children Follow Rules*. Oxford: Oxford University Press.

Uslaner, Eric M. 2002. *The Moral Foundations of Trust*. New York: Cambridge University Press.

Uslaner, Eric M. 2008. 'The foundations of trust: Macro and micro.' *Cambridge Journal of Economics* 32: 289–294.

Uslaner, Eric M. (ed.). 2018. *The Oxford Handbook of Social and Political Trust*. New York: Oxford University Press.

Valentino, Nicholas A. 2001. 'A spiral of cynicism for some: The contingent effects of campaign news frames on participation and confidence in government.' *Political Communication* 18: 347.

Valiyev, Anar, Axer Babayev, Hajar Huseynova, and Khalida Jafarova. 2017. 'Do citizens of the former Soviet Union trust state institutions and why: The case of Azerbaijan.' *Communist and Post-Communist Studies* 50(3): 221–231.

Van Berkel, Freek, Julie E. Ferguson, and Peter Groenewegen. 2019. 'Once bitten, twice shy: How anxiety and political blame avoidance cause a downward spiral of trust and control in the aftermath of failed public projects.' *Administration and Society* 51(4): 545–580.

Van de Walle, Steven, Steven van Roosbroek, and Geert Bouckaert. 2008. 'Trust in the public sector: Is there any evidence for a long-term decline?' *International Review of Administrative Sciences* 74(1): 45–62.

Van der Meer, Tom. 2010. 'In what we trust? A multi-level study into trust in parliament as an evaluation of state characteristics.' *International Review of Administrative Sciences* 76(3): 517–536.

Van der Meer, Tom. 2017. 'Dissecting the causal chain from quality of government to political support.' In Carolien Van Ham, Jacques Thomassen, Kees Aarts, and Rudy Andeweg (eds.), *Myth and Reality of the Legitimacy Crisis.* Oxford: Oxford University Press.

Van der Meer, Tom. 2018. 'Economic performance and political trust.' In Eric Uslaner (ed.), *The Oxford Handbook of Social and Political Trust*, pp. 599–616. New York; Oxford: Oxford University Press.

Van der Meer, Tom, and Paul Dekker. 2011. 'Trustworthy states, trusting citizens? A multi-level study into objective and subjective determinants of political trust.' In Sonia Zmerli and Marc Hooghe (eds.), *Political Trust. Why Context Matters.* Colchester: ECPR Press.

Van der Meer, Tom, and Armen Hakhverdian. 2016. 'Political trust as an evaluation of process and performance: A cross-national study of 42 European countries.' *Political Studies* 65(1): 81–102.

Van Deth, Jan, Jose Ramon Montero, and Anders Westholm. 2007. *Citizenship and Involvement in European Democracies: A Comparative Analysis.* New York: Routledge.

Van Erkel, Patricia, and Tom Van der Meer. 2016. 'Macroeconomic performance, political trust and the Great Recession: A multilevel analysis of the effects of within-country fluctuations in macroeconomic performance on political trust in 15 EU countries, 1999–2011.' *European Journal of Political Research* 55(1): 177–197.

Van Ham, Carolien, Jacques Thomassen, Kees Aarts, and Rudy Andeweg (eds.). 2017. *Myth and Reality of the Legitimacy Crisis.* Oxford: Oxford University Press.

Van Hoorn, Andre. 2014. 'Trust radius versus trust level: Trust radius as a distinct trust construct.' *American Sociological Review* 79(6): 1256–1259.

Voeten, Erik. 2016. 'It's actually older people who have become more cynical about U.S. democracy.' *Washington Post/Monkey Cage*, December 14, 2016. https://www.washingtonpost.com/news/monkey-cage/wp/2016/12/14/its-actually-older-people-who-have-become-more-cynical-about-u-s-democracy/.

Voeten, Erik. 2016. 'That viral graph about millennials' declining support for democracy? It's very misleading.' *Washington Post/Monkey Cage*, December 5, 2016. https://www.washingtonpost.com/news/monkey-cage/wp/2016/12/05/that-viral-graph-about-millennials-declining-support-for-democracy-its-very-misleading/.

Volodin, Dmytro. 2019. 'Deliberative democracy and trust in political institutions at the local level: Evidence from participatory budgeting experiment in Ukraine.' *Contemporary Politics* 25(1): 78–93.

Wagner, Alexander F., Friedrich Schneider, and Martin Halla. 2009. 'The quality of institutions and satisfaction with democracy in Western Europe: A panel analysis.' *European Journal of Political Economy* 25(1): 30–41.

Wallace, Claire, and Rossalina Latcheva. 2006. 'Economic transformation outside the law: Corruption, trust in public institutions and the informal economy in transition countries of Central and Eastern Europe.' *Europe-Asia Studies* 58(1): 81–102.

Wang, Z., and Y. You. 2016. 'The arrival of critical citizens: Decline of political trust and shifting public priorities in China.' *International Review of Sociology* 26(1): 105–124.

Warren, Mark (ed.). 1999. *Democracy and Trust.* Cambridge: Cambridge University Press.

Weatherford, Stephen M. 1987. 'How does government performance influence political support?' *Political Behavior* 9: 5–28.

Webster, Steven W. 2018. 'Anger and declining trust in the American electorate.' *Political Behavior* 40: 933–964.

Weil, F. D. 1989. 'The sources and structure of legitimation in Western Democracies: A consolidated model tested with time-series data in six countries since World War II.' *American Sociological Review* 54(5): 682–706.

Whitefield, Stephen, and Geoffrey Evans. 1999. 'Political culture versus rational choice: Explaining responses to transition in the Czech Republic and Slovakia.' *British Journal of Political Science* 29(1): 129–154.

Wilson, Rick, and Catherine C. Eckel. 'Political trust in experimental designs.' In Sonja Zmerli and Tom Van der Meer (eds.), *Handbook on Political Trust.* New York: Edward Elgar.

Wong, Timothy, Po-san Wan Ka-ying, and Michael Hsiao Hsin-Huang. 2011. 'The bases of political trust in six Asian societies: Institutional and cultural explanations compared.' *International Political Science Review* 32(3): 263–281.

Wood, Danielle, John Daley, and Carmela Chivers. 2018. 'Australia demonstrates the rise of populism is about more than economics.' *Australian Economic Review* 51(3): 399–410.

Wright, Joseph, Erica Frantz, and Barbara Geddes. 2015. 'Oil and autocratic regime survival.' *British Journal of Political Science* 45(2): 287–306.

Wroe, Andrew, Nicholas Allen, and Sarah Birch. 2013. 'The role of political trust in conditioning perceptions of corruption.' *European Political Science Review* 5(2): 175–195.

Wu, Cary. 2021. 'Education and Social Trust in Global Perspective.' *Sociological Perspectives.* https://doi.org/10.1177/0731121421990045.

Wu, Cary, and Rima Wilkes. 2018. 'Finding critical trusters: A response pattern model of political trust.' *International Journal of Comparative Sociology* 59(2): 110–138.

Yakovlev, Pavel, and David Gilson. 2015. 'Public trust and press freedom.' *Economics Bulletin* 35(1): 214–219.

Yamagishi, Toshio. 2001. 'Trust as a form of social intelligence.' In K. Cook (ed.), *Trust in Society.* New York: Russell Sage Foundation.

Yamagishi, Toshio. 2013. *Trust: The Evolutionary Game of Mind and Society.* New York: Springer.

Yamagishi, Toshio, Masako Kikuchi, and Motoko Kosugi. 1999. 'Trust, gullibility and social intelligence.' *Asian Journal of Social Psychology* 2(1): 145–161.

Yamagishi, Toshio, and Midori Yamagishi. 1994. 'Trust and commitment in the United States and Japan.' *Motivation and Emotion* 18(2): 129–166.

Yang, Qing, and Wenfang Tang. 2010. 'Exploring the sources of institutional trust in China: Culture, mobilization, or performance?' *Asian Politics and Society* 2(3): 415–436.

You, Jong-sung. 2018. 'Trust and corruption.' In Eric M. Uslaner (ed.), *The Oxford Handbook of Social and Political Trust*. New York: Oxford University Press.

Zak, P. J., and Stephen Knack. 2001. 'Trust and growth.' *Economic Journal* 111: 295–321.

Zaller, John. 1998. 'Monica Lewinsky's contribution to political science.' *PS-Political Science and Politics* 31(2): 182.

Zilinsky, Jan. 2019. 'Democratic deconsolidation revisited: Young Europeans are not dissatisfied with democracy.' *Research & Politics* 6(1): 1–10.

Zmerli, Sonia, and Marc Hooghe (eds.). 2011. *Political Trust: Why Context Matters*. Colchester, UK: ECPR Press.

Zmerli, Sonia, and Kenneth Newton. 2008. 'Social trust and attitudes towards democracy.' *Public Opinion Quarterly* 72(4): 706–724.

Zmerli, Sonja, and Kenneth Newton. 2011. 'Winners, losers and three types of trust.' In Sonja Zmerli and Marc Hooghe (eds.), *Political Trust: Why Context Matters*, pp. 67–94. Colchester, UK: ECPR Press,.

Zmerli, Sonja, and Tom Van der Meer (eds.). 2017. *Handbook on Political Trust*. New York: Edward Elgar.

Index